Our Ordered Lives Confess

Harvard Studies in American–East Asian Relations 8

The Harvard Studies in American–East Asian Relations are sponsored and edited by the Committee on American– Far Eastern Policy of the Department of History at Harvard University.

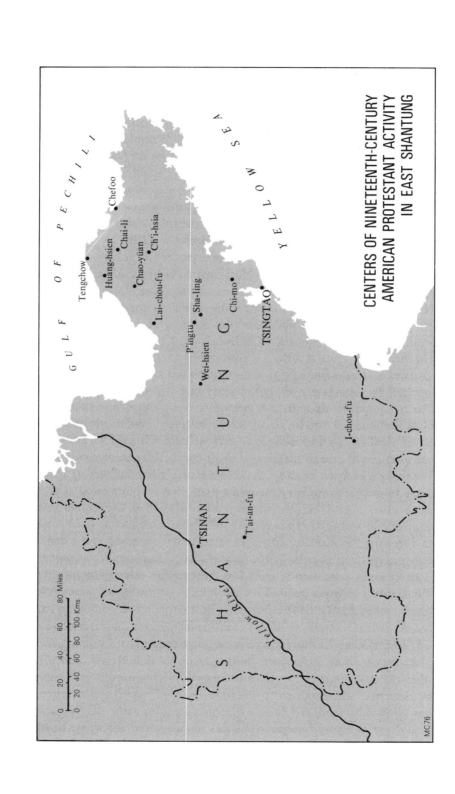

CENTERS OF NINETEENTH-CENTURY
AMERICAN PROTESTANT ACTIVITY
IN EAST SHANTUNG

GULF OF PECHILI

YELLOW SEA

SHANTUNG

Chefoo
Chai-li
Huang-hsien
Chao-yüan
Ch'i-hsia
Tengchow
Lai-chou-fu
P'ingtu
Sha-ling
Chi-mo
TSINGTAO
Wei-hsien
I-chou-fu
TSINAN
T'ai-an-fu

Yellow River

0   20   40   60   80 Miles
0   20 40 60 80 100 Kms

MC76

Our Ordered Lives Confess

Three Nineteenth-Century
American Missionaries
in East Shantung

Irwin T. Hyatt, Jr.

Harvard University Press

Cambridge, Massachusetts
and London, England
1976

Library of Congress Cataloging in Publication Data
Hyatt, Irwin T   1935–
  Our ordered lives confess: three nineteenth-century
American missionaries in East Shantung.
    (Harvard studies in American–East Asian relations; 8)
    Bibliography: p.
    Includes index.
    1. Crawford, Tarleton Perry, 1821–1902. 2. Moon,
Charlotte, 1840–1912. 3. Mateer, Calvin Wilson, 1836–
1908. I. Title. II. Series
BV3427.A1H9   266'.0092'2 [B]   76–7515
ISBN 0–674–64735–1

To Ida Pruitt

Europeans never understand anything of China that does not resemble themselves.

————André Malraux

No two men, indeed, can find the same traits of character in any country, because at bottom as we look at the world, we find only ourselves.

————George Kates

Preface

This book is a study of the adjustments of three nineteenth-century American Protestant missionaries to life in east Shantung province. More generally the subject is international relations of the person-to-person kind, based on living experience abroad, that Americans like to think of as really getting to know another people.

Understanding other peoples is by common agreement necessary for living in the same world with them. As a practical proposition understanding seems highly problematic, or at least different people seem to come up with widely differing understandings. Blame is typically placed on lack of appropriate information, on prejudice, or on the crisis attention span that afflicts international concern. Another difficulty is that people often do not even understand themselves, let alone others.

This problem of understanding is what the present study tries to examine, in a specific situation involving Americans and Chinese. As Protestant missionaries the subjects represent the largest body of Americans that has historically tried to get through to the Chinese as people. Together with Protestant and Roman Catholic evangelists from European nations, these Americans learned the language, settled widely, and for more than a century were for many Chinese the living face of a new international order. As teachers, as publicists, and simply as privileged foreigners living there, they contributed to the processes of modernization and nationalistic self-discovery in that country. As objects of prayerful concern and of money-raising efforts at home, and as indefatigable reporters on the Chinese scene, they also contributed to American opinion and policy regarding China.

The study's geographic setting is a city in northeast China known in the nineteenth century as Tengchow. Known anciently (and again today) as P'eng-lai, after its hsien or district name, Tengchow stood "on a rocky hill by the sea, facing Manchuria, on the peninsula of Shantung province which reaches out into the Yellow Sea toward Korea."[1] According to popular legend Tengchow's history went back more than two thousand years to the reign, depending on which story one stresses, of either Ch'in Shih Huang-ti (221–210 B.C.) or Han Wu Ti (141–87 B.C.).[2] Each of those great emperors reportedly made local visits in search of five "eastern isles" inhabited by immortal beings. Both were really seeking immortality for themselves, and both were disappointed.

A city did grow from these royal visitations, and since its earliest days "P'eng-lai" has been famous in Chinese folklore. Ch'in Shih Huang-ti, for example, is said to have dispatched from the site three thousand young men and women who became the progenitors of the Japanese people. In the waters below the Temple of the Blessed Isles, for a thousand years the city's clifftop landmark, magic dolphins have played; and in the offshore mists men have glimpsed islands where "men and animals never die and where the palaces are of gold and silver." The great poet Su Tung-p'o saw in these waters the Eight Immortals floating on lotus thrones and in 1085 wrote "Mirage at Sea" in commemoration. More recently, in one of the memorable passages of modern Chinese fiction, a famous traveler saw in the same waters a vision of the impending shipwreck of China's traditional civilization.[3]

By mid-nineteenth century, when Christian missionaries arrived with a new kind of immortality, magic P'eng-lai had indeed fallen on hard times. As Tengchow it was still the civil, military, and educational capital of a prefecture (also called Tengchow) that included nine districts and one department (chou). This amounted to an overall area of about 5700 square miles and 3,000,000 people, mostly peasant farmers. The city itself was surrounded by a forty-foot wall that was three miles around and by repute one of the oldest, thickest, and most masonically excellent in China. Within the wall, however, was a population that seems to have been declining throughout the nineteenth century, to a total of just over 40,000 by the 1890s.[4]

Economic depression was the problem most often cited. The city's harbor had been ruined by natural causes, and its trading importance was undercut by the development of Chefoo (Yent'ai)—a treaty port fifty-five miles to the east—and later of Tsingtao to the south. An American observed in the 1880s that Tengchow's many public buildings were all in various stages of collapse. As for the common people, their "whole time and all their thoughts" were occupied by the struggle simply to stay alive. In a city "without commerce and with little local trade," most were "poor and growing poorer every day." [5]

Tengchow was in short a decaying, backwater place from the time the Conventions of Peking opened it to missionary activity in 1860. Things continued downhill for the next fifty years, the period covered in this book. The most punishing aspects of local life to Western missionaries were Tengchow's loneliness, its stagnant aura, and its low level of religious interest, or of professional stimulation. As an official examination center the city was conservatively oriented, and antiforeign tendencies were evident from the first. With Chinese friends hard to find, foreigners thus depended for reinforcement mostly on each other. Husbands were thrown on wives, wives on husbands, and younger people on older hands, to a degree that was to say the least emotionally problematic. In an age and in a type of work where strength—of character, of devotion, of sheer physical endurance—was a paramount American virtue, it was a life that could literally destroy people.

On the other hand, to those who were both sensitive and tough, it was by no means an impossible life. Tengchow's very stagnancy meant that foreigners had an environment that would not suffer unsettling change. Once certain ground rules were learned, they discovered, it was also possible to live with the city's antiforeignism. With so many officials about, the local people were actually peaceful and lawabiding; in the whole decade of the 1870s there were only four murders in town, and vices like thievery and opium addiction were always rarer than in more lively ports.[6] Outside Tengchow's wall were moreover hundreds of thousands of people who proved "simple, kindly, well-disposed to foreigners, industrious, and fairly reliable with a good deal of character." For many years the city's itinerant missionaries had the additional advantage of being the first and only Westerners most of those people ever saw.[7]

In emotional terms, too, there could be rewards. The closeness of some missionary marriages and friendships at Tengchow was legendary. By luck and circumstance, by trial and error—but mostly by hard work and intelligent study of one's options—it was also possible to find enjoyable and professionally significant work. By some social reeducation one could even make real Chinese friendships. Such friendships came to fortunate Americans as a kind of marriage between their own Christianity, which always emphasized the hidden potential of any individual soul, and the equally mystic, profoundly personal Chinese notion of *yüan-fen,* the idea that certain individuals are fated to be brought together even "though separated by a thousand li." The nurtured loyalty of some of these relationships, where each party at some level believed that one friend had been brought half way around the world specifically to find the other, makes poignant reading.

Another opportunity in Tengchow was the personal growth it could facilitate. Included here was the influence of Chinese friendships, but there was much more, beginning with study of the unique native language. With a little Mandarin and with knowledge of a few basic social principles, a foreigner—if he took the principles seriously and meant what he could haltingly say—was able to begin a fascinating lifetime of exploring the majestic web of personality and lore about him. Linguistic or philosophic brilliance was not required. What was necessary were personal traits like tact, dependability, and genuine interest in other people. If he had such traits abundantly, a foreigner could start with a strange new name and acquire in time, by imperceptible accretions, a new and fuller identity.

None of these rewards came easily, and which way a foreigner's total experience went depended largely on his own physical and spiritual resources. The Americans in nineteenth-century Tengchow were all confident children of their own civilization; they had come to China to teach and save and grow in grace, not to be taught or reshaped by the Chinese. In Tengchow they ran head on into self-doubt—the first such encounter, apparently, for many—and a situation that would inevitably change them, if they stayed, no matter how strong they were. In consequence only fifteen American missionaries stayed ten years or longer, out of more than a hundred who at some point between 1860 and 1900 lived in Tengchow. The others mostly transferred to more promising places. About a dozen, however, gave up missionary work entirely after a year or so in Tengchow, and an equal number quickly died there. To some who tried to stay strange things happened: one man coped by never getting out of bed, another by endlessly counting the city's paving stones, and so on with several cases of advanced "brain trouble."

The basic choice that had to be made in Tengchow, however unconsciously, was whether to stagnate like the city itself—in self-pity and cultural arrogance—or to try to become a bigger and necessarily different person. The second alternative could by diligent application enable these specialists in being born again to be reborn themselves, to find in China a kind of divine grace and personal confirmation that in their earlier lives they had missed. The rub was that the second course was much harder to pursue.

What follows amounts to successive accounts of how three Americans managed to stay, of how they individually responded to the problems and opportunities just mentioned. Two of the subjects, T. P. Crawford and Lottie Moon, were missionaries of the Southern Baptist Convention; the third, Calvin W. Mateer, represented the Presbyterian Church U.S.A. (North). As a group the three represent a total of 135 years of life in prerevolutionary

China. Almost all those years were spent in the same place at roughly the same time, dealing generally with the same Chinese. All three moreover became missionaries of renown back home, to the extent of being memorialized with biographies of the hagiographic type.

The chief intention is simply to recount what seem to be three interesting stories. Otherwise the hope is to suggest a few points about missionaries and about people-to-people Sino-American encounter generally. Among included topics are such matters as the diversity of Christian witness in non-Christian lands, the differences in how male and female Americans responded to life in such places, and the difficulty of transmitting lessons learned by individuals abroad to Americans at home. The main overall topic, however, is one that has interested me particularly since living in Taipei in the late 1960s: how is it that of Americans placed among Chinese, starting out more or less equally, some—and not necessarily the brightest or most professedly tolerant—will find friends and a new appreciation of life, while others seem mostly to find rudeness, deceit, and health worries?

Since each of the book's three parts is preceded by a separate preface, this one will not be prolonged beyond a few advice-to-the reader remarks. First, Part III is proportionately longer than Parts I and II, because the scope of Calvin Mateer's activities was simply much greater than that of T. P. Crawford or Lottie Moon. To keep within a reasonable length, on the other hand, and because emphasis is placed on Mateer's development as a person, several important aspects of his work are only incidentally treated. It will also be noted that Part II treats rather extensively some matters not directly connected to Lottie Moon; here I can only ask the indulgence of being permitted to place Miss Moon in what to me is the most significant perspective.

Regarding source material, I have for some purposes—as for information on the subjects' lives before they came to China— relied heavily on their earlier "hagiographic" biographies. Much the greater portion of the book is based on Presbyterian and Southern Baptist archival materials; on letters, articles, and books by the missionaries themselves; and, in Calvin Mateer's case, on writings in Chinese by Chinese Christians. In all three cases a different sort of person emerges from that described in the official biography. In Miss Moon's case the earlier biography itself becomes a subject of study.

In romanization of Chinese words, a few well-established archaisms are used, such as Kiaochow and Tsinan instead of Chiao-chou and Chi-nan. Proper names of individual Chinese, where Chinese written characters are available, are represented in the standard form (for example, Miao Hua-yü). Where characters are not available, the most commonly employed contemporary romanization is used, as in Kao Ku San. Finally, the reader may assume that Tengchow, unless specifically noted otherwise, always refers to the city of that name and not to Tengchow prefecture. He may also assume that Tengchow and all similar representations (Tung-chow, Tung Chow Foo, Tengchowfu and so on) that appear in quotations refer to the city in Shantung province—and in *no* case do they refer to the town of Tungchow (T'ung-chou) near Peking or to Tungchow (Nan-t'ung) in Kiangsu province.

As for acknowledgments I am in a quandary. I have certainly received an unusual amount of help on this book, from many generous people. At the same time the book is of such a character that it seems especially advisable for me personally to assume full responsibility for all views expressed. For making available indispensable source materials, I must at least express my great indebtedness to Madeline Brown of the former United Presbyterian Mission Library; to Nancy Nell Stanley, Director of Library and Archives, Southern Baptist Foreign Mission Board; to Barbara M. Hayes and Harold F. Smith for use of personal documents; and to the staffs of the Missionary Research Library, of the National Archives, and of the Perkins Library at Duke University (Manuscript Department). For immensely helpful readings of the draft I must thank Redmond and Suzanne Barnett, Adrian Bennett, Paul Cohen, and K. C. Liu. For financial support I am indebted to the East Asian Research Center, Harvard University; to the Committee on Exchanges with Asian Institutions, Social Science Research Council; and to the Emory University Faculty Research Committee. To my mother and father, to John Fairbank, and to my wife Margaret I owe debts that could never be enumerated.

Contents

I /

Tarleton Perry Crawford

The crank microbe flourishes in isolation, and the inbreeding of one's own thoughts brings suspicion and prejudice.

———*Anna Seward Pruitt*

1/

Battering Satan's Ramparts:
A Missionary's Formative Years

The Southern Baptist Convention is America's largest and most vital Protestant denomination, with today's biggest foreign missions program. As Baptists the SBC's 12,700,000 members take their Christianity seriously and evangelically. They are, as one Baptist minister's son has observed, "a people of monumental earnestness," and in the south they are collectively "a little like China; there are immeasurably more of them than anybody else, and they tend to regard themselves as the center of the universe." [1]

So perhaps it is not by pure chance that there has been a certain affinity between Southern Baptists and China. The first officially appointed missionary of the SBC's Foreign Mission Board—the Reverend Samuel C. Clopton—was posted to Canton in 1845. Mr. Clopton quickly died of sunstroke, however, and for many years Southern Baptists lagged embarrassingly behind more experienced Protestant efforts. In 1900 there were still only 49 SBC missionaries in China, including wives and single women, whereas northern Presbyterians and Methodists each numbered more than a hundred by 1890.

Better money-raising and recruitment brought significant Baptist growth. An impressive peak of 287 missionaries was achieved by 1924 (still only about half northern Presbyterian and Methodist strength), and as late as 1948 the SBC had in China a 220-

person contingent supervising a native church membership of 123-000. Adapting at that point to changing Chinese political conditions, attention shifted to other areas. A new Taiwan effort—beginning in 1949 with a South Carolina lady and 48 Chinese Baptists—grew even so by 1970 to 69 missionaries, 10,000 converts, and 100 churches and chapels; and longer established work in Hong Kong and Macao increased at the same time to 79 missionaries and over 20,000 church members.[2]

These statistics are offered simply as background to the point that China—no matter what the Presbyterians, Methodists, or any others did there—has historically had a special importance to this late-blooming but most persistently missionary-minded of American churches. Attracted by China's size, huge population, "relatively advanced" culture, and ease of missionary access, the SBC for over a century gave to that country the greatest concentration of its missionary money and attention.[3] Out of the encounter has come a little studied but immensely rich historical and human experience. At home Southern Baptists have always tended to symbolize, to make their religion an extension of deeply felt moral convictions and social anxieties; in the China field this tendency has produced stories dramatic enough to be taken by Baptists as lessons in universal truth.

Two of the three stories in this book are cases in point. The Reverend T. P. Crawford, the case first in hand, was a missionary in China during the slow, difficult period of early Baptist work. Forty of his fifty preaching years were spent in Shantung province, mostly at Tengchow. There Crawford observed and analyzed what he thought was the "most remarkable half-century in the history of the human race." As a devoted but totally reactionary evangelist, he saw nothing but evil in the social gospel type of Christianity that developed toward the end of that time. He never liked the Chinese very much, and sometimes one feels that there were not many people whom he did like. Fortunately, perhaps, Crawford was so intemperate in urging his personal enthusiasms on other Southern Baptists that he finally "threatened the very existence of the Convention," not to mention its China missions, and his church had—as he termed it—to "refrigerate" him.[4]

Nonetheless T. P. Crawford had for a time the "attention of many learned audiences," and he was the recognized leader of a Baptist "revolution." He stated that he had been led to his revolutionary convictions by the divine hand; but he also said that his convictions were strictly rational, or "forced upon me, one after the other, by actual experiences in my missionary work and its environments."[5] To an extent the historical record supports his claims. Certainly his experiences testify eloquently to the fact that eccentrics generally have logical reasons for thinking as they do. How that logic evolves is what this study is about.

America, 1821–1851, and Shanghai, 1852–1863

Tarleton Perry Crawford was born May 8, 1821, in Warren County, Kentucky. He was the fourth of seven sons of John and Lucretia Kemble Crawford, pioneer farmers. Growing up on Pilot Knob, an "interesting and romantic spot" near Bowling Green, he spend his childhood mostly at farm work or in the woods. He did not spend much time in school. Education came chiefly in the evening from his mother, who was known for deep faith and "unusual mental endowments and an insatiable thirst for knowledge."[6]

As a boy Tarleton was known as something of a free thinker. His conversion experience occurred at the age of sixteen, as he stood on a stump mimicking a local preacher. Someone called to him that he was committing a grave sin. Stricken with fear, he was unable for a week to do anything except read the family Bible. Out of this experience, and encouraged by his mother's counsel, he resolved to give his life to God as a "poor despised Baptist preacher."[7]

Leaving home with two and a half dollars in his pocket, young "T. P." farmed, studied, and did odd jobs for eleven years in a number of Kentucky and Tennessee communities. In 1851, at age 30, he secured a college degree from old Union University at Murfreesboro, Tennessee. His Baptist professors at that church school had reservations about his future as a preacher. His elocution, they thought, was unattractive, and "indeed, he seemed never to have bestowed a thought on the subject of how his message was to be delivered." But his academic record was the best in his class, and everyone was impressed by his piety and unyielding determination.[8]

As far back as 1847 T. P. Crawford had been thinking of missionary work, and while at Union these ideas took definite shape. For two years he hesitated, feeling himself not intelligent enough and generally incompetent to the task. But as he considered the strength of his convictions he felt better equipped, and a year before graduation from college he wrote the Southern Baptist Foreign Mission Board that his mind was made up. He cited three reasons: "The first and principal one, a desire to please Christ . . . Second, sympathy for the perishing heathen, especially the female portion. Theirs is a hard lot, particularly in China. Third, a desire to labor in such a place, and in such a manner, that the influence of my example may continue to live and be productive of good, after my sufferings and toils on earth shall have ended."

Why he chose China as his preferred field is not very clear. He was convinced, however, that he was "not actuated in the least by a spirit of romantic adventure," and he had made a close study of such pertinent literature as he could find. In one letter to the board he enumerated a list of obstacles he would probably meet in China; these included unfriendly officials and higher classes, an unhealthy climate, and a particularly difficult language. He also had forebodings about having to deal with China-coast Westerners—traders and sailors—whom he seems to have disliked well in advance of knowing any such people.[9]

In due course Crawford was appointed to Shanghai, with his support guaranteed by the Big Hatchie Association, a power among Tennessee Baptist groups.[10] All he lacked, the board told him, was a wife to assist and comfort him in his hard life in the foreign field.

At this point T. P. Crawford's life intersected with that of a young woman named Martha Foster, from Tuscaloosa, Alabama. Miss Foster, who by 1851 was twenty-one years of age, had been struggling for five years—despite the fact that she came from a relatively prosperous, devoutly Baptist home—with feelings of social and intellectual inferiority and with a constant sense of guilt because she did "not much enjoy religion."[11] As things turned out, Miss Foster and T. P. Crawford were answers to each other's problems.

Actually Martha Foster was a very religious person, particularly since the fall of 1849. In October of that year, having just recovered from a long, almost fatal illness (and still shaking with chills), she had attended a revival with her family. Martha and two of her brothers had been deeply affected by the revival, and a series of powerful family prayer experiences followed, culminating on November 14. On that night, during a terrific thunderstorm, Martha distinctly felt "the finger of God" directing her "to a heathen world."[12] Never before, apparently, had the idea of being a foreign missionary seriously entered her mind.

Interestingly, Martha Foster first wrote in her diary that God from that point wanted her to be a missionary's wife, which she later crossed out and changed to read "become a missionary"; this was typical of the identity, or perhaps role, conflict that was much in her thoughts during those years.[13] Throughout the 1846 to 1851 period (age sixteen to twenty-one) she was preoccupied both with religion and with love for various young men. There were five for whom at one time or another she had such affection, and she received proposals from two of them. Terrified by the repugnant possibility of winding up an old maid, and much enjoying hugging, kissing, and romantic conversation, she yet feared further sexual intimacy ("a serpent, a fiend intruding upon me").[14] She also deeply resented the role that both her religion and her society would thrust upon her as any man's wife ("To be called inferior! Inferior! In what?").[15]

Martha had always wanted to do something important in life on her own. As a male relative saw her, she had a "restless longing for something," a kind of "yearning that the world might be made better through her living in it."[16] She herself said shortly before her 1849 revival experience, "Is it presumption?—is it an idle fancy? it is *something*—I have long felt it—without knowing whence it came, how or when. There is something within that tells me there is much in store for me in this life. That my future will be full of events—and everything now is preparing me for it. I have no idea as to the sphere, yet it seems some station is designed for me by Providence, either conspicuous or useful. I commit myself into Thy charge, O Father!"[17]

Unable to bring herself to marry any of her suitors, and discouraged by her church from trying to become an unmarried missionary, Miss Foster had taken up teaching in the fall of 1850. She found the work generally unrewarding. She also found herself unable to shake off caring about men and their attentions to her—a rich bachelor merchant, a Peeping Tom tailor, and a traveling fiddler whose music filled her "with a wild painful rapture." By February 1851 her diary entries reflected a longing for direction that bordered on hysteria. "Forsake me not, O my God," she wrote on St. Valentine's Day. "The withdrawal of Thy face has been long . . . My Father Thou hast promised, and wilt not Thou perform?"[18]

As Martha struggled at this time with her urges, she discussed with a local pastor the possibility of becoming a missionary. The pastor communicated her concern to the SBC Foreign Mission Board, where it was now seen as a possible solution to the newly appointed T. P. Crawford's need for a helpmate in China. Crawford saw all this as an intervention by the divine hand. Making his way by train, horse, and foot to Tuscaloosa, he presented himself to Miss Foster four days after her Valentine's plea for divine help.

Crawford's arrival, with the message that God had sent him to marry Martha Foster and take her to China, threw Martha into a state of "numbness." Her mother declared, *"It shall never be,"* and the family generally thought the whole idea "madness." Martha, however, saw Crawford as a "self-made, easy, everyday kind of fellow," and this judgment—together with the likelihood of Providential involvement—led to their marriage some three weeks after meeting each other. During the ensuing honeymoon trip Mr. Crawford confided to a Big Hatchie friend that his marriage "altogether [had] been rather peculiar." To which the friend replied, "Otherwise it would not be like my brother Crawford."[19]

After a number of Baptist meetings and 102 days at sea the Crawfords arrived in Shanghai in March 1852. The Southern Baptist mission had been locally established for five years. In T. P. Crawford's eyes, however, things were still very much in an "experimental or formative stage"; the treaty-port air was "throbbing with hopes, fears, and suspicions." From the first he had no doubt that a Christian China could be built from this situation—the only question was how to do it.[20]

He and his bride quickly found that converting the Chinese was only one of the problems of missionary life. The little Southern Baptist community, for example, they found to be split in a bitter feud between its two senior members, Matthew T. Yates and Jehu Lewis Shuck. The Reverend Mr. Yates and his supporters were trying to force Shuck to leave the field; they accused him of unseemly financial activities and of sexual misconduct with several Chinese women. The Crawfords prudently refused to be drawn into this mess of "slanders and heartburnings" and struggled instead with the Chinese language.[21]

The language proved even more difficult than Crawford had feared. He studied hard but for many months got only headaches and "days of gloom" in reward. Not only did his health suffer, but he could not suppress a feeling of resentment at the swifter progress of his young wife Martha. Mrs. Crawford, who was by this time thoroughly devoted to her husband, was very distressed: "He said he could never speak the Chinese language with any degree of ease —that his progress would be slow—that it would be the reverse with me—I would speak easily and learn more rapidly. The contrast would be observed always unfavorably to him. It would be bitter that he [be] in any respect inferior to his wife. It would be a continual trial. This was unexpected to me. I had prayed long and earnestly that God would make me willing to see my husband daily outstripping me . . . But O I was not prepared for this."[22]

Fortunately Mr. Crawford came soon enough to a point where, as his wife put it, he had "no occasion to be ashamed of his Chinese speaking abilities."[23] He continued to have trouble penetrating the written language, but this he handled partly by continuing to study and partly by taking the attitude that he did not need to be able to read much anyway. He decided that the difficult Chinese characters were "hieroglyphs" that were "doomed to the tomb and the antiquary"; to hasten this along he began in September 1852 to work personally on a new script for missionaries to offer as a replacement. The resulting Crawford Phonetic System—devised with a crew of Chinese helpers over the next few months—provided an alphabet of hooks and slashes whereby an illiterate could write Chinese "in a week or two." [24]

To Crawford's disappointment few people, Chinese or foreign, saw his phonetic system as more than a curiosity. But by 1853 his spoken Chinese was good enough to do considerable preaching to "great crowds of raw heathen," among whom he again came up with methodological views distinctly his own. He was different now in his attitude toward the use of native preaching assistants; he disagreed with the missionary majority who reasoned that such helpers knew the people and could be usefully employed to gain access to their hearts. Crawford reasoned rather from the example of the celebrated, recently deceased Karl F. A. Gützlaff, whose many former helpers were now discovered to be engaged in un-Christian and in fact depraved pursuits. Arriving just at the moment of this exposure, Crawford's "unsophisticated Baptist mind" perceived at once (so he later stated) that the prevailing system was utterly corrupt. Natives who took money to spread the gospel were "inferior moral characters . . . simply foreign employes, on so many dollars per month to gather in converts for the satisfaction of their masters."

The missionary community was quite upset by the Gützlaff case. When T. P. Crawford proposed putting all assistants on self-support, however, the response was even cooler than that received by his phonetic system. In fact, Crawford once recalled, his suggestions "brought upon my poor head a vast amount of odium." Few agreed with his contention that "a hireling ministry implies a corrupt membership"; this reflected on lands other than China, and also no one could think of an alternative. Hirelings the helpers might be, but without them there would be no help at all. [25]

Rebuffed by his colleagues, Crawford set out to prove that he could succeed entirely on his own. Failing in the streets of Shanghai, he was soon in the suburban countryside preaching to farmers. There his most promising village was taken away from him by Episcopalians, who paid a local couple to open a school. The Episcopal hirelings, Crawford heard, turned out to be "miserable hypocrites and opium smokers" who as a sideline did "a horrible business in supplying *women*."[26]

While her husband battled such "pecuniary inducements," Martha Crawford quietly conducted a small girls' school in the city. She paid her pupils ten cash, a little less than a penny a day, to attend. The school's Chinese teacher, as Mr. Crawford had predicted, stole the girls' cash to buy opium, but Martha Crawford trustingly engaged two more teachers. One of these new employees —a Mrs. Yee— became the first woman to be baptized in Shanghai (1855). The other, a man named Wong Ping San (Huang P'insan), became the first permanent member, and later pastor, of the Shanghai Baptist Church.[27]

Although Crawford later condemned his wife's school as a mistake, he remembered the acquisition of Pastor Wong as the most important event of his work in Shanghai.[28] Wong's conversion took place not long after he became T. P. Crawford's paid personal language teacher. It also occurred during one of the periodic sieges that punctuated the Crawford's Shanghai years; with artillery in his ears and Crawford phonetic tracts before his eyes, Wong had what Mr. Crawford identified as a real old-fashioned conversion.[29]

Military threats to Shanghai, of course, came from a number of directions during the 1850s and 1860s—from Red Turbans (alias Small Sword or Triad Society) rebels, from counterattacking imperial armies, and always in the background from the great Taiping Rebellion. Like many missionaries T. P. Crawford was fascinated by the Christian elements in the Taiping story. Once he hid two young Taiping "princes" for several months in his home, and on another occasion he visited the rebel capital at Nanking. Such contacts came through the agency of the Reverend Issachar Roberts, a sometime Southern Baptist missionary and Taiping adviser. For a time Roberts had a strong influence over Crawford, to the considerable unhappiness of Mrs. Crawford; but both Roberts and the Taipings eventually lost their appeal, as they came alike to seem too "fanatical." [30]

During these turbulent years Crawford slept for safety with a hatchet under his pillow. He was never prevented, however, from spending most of his time in Shanghai's troubled rural suburbs. There he preached and built up contacts, and he established himself as a private mail service. His home became a repository for the valuables of Chinese acquaintances living in exposed areas. Crawford also prepared himself well, as things turned out, for the American Civil War, which at certain periods cut off southern missionaries from home support. For a monthly fee of ten dollars, for instance, he gave nightly English lessons to local businessmen. More important he began as a real estate agent in the fall of 1861 to "aid the Chinese owners to sell their lands to foreigners."

For a skillful real estate agent, it should be noted, Shanghai was now a good place. Foreign trade was shifting there from Canton, while rebellions dislocated the local Chinese. T. P. Crawford thus could buy property from natives in distressed circumstances, and as land values rose he did very well indeed. In an eighteen-month period (1862–63) he cleared about US $6600, which he reinvested in local land. These properties he then leased out, and the rents added to his and his wife's missionary salaries—when those got through—to give them an annual income of US $3000. If not exactly a killing, this was certainly a windfall; it was three times what the Crawfords had made strictly as missionaries, and it enabled them to live nicely and with an unusual amount of independence. Holding onto his increasingly more valuable Shanghai properties, Crawford enjoyed for the rest of his life—the next forty years—a "comfortable living apart from any support from the Board."[31]

In 1863 the real estate business began to fall off, and T. P. Crawford contracted cholera. Mrs. Crawford moreover developed liver trouble, and they decided to leave Shanghai for some healthier place.[32] Also, Mr. Crawford was keenly aware that as a missionary he had not made much of a mark in eleven years in Shanghai. He felt he had not had a fair chance: the times had been unsettled, the overall environment and local mission work were both highly commercial, and circumstances had kept him from devoting all his energies to evangelism.

Most of all, Crawford had never had a real work of his own. The Shanghai Baptist Church belonged to his senior colleagues on the field, first Shuck and later Yates. Crawford naturally had a hand in this work, and in later years he would claim credit for most of the Baptist conversions that took place during his Shanghai years. But somehow he was usually on the fringes, preaching out in villages. And the notion of his seniors that missionaries should have "all things in common"—including converts and mission money—meant to Crawford only that "no one had any individuality." As a man who thought of himself as "something like the apostle Paul, not liking to build on another man's foundation," he did not like being an assistant.[33]

For all these reasons the Crawfords left Shanghai in August 1863 for the recently opened province of Shantung. There everything was just beginning, and Crawford could reasonably expect to win souls and be pastor to a flock of his own.

Beginning in Tengchow

When the Crawfords reached Tengchow, their new station, the situation was still not as they ideally would have had it. Another Baptist minister, Jesse Boardman Hartwell of Darlington, South Carolina, had been on the scene from the opening of the province two years before. Mr. Hartwell already had a little church in hand, and there was also a Presbyterian mission. Discouraging, too, was the attitude of the community's leading Chinese citizens, who were reported to have resolved "in council assembled . . . to discourage all intercourse with the outsiders and to render their stay as inconvenient and unpleasant as possible." [34] Early in 1864, however, J. B. Hartwell—who was having difficulty receiving his missionary salary—left town to take work as interpreter for the Shanghai Municipal Council. Crawford became pastor of the Tengchow Baptist Church, which made him the only Southern Baptist pastor north of Shanghai. Things were looking up, and with Mrs. Crawford he settled down to work on the intransigent natives.

In a little less than two years the Crawfords reportedly added eight new baptisms to the fifteen members Hartwell had left them. The church seemed to be doing well. But when the war in America ended Hartwell quit his Shanghai job, and in December 1865 he returned to his Tengchow pastorate. Crawford reluctantly went back to being an assistant. The congregation, including the new members, quickly gravitated to the paternal Mr. Hartwell; and as other missionaries noted admiringly, they "leaned on him, clung to him as to a father." [35]

All this time the Crawfords had been living in the Hartwell home, which was a fine arrangement as long as the Hartwells were in Shanghai. But now the two families were crowded in together. Trouble quickly developed between Eliza Hartwell and Martha Crawford, who was irritated by her hostess's patronizing manner. Mrs. Hartwell returned Mrs. Crawford's dislike, and she moreover did not like Mr. Crawford, whom she described to other missionaries as an un-Christian and ungentlemanly person. [36]

In addition to these problems T. P. Crawford fell immediately into an unhappy relationship with J. B. Hartwell. On Hartwell's first Sunday back from Shanghai he fiercely upbraided Crawford for making certain changes in his church's worship service; Crawford's additions, said Hartwell, were "mummery and nonsense." Later he accused Crawford of scheming to steal his parishioners and to turn other local missionaries against him. Crawford took these and other "oft-repeated undefinable offenses" for several months. Then, calling Hartwell aside one day, he let him know how he felt: "I told him that he was the subject of a peculiar kind of selfishness, ambition, and pride which made it difficult for me to get along with him; and that I had reason to believe others had also experienced something of the same. He denied the correctness of my judgements in the matter. I endeavored by examples, illustrations, and in other ways to convince him of the fact. I also requested him to take it kindly . . . It was too much for him—he couldn't stand it: Next morning his countenance was changed towards me and lowering." [37]

It was agreed that the quickest solution to all these difficulties would be for the Crawfords to find another house and church. The first problem being particularly pressing, Mr. Crawford commissioned his literary assistant to find a way of getting around the community's strict ban on further leasing to foreigners. The assistant, a man named Chao Ting Ching, was a newcomer, too. Unable to find anything as Crawford's agent, Chao resorted in April 1866 to a favorite dodge of the period: he rented a house—a large and conspicuous one in this case—in his own name and sublet to Crawford. As Crawford saw it, "Notwithstanding treaty rights this seemed the only way." U.S. Chefoo Consul E. T. Sandford later added, Crawford knew "that he had done wrong to take this underhanded course in obtaining a house, but the temptation was too strong for him to withstand." [38]

The resulting uproar was in the classic *chiao-an* (missionary incident) style. Fifteen individuals had witnessed assistant Chao's negotiation of the original lease, and these and other concerned neighbors—including the landlord—now felt that they had been deceived. Physically prevented from taking occupancy, Crawford appealed for help from Consul Sandford and fellow local missionaries. Everyone seems to have been eager for some sort of confrontation, and this came one day late in April. Accompanied by Sandford, Hartwell, and another missionary, Crawford raised an American flag over the disputed property, an act which at once drew an angry crowd. The crowd reportedly beat gongs and did a lot of "jumping and hooting." One man even dared Mr. Crawford several times to "come on"; Crawford drew a pistol, and for a moment it looked to all as though he meant to shoot the person. "But fortunately," recalled E. T. Sandford, "he did not." Instead Crawford led the Westerners in a charge against the Chinese crowd, he and Hartwell with pistols and Consul Sandford and the other missionary with rolled-up umbrellas. The Chinese charged, too, reported Crawford, and "a number of these did with a yell rush violently upon me and the Rev. J. B. Hartwell and seize my person. Only by a powerful effort was I able to escape with my life out of their hands." [39]

Out of this scuffle came a short-term victory for the Americans. The native crowd retreated, and Crawford recalled that "we kept them at bay for an hour or two." Sandford put diplomatic pressure on the local authorities, and after ten days the Crawfords were finally able to occupy their house. The district magistrate had the landlord's family bodily evicted from the place, a Chinese military guard was posted, and proclamations were issued enjoining the people not to molest foreigners. So Crawford had won. He was troubled, however, by a feeling that if the affair could have been handled in a "different manner and spirit" the natives would perhaps have been left with "much more favorable impressions." [40]

Crawford's misgivings in no sense detracted from his enjoyment of his new home. The house gained by so much struggle quickly turned into a large compound, two-storied in part, with thirty-four rooms arranged around a total of seven interior courtyards. In addition to several rooms for each of the Crawfords, Mrs. Crawford's diary reveals, quarters were soon available for foreign and Chinese guests and for live-in servants, teachers, church deacons, school pupils, and all the other types expected to gather around. In the courtyards were porticoes, piazzas, a well, and seven different kinds of trees. By all accounts it was an impressive place. [41]

The purpose of all this was not so much comfortable living as to have an establishment that would attract membership for a new church, separate from Hartwell's. By December, eight months after taking occupancy, Crawford felt secure enough to announce the formation of such an enterprise. He called it the Monument Street Baptist Church, emphasizing its distinctness from Hartwell's address on North Street. Three Chinese at once transferred their memberships from North Street: Crawford's assistant Chao Ting Ching, his wife's helper Mrs. Liu, and a Presbyterian defector named Wong Wha Yuan. Other founding members were Mrs. Crawford, Mrs. Sally Holmes (an American missionary widow), and a Dutch drifter named deGrew. Mr. deGrew, an acquaintance from Shanghai days, had a Chinese mistress who became a member when the Crawfords got them married. [42]

From this base T. P. Crawford pursued a routine of street

preaching and noon services on market days. Meeting little further encouragement and a good deal of hostility in Tengchow city, however, he soon did as in Shanghai. With Chao Ting Ching and another assistant, this one a degree-holding scholar named Lu Mingchao, he went into the outlying rural areas. As Crawford described it scripturally, "The people finally treated my labors with so much indifference that I turned to the country, shaking, as it were, the dust from my shoes as a witness against the city."[43]

Proceeding to various nearby market towns, Crawford quickly found his witness more warmly received. In Huang-ch'eng—sixteen miles south of Tengchow—he struck up a fruitful relationship with a schoolteacher named Sun Chang Lung. Though "proud, tyrannical, bigotted, and exacting," Sun had strong truth-seeking inclinations. He was also "whe teu" (*hui-t'ou,* headman) of a family which spread over nine villages and which faithfully followed his lead in spiritual matters. In 1867 Sun became T. P. Crawford's first real convert in Shantung; he evicted a Buddhist bonze from his family temple at Ma-chia village, turned the place into a Baptist outstation, and over the next few years presented Crawford with nineteen relatives and friends for baptism. Two of these people, Sun Kyi Di (Sun Chang Lung's son) and Chang Yun Who, became the first deacons of Crawford's church.[44]

The year 1867 also brought raids by Nien rebels, and thereby another important convert in a refugee named Meng Kyü Wha. Described as "a lovely earnest old man," Meng was locally respected as a lineal descendant of the sage Mencius. After the Nien raiders had gone, Meng enthusiastically introduced Crawford to his home village of Meng-chia-chuang, ten miles southwest of Tengchow. At the end of this first year of his independent pastorate Crawford claimed twenty-two baptisms; and although the Foreign Mission Board only gave him credit for five baptisms, it agreed that his country evangelism did look promising. Villages were opening up, and the villagers—who at first "did not seem to understand the object"—were now telling him, "You are like our own sage Confucius, who went in his cart from village to village exhorting the people to morality."[45]

As Mr. Crawford exhorted the country folk his wife Martha employed herself usefully at home. Her first noticeable Tengchow work, accomplished in 1866, was an interesting bicultural literary endeavor. In order to communicate better with her now sizable domestic staff—and to help other foreign wives with similar problems—she wrote a book called *Tsao yang-fan shu* (Foreign Cookery in Chinese). The book provided some 270 exotic recipes, including such Tuscaloosa specialties as frizzled beef and fritters, sour milk biscuits, perfumed toilet soap, and a disinfectant in which to boil American men's long underwear. It also advised the Chinese reader on general matters like not forgetting to wash often and not throwing garbage into an employer's courtyard.[46]

With the cookbook finished, and with female evangelism moving slowly, Mrs. Crawford asked her husband if she could now start a small boys' boarding school in their home. Eliza Hartwell had been operating a girls' school since 1863, giving her husband's church an attraction that Crawford's lacked, and Mrs. Crawford's friend Sally Holmes did some teaching independently. T. P. Crawford told his wife that straight preaching, as far as he was concerned, was the only work a missionary should do. He did not object to having a few boys around, however, and he agreed to allow the school on the condition that he be personally involved in no way.

Martha Crawford began her school with six little boys in 1867, just as her Tengchow Presbyterian neighbors Julia and Calvin Mateer were doing at roughly the same time. In two years the number was up to fourteen. Mrs. Crawford was disappointed in her hope of using the school to gain access to city homes, but her country boarders were well-behaved and hard working. She did not at first intend to do much; the object was simply to get the boys under "hold" and give them a few characters and some scripture. Then, having no children of her own, she found herself becoming attached to her pupils and interested in their possibilities. She had no particular curriculum, she said, but just "took them farther and farther along in what text books I could get."[47]

As the school prospered T. P. Crawford emerged as one of its strongest supporters. He professed to see a connection between his wife's work and his own access to her pupils' country villages. He also agreed with her that educational services seemed to damp down hostility and attract favorable attention. For a Baptist journal he wrote an article describing how Tengchow Baptist and Presbyterian missionaries helped each other in their educational programs. Missionary education, he said, was a long-felt want, and on several occasions he wrote urging young ladies at home to come out and join the work.[48]

From a number of perspectives the Crawfords' Tengchow work seemed to be developing nicely. By the end of 1868 Mr. Crawford felt able to describe his prospects with downright exuberance: "Thus my little church is steadily growing in numbers and moral power . . . In fact, there are many, both men and women, in an interesting state of mind, and of whom we have hopes of an early conversion. In short, I see a great and *radical change* coming over the public mind, and have never been so encouraged since I arrived in China." [49]

Some Ugly Characters and How to Deal with Them

Despite the encouragements just described, certain rather serious problems also appeared in T. P. Crawford's life during the late 1860s. One problem had to do with his attitude toward his expanding country work—the fact that he regarded it, as in Shanghai, as an opportunity for combining profit with preaching.

As he opened up villages Crawford thus tried for a time, apparently without much success, to recruit local farmers for contract labor in America.[50] As early as the summer of 1866 he was also being paid by foreign merchants in Chefoo to investigate a rumored coal deposit at Lai-wang-kou, between Chefoo and Tengchow. Over the next two years he tested minerals, solicited help from various people, rented a hill and hired men to dig in it, and wound up struggling with "powerful, hostile, and dangerous" natives. The Lai-wang-kou people, claiming that Crawford's diggings were disturbing ancestral graves, asked their district magistrate in 1868 to stop the missionary's operations. Knowing he had no treaty right to do mining work (and having already failed in attempts to get special permission), Crawford maintained that he "never *intended* anything by it but a geological examination." Objections to his activities, he stated, were part of a general conspiracy to run foreigners away.

This conflict came to a head in August 1868. At that point the magistrate arrested Crawford's assistant Lu Ming-chao—his degree-holding scholar—who was supervising whatever was in fact going on on Crawford's hill. Official stone monuments were erected, at the site and in Tengchow city, accusing Lu of illegal mining and warning others against "hooking themselves to Lu Ming-chao." Lu was described as one of a band of lawless sharpers *(wu-chih kun-t'u)*, or "low class persons coveting exorbitant gains." T. P. Crawford was outraged, not on Lu's account but because he read all this as an attack on himself. As he saw it, he had "treaty rights in Lu Ming Chau's reputation . . . To defame him is by implication to defame me." In the same spirit he met the next official move, which was an attempt to make him give up his coal hill: "The magistrate's runner brought them both [Lu Ming-chao and the original hill owner] to my study, and they there begged me by their lives, and the lives of their mothers, wives, and children to give up the title deed—the landlord on his knees— The runner spoke for his master and said if I would only grant this petition I would show great mercy, and be the cause of saving their lives, together with many other like words. Of course I refused to give up the deed."

Crawford's interest lay rather in recovering his own reputation and punishing those who, as he put it, had "calculated to vilify and slander me before the people." Up to the spring of 1869 he pressed through American diplomatic channels for destruction of the offensive monuments, a monetary indemnity, and freedom to go on with his geological exploring. In February he was advised by the U.S. Legation in Peking to "let the whole matter drop," because he had no real case and had himself given the "handle" to anyone who wanted to vilify him.

Mr. Crawford heeded this counsel. Included in his dropping was Lu Ming-chao, who had by March been stripped of his literary degree and was reportedly under sentence of death, but who had somehow escaped and taken sanctuary in the U.S. Consulate at Chefoo. After some weeks Vice-Consul Samuel A. Holmes wrote Crawford asking advice on what to do about his man Lu, or whether Crawford could somehow help the consulate with his case. Crawford replied that Lu Ming-chao definitely had a problem ("if you release him now his head will come off as certain as fate"), and so did the concerned consular officials. But for himself, "I can only say that you have him in charge. I place him in your hands as my Consul . . . The responsibility rests with those who represent the government of the United States in China. I am a law abiding man, and this is a treaty port." [51]

At this point Mr. Crawford's correspondence with the consulate terminated, leaving Lu Ming-chao's fate still very uncertain. Crawford was apparently now preoccupied with "heartburnings" in his Monument Street church congregation, which was after all his primary interest. Problems here centered partly around questions of leadership within the church, and partly—as in Lu Ming-chao's case—around the fact that Crawford often formed business relationships with his parishioners, as their employer or sometimes partner.

In the latter area a dispute had come up involving Wong Wha Yuan, the ex-Presbyterian deacon who had been a Monument Street founding member. In addition to moving quickly into a leading role in the congregation—now considerably expanded by recent country work—Wong had opened a store in which T. P. Crawford was an investor and silent partner. When Wong in 1868 brought into the store a third partner, a non-Christian Chinese, Crawford was infuriated. As pastor, he brought Wong before the whole congregation for trial on a technical charge of Sabbath-breaking; the idea was that Wong would either get rid of the new partner (who ran the store on Sundays) or be himself excluded from the church. The Chinese members of the congregation refused to vote on this issue. Mr. Crawford then called on Mrs. Crawford, and on the strength of her one vote he ruled Wong democratically excluded.[52]

Subsequently a case arose involving Chao Ting Ching, Crawford's preaching assistant, who also had a high place in the esteem of the Chinese membership. By 1869 the Crawfords thought Chao had "become vain and puffed up and needed to know that he was not indispensable to us." Before he could be "sent off to rough it awhile" it was apparently necessary to convict him of an offense graver than vanity. Chao was accordingly soon tried for adultery with the wife of another leading church member (an "ugly" character himself). Evidence added up to a lurid tale of "uncontrolled passion," wrote Mrs. Crawford, "that almost drove me mad." After his trial Chao roughed it for good, or at least he appears no more in the record.[53]

Each of these dismissals—whatever the specific charges—illustrates a single major difficulty in T. P. Crawford's church, which was his inability to get along with the natural leader types in his congregation. This was an important matter in all missionary churches, the need for the foreign pastor to harmonize his own authority with that of his most attractive, energetic parishioners. The missionary definitely needed such people. Mrs. Crawford wrote, "The Chinese *must* have it seems a native they can look up to as a kind of second pastor—we are so far superior to them they dare not try to imitate us, and are greatly under the influence of the man among themselves who has the first place." [54] Those who successively had first place under Crawford, one gathers, managed invariably to cheat, prevaricate, backbite, or otherwise so challenge his authority as to make their exclusion inevitable.

Crawford also continued to have difficulties with his chief American associate, J. B. Hartwell. As Crawford saw it, Hartwell never forgave him for their traumatic confrontation of 1866, when he had spoken to Hartwell about the latter's "grasping disposition." For almost two years after that the Hartwells had refused to attend social gatherings at which either of the Crawfords were present, to the embarrassment of the Crawfords and of others in the area's foreign community. In February 1868 the Reverend Charles Mills of the Presbyterian mission arranged a mediation between the two Baptist families. All parties made apologies and promised friendship. But Mrs. Crawford heard herself being patronized again by Mrs. Hartwell, and Mr. Crawford read aloud from personal letters that made him sound good at the Hartwells' expense. The breach remained and infected the work of the two men—to the extent, Mrs. Crawford's diary suggests, that they were competing to win souls not only for Christ but as marks of His favor in their struggle against each other.[55]

Mr. Hartwell seemed in the late 1860s to have a definite edge in this competition. Assisted by an energetic staff of paid lay preachers, he built his North Street Church into a group that was both larger and considerably more congenial, apparently, than Crawford's. The acknowledged star of Hartwell's team—in fact of the whole Tengchow Christian community—was a man named Wu Tswun Chao. Converted by Hartwell in 1866, Wu rose rapidly from "part teacher, part deacon" to directorship of an evangelistic enterprise that spread over three local hsien (districts). By 1870 he, together with Hartwell and four Chinese employees, had increased North Street membership to fifty-six. Crawford, from a perspective formed by administrative heartburnings and more modest growth, regarded "hireling" Wu with a sort of wistful suspicion: Wu Tswun Chao served Hartwell with vigor and competence, and also with loyalty and obvious personal affection.[56]

In 1870 some unexpected events suddenly changed the picture. In the fall of that year the Tengchow foreign community, frightened by local unrest stemming from the Tientsin Massacre in June, refugeed en masse to Chefoo. At the same time Eliza Hartwell died in childbirth, still refusing to let the Crawfords enter her house, and early the next year J. B. Hartwell took his four little children home to America. This left T. P. Crawford, as in 1864-65, again the only ordained Southern Baptist missionary in the north China field. Hartwell, however, was unwilling this time to allow his church to be placed in Crawford's charge; instead he hastily ordained Wu Tswun Chao, his trusted assistant, as his ministerial successor at North Street and as the first ordained Chinese Christian minister in Shantung province. Hartwell assured everyone that Wu was a "very reliable, earnest, intelligent, and (for a Chinaman) well-informed Christian."[57]

Crawford took this last development quite gracefully. He preached at the Reverend Mr. Wu's ordination, gave him a new Bible and the "right hand of fellowship," and resolved to have a "very tender Christian feeling" for the North Street group and its new pastor. "If they would only allow me," he offered, "I should delight to lead them in the way of holiness and peace."[58] With Hartwell gone there would perhaps be opportunities to teach such things to Wu's people, even to win the esteem of Wu himself. In any case the North Street church no longer seemed quite so threatening, and Crawford could devote all his emotions to a fresh start on his own work.

From the early 1870s T. P. Crawford thus pushed with renewed vigor along several church-building lines. One of the most important of these, in Crawford's view, was to build a church in the physical sense—to have a real Monument Street religious center, separate from his own home and more impressive than the North Street structure. When the Foreign Mission Board was slow to answer an 1871 request for funds, Crawford paid for the $3000 edifice himself. On account of this and other reports the board wrote in 1872 asking Crawford if he were getting "rich" in China. Somewhat hurt, Mr. Crawford asked his Presbyterian friend Charles Mills to set the board straight on "rumors of his great wealth." Mills obligingly wrote that Crawford had made modest sums in Shanghai and elsewhere because of his thrift and financial skill, but that he was rich only "in faith and good works."[59]

The new Monument Street Church, opened in 1872, stood on a nearby lot facing the ancient Ch'i family memorial arch, a Tengchow landmark from which the street took its name. The location created a geomantic confrontation of some local interest, between the church's lofty tower steeple and the spooky influences believed to emanate from the memorial arch. Very proud of his building, Crawford held services frequently and with a bit of fanfare; for the main Sunday morning meeting he designed a large white flag, proclaiming Day of Rest in Chinese characters, which he flew from a staff in the churchyard. Anticipating a growing flock, the new church had seats for 280 worshipers. By 1875 a total membership of 57 was claimed.[60]

Another interest during these years was refinement of his preaching and pastoral style. As a preacher Crawford strove mostly for "great force and effect," not homiletic polish. Since his Shanghai days he had felt that Chinese audiences "could not fix their attention, nor remain quiet long enough to understand a connected discourse," and he now abandoned virtually completely the sermon structuring taught in home seminaries. His approach was rather "assertion of a truth pointed by a striking illustration," or by strings of anecdotes and ideas drawn from notes on a great variety of subjects. It all sounds much like the technique that had so distressed his professors at Union University; but according to some colleagues, it could be quite effective in China: "Crawford was a great preacher in Chinese, and this in spite of the fact that his knowledge of the Chinese language was only ordinary . . . In the church I have seen him hold crowds that would have left others. On the streets I have seen him collect his audiences solely by the powerful way in which he could handle certain topics. In his day few people in the city of Tengchow could say they had never heard the gospel." [61]

As a pastor Crawford talked increasingly about being "democratic," but basically he was always an exhorter and a disciplinarian. This was in line with another long-held view, confirmed by experiences in the late 1860s, that "the best of the Chinese as yet are but children." A great deal of his energy seems to have gone simply into making his people behave in church, no small task in a congregation always "rather floating and uncertain" and without churchgoing traditions.[62] His attitude and some of his problems, perhaps, are reflected in a handout of 1870: "Churches are places for serious worship and must be run by definite regulations. Men and women must be seated separately, and when the time comes to stand or kneel, this means everybody. There must be no smoking, talking, or other noisemaking, no leaning back in the benches, no moving around. When the pastor is preaching, the congregation shall not read books nor look around at each other, but shall look at the pastor and listen attentively to his words. Only when he has finished speaking is it permissible to leave." [63]

Beyond decorum Crawford had strong ideas on the church as a social institution. Many of these ideas came out of the frontier matrix of Southern Baptist experience in America; the local church as T. P. Crawford had known it at Sinking Springs, Kentucky, was not only the body of the neighborhood elect but a whole community in itself. To its members it was a better business bureau and an informal court of law, as well as a place for spiritual comfort and entertainment. Quoting Matthew 19:15-17, Crawford thus told his Tengchow Baptists to bring all their social and business difficulties to church, where hearings, witnesses, calm discussion, and democratic voting would work things out. In irresolvable conflict Pastor Crawford would rule—something like a Chinese sect or clan leader—with "a kind but steady nerve." [64]

Crawford's understanding of democracy has already been demonstrated. His theology, quite apart from his commercial involvements and leadership anxieties, perhaps limited his ability to make Christianity a real harmonizing agency. Meng Kyü Wha's family, for instance, once wondered why Baptists could not "yield just a little of right and justice for the sake of peace."[65] The answer was that Crawford tended to turn all problems into issues involving his faith's doctrinal purity, which made it very difficult for him to operate in the compromising Chinese fashion. He often stated that he had no objection to Chinese old custom *per se*, but at the same time he intended "not to engraft Christianity upon heathenism, but to uproot the one and plant the other in its place." [66]

These contradictions continued to present him with pastoral problems. To get his views across better—perhaps also to take his mind off other things—Crawford returned during this period to literary work, an area in which he had been inactive since the 1850s. Some of his new writings bear obviously on his pastoral situation. His *Christian Ritual*, for example—an 1870 handbook for Mandarin-speaking Baptists—deals considerably with behavior problems; most of it, a little curiously, deals with how to conduct a proper funeral service, stemming from Crawford's fear that his people were grafting Christianity onto Chinese ancestor veneration. [67] He did a hymnbook in the same year, many of the hymns original, and a *Mandarin Grammar* for use in schools like his wife's. In English he turned to scriptural interpretation, as in an 1874 essay on "What Caused the Sudden Death of Christ?" These last efforts drew a somewhat critical reaction from missionary colleagues; as one friend observed, T. P. Crawford had some very original ideas, and he "dearly loved to get hold of odd views." [68]

Crawford's most noteworthy writing of this period was an 1873 book called *Ku kuo chien lüeh* (Brief history of the ancient world). This was again done partly for use in Mrs. Crawford's school, but it also represents an attempt to impress the Chinese scholars who came to Tengchow to take examinations for official service. The book's China section is on the whole accurate, if a bit sketchy, and shows knowledge of sources like the Bamboo Annals and Ssu-ma Ch'ien. Its effect on Chinese scholars must have been limited even so; a little too much weight seems placed on immoralities in China's past, and on the "300,000 false gods and idols" still around.[69]

The great seriousness with which T. P. Crawford took himself as a Christian professional—as one called by God "to batter these ramparts of sin and Satan"—at times strikes one as something of a paradox. Numerous missionaries who knew him well described him as a man of "wonderful vivacity," an entertaining and even delightful personality. Already rather patriarchal in appearance by the 1870s, he strode about with a long stick fashioned like a Biblical shepherd's crook. Sometimes he dressed in Chinese style, but by preference he wore a trailing Prince Albert coat open at the neck to accommodate his long beard. He spoke like a minor prophet, in scriptural clichés, with occasional nonscriptural prophecies ("This dynasty will die nasty") that struck his colleagues as amusing. By all foreigners except the Hartwell family, apparently, he was regarded as a Baptist of "real sociability," and as close in most ways to his own 1874 definition of the ideal missionary: "a man with good hard common sense, a tough heart, and generous nature, one who will doctor away whether his patients get better or worse, and like Abraham, walk by faith, and hope against hope."

Still, something hard to define but sadly vital was lacking in this faithful heart. One of the friends who thought him "always interesting" felt also that "his character was more of the robust than of the winning type. One was not easily drawn into a feeling of intimacy with him." Martha Crawford's father, alarmed by frequent letters about turmoil among the Tengchow Baptists, feared his daughter's husband lacked "that *humble devotedness*" proper to the pastoral calling. Almost everyone contrasted his working style with the folksiness of his "widely and greatly beloved" wife Martha. No one ever wrote about him—as some did about his colleague Hartwell—that the Chinese loved him or that "he loved the Chinese, and they recognized the fact." [70]

2/

A Stranger in a Strange Land: Crawford's Difficulties Multiply

While T. P. Crawford busied himself at writing and pastoring in the early 1870s, a new "heartburning" was slowly building to flash point. By the middle years of the decade he had become thoroughly enmeshed in the most serious of many social traumas that intruded on his long career, a struggle from whose effects he would never really recover. It involved all the usual elements—money, pride, and J. B. Hartwell—and perhaps by this point Mr. Crawford should have been wise enough to avoid such trouble. On the other hand, it was perhaps a logical outcome of behavior patterns that could have led nowhere else.

The Kao Ku San Affair

The principal actor in this drama, apart from T. P. Crawford, was a Chefoo Christian merchant named Kao Ku San. Among Shantung Chinese Baptists Kao had a status somewhat comparable to that of Wu Tswun Chao: as Wu was the most prominent native administrator, Kao was important because he had more money than anybody else. Enjoying close relations with both Wu Tswun Chao and J. B. Hartwell, Kao annually donated US $300 to the North Street Church in Tengchow, which he frequently visited as an honored out-of-town member. Kao's support was crucial to North Street activities, particularly when Hartwell left in 1871.

There was good reason for Kao Ku San's generosity to the church. His money came from a number of sources, but it had all been made recently by capitalizing on his status as an early Baptist convert. His rise from impoverished obscurity had come specifically through association with the ubiquitous Holmes family —three Baptist brothers from Virginia, who as missionaries, diplomats, and businessmen seemed to be into everything in Chefoo in the 1860s. Converted to Christianity in 1860 by the Reverend James L. Holmes, Kao found employment and soon worked up to full partnership in brother Matthew G. Holmes's trading company. As the firm, called the Ch'ing Mei Hong, prospered, it opened branches in Tientsin and Shanghai. Kao Ku San acquired ownership of the *Dragon,* the hong's ocean-going steamer, and he invested extensively in Chefoo real estate.[1]

T. P. Crawford, impressed by the Ch'ing Mei Hong's success, invested in the late 1860s some 5900 taels (equivalent to about US $10,000) in the form of a loan at 12 percent interest. This money went to expanding the firm's operations at Shanghai, headed by one Li Chin-yü. Crawford was in no hurry to be repaid his principal. In 1871, however, he was troubled by reports that Matthew Holmes was putting his estate in his wife's name and making hasty preparations for a trip to America. Crawford had a talk with Holmes, and together they talked with Kao Ku San. Details are unclear, but the upshot was that Kao signed an English-language agreement whereby he took over the hong and assumed personal responsibility for its debts. Apparently in exchange for an extension on the debt owed to Crawford, he mortgaged the *Dragon* and several of his properties, including his own impressive home, to Crawford.

Crawford was apparently not at great pains to explain to Kao just what he was signing. Kao seems to have been somewhat disingenuous, too, in that he did not tell Crawford that the hong had fallen into difficulties, with several other creditors already pressing him. In any case Matthew Holmes sailed away in December 1871, never to be seen in China again. Crawford and Kao Ku San were left with an agreement which neither entirely understood, and which would eventually bring disaster to both.[2]

A critical third ingredient was added to this relationship in 1872, when J. B. Hartwell—much to everyone's surprise—suddenly reappeared after only a year in America. He had found a new wife in the person of his former wife's sister, and this time he decided to locate in Chefoo rather than in Tengchow. This, he said, was because Chefoo was now a more important place, and because his friend the Reverend Wu Tswun Chao was already handling Tengchow with "a great deal of discretion and propriety." Actually, most of the members of Wu's church, as in all Tengchow churches at the time, were natives and part-time residents of country villages scattered all over east Shantung—many of them closer to Chefoo than to Tengchow. By setting up in Chefoo Hartwell was thus in a sense as close as ever to his old congregation. With the full cooperation of Wu Tswun Chao, he quickly resumed an advisory relation with the North Street church, amounting to "constant counsels and occasional presence."³

The assistants who had originally helped Hartwell assemble the North Street congregation moved (except for Wu Tswun Chao) to Chefoo to assist him again. A kind of two-pronged Hartwell operation now went forward—new work actually in Chefoo, plus the Tengchow work technically headed by Wu. Financial support of the Tengchow branch came partly from generous individuals like Kao Ku San, but mostly from the Foreign Mission Board via Hartwell's Chefoo appropriation. This money went not only to pay Pastor Wu's salary of 108,000 (later 150,000) cash—sums in excess of US $100—but also to things like a North Street entertainment fund and to personal loans to four leading Baptists of Chao-yüan district.⁴

T. P. Crawford, who was trying to establish strict self-support at his own Monument Street church, looked on these developments with alarm. He saw in Hartwell's counsels "a hostile *regnum in regno*," and in Wu Tswun Chao's activities a burgeoning money-changing operation.⁵ Most of all, he was galled by the claims of Hartwell and Wu that the North Street "church without foreigners" was an indigenous Christian body needing no outside help. Crawford could only interpret this as a deliberate falsehood aimed at concealing Hartwell's renewed competition with him in Tengchow; particularly irritating was the fact that the self-support money was advertised as coming from Kao Ku San, a man deeply in Crawford's debt.

Out of this background Crawford began late in 1872 to put strong pressure on Kao Ku San to pay back all that Kao owed him. Kao, however, was now in worse financial shape than ever. As Crawford gradually discovered, the real reason for Matthew Holmes's departure—and for Kao's difficulties—was that the Ch'ing Mei Hong had been stolen blind by Li Chin-yü, its Shanghai manager. This individual was now revealed to be "Wild Calf" Li of Huang-hsien, a notorious swindler. Although the hong's books were "utterly false and unintelligible," it was estimated that the Wild Calf had gotten away with as much as 40,000 taels, more than enough to ruin Kao Ku San's firm. Kao—or rather Crawford, now—did not even own the *Dragon*, because Li Chin-yü had absconded with the money sent to complete payment on the steamer.

Because of these difficulties Kao Ku San told Crawford he could give him nothing but a thousand taels' worth of marble tombstones that happened to be on hand. Crawford took the

tombstones to Shanghai, where to the large amusement of the foreign business community he tried to sell them on speculation. Unsuccessful, he came angrily back to Tengchow to demand his money
again. At this point lack of understanding became crucial. The
interest rate on the original loan, compounded, had increased Kao's
debt to a figure that Kao professed to find incomprehensible.
Crawford was similarly unable to understand when he himself was
presented with a bill for US $847, as money owed to associates of
Kao who had supposedly been his and Kao's middlemen.

By the beginning of 1874, as J. B. Hartwell put it, "Passion
as well as a sense of justice had begun to speak loudly in the breasts
of both." Kao was circulating "all sorts of slander" about Crawford, while the missionary reported that Kao was smoking opium
and gambling. In the summer of that year, against Hartwell's
advice, Kao Ku San finally brought a suit against Crawford at the
American consulate in Chefoo. Available evidence indicates that
the suit amounted to an extortion attempt. Kao charged that
Crawford had tricked him in their original paperwork, and that
Crawford now actually owed him, Kao Ku San, 3000 taels for
properties already transferred to the missionary.

All the documents supported Crawford, but at the trial
Kao produced two witnesses—both Chinese Christians of Hartwell's group—who swore that Crawford was a thieving liar and
that he had swindled Kao Ku San. One of the witnesses was a son-
in-law of Kao, but the other was Liang Wei Shing, Hartwell's current chief assistant. This man—whom Hartwell had just arranged
to have supported by the Chestnut Street Baptist Church of
Louisville, Kentucky—told Crawford privately that if he did not
pay 10,000 taels (about US $15,000) to him and Kao he would
make disclosures that would ruin Crawford's ministerial character.

Kao lost the suit, and Consul Eli Sheppard warned him that
if he did not repay Crawford in two years the missionary could
take possession of properties including Kao's home. Kao, "mad-
dened by defeat," told Crawford he would kill him. Crawford
responded (so Hartwell reported) with violent gesticulation and
unseemly swearing. Late in 1874 Kao came up to Tengchow armed
and "prepared for murder"; but Crawford hid while local Christians put physical restraints on Kao and escorted him back to
Chefoo. Crawford appealed to the Chinese authorities, and then
to Consul Sheppard, to have Kao arrested or at least bound over
to keep the peace. The Chinese refused to take action. Hartwell
persuaded Sheppard not to press the matter, on the theory that Kao

had been provoked by Crawford and that he was in any case repentant now.

Frustrated by the civil authorities, Crawford made an appeal for justice before the North Street church in Tengchow. He asked that it take action against its members Kao, Liang Wei Shing, and Chao Shang Ching (Kao's son-in-law). This proved to be another fiasco. Crawford had just committed the indiscretion of intercepting and reading a letter from Hartwell to Wu, and when he asked Wu's church to censure Kao Ku San, Pastor Wu countered by proposing that Crawford be censured instead, for reading another minister's mail. Violent scenes followed as Crawford accused Wu of conspiring against him, and Wu "shook his fists, threatened and screamed." T. P. Crawford was the one finally censured, and the split between the two Tengchow Baptist churches was complete.[6]

In Chefoo the distressed missionary community made a last effort to get things straightened out. Crawford was persuaded to have one more talk with Kao, at the home of the English Baptist Timothy Richard. This meeting turned out to be a sort of last straw. Enraged by ostentatious praying and repentance on Kao's part, Crawford apparently suffered some kind of stroke. As Hartwell described it, Crawford became "very much flushed and had a swelled and bloated look about the face." After he had "gesticulated and stamped around and talked loudly," he claimed to be worn out from nervous exhaustion and "softening of the brain." [7]

Crawford soon recovered his composure, but the strain of recent events had in fact worn out a number of people. A little unexpectedly, Hartwell was the first principal participant to become a casualty. His second wife, who had apparently been unprepared for the combative aspects of missionary life, had fallen into chronic illness and was already putting pressure on her husband to take her back to America. Early in 1875 he acceded, and for the third time in four years the Southern Baptist situation was turned upside down by an abrupt Hartwell move. His Chefoo work quickly declined, as his team of assistants—now seeing themselves as "a head without a tail"—scattered to secular employments. Kao Ku San went quietly back to work, and Wu Tswun Chao was again thrown on his own resources.[8]

As the Kao Ku San affair at last began to recede, a number of people also wrote lengthy letters to the Foreign Mission Board, which been hearing rumors of a "deadly war" in its North China Mission. Crawford reported that Kao and other renegades had perpetrated "crimes of the deepest dye" against him, at the instigation of J. B. Hartwell. In his view Hartwell had been in "a passion of hostility and dislike" ever since their falling out a decade before. "By some means, I say not how," Crawford wrote, "he has prejudiced most of his people against me . . . Here is the root of my difficulties with Kao Ku San." [9] Hartwell maintained that Crawford's complaints were alibis. Before leaving China he wrote the FMB that Crawford had never been able to get along with Chinese people; that his business activities were ruining mission work in Shantung; and that regarding the Kao case, "the fact is Mr. Crawford's mind works morbidly on the subject of Kieu San and his money." The true root of Crawford's difficulties, Hartwell stated, was that Kao and other Chinese "had formed their opinion of him from their own observations of his character." [10]

In the correspondence of the two men, and apparently in their conduct as well, certain differences existed that gradually won Crawford the sympathy both of most other missionaries and of the home board. Hartwell's attitude had from the first been one of sanctimonious self-righteousness, and sometimes, toward T. P. Crawford himself, he displayed what can only be called sadism. To the FMB he wrote, "I feel heartily sorry for Bro. C. and for the sad state of things he has brought about," while to Crawford he sent a one-line note: "When you get to Heaven, I hope there will be no 'softening of the brain' there." [11] Crawford, even as he accused Hartwell of prejudicing people, added, "We are morally and in many other respects *both* worthy . . . Oh, brethren, pity our *weakness,* and try by some means to get us out of this strife." Hartwell moreover began making all sorts of accusations early in 1874, while Crawford never mentioned Hartwell to the board until specifically asked for his side of the story in 1875. [12]

Another side of the story, which no doubt leaked out, was that in denouncing Crawford Hartwell made personal insinuations about several other missionaries who were taking Crawford's side, and he accused U.S. Vice-Consul Samuel A. Holmes (the third Holmes brother) of conspiring with Crawford to defraud Kao Ku San. What most impressed their local associates, however, was that Crawford—although volatile in the presence of his opponents— made no representations to outsiders that he had not already (as Hartwell indignantly reported) made even more strongly to his opponents' faces. Hartwell by contrast slyly encouraged his Chinese to resist Crawford and fired off self-serving letters in all directions. As Miss Lottie Moon, a Tengchow Baptist, observed, "While the one party has bruited it in correspondence from one end of China to the other, a dignified silence has been preserved by the other party. While the one, by a shrug or a sneer, has given the cue of scorn and contempt to the native Christians of our church, the other has remained absolutely silent or has resolutely upheld the Christian character of his opponent . . . What *could* be more disgraceful?" [13]

In the spring of 1875 the Foreign Mission Board directed Matthew T. Yates, now its senior China missionary, to go up from Shanghai and try to bring about an "amalgamation," under Crawford, of Crawford's Monument Street Church with Wu Tswun Chao's North Street congregation. Hartwell, writing from America, tried first to block these discussions and then to prejudice Yates against Crawford. He also sent to Wu Tswun Chao money drafts on the FMB totaling over US $500, to keep self-support alive at North Street and to frustrate interference by Crawford. As Yates gradually got the picture—in Tengchow and by correspondence from elsewhere—he reprimanded Hartwell for inciting his adherents against another missionary, and for allowing money to become so important in the activities of the North Street Church. [14]

By the beginning of 1876 T. P. Crawford had thus been vindicated before his fellow missionaries. Things had gone much too far, however, for an amalgamation of his church with Wu's; the whole spirit at North Street, he reported, was far too hostile for such an effort to succeed. He had also fallen into a new dispute with a Chefoo Presbyterian, involving alleged theft of a Presbyterian convert for his own congregation. [15] Even worse, as he reapplied his energies to his own pastorate, he found the Monument Street group in a state approaching chaos. The two leading elders, Sun Chang Lung and Meng Kyü Wha, had fallen out with each other in 1872, and by 1874 earnest old Meng had withdrawn with all his family. Mrs. Liu, longtime director of woman's work, had by her "wicked temper and perverse ways, her jealousies and bickerings" driven away more women than she attracted. By 1876 she had been turned out of the church along with her son and husband. [16]

In this situation, and with news arriving of a fresh and even worse feud splitting the entire Christian community at Chefoo, Crawford began to "try to save the pieces" at Tengchow. Openly hated by half the Chinese Baptists of his city, he felt many fears regarding the future. Actually—due to brain softening and other physical problems—he anticipated being dead within five years. In the meantime he apparently saw little else to look forward to: "Life in a heathen land is hard on the *heart*. To live from year to year without the least sympathy from those all around you! To always impart and never receive! To love and never be loved! To know but never be known! A stranger in a strange land!" [17]

Events of 1876: Problems with Church, School, and Health

From 1876 one discerns in T. P. Crawford's life a kind of pendulum or cycle phenomenon. At times, as at the beginning of 1876, he appears so despondent as to be on the verge of break-down. At other points his spirits rally, as some unexpected development brings notable happiness. In between come months or even years of the "long pull at dull, monotonous heathenism"—long stretches of nothing, as Mrs. Crawford said, except abominations, when she and her husband "wept our souls *dry*" from lives totally devoid of "freshness and elasticity." [18] For at least the last five years of the 1870s one sees both Crawfords on an emotional roller coaster that would truly have destroyed any but the toughest of hearts.

The year just begun was a particularly severe one. Ignoring the cold and uncourteous treatment accorded him by Wu Tswun Chao's followers, Crawford worked to get his Monument Street group back into order. It was a dismal experience. New trials and dismissals were found necessary. These were accompanied by numerous voluntary resignations, plus a general decline of religious feeling among members still around. One of Mrs. Crawford's favorite younger converts told her in May that he felt hypocrisy all about him: "He seemed reluctant to speak—but after some hesitation said in substance that . . . for himself he felt not a particle of that warmheartedness Christians ought to have—or desire to teach and lead others. He was not in a warmhearted frame of mind—and no one else was. He had noticed for several years not a member of the church was in that state." [19]

One factor seems to have been the congregation's inability to understand T. P. Crawford's policy on money matters, or rather to square his stated position with his observed practices. From conviction and from recent experience with Hartwell's people, Crawford said, it was his position to keep Christianity and financial gain separate—to make it a rule to have no Christian hirelings and to "not lend money to Chinese, it was full of evils." To some of his members, however, he had revealed a willingness to hire or to lend to virtually anyone when it promised profit to himself. Only when such associations became unprofitable or embarrassing—as Lu Ming-chao and Wong Wha Yuan had found out—were the pastor's principles so finely drawn. Then they were employed to justify abandoning or excluding some formerly leading personality, or to draw the congregation into conflict with Crawford against an outsider like Kao Ku San.[20]

This issue came to a head in June. At that time a group led by Deacon Sun Kyi Di submitted a request for a church loan to "help eight country brethren who were in straits." The problem was that the wheat crop had failed—the onset of a great famine that would eventually take 13,000,000 lives in north China. Crawford opposed the loan on principle, deploring "the evils of giving" and "the idea that the church is so much of a money concern." He suggested that the eight country brethren, far from being in any real need, were trying to pad their already affluent circumstances. The contrast between the circumstances involved and the pastor's own comfortable situation—and between his attitude and the support his people had given him in the long struggle with Kao and Wu Tswun Chao—greatly angered a number of members. This was also the beginning of a rift between Crawford and the Sun family, for many years his leading supporters.[21]

As old converts fell away they were not replaced by new ones. Years of quarreling had closed many villages that had produced Baptists in the 1860s: Meng Kyü Wha, for instance, would now not let Crawford evangelize in Meng-chia-chuang, and in Chao-yüan and Huang-hsien he was kept out by friends of Hartwell and Wu Tswun Chao. A preacher training (lay evangelist) program foundered at about this time on Crawford's refusal to aid the evangelists financially. He urged them to emulate the farmer preachers of Tennessee, who supported themselves and preached for the love of God. If one preached well, Crawford explained, bands of adherents would arise to support him, or "such at least is the theory." On this theory Crawford quickly lost his preachers because, Deacon Chang Yun Who said, a part-time farmer in Shantung would starve waiting for such support.[22]

Another problem centered around Martha Crawford's school for boys. The school had been going now for a decade, and to Mrs. Crawford's gratification it was a definite success. Enrollment had increased to twenty, the curriculum had expanded, and some of her original pupils were themselves teaching the smaller boys.[23] T. P. Crawford's earlier enthusiasm for education, however, had by 1876 diminished. Several factors were involved, but the most evident is that he had come to feel the school simply took too much of Mrs. Crawford's attention. It was his feeling that she should do more of strictly evangelistic work, preferably together with himself.

Martha Crawford's 1876 diary entries do show her absorbed by her pupils to the virtual exclusion of other matters. In particular—and this seems to have bothered T. P. Crawford most—she was absorbed by an older student named Kwo Yu Yoong, a youth of great precocity but uncertain physical and spiritual health. Over a seven-year period Mrs. Crawford had developed toward Kwo feelings which she found difficult to analyze, except, as she put it, "I have never been so attached to any Chinaman before." [24]

An outsider surmises from her "great deal of happiness" and many heartaches over Kwo that Martha Crawford was giving to this young man some of the affection that she had learned long ago in Shanghai she would never be able to give to a child of her own. In any case she obviously cared greatly for Kwo Yu Yoong, a feeling he also obviously returned. She hoped that he would soon take over her school as head teacher, and someday become a minister. Unfortunately, Kwo's affection for Mrs. Crawford did not extend to her husband, and he was known in the church as a critic of T. P. Crawford's pastoral style. The combination of factors bothered Crawford considerably. Also unfortunately—in the eyes of both Crawfords—Kwo was becoming romantically interested in a girl named Mary Kiang. Miss Kiang had for some time been a prominent member of Wu Tswun Chao's church, and she had been a particular favorite of the Hartwell family.[25]

Crawford coped with all these problems in several ways. One way was by returning to literary work, as in his difficult period of the late 1860s. In 1876 he thus completed an English-language book begun several years previously, *The Patriarchal Dynasties*. Here he applied himself to "the great question of the age," identified as the exact age of the world, and to proving that ancient Chinese chronology was the Book of Genesis in disguise. His studies were based on Genesis, on a Ming dynasty Chinese scholar named Wang Shih-ching, and on "Berosus, the great Chaldean historian." The finished book maintained that the age of the world was 14,376 years and, among other discoveries, that the Garden of Eden was a theocratic confederacy with a population of 1,174,-405,120. His work, he believed, ended all false notions on a number of subjects and necessitated "the modification of many opinions, the fall of many theories, the revision of many books, and liberty for all to believe both in the Bible and in modern discoveries." [26]

Of several obvious comments that could be made about *The Patriarchal Dynasties*, the most pertinent is that it suggests that something really was happening to Crawford's brain. As early as 1874 readers had remarked that Crawford's scholarly points were either so eccentric as to be incomprehensible or so obvious as to be not worth making. Moreover, one reviewer had observed, they tended to be proved by mistranslations, quotations out of context, and sometimes by statements exactly opposite to what a reported source had said.[27] But at least he had had a more modest perspective. Now, with this new book—which readers clearly regarded with amused incredulity—he seemed to be losing a certain ability to distinguish reality from fantasy. For a man who liked to be known as "honest, intelligently honest, perseveringly honest, if he was anything" to predict "mighty consequences" from such stuff seems a rather unhappy development.[28]

Otherwise he moved to clear up two specific grudges. One of these was Kao Ku San, whose two-year grace period expired in the summer of 1876 with his debt still unpaid. Crawford badgered the Chinese authorities first into making Kao turn over most of his properties to the missionary, and then, in September, into putting him in jail for insufficient payment. At the same time he took Mrs. Crawford on an extended trip to Japan. Martha Crawford's diary notes that the trip was to be a rest ("Mr. C's brain is troubling him") and an escape from "the great weight of being hated." It also took her away from her school and from Kwo Yu Yoong; and while in Kyoto Crawford located two English orphans whom he and his wife precipitately adopted. For a number of reasons Mrs. Crawford questioned the wisdom of taking on these children, but T. P. Crawford apparently won her over. They would be good for "our spiritual and mental health," it was suggested, and to counter Chinese views that childlessness was evidence of divine displeasure. They would also permanently divert Mrs. Crawford's emotions from Kwo Yu Yoong.[29]

The year ended on an ambiguous note. On the one hand, Crawford had his final revenge on Kao Ku San. As Kao spent the fall in prison, Crawford quietly took possession of all his properties except his own home. Then, on the day Kao was released—the last day of December 1876, as it "snowed a deep snow"—Crawford had Kao's family and all their belongings turned into the street. Other missionaries sent notes "begging for pity for Kao," and Kao Ku San eventually came himself to seek Crawford's mercy. Angered by all this "hue and cry of oppression," Crawford refused to see Kao and sold the home to another party. "Thus his righteousness in the matter is manifest," Mrs. Crawford observed.[30]

The physical and mental condition of both Crawfords simultaneously continued to deteriorate. T. P. Crawford now felt "nervous paralysis" in his lower extremities, as well as feeling that "we scarcely dare to hope . . . all sorts of indescribable difficulties beset our paths." Martha went from being "so absent minded as to be almost useless" in July to experiencing "dizziness so I am not able to concentrate" in November. More significantly, perhaps, her husband had begun clearly to display the deviousness, cruelty, and overwhelming self-centeredness for which they had so despised J. B. Hartwell.[31]

Crawford Articulates a Philosophy and Breaks Down

The next eighteen months were another critical period for T. P. Crawford. After a generally frustrating year in 1876, he found 1877 to be much more rewarding. Maintaining the aggressive style that had disposed of Kao Ku San, he attacked several other threats and won victories over most. He also took stock of his quarter-century in China, organized his reflections, and articulated a personal philosophy before an important assembly of his colleagues. At the same time he became increasingly more narrow-minded and vindictive. Given his established up-and-down pattern, the consequences were dreadful.

As the new year opened, Crawford was already working to eliminate a leadership problem in his church. The difficulty this time was with Sun Chang Lung, the congregation's senior surviving member. As a mission schoolteacher and family head, Old Sun had lately become too puffed up ("first in scholarship, first in wealth and position, first in his own estimation and demands"). The technique here was first to dismiss him from his teaching job, which got his followers "very much put out," and then, at the Chinese New Year, quickly to lay what amounted to a trap to catch him presiding over family ancestral rites. For years it had been conceded that at such times Old Sun could discreetly "have out his ancestral paraphernalia"; now it became a matter where "the purity of the church is at stake," requiring a trial. By telling the members that God expected them to exclude idolaters, Crawford achieved a state of confusion and, after some months, Sun's dismissal by a close vote.[32]

While the Sun Chang Lung case went on Crawford launched a general campaign to trim the educational program. The stated reason was that it had become unreasonably expensive; for several years the value of silver in Shantung had been falling in relation to copper cash, and it happened that missionary salaries were paid in silver while schools operated on cash. Crawford calculated that his own salary had been effectively reduced by 30 percent, and that the mission's various teachers and pupils were thus profiting at his expense.[33]

The school for girls supervised by Mrs. Sally Holmes broke up with the firing of Old Sun. To deal with Martha Crawford's boys' school, Mr. Crawford summoned its parents and teachers to a January consultation. Here he reminded the parents of his mission's past generosity in educating their children free of charge, even though "right principle" dictated that people should pay for services received. He than announced a progressive pay scale whereby each schoolchild would pay 1000 cash (*ca* US $1.00) immediately, 2000 cash by the end of the year, 4000 in 1878, and more to be determined after that. The Chinese teachers—who were, by comparison to foreign teachers, persons "of inferior qualifications and utility" anyway—would have their salaries reduced. Mrs. Crawford seems to have been somewhat stunned by all this, but she and a reduced group of patrons went along with her husband's plan.[34]

The coming of spring brought additional satisfactions. Minnie and Freddie—the two Caucasian orphans—arrived from Kyoto in April, and Mrs. Crawford, now forty-seven years old, soon had her hands full with mothering. Back in America the Foreign Mission Board had also terminated J. B. Hartwell's money drafts to China, bringing hard times to his former followers. By May Wu Tswun Chao had closed down the entire North Street operation. His assistants and his congregation, he stated, had deserted him, enabling Crawford finally to write, "Thus the artificial arrangement of a 'self-supporting church with a native pastor' has broken down for want of *vitality* and *foreign money* . . . a good thing for the church." Later they heard that Wu had moved into Buddhism, selling incense and funeral supplies.[35]

As Wu Tswun Chao closed his church the Crawfords were en route to Shanghai, to attend the first General Conference of Protestant Missionaries in China. This gathering (May 10–24, 1877) was attended by 126 missionaries representing 21 European and American societies. Numerous papers, resolutions, and committees resulted, and the meeting was widely recognized as a significant, if very tentative, ecumenical beginning; it proved such a gathering could at least take place without breaking up in quarrels, which had been the anticipation of some on hand. Martha Crawford, who prepared a paper on "Woman's Work for Woman," was one of four women admitted onto the forty-five paper program. T. P. Crawford got a spot, too, on the subject of "Advantages and

Disadvantages of the Employment of Native Assistants." The topic
was one on which he had long had an attentive eye, and from
which he could digress to offer a variety of strongly felt views.[36]

In Shanghai Crawford learned that J. B. Hartwell had been
sending around a fresh wave of "dastardly" correspondence about
him. He further learned that Hartwell was attacking him at home
before the FMB, dragging up the old coal hill story and many
other slanders. It had taken one board member ten hours, Crawford heard, simply to read through all the charges Hartwell was
making against him.[37] This news no doubt added to Crawford's
already strong convictions regarding native hirelings. In conversation with other conferees, however, he found encouragement in
his own views, and on May 18 he commented, "The peculiarity of
my position has cost me a good deal of mental suffering. It is far
more pleasant to find oneself in company with others . . . I am
rejoiced however to find since coming to this Conference that the
tide is turning among the missionaries in favor of the voluntary
principle of labor. Let the reformation go on."[38]

On the following day Crawford presented in his speech an
outline of matters needing reform. His main point was that at least
one in every fifteen Chinese Christians was in some kind of full-
time mission employ, even though scarcely any of these "semi-
converted, half-Christianized" individuals were worth employing.
Most of them knew nothing about Christianity, really, except that
it paid well for a very vague and loosely regulated sort of work.
Crawford obviously had in mind Tengchow's North Street Church
as his case study in religious racketeering—proof that foreign
money "always before their eyes and clinking in their ears" attracted grasping, dishonest converts and earned for Christianity the
contempt of the Chinese public.[39]

The mission cause would surely fail, the speech went on, unless
missionaries kept remunerations "so small as to leave a liberal margin for the play of the voluntary principle." Experience demonstrated that Chinese people by nature lacked moral, spiritual, and
altruistic qualities; indeed, they were mentally unable even to
think about things in "those pure regions which lie above all human
traffic." As Crawford added in response to two other papers, the
natural religion of China was "a bowl of rice with two chopsticks
in it," from which came the fact that "with the Chinese the philosophy of life is to eat." Christianity's task was not to cater to all
this but to "beget higher and holier aims and thereby overthrow the
foundation of all their systems." His own work bore this out: "We
try to maintain strict discipline among the members, believing

that religion is ordained to work the fear of God and the elevation of conscience. Education and science utterly fail in this particular. Success is small and growth slow here, but everything else is fallacious. We must teach them to fear God and keep his commandments, not only for wrath but for conscience sakes. Such teachings can never fail . . . Merchants may break and steamers explode; but moral and religious instruction will remain forever." [40]

Reaction to Crawford's view was mostly disapproving. Samuel Dodd, a Presbyterian, said that Crawford was trying to make himself look good by making the Chinese sound impossible, and that his speech was "calculated to do much harm." Another critic called him self-contradictory and destructive. A third wondered if Crawford had heard of love, the "Christian principle that should override all others." Crawford argued vigorously with these critics, to the point that Mrs. Crawford feared "danger of some unpleasantness." Afterwards, in the published *Records* of the conference, his paper was printed with a special editorial disclaimer. [41]

T. P. Crawford took a sanguine view of his conference experiences, and back in Tengchow he continued to be "warmly cheered" by certain events. In Richmond the FMB had tired of reading J. B. Hartwell's allegations, and also of being embarrassed by reports of angry Hartwell speeches before the home churches. By the summer of 1877 Baptist pastors, appalled by his tales of missionary strife, were asking the board to send Hartwell to some distant post as quickly as possible. [42] By early 1878 he had been reprimanded, and the following summer he resigned from the FMB to move to California, where he would take up work among Chinese immigrants. There the second Mrs. Hartwell, who had always "disliked the Chinese exceedingly," at once fell ill and died. [43]

By February 1878 Crawford was already so encouraged as to reattempt an amalgamation of all the Tengchow Baptists. With Hartwell and Wu Tswun Chao both out of the picture, Mrs. Crawford wrote, "a sort of bitterness seems to be plucked up." As Crawford attempted to take over the property and assets of the North Street Church, however, some of its former leading members—now back in their native Chao-yüan district—resisted vehemently. Anticipating that Crawford would try to collect the personal loans they had taken out of North Street funds, these men sent anguished protests to the *lao-hui* (home church) via J. B. Hartwell. Four of these lengthy letters were translated and sent to the FMB by the obviously delighted Hartwell. In addition to trying to steal their money and their church, the letter writers reported, Crawford was "oppressing the brethren and cooling off the hearts of all the members, by evil deeds, . . . that he may obtain the glory of this world." [44]

In response Crawford simply declared this group to be a Chinese guild or trading company—not a religious interest—and unilaterally merged the two former churches in a new Tung Chow Baptist Church. In an immediate tactical sense he won: the Chao-yüan Baptists soon turned to fighting among themselves, dropped their Christianity, and faded from the scene.[45] He never collected the debts, however, and in another sense the whole episode was disastrous. Months of renewed feuding brought out a whole accumulation of grievances, in Crawford's own adherents as well as in the former North Street people. Ever since the trial of Old Sun certain members had spoken "coldly" to him, misbehaved during his sermons, and relapsed into cursing and other bad habits. Now people even complained that he served inferior food at social events, and his few North Street recruits had clearly come expecting another "bank with dividends." It was not an auspicious beginning for the new union church.[46]

Other problems developed simultaneously. Most seriously, things were not going well with Mrs. Crawford. Years of worry over her husband's difficulties—from being "beside [her] self with grief and anxiety" over Kao Ku San to coping with the "great deal of confusion" in the new merged church—had worn her out. She still worked almost as much as ever in her school, and now she had their adopted children. Minnie and Freddie had turned out to be "not bright" mentally, and caring for them added one more burden that threatened, Mrs. Crawford wrote, to be "more than my nerves can stand." [47]

By March 1878 the Crawfords also sensed a "drift" in their relations with each other. T. P. Crawford blamed this on the effort Martha continued to invest in the school. He had been particularly upset since the preceding fall, when a recent graduate had reportedly cheated him on a business loan; in addition, Kwo Yu Yoong was still around, and Mrs. Crawford continued to worry over him. In any case Crawford began telling his wife in March that their feeling of separation was due to her absorption in schoolwork, and that as a missionary she should spend her working time in a more directly evangelistic way. Mrs. Crawford was distraught over the choice—husband or school—that she was being asked to make. Of her husband's demand that she close the school she wrote, "I should deplore this. The very thought of it seemed like amputating all my limbs. I hardly think it necessary." [48]

As T. P. Crawford struggled that spring with his work and

his marriage, a host of unsettling influences apparently bore down on him. In many ways his and his wife's whole home life had been in turmoil for two years. In the streets and at the door they had had to fend off "troops of beggars" (famine refugees), and in the compound Mrs. Crawford's female servants and their two families fought constantly. Mr. Crawford's current male servants—two cousins named Fung—were thieves, he thought, and they treated him contemptuously, as a "foreign devil." [49] For at least a year visiting missionaries had been telling each other that T. P. Crawford was about to fall apart, and he himself was convinced that he had "trouble with his brain of years standing." So not very surprisingly, perhaps, he was suddenly seized late in May with another attack of numbness, increasing this time to the point of real paralysis, in his legs. On June 22 he literally fled from Tengchow. He departed, Mrs. Crawford said, going "he knows not where." [50]

3/
Blowing The Gospel Trumpet

After some months Mrs. Crawford, who had remained in Tengchow, received news of her husband's whereabouts. He was in San Francisco, where he stayed throughout the fall of 1878. T. P. Crawford was now fifty-seven years old and had not been home in twenty years, since a brief furlough during his Shanghai period. California was serving as a kind of decompression chamber, where he tried to shake off the long pull at heathenism and, as he put it, get his mind "into line with our [own] people." [1]

Lonely and out of touch with American life, Crawford now connected both his brain trouble and his feeling of alienation from America with his years of isolation at Tengchow. "I have suffered very greatly," he wrote, "for the want of suitable *mental* companionship—constantly and always at hand—men to whom I could go for unreserved interchange of thought and feelings." The only such friend he could recall was A. B. Cabaniss, a former Shanghai missionary who had been gone from China since 1859. "Even to this day I find myself weeping over his absence," Crawford remarked; "Pardon this unexpected digression." [2] In December he at length headed for the east coast and Southern Baptist country. As his wife wrote him, California was probably still too close to China anyway. [3]

From this point T. P. Crawford's life moved into a new and final phase. He would live, to his continuing surprise, for almost another quarter century. As in the past he would experience elation, depression, and breakdowns. But things would move more slowly, with longer periods of remission between his highs and lows than in the turbulent 1870s. By one way of looking at him, he had already lost any chance he had of professional success, and he was now simply stumbling through a kind of twilight agony. At the same time he managed to connect his own past misfortunes in China with certain unrelated apprehensions at home, and he won a brief fame out of all proportion to his real achievements. He became more controversial than ever and remained, to those who had to deal with him, always interesting.

42

A Healing Furlough and a Struggle Renewed

Wanting to "get under the influence of the eastern states," Crawford spent the winter of 1879 traveling from one to another of the larger seaboard cities. During this trip he spoke before churches and mission boards in Boston, New York, Philadelphia, and Washington. His standard presentation was a series of three talks called "The Races of Men," each of which included pertinent digressions into missionary matters. The reason for the emphasis on race was the subject's topicality, due to public agitation on the issue of restricting Chinese immigration. Crawford reportedly opposed restriction, and his talks were designed for "removing race prejudice and making the hearer feel that all men are brethren—children of one Father, and equally in need of the gospel." [4]

This being the stated purpose, the actual message must have been confusing to some hearers. Crawford had already expressed in earlier scholarship his opinion that the Chinese people were the "living mummies of the past"; now by extension all Mongolians became "the race of the past, nothing [Mongolian] being worthy of consideration unless it be hundreds of thousands of years old." Uncreative, stubborn, without music or poetry, all these people were seen by the veteran missionary as sunk in a stupified sloth imposed by "the most primitive forms and symbols of human thought and speech."

This unflattering Mongolian picture would be compared on the following evening to one of the black race, which, except for musical rhythm, was represented as having no traditions at all even though "unchanged for the past 3000 years." Both would then be contrasted with the Caucasian race of the future. Although Crawford stated that it probably takes all kinds to constitute God's complete ideal of humanity, he made it clear that white people—by their superior intelligence and determination—have a godly mission to uplift the other races by hitting their defects like "a ball of iron." [5]

An impartial reading suggests that anyone who would have admitted Crawford's Mongolians or Africans to the United States would not have been a very loyal citizen. What one really sees here are not immigration talks but an illustration of how some typical Social Darwinist racial views could develop, out of frustrating personal experiences, in a man who rejected evolutionary theories completely. In his earlier years Crawford had been more tolerant, and he did not presume to lecture as an expert on such matters. The "Races of Men" became from this point one of his stock furlough presentations, reportedly attracting much attention both in the east and throughout the south.

Whatever his point in all this, Crawford by all accounts impressed many audiences with his anecdotes and returning good humor. By the time he reached his own mission board in Richmond he was enormously cheered, to the extent that he had sketched out a unique proposal for a general meeting of all Protestant mission directorates. This would be a high-level version of the 1877 conference he had attended in Shanghai, but devoted to the single subject of his own 1877 address. The conference would be sponsored by Southern Baptists, he hoped, on the theme of "levying the natives." The goal was to eliminate grasping Christians like those he knew in Tengchow—and missionaries like Hartwell who catered to them—by establishing as policy the idea that "foreign funds go to support the work of foreign missionaries, and let the natives look to themselves." [6]

His conference proposal was turned down, but Crawford's furlough was a rewarding experience nonetheless. His practical-minded views on mission method—summed up in his slogan, "I don't believe in drawing the wagon while the natives ride"—had attracted smiles and applause over a wide circuit. He was also privately congratulated and thanked by the FMB for "the whole course of his conduct" in his difficulties with Hartwell.[7] And finally in the spring of 1879 he received a Doctorate of Divinity from Richmond College, an honor he had been soliciting for several years. As he had said in 1874, such recognition would be "peculiarly appropriate in my case; for I have been doctoring away on the diseased divinity of China long enough surely to justify anyone in giving me the title." [8]

As he returned to China Dr. Crawford thus felt greatly reinvigorated. His numbness had disappeared and, away from the complexities of daily life in Shantung, he had been able to put his career in perspective. In fifteen years in Tengchow he had probably lost more converts than he had gained; but he had mastered the workings of the native mind, and with rededicated discipline he would build a new and better church. Strong evidence of divine support came on his return voyage, when he was acclaimed as a hero during a typhoon off Japan. As his ship's frightened crew scrambled into lifeboats, Crawford reinspired them with cries of "Never give up the ship" and "Pass on the buckets." He reached Tengchow in August, surprising his wife by arriving early and by looking "so much fleshier and more cheerful than I had seen [him] for years." [9]

After fourteen months' absence Crawford found the church situation calmer but not really encouraging. Kao Ku San was also making new pleas for mercy, requiring a reminder, as Mrs. Crawford put it, that "Mr. C. of course refuses to have anything to do with such a man." [10] But the really big development, Crawford discovered, was that his mission's whole identity had come to be centered on its educational program. Despite the new fee system, his wife had increased her school's enrollment to a record total of twenty-two. Mrs. Holmes had also reopened her girls' school, and Lottie Moon was teaching, too. Altogether the three institutions had fifty-seven pupils. Other missionaries congratulated T. P. Crawford on Mrs. Crawford's work in particular; by common agreement she had built—under difficult financial conditions and with two new children of her own—a fine school by her personal "industry, patience, tact, and fine education." Three of her graduates had become Christian teachers themselves, and Kwo Yu Yoong had become head teacher in her own school. [11]

Crawford remained silent for some weeks, but the situation concerned him greatly. Soon he began to reapprise his wife of his own view, firmed up in speechmaking at home, that schools were simply a kind of bribe to draw mercenary converts. Mrs. Crawford's happiness at his cheerful return—that "the long dreary days of absence [were] ended"—was quickly cooled by his reiterated insistence that she terminate her school entirely. As one colleague observed, Martha Crawford was "an excellent strong woman," and she and her husband had "many heart searching talks on the subject." [12]

Now more involved than ever with her pupils, Mrs. Crawford tried to temper T. P. Crawford's intensity by making compromises with him. She reduced her school time somewhat, and in the fall of 1879 she gave up entirely her "medical practice." The latter was another form of bribery by which Mrs. Crawford normally dosed or advised "not less that 1500 or 2000 patients per annum." With the time gained here she met with her husband for an hour's daily Bible study together, and she also greatly increased the rural evangelistic work that he wanted her to do. In 1880 she presented the gospel message to the women and children of 315 different villages. [13]

These concessions failed to satisfy Crawford. Since Mrs. Crawford's diary became one of the casualties of her new work load, her own feelings are not so clear. On the one hand she had not—except for the day of his return from America—written about her husband for at least ten years with the sort of affection ("all my earthly happiness is so twined about him") that had been prominent in her Shanghai journal. She also greatly cherished the students and parents of her school; she had such friends, a fellow missionary said, because the Chinese knew she "attached her friends to herself with hooks of steel." [14] On the other hand she worried a great deal about her husband's physical and mental health. She had been highly conscious since her early Shanghai days—when she watched the icy-hearted Issachar Roberts turn his wife into a suicidal "raving maniac"—of the absolute emotional interdependence of the foreign husband and wife in China.[15]

Martha Crawford was thus cruelly torn between conflicting loyalties, to her husband and to her pupils and their families, who by this point—together with the patrons of the Holmes and Moon schools—made up virtually all that was left of T. P. Crawford's church. In this situation she rapidly broke down both physically and emotionally. Her liver became "deranged," and she suffered from being "always most obstinately constipated." The latter complaint—a little discussed but common problem of modest Westerners in primitive sanitational circumstances—was of course aggravated by all the country work she was now doing. She also worried over new quarrels in the congregation, and she was depressed by the retirement in July 1881 of Sally Holmes, her fellow teacher and closest friend for eighteen years.

Mrs. Crawford stayed on until October of that year, to be present at the marriage of her adopted daughter Minnie, now nineteen, to the English Baptist Alfred Jones. Then, with twelve-year-old Freddie sent away to boarding school, she left Tengchow as precipitately as her husband had in 1878. Also like him she experienced severe initial culture shock in America. "I feel lost," she wrote in San Francisco; "I know how to get hold of nothing." [16]

Back with American friends and relatives Martha Crawford was soon quite happy, to the point of weeping "irrepressible tears of quiet joy." [17] She was gone from Tengchow for two years, and for a time there seems to have been some doubt that she would return. In any case T. P. Crawford closed her school soon after her departure; as one of Mrs. Crawford's friends observed, the headmistress's absence "added fertility to the doctor's self-support tendencies, which grew with a courage comparable to Jack's famous bean stalk." [18] Such a protest arose from the Chinese patrons and other missionaries, however, that Crawford allowed Kwo Yu Yoong to reopen classes on condition that fees be raised, and that certain changes be made in the curriculum for 1882.

From this point the school remained technically open but still caught in a "pangs of death" situation. T. P. Crawford's most startling curricular innovation was to insist that English language instruction be added, a controversial step that Mrs. Crawford "exceedingly deplored" by mail. Crawford's logic was that her students had always come for mercenary reasons anyway, and that it made more sense to teach them English and lose them to treaty-port business than to educate them only in Chinese and have to put up with their cries for mission employment. The change would also supposedly attract more respectable patrons, who would pay more, and the English teaching could be done by two new missionary arrivals, Cicero W. Pruitt and N. W. Halcomb. Crawford would not have to participate himself, and Kwo Yu Yoong—whose specialty was classical Chinese—would presumably soon be squeezed out.[19]

The result was that the school quickly lost about half its students. The former "dead poor" boys could not all pay the raised fee, and the anticipated wealthier entrants failed to materialize. Crawford lost interest, closed the whole program down again, and finally agreed to let Pruitt and Halcomb carry it on if they would get it off his property. The 1882 school year ended with Mr. and Mrs. Pruitt, Weston Halcomb, Kwo Yu Yoong and another Chinese teacher, and twelve schoolboys crowded into the Pruitts' small house. The school had occupied nine rooms and two courtyards in the Crawford compound.[20]

At the end of 1882 Crawford also received an important letter from his wife, one that brought him "inexpressible delight." Mrs. Crawford wrote that she missed him greatly and that she had decided to "come back to China to be a good wife, and cooperate with him in all his self-support ideas." [21] Crawford took this as her agreement to "cast mission schools overboard," which he quickly did by making no request for her school in his 1883 estimate submitted to the Foreign Mission Board. Weston Halcomb and Lottie Moon managed to keep it going for a time by writing letters of protest, but Mrs. Crawford's return finally ended the whole issue. As she had promised, she "carried out to the letter" her surrender by dismissing all the students and teachers and by writing the FMB to express full support of her husband's views. The school closed for the last time in January 1884.[22]

This complicated story had significant consequences. The protracted school conflict of the early 1880s lost Crawford the respect of his church's remaining members, in addition to removing its most attractive activity. He also lost here the trust of Miss Moon, who had supported him so loyally against Hartwell, and of the two new men. The most remarkable result, however, was the change that now took place in Martha Crawford. She continued to maintain contact with her former students, one of whom wrote as late as 1913 that "all he was that was worthwhile was due to the influence of Mrs. Crawford." [23] But never again in her remaining twenty-five years did she do school work. Instead she assumed what amounted to a whole new way of life, consisting of Chinese dress (which she had never worn previously), constant country itineration, and devotion to female evangelism exclusively.

To T. P. Crawford it all seemed a great victory. His wife was back and at last properly employed. Lottie Moon had also terminated her school, partly because she wanted to do country work and partly because she was weary of Crawford's own "ever-repeated annoying demands." [24] With Sally Holmes gone, the once thriving Baptist educational work was thus totally eliminated. Crawford took this to mean that he had finally "overthrown the tables," that he had cast out the last money changers in his personal temple. To him these schools had represented "a question of life or death to our type of Christianity," a great battle for which, as he put it, "my whole manhood rose up ready for action." [25]

A number of factors had contributed to Crawford's curious intensity on this logically modest issue. In addition to his belief that his wife's school had alienated her from himself, he identified the whole school idea with the J. B. Hartwell "subsidizing" style. He was also considerably troubled now by the success of his Presbyterian contemporary Calvin Mateer, who by "carrying on large operations" educationally was raising up "stall fed congregations." Hartwell and Mateer, Crawford reasoned, had between them poisoned the Tengchow field against his own efforts to implant self-reliant "bed rock" Christianity. [26]

Schools had thus become an important symbol to Crawford. On the one hand they represented an unscriptural and corrupt philosophy of mission work. On the other hand they symbolized his personal failure as a missionary, by comparison to several colleagues including his wife. On both counts schools had to be abolished. The sterile state of Baptist evangelistic endeavor—plus his own poor health, Crawford now felt—came directly from "the difficulties and burdens of holding out against this hot house system." First by Hartwell and then by Mateer, he wrote, "the aim of my life seemed to be stalemated." [27]

Crawford's own course was righteous, perhaps, but it was also very counterproductive. In the spring of 1884 Weston Halcomb reorganized the former North Street Church, and by the next year it was reconstituted around a largely self-supporting elementary school.[28] And in winning his wife away from her schoolboys Crawford in a sense lost her himself. In her articles and public statements she certainly supported him; but in pursuing her new country work she spent up to five days a week away from home, and he saw less of her than ever. In striving for closeness to those among whom she worked, Mrs. Crawford moreover became so Chinese in dress, appearance, and general manner that even C. W. Pruitt—to whom "her life was a benediction"—felt she came to have "a somewhat sinister effect." As for T. P. Crawford, Pruitt thought, "He must have been a sadly disappointed man." [29]

The Terrors of the Refrigerator: *Focusing Resentments on the FMB*

The disappointing consequences of T. P. Crawford's austerity program quickly became evident. At the end of 1884, the first full year without schools, Crawford reported that he was experiencing "hard trials, hard work, and little apparent success." He had finally got rid of corrupt practices, he thought, but as a result his people had "ceased to come about." Numbers had openly "thrown down" their Christianity, and so few of the church's 103 listed members attended services that a wall was put up "dividing it into two rooms, that the small congregation might look less lonely." Even those who remained active, Crawford believed, were only putting on a show as they waited for him to die, hoping that the next pastor could be induced into "liberal use of money." [30]

Crawford responded to all this in established ways. In a burst of zeal he bought a large, specially designed tent for country evangelism, and for a time he preached with renewed intensity. Thieves looted the tent one night, however, and while riding home penniless the missionary fell off his donkey and suffered a painful injury. Upon discovering the tent's contents in the homes of Chinese acquaintances who "well knew their ownership," he seems to have given up country work.[31] In his literary studies, on the other hand, Crawford was by this time finding chapters of the Bible *"in their entirety"* in Chinese historical documents. Encouraged by this "most valuable discovery of the age," he applied his time increasingly to a large new work to be entitled *The Reign of Man*. He hoped his scholarship would "settle or clear up many difficulties in history, theology, and chronology." [32]

As Crawford carried on in such fashion, most of his missionary colleagues fell into despair. Unable to make any kind of positive local impression, they came to feel that a sort of special curse hung over Baptist work in the Tengchow area. The common Chinese response, as a distressed 1884 newcomer noted, was to "call us 'devils' every day and hate us every hour." Several Southern Baptist missionaries died at this time in particularly horrifying ways, as in convulsions or after days of massive hemorrhaging. Visitors from America were shocked by the whole scene; as one who stayed in the Crawford compound said, he had never experienced an environment "so lonesome, so repulsive, so wearing to the body, and so harrowing to the spirit." Of seven new missionaries assigned to east Shantung by the FMB only C. W. Pruitt survived to 1890, all the others either dying or succumbing to nervous breakdowns. The common experience was summed up by young Enos E. Davault, who, the board noted, closed his deathbed letter "with the touching cry 'Help! Help! Help!' " [33]

Crawford's stated view here was that only a missionary who could "fall as flat as a pancake" and get back up should come to his rugged field.[34] The younger Americans, while they granted Crawford's own ability to do this, did not generally appreciate his attitude. As they reflected on the "paralyzing effect of conditions around them," they also rejected his ideas on schools and on assuming that Christian Chinese had to be treated like juvenile delinquents. His insistence, as mission chief, on dictating even how they spent their own salaries was taken by most as a personal insult.[35]

The result was that the younger people all moved rapidly to interior locations. Life with T. P. Crawford, Lottie Moon wrote, had become too much "a constant matter of humiliation," as he tried to make all around him "stultify themselves by absolute submission." [36] Unfortunately, as the mortality figures indicate, only Miss Moon and C. W. Pruitt were tough enough to survive interior life. Weston Halcomb carried on the new North Street work for three years by moving it all to a country village but left in pathetic condition after his young wife died.[37]

Crawford was at times obviously shaken by the lack of respect and high rate of attrition displayed by these junior associates. Once in 1884 he told Miss Moon that he was "not only unable to get on with his fellow missionaries, but that he had alienated the Chinese from him and that his withdrawal was absolutely essential." [38] He also offered several times in 1884 to turn over his Monument Street pastorate, or mission leadership, to C. W. Pruitt. Pruitt perceived, however, that Crawford only intended that he be a figurehead to disguise Crawford's own continuing authority. So Pruitt instead moved in 1885 to the country town of Huang-hsien, where he quietly administered what his colleagues soon regarded as the real mission headquarters.[39] As this gentle, widely respected man told the old chief, "Men have a profound philosophy in rejecting most cordially your views . . . The greatest part of life is in other directions."[40]

With Crawford's work totally destroyed and his wife and comrades gone away to escape his company, the stage was set, perhaps, for a new crisis. This began early in 1885, when he happened on a book that advanced some general views much like Crawford's own, but derived from the experiences of a Baptist missionary in a different locale. The book dealt with the work of E. L. Abbott, a veteran American Baptist (North) missionary in Burma. Crawford was impressed by Abbott's use of strict self-support regulations to keep the cupidity of the Burmese Baptists under control. It seemed like what might have happened in Tengchow: without J. B. Hartwell, Calvin Mateer, and their "army of native parasites or weak-kneed dependents," Crawford reflected, he might likewise have recruited "numerous bands of manly, self-supporting, self-propagating native Christians." He was also struck by the fact that E. L. Abbott's views had apparently been totally rejected by Abbott's home board.[41]

Thinking about how this other missionary had seemingly been "suppressed, ostracized, and refrigerated" by his organizational superiors, Crawford had what can only be called a fateful brainstorm. The subsidized success of "large operators" like Hartwell and Mateer, Crawford now perceived, were actually created—or fabricated—by the mission boards behind them. The boards actually did the extracting from American church members of the money disposed of by such men. The field agents then spread these sums about—on "costly schools of various kinds, native preachers, Bible women, dispensaries, hospitals, patients, and other hangers-on to mission funds generally"—and gathered data for glowing reports. The reports went back to the boards, who used them to impress the church members, collect more money, and start the cycle over again. Ambitions were fed and pockets lined at every level except that of the deceived home church members, who were paying for it all.[42]

This work of "carrying on grand enterprises for the benefit of mankind" was thus only a grand confidence game, a self-serving secular business totally alien to the proper missionary spirit. Strict soul-winners like Crawford and E. L. Abbott threatened the whole industry, which was why they wound up refrigerated, or frozen out. They were victims not of bad luck or personal mistakes, but of a "money makes the mare go" mission methodology. The only question was whether it was a deliberate conspiracy or an unintended perversion.[43]

To get an answer to this question T. P. Crawford determined in March 1885 to go in person before his home board. Since he was not due for furlough he came at his own expense, with Mrs. Crawford again remaining behind. From May to October he toured churches and denominational meetings from Texas to Virginia, explaining to Southern Baptists what was happening to their missionary contributions. By the time he reached the Foreign Mission Board, he believed, it had hostile observers following him around. In any event the FMB quickly appointed a special committee to meet and deal with Crawford.

By October 12, when Crawford appeared in Richmond, correspondence had also arrived that put his trip into clearer focus for the board's special committee. Lottie Moon wrote that other Shantung missionaries were enjoying Crawford's absence, but that none shared the "peculiar views on mission policy" that he seemed to be publicizing at home. All were in fact heartily tired of his "worse than profitless discussion of the same ever-recurring themes." Especially not to be believed were any statements he might make about schools, because the rest of his mission "saw as the result of schools the best and most efficient members of our church." [44]

Miss Moon's letter revealed not only that Crawford was alone in his views but also that he was apparently not a man entirely to be trusted. The board had asked him previously to clarify his mission's school policy, and he had stated that there was no policy, that "we claim no power and make no attempt . . . to control the particular labors of anyone." [45] Miss Moon, on the other hand, said that he constantly "*demanded* in the most imperious manner that [others] should definitely pledge themselves to his views" and that because he had "utterly failed to carry with him the judgment of his associates, we do not think it right that he should try to force his views upon us practically without our consent, by going home to influence the Board in person." Crawford had in fact misrepresented the purpose of his trip to his associates, and their feeling was that he had not kept faith with them.[46]

Thus advised the Foreign Mission Board gave Crawford a hearing. At the first session Crawford spoke extemporaneously, reminding the board of its obligation to economize with the money of the home Baptists as it spread abroad "our peculiar type of Christianity." The next day he submitted an essay and recited an original poem. The essay described schools and native assistants as great "wens" on the back of the missionary effort, crushing it down. "I would say, Baptists of America," he said, "dump your subsidy loads, and blow ye the gospel trumpet, blow." All non-Baptist denominations were "bound hand and foot" already. Specifically, he urged the FMB to draw up a new set of regulations, using its "hold upon the missionaries" to ensure that self-support became general practice.[47]

Crawford was then subjected to close questioning, giving him the impression that his painfully acquired knowledge was being dismissed as "a theory to conjure with." His request for self-support regulations was received particularly poorly. When the committee made its report on November 6, it based its rejection of his arguments mostly on the inflexible law under which it seemed he wished all missionaries placed. Not only were his proposals undemocratic and arbitrary, the report said, but they were grounded on an unreasonable assumption that conditions were exactly alike in all mission fields. Theologically, Crawford's regulations implied a distrust of God as much as of natives or fellow missionaries, a presumption that God's grace was insufficient to lift His children above the corrupting influence of money.[48]

Finally the board in effect censured Crawford by resolving that he be "kindly requested" to stop speaking before home churches and return to his mission station. Crawford responded by denouncing the committee for "unbaptistic" conduct and for trying to gag him. Then he went to the home of an acquaintance in Manchester, Virginia, where he sorted out his thoughts on "the terrors of the refrigerator." Perceiving an analogy between his own experience and the treatment accorded Jesus by the Sanhedrin, Crawford resolved to win victory "over all personal considerations, over the terrible ostracism, refrigeration, and extermination that clearly awaited me." The Foreign Mission Board, he vowed, would rue its attempt to suppress him as "the beginning of the end of the whole Board system among American Baptists."[49]

From this point T. P. Crawford ignored his board's instructions by lecturing for approximately another year in the American south. He took his views to "pastors and brethren everywhere," struggling all the while, he thought, against FMB attempts to destroy him. The board did publish certain letters from China missionaries who opposed Crawford's ideas.[50] It also issued a new set of "Rules for Missionaries" in February 1886. To Crawford's dismay the changes were not at all the ones he had wanted; instead he found an amendment prohibiting active missionaries from amassing secular wealth, and another stating that "no missionary shall abandon his station, or return to the United States, even at his own expense, except on account of sickness of himself or family, without permission of the Board."[51] Crawford additionally found himself ostracized at large denominational gatherings. As his circuit narrowed to places like Farmville, Virginia, and Big Hatchie, he began to send unsigned letters threatening individual FMB members with libel suits.[52]

The last tactic tried by Crawford was a personal appeal to the president of the Southern Baptist Convention, Patrick H. Mell. He sent Mell an autographed picture and a message informing him that he was "authorized to disbelieve all newspaper and private reports" unfriendly to Crawford. He also enclosed a set of *"laws"* under which he desired "to see our foreign missions placed by the action of the Convention, voicing the will of the denomination." His own travel observations, he reported, had confirmed that Baptists everywhere were rising against the Foreign Mission Board and its "free ticket" system. With subsidizers clearly out of control in the foreign field, the people themselves were demanding laws like the "just, wise, and good" ones he was submitting.[53]

Mell seems not to have replied, and in September 1886 Crawford departed for his mission station. He returned by way of Europe, where he observed that Baptist converts in Italy seemed even more corrupted by "pious gold" than those in China. He reached Tengchow in December, having been away for over a year and a half. In America his trip was nicely summarized by the FMB *Foreign Mission Journal:* "It is a great grief that one so long, so much, and so justly beloved and honored by Southern Baptists, should seem in his latter years to be destroying what he had done so much to build up, and that he is using . . . his position to substitute a wild and barren theory for the practical plans which experience has developed." [54]

Self-Support Runs Mad

T. P. Crawford at least returned to China with his earlier question answered. His board's casual attitude toward his 1879 conference proposal, followed by its recent effort to refrigerate him, indicated that he was opposed by a corrupt but powerful "syndicate." He intended to speak out further; but he did not know exactly what to say, and he wanted his enemies to show their hand before he made up his mind. For the next two years he accordingly sent home very terse reports. He was simply sowing the seed in Tengchow, he said, while Mrs. Crawford was "cultivating her patch" in the country.[55]

Baptist work in Tengchow remained notably unsuccessful. Reporting for her husband in 1888, Martha Crawford stated that after thirty years' work, and an aggregate of 130 man-years of labor, Southern Baptists had still made no visible impression. Although personally "not much accustomed to theorizing," she went on to convey T. P. Crawford's explanation of what was wrong. Mateer's Presbyterians, with their "imposing male and female schools, their host of native assistants, [and] their hospitals with other pecuniary inducements," had convinced the community that Christian conversion meant joining an army of parasites. By the spring of 1889 things were so discouraging, Mrs. Crawford wrote, that she and her husband were ready "to withdraw entirely from this field [rather] than to keep on longer at this poor dying rate." [56]

By the time of the latter report T. P. Crawford was again in a state of deep depression. The FMB had still not divulged its designs on him, and his relations with his associates in China were not happy. Various "mental torments" were moreover troubling his brain. Unsure of what to do, Crawford in March sent a confusing letter to C. W. Pruitt, asking him, apparently, to take over officially as mission head. Crawford's torments required that he himself stop working, and he offered to give up his salary and mission voting privileges. On the other hand he would not leave the field, because he had nowhere else to go. In this connection he reviewed his life at some length for Pruitt, to show how it had been "one of the hardest that ever fell to the lot of mortal man." The problem was that he had always been "a minority consisting of one" engaged in a "desperate struggle for existence." The hardest part was that scarcely anyone had seemed to feel any affection for him. "Oh, wretched man I have been!" Crawford concluded; "Even Paul knew nothing of such a trial." [57]

Unable to understand what Crawford wanted him specifically to do, Pruitt replied with a kind note designed simply to cheer him up. As paralytic seizures set in again, Crawford abruptly left in May on another trip to America. The object was to get away from China and to rest. As soon as he reached the southern states, however, he felt restored to his "full vigor." By July he was again exhorting home congregations to "strike for a thorough *Revolution* . . . to raise the cry, Down with the Board and the subsidy system." [58] Almost immediately he got the impression that the pastors of these churches were prejudicing their people against him. Then, after being repeatedly rung down for being out of order at a large denominational meeting, he perceived that "the host of secretaries and editors" had conspired to have him refrigerated wherever he appeared. Falling now into a state of collapse, Crawford went to the home of a relative in Gatesville, Texas. For seven months— from October 1889 to April 1890—he was unable to make his brain function, he said, or apparently to do even the simplest tasks except chop wood in the yard.[59]

Still not much improved, Crawford went back in July 1890 to seek his wife's care in China. This time he found the situation changed in an important way. The FMB, determined to rebuild its decimated North China Mission, had just assigned eight new recruits to Tengchow. With Lottie Moon and C. W. Pruitt busy with country work, it fell to the two Crawfords to shepherd these young people through their accommodations to missionary life. Displaying some of his old geniality, T. P. Crawford was soon highly popular, particularly with George P. Bostick, the dominant personality in the new group. Bostick, a red-bearded extrovert from North Carolina, showed great deference to the "aged servant of God," so apparently weary and wise through his holy labors.[60] By a happy coincidence Bostick was already theologically an extreme fundamentalist. Somewhat to Crawford's amazement, it seems, the old missionary found him to be in total agreement with his own views on self-support, native discipline, and many other matters.

Amid such encouragements Crawford's spirits again rallied remarkably. His loyal wife, now home again for a while, greatly impressed all their young charges. In G. P. Bostick he had moreover acquired a kind of executive officer, a man who would enforce the orders Crawford himself was too exhausted to reissue. The upshot was that by the fall of 1890 Pruitt and Miss Moon, coming in from their interior posts, found themselves outvoted on matters of longstanding controversy. At one such 1890 meeting Crawford and Bostick secured passage of a blanket prohibition against spending any money at all on "natives"; it was the first time Crawford had ever really won such an issue democratically.[61]

More good fortune followed. In the summer of 1891 Bostick discussed with Crawford a letter received from a church congregation in North Carolina; the import was that the church wanted to support Bostick as its own independent missionary. To Crawford this at first indicated simply a laudable spirit of congregational autonomy, a quality he had thought destroyed by the various directorates. Reflecting further, he suddenly saw an idea for a whole new scheme of missions. He began writing widely to home churches in search of more offers of independent support. Fusing this idea with his earlier self-support preoccupation, he urged the churches to stop being "mere tributary appendages" and to put their missionary money into nonsubsidizing individual evangelists like himself. At last he had a real strategy, something beyond convert horror stories, with which to attack the FMB.

Crawford's enthusiasm reached a peak in January 1892 when he mailed to southern churches 1000 copies of a pamphlet entitled, "Churches, To the Front!" The pamphlet was supposed to be only a preliminary statement, and it said little about actual mission work. What it mostly did was to attack the Foreign Mission Board, described as "wheel within wheel, delay, friction, and waste everywhere." Board operations, Crawford stated, were distinguished chiefly by serious blunders, particularly in personnel selection and use of money. Church boards generally, in fact, were shot through with secularization, "ring-government" of the Boss Tweed type, plutocracy, nepotism, ostracism, suppression, refrigeration, and many other unattractive phenomena. Crawford suggested that Baptists throw down their support of such institutions and join the growing revolt against "the dangerous tendency of our times towards centralization." Attention should be refocused on local churches, the only places where Baptist "spirituality, soul-liberty, and religious simplicity" still existed.[62]

Having tolerated T. P. Crawford's irregularities for seven years, the FMB now dropped him from its rolls. As the board explained, it had no other choice. In the United States Crawford's "revolution towards simplicity" implied that the Southern Baptist Convention should cease to exist. In the mission field it represented "the self-support idea run mad." As faith without works is dead, the board editorialized, so "bare trust in God without the use of means suggested by sound common sense is fanaticism."[63]

Soon "Crawfordism" was the talk of Baptists throughout the south. Despite this, and with his Shantung admirers even calling themselves Crawfordites, T. P. Crawford fell almost at once into a new depression. In the spring of 1892, at a party given to celebrate the Crawfords' fortieth missionary year, he startled the group with a singularly lugubrious speech of thanks. His whole career, he recalled, amounted to constant self-sacrifice amid scowling faces, frightened children, and barking dogs. G. P. Bostick only made things worse by urging him to lead them to Szechwan province, or some similarly distant challenge.[64]

With Crawford unable to decide what to do next, the FMB counterattacked brilliantly. Early in 1893 reports went out that the Reverend Dr. J. B. Hartwell, after nearly twenty years' home service, was returning to China. With a force of "ten of the most promising young pastors in the south," it was said, Hartwell would reassume directorship of the Shantung work he had founded so long before. On receiving this news Crawford began making plans to leave the area.

Hartwell arrived in August with a certain fanfare, displaying his pastoral task force and current wife. His old Chinese followers, most of whom had not been in a church in years, at once began rallying to his service. Crawford reported Hartwell absorbed in recruiting hirelings; Hartwell reported only that his old Baptists flocked about him with shouts of joy, while Crawford's few adherents took "most kindly, to say the least" to the news that their pastor was leaving.[65]

Within a month Crawford had left Tengchow for the last time. With him went a band of ten American Crawfordites, including Mrs. Crawford. Apparently not having any fixed destination, this "Gospel Mission" group spent the winter in a remote part of P'eng-lai hsien. Continuing westward in the spring of 1894, they finally settled at the foot of T'ai-shan, Shantung's sacred mountain. For a time the natives resisted vigorously, and Crawford experienced feelings "closely bordering on despair." As paralysis returned, however, the resistance slackened, and Crawford's health improved. By fall the Gospel Missionaries were hard at work among the "dense, ignorant, heathen, and suspicious" local folk.[66]

Crawford lived on at the town of T'ai-an-fu for another six years. He never won many converts, but surrounded by his Gospel Missionaries—"choice spirits" of similar convictions—he seems to have found a measure of peace. He wrote letters praising his followers for their cheerful, self-denying service and for their style of "going down to the people," or wearing Chinese clothing. A continuing series of reports went back to the home churches, soliciting funds under slogans like "Responsibility is the mother of activity" and "Let modern adjuncts alone." [67]

The Boxer outbreak of 1900 ended Crawford's missionary career. Forced to leave the interior, he and Mrs. Crawford returned to America, where for a year and a half they traveled about the south. Crawford gave lectures on the Boxers and on the Gospel Mission philosophy. After several unfriendly receptions in the Smoky Mountains he suffered a final depression; the "Convention Board system," he wrote, had destroyed the Baptist character.[68] Sick and unhappy, he moved to Dawson, Georgia, where with relatives of Mrs. Crawford he took up his last residence.

Crawford and Crawfordism

T. P. Crawford died of pneumonia in April 1902. Although Mrs. Crawford was now seventy-two and in poor health, she returned to T'ai-an-fu in the fall. For seven more years she carried on the "pure evangelism" of the Gospel Mission. It was the kind of life she had led for the past quarter-century anyway, and, as she told a concerned relative, "The Lord called me to labor in China, and that call has never been revoked." By the time Martha Crawford died in her fifty-eighth missionary year most of the other Crawfordites had already returned, somewhat chastened, to the service of the Southern Baptist Foreign Mission Board. After 1910 Crawfordism and the Gospel Mission existed mostly as memories. [69]

For a few years T. P. Crawford's activities had nonetheless given real concern to his former board and to the Southern Baptist Convention. In Shantung it took Baptist missionaries almost a generation to overcome the effects of his feuds, his unattractive social philosophy, and his refusal to give sensible leadership training to Christian Chinese.[70] Both as a practicing missionary and as a Baptist theoretician he had been, perhaps, a living repudiation of the pristine faith he claimed to be reviving. But there was still a certain logic to the public lessons he drew from his long career, and his church worried with good reason about his influence.

Most of the attention attracted by Crawford's Gospel Mission came in the late 1890s from the Mississippi valley area. In that territory congregational independence had always been an especially sacred Baptist principle; a doctrine called Landmarkism, which vehemently articulated the idea, had in fact flourished at Union University during Crawford's days there. The appeal of Crawfordism itself, however, seems more closely tied to a broader kind of malaise, one of more recent development. What one really sees in statements by Crawford's home supporters is a deep anxiety over the corporate drift of modern life generally. The dominant impression is of a kind of nostalgic distemper, a claustrophobic reaction against the late nineteenth-century's "insane rush for organization in all departments of active life." [71]

By calling attention to octopus-like church syndicates Crawfordism simply turned this in a specifically religious direction. The church world was obviously as guilty of "large gatherings, magnetic speeches, enthusiastic hearers, large collections of money, etc." as were other burgeoning mass enterprises. To Southern Baptists, among whom personal soul wrestling and congregational "revival power" were particularly important, any kind of bureaucratic manipulation was a special threat. Appealing directly to that fear, Crawford suggested that a conspiracy of "evilly disposed leaders" was for its own enrichment and glory using church boards to bureaucratize Southern Baptists. The Foreign Mission Board—with its programs, regulations, "itching ears," and drift toward humanitarian do-goodism—served to epitomize the "mechanical means and novel methods" by which such centralizers worked.[72]

As things turned out, Crawford greatly misread his Southern Baptists. The overwhelming majority had sufficient intelligence and humanity to see through his message and reject it. Some fifty trans-Mississippi churches were influenced, but not as Crawford anticipated. Although they revolted and seceded from the SBC, they showed little interest in supporting Gospel Missionaries in China. Theirs was an isolationist and even antimissionary movement, which —as one true Crawfordite complained—was "more political than religious in its natural distaste for an oligarchy, and which missed entirely the deeper meaning of self-abnegation."[73] Even among Southern Baptists religion was only one of the emotional fuses Crawford was lighting.

T. P. Crawford as an individual can of course be seen in a number of ways. To an American southerner his Quixotic career suggests what W. J. Cash called the "hell of a fellow" (Pickett's Charge) tradition, a mode of behavior where one resolves that "nothing living [can] cross him and get away with it."[74] More fairly it suggests the intensely personal quality of old-time southern fundamentalism, where one has something, perhaps, that is "really a form of faith in one's self, an extension of ids and egos." Crawford truly was a man who had "met God in a personal way out in the woods," who had even felt "God's tap on the shoulder" while mocking Him on a treestump.[75] It was a faith that was subsequently his strength—to become a college man, a poor despised Baptist preacher, and a gospel fighter across the waters.

In China this kind of faith, because it centered so completely on himself, was to Crawford's disadvantage. When the "natives" failed to heed his words of life they were rejecting him personally, telling him he was not the divine agent he believed himself to be. In critical addition to this common missionary frustration—and to a degree happily uncommon among most missionaries—Crawford had to contend with such Christian brothers as J. B. Hartwell and Hartwell's Chinese adherents. In that protracted struggle, which was the central experience of his missionary life, Crawford was unquestionably treated despicably by the unctuous Hartwell. He also appears to have been at various points swindled, slandered, sued,

censured, blackmailed, and threatened with death by a very un-
regenerate band of converts. His physical strength failed, and (as
Hartwell cruelly reminded him) it seemed his brain was softening,
too.

In the last connection one could make a case that Crawford
was simply a sick man, particularly in his last quarter century. In
addition to unreasonable stubbornness, he displayed something
suggestive of paranoia ("I have looked over the whole course of my
life, and I confess to a feeling of opposition"). He even claimed at
times to act solely by divine inspiration, never out of human
weakness ("I do not suffer such carnal desires to take possession of
my mind or in any way control my actions"). The ferocity of his
struggle with the Foreign Mission Board—when "victory or defeat
[did] not enter into the consideration"—reads suicidally. One also
has to remember his many bouts with numbness, paralysis, "slug-
gish" thought, feelings bordering on despair, and so on.[76]

However much sympathy one feels, T. P. Crawford's tragedy
was nonetheless overwhelmingly self-inflicted. His early work was
frustrated largely by his avaricious interest in secular business,
where both as a Christian minister and as a "law abiding man" he
stretched the rules considerably. Much more important, he was deficient in personal relations, the *sine qua non* of life in old China.
In old-fashioned American language—the kind Crawford used—
he was a hypocrite and a deceiver, in more ways than it seems
worthwhile to enumerate. The point is that while he hurt himself
he hurt others, too, people who trusted and depended on him. To
individual Chinese like Lu Ming-chao, Wong Wha Yuan, and Sun
Chang Lung he was disloyal to the point of treachery. To at least
a dozen young Americans in the 1880s and 1890s his selfish vanity
helped bring death or sidetracked lives. What he did to his wife is
a story in itself.

Crawford did have appealing traits. One finds, for example,
some very tender letters to his adopted son. Another letter details,
at length and with truly affecting poignance, an 1886 encounter
in Alabama with an old black woman who had known Martha
Foster as a child.[77] But the attractive aspects of his reputation—
the wisecracking geniality and moments of avuncular kindness—
unfortunately do not come across very often in the written record.
What one does find is a personality of such cumulative repellence
that one is finally amazed that so many human beings could stand
T. P. Crawford's company, let alone accept his God and worship
in his church.

Crawford's story is so depressing that one who dwells on it

wonders if he himself is a sadist. It seems necessary to understand his problems as fully as possible, however, to see how such stereotypes really could exist, and to help understand the reactionary sort of philosophy identified with Crawford's memory. Basically T. P. Crawford was a man who never came to terms with the life he had chosen for himself. The Chinese did not measure up to his designs on them, so he wound up despising the Chinese and hunting witches among well-meaning fellow Americans. His life seems sadly summarized by his last words, spoken as he died rocking on a south Georgia porch: "Friends, go away!" [78]

II /

Charlotte Diggs Moon

God rather desires in us fidelity to those little things
which he does place under our control, than an
ardour for great things which do not depend
upon us.

> ———*translated from St. Francis de Sales;*
> *copied by Lottie Moon in the*
> *margin of her* Imitation of Christ

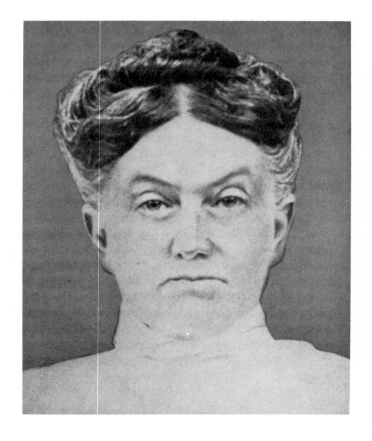

4 / Woman's Work in East Shantung

Martha Crawford's friend Sally Holmes, it will be recalled, left the Southern Baptist North China (east Shantung) Mission in 1881. Among other friends left behind by Mrs. Holmes was a young man named Wang, who had been her pupil as a child and whom she had taught to speak English. By the early 1890s Wang had become a well-to-do businessman associated with Jardine, Matheson and Company in Tientsin. Hearing in 1893 that Mrs. Holmes was in poor health and destitute circumstances in America, he wrote asking that she come back to China and allow him to care for her, as she once had cared for him. Mrs. Holmes declined the offer, but Wang, to "express the gratitude in his heart," from that time supported her with a gift of six hundred American dollars each year. After Wang died around 1900 his wife, following his instructions, continued to send the same generous amount annually until Mrs. Holmes also died.[1]

This story, which understandably was widely recounted in Shantung missionary circles, might be used to develop a number of points about American missionaries in China. Certainly it underlines the fact that the lonely bitterness found by T. P. Crawford was only one face of the missionary experience—an extreme one, probably, which was balanced even in his own field by human relationships exemplifying the finest ideals and dearest dreams of Chinese and Americans alike.

The story of Sally Holmes and the child she had befriended also underlines the intensely personal, emotionally charged nature of an entire face of missionary endeavor, a very special one called woman's work. Woman's work—work by female missionaries with native women and children—grew up in China as in many other fields during the period dwelt upon in this book, the last four decades of the nineteenth century. As an influence both on missions and on American opinion about China woman's work has been enormously important, and it also constitutes a fascinating and significant aspect of United States social history. A recent survey of this type of work, breaking ground from the angle of institutional development, claims quite simply that "no other form of American intervention overseas has made a more powerful cultural impact." [2] Another survey, this one a history of American women, notes that we have here "the first area of American life where women achieved a more or less equal professional status with men." [3]

So the type of work done by Martha Crawford, Sally Holmes, and many other American women in China seems from a number of angles well worth studying. One could examine the propositions, for instance, that it eventually produced such phenomena as Chinese feminism, the Soong sisters, and Pearl Buck. Yet although large and accessible quantities of documents exist, they remain mostly unstudied; it seems, as one observer comments, that "as far as academic history is concerned it is as if all this had never happened." [4]

Given the current increased interest both in China and in American feminine history, this situation will no doubt be corrected soon. But at present it still seems necessary before discussing Miss Lottie Moon to indicate what her kind of work involved.

Development in America and in the Field

One expeditious way to approach woman's work is through the writings of Helen Barrett Montgomery, one of its great home-front organizers and publicists. In her *Western Women in Eastern Lands,* an influential 1910 historical work, Mrs. Montgomery explains the growth of female missionary endeavor as simply one aspect of an entire century of revolt by Western women against the "cribbed, cabined, and confined sphere to which the natural prejudices of a man-monopolized world had assigned them." Other aspects were causes such as abolition, temperance, and inheritance rights. But missionary activism, from Helen Montgomery's Christian perspective, was the ordained crowning glory of the whole "woman's century" process.[5]

An event of watershed importance, apparently—at least for American women—was the Civil War. There had been many female missionaries, including some well-publicized ones, prior to the 1860s, and women's groups had always raised an "astonishing proportion" of the funds that financed American missionary activity. Compared to later nineteenth-century woman's workers, however, the earlier field representatives seem mostly to have led lives still rather cabined and confined, and home-front work was small-scale and unfocused. What the Civil War did was to initiate a process of consolidation at home and of raised expectations both there and in the field. As Helen Montgomery put it, the war gave to American women in both sections a "baptism of power," a situation in which they were "driven to organize, forced to cooperate by their passion of pity and patriotism."[6]

By the 1870s this new sense of power had significantly stimulated both the feminist spirit and the impulse to religious mission. These two ideas fused in a growing conviction that worldwide female uplift was identical with worldwide Christian evangelization, that "the pure religion of Jesus" provided not only spiritual salvation but a "Magna Carta of Womanhood." Women in the United States and Europe were perceived as gaining equality through feminist reforms "based squarely on the principles of the Bible." In Eastern lands, on the other hand, where "no clear gospel" existed for emancipation—or where existing gospels ran exactly counter to the desired message—millions of women and children, too, remained in "slavery" to men. In this situation Western women had a clear duty, Helen Montgomery summarized, to "put within the reach of their sisters in other lands this good tidings of great joy."[7]

Emerging as a logical vehicle for advancing several good causes, missionary service became in the latter decades of the nineteenth century an attractive prospect for numbers of American girls. Such service was of course not thought of by those who undertook it—either male or female—as a rationally calculated career. It was something chosen consequent to individual call experiences, spiritual crises that made one "set apart" from home comforts for lives of sacrifice, toil, and adventure in alien lands.

Calls could be either sudden or protracted and could come at any time. Judging from woman's workers in east Shantung province, an individual's call typically came in her early twenties. As the case of Martha Foster Crawford demonstrates, a variety of factors including great inner turmoil could be involved. Other common influences illustrated by the same case are the importance of having been raised in a strong Christian atmosphere and of receiving a timely marriage proposal from an aspiring male missionary. Martha Foster was not, perhaps, as emotionally deprived in childhood as seems to have been the case with her many later co-workers who had grown up either as orphans or without fathers. She did, however, display the typical restlessness of the whole nineteenth-century Shantung group: virtually all came from small-town or farm backgrounds, and dissatisfaction with the narrow horizons of such life were frequently expressed.[8]

Arriving in China in 1852, Martha Crawford was distinctly a pioneer. During the 1860s and 1870s many more Christian women chose such lives. The first comprehensive statistical survey of China missions, undertaken in 1877, showed 344 American and British missionary wives in the field. This represented an increase of about 190 over a rough count made in 1859. There were moreover almost as many single women (63) as there were bachelor missionaries (66). By the time of the next survey in 1890 women outnumbered men by 707 to 589, with 316 of the females being unmarried. By a third tabulation in 1907 the women had increased to 2481, of whom 1038 were single. These figures fail to reflect a considerable number who had arrived and either died or returned home between surveys.

American missions in east Shantung figured very importantly in this increase. In the half century between 1860 and 1912 a total of 119 women began their missionary careers at the Presbyterian stations in Tengchow or Chefoo or at one of the posts of the Southern Baptist North China Mission. Of this number seventy-one came as single women, with sixteen marrying eventually in the field. Some stayed only a few months or even weeks, but most remained longer. A few, like Martha Crawford and Helen Coan (Mrs. John L.) Nevius, became virtually part of the landscape.[9]

Shantung women missionaries were also influential in ways that statistics do not reflect. Helen Nevius's Chinese-language Christian literature for women, for example, constitutes probably the most noteworthy body of such material ever done by one individual. Julia Mateer justly shared credit with her husband for the good work of the Presbyterian Tengchow College, and Annetta Thompson (Mrs. Charles R.) Mills pioneered modern linguistic and vocational training for the Chinese deaf. It will be recalled that Martha Crawford herself, at the 1877 General Conference—where her husband spoke on native hirelings—contributed a paper on "Woman's Work for Woman." There were special factors behind Mrs. Crawford's sudden professed concern for work other than teaching, but her paper was still quite significant as an expression of the widening vision of women missionaries; its real point was simply that women should think in more ambitious terms. Encouraged by General Conference contacts, the women established their own magazine, *Woman's Work in China,* and the leading article in its first issue was a long letter from Julia Mateer. Here Mrs. Mateer joined Martha Crawford in encouraging women missionaries to become more active and versatile.[10]

Martha Crawford and Julia Mateer certainly did not invent female missionary work in China, but more than most they did represent a new approach to it. The new approach amounted chiefly to a more cheerful attitude and to a greater involvement in Chinese life. Phasing out from respectability was the treaty-port parlor ornament, a ladylike type who spent her days waiting to "break down." Breakdowns, Mrs. Crawford suggested, came to women who secretly wanted them. Julia Mateer stressed duty to God and helpfulness to one's husband, but mostly she recommended forgetting one's personal pains through hard work. A good start, she thought, was to learn the Chinese language, if only to be aware of what one's houseboy was teaching her children.[11]

For the missionary wife who had no children there was frankly not much to do except either work or lie about. It seems hardly coincidental that of the three best-known nineteenth-century Shantung woman's workers—Helen Nevius, Julia Mateer, and Martha Crawford—only Mrs. Crawford had children, whom she adopted after a quarter century in China and who seem to have spent relatively little time in her home. But with full-time amahs and cooks available at five dollars a year plus board (and seamstresses and washerwomen for a dime a day), even American mothers of seven and eight children had time for outside careers.[12] Realization came rapidly that "a woman with a little strength and skill can make even a pig-pen comfortable," and that "we can have a home with its comforts and live nearly as we would in our native land, and still have our hands free to prepare for and do the great work for which we came."[13]

Woman's work still did not turn into a movement until aided by several additional factors. The first of these was the opening of the Chinese interior to missionary work, beginning with the treaties of Tientsin and Peking. Presented in the 1860s with vast territories to be worked, male missionaries needed assistance. From their frustrations with treaty-port Chinese menfolk many were already convinced that more attention should be given to the country's secluded women; by their conspicuous support of popular Buddhism the females seemed to demonstrate a higher religious consciousness, and the material and emotional deprivation of millions among the poor obviously needed uplift. If wives and mothers could be won, the theory went, their men might well follow them to Christianity.

Another influencing factor was the snowballing effect of reports sent home by woman's workers already in the field. Even today these documents are an exciting reading experience, as one finds the plight of Chinese womanhood described with great indignation. The indigenous religions are of course severely criticized; but the real trouble is clearly the indigenous male sex, which is represented as subjecting its women to an almost limitless variety of cruelties. Female missionaries in Tengchow and Chefoo reported regularly on shocking occurrences in which the women and girls of their areas were tortured, thrown to wild animals, sold into male servitude, driven to suicide, or murdered outright.[14] Quite apart from other benefits, Chinese women apparently needed Christianity as a consciousness-raising self-defense weapon.

From a number of angles, then, the great Christian duty and opportunity in China very likely lay in work with women. By contrast with the male Chinese predisposition—which was "to have nothing to do and have your belly full of rice"—the women were "much superior to the men in the matter of *heart*." Or as Julia Mateer observed, the situation was basically similar to that in America: there were "more warm-hearted, pious, self-sacrificing women than men of like mind."[15]

The Culture Gulf

Female missionaries had traditionally gravitated to teaching because it was physically and emotionally the easiest type of work available. Schools were "accessible and regular, with more immediate results."[16] But the indirect, long-term evangelistic benefits of primary education did not easily reach natives who had already grown up. The distinctive concern of the expanded, post-1860 woman's work movement was accordingly for massive evangelistic contact with adult females.

Generally speaking there were two ways of making such contact. Visitation, or house-to-house calling, had been practiced to a limited extent all along, and it remained the obvious method for urban use. Itineration (country preaching tours) became feasible only as the country opened up and as the female sense of mission expanded. Rural itinerating demanded skill in open-air discourse, considerable physical stamina, and a winning personality. Wherever work was carried on—in the missionary's home, in a Chinese dwelling, or under a roadside tree—the biggest problem was always simply getting one's listeners to comprehend the message. Success here depended largely on how well the individual missionary coped with the cultural and social gap—gulf, really—that separated her from her audience.

The magnitude of this separation is graphically revealed in itineration reports from east Shantung woman's workers. To begin with, their tours carried them into areas where few if any white females had been seen, and one could never tell just what would happen. Through the late 1870s local females often would hide from the foreigners, and the males might display marked hostility. But this was never entirely the case, and the curiosity of both sexes increasingly brought them out in sizable numbers. Such curiosity occasionally had bizarre origins, as in one Shantung district where a French commercial traveler had sold peepscopes showing European women in erotic poses; but usually the interest came from nothing more than the novelty of the foreign intrusion into village life.[17]

The typical first meeting amounted to a sort of good-natured collision, and the missionary's first job was to organize this into a coherent encounter. Each new crowd had first to be allowed to satisfy its curiosity regarding Western hair style and clothing. This meant being pinched, pulled, and otherwise roughly inspected, and hats were sometimes lifted off and tried on all around. When these things ended, the missionary in charge would suggest that the group withdraw to someone's home, or, if no invitation were forthcoming, to some common gathering place. Then would begin the difficult process of trying to convey why the foreigners had come: "Mrs. Mateer would often begin by asking if they knew why we had come to their village. Generally someone would say 'to make merit.' 'No,' Mrs. M. would say: 'We have come to teach you the best news you have ever heard; the most important thing you will ever hear. We come from far away because we know it to be good and true and the only thing to make you happy, here and hereafter. Can you tell where you will go when you die?' Then someone will say: 'Oh, we don't know anything; we're stupid!' And another says: 'Who knows?' Then Mrs. M. will say: 'I know,'— and someone will call out: 'These foreigners know everything!' "[18]

Although interruptions would be "numerous and distractingly foreign to the subject," the speaker would press on patiently. The technique was to answer enough questions to keep one's audience from leaving, but gradually to bend the dialogue in a more spiritual direction. If things went well the missionary would talk for perhaps an hour on sin, the future life, and the love of God the Father. Also a definite effort would be made to get into a specific home at some later time, when instruction could be pursued with a smaller group of the genuinely interested.

For the unacclimated or squeamish foreigner it could all be very unsettling. Jennie Anderson of the Chefoo Presbyterian station, for instance, felt most uneasy when she first found herself alone in a room filled with unwashed and apparently uninhibited Chinese women and children. She appreciated the relief this gave from outdoor skirt-pulling, but she recoiled from "smoking their dirty old pipes, and [drinking] the soup out of their odoriferous kettles." She was also distressed by the lack of clothing on younger children. Even worse than a Chinese home, Miss Anderson found, was a Chinese inn; in such places of "utter desolation and repulsion" cows and other animals sometimes wandered about, and rude males might invade one's audience. To disperse such nuisances required nerve and "muscular force." Ever-present stacks of stinking Shantung beancake were a nuisance impossible to disperse.[19]

Woman's workers thus constantly had to remind themselves of their duty, the need to "feel deeply the worth of *one soul*." Veterans liked to quote the words of Sir Astley Cooper, the famous anatomist, to his students: "My advice to each of you [is] learn to disregard your nose." [20]

Bible women were another test of the female missionary's devotion. Bible women were Christian converts who were employed to open up new areas and develop old ones. Typically they were semiliterate, low-paid females who located audiences, made contacts, gathered and led meetings, taught and counseled in homes, and sometimes preached in the streets. In theory the Bible woman's relationship to the woman missionary was that "hand-in-hand, in Christ's name, they go out . . . on a combination camping trip, exploring adventure, preaching tour, and social welfare adventure" —sustained by the missionary's "tender, heart-quivering, admiring, leaning love" for her native sister.[21] Actually, going hand-in-hand was often considered rather too close: "I do not much enjoy going about with a native woman. We can seldom if ever get two rooms, and the old woman had then to sleep with me. If the kang [bed] is narrow, she had to get close to me to keep from falling off. Well, it is sufficient to say that every small thing that lives and breathes is on intimate terms with the natives, and the romance of this part of missionary experience can be appreciated by every American lady." [22]

The most distressing discovery of all was that religious consciousness—despite all theories and advance intelligence—did not seem to exist in the great mass of Shantung women. Helen Nevius discovered in her first Tengchow visitations (1862) that she and the Chinese were on somewhat different wave lengths. She asked a typical girl to state her conception of the "Great Creator," and the young woman replied that she had never thought much about Him. To an elderly female Mrs. Nevius said, "I do so want you to believe what we tell you about Jesus," to which the person answered, "Why, of course I'll believe; why shouldn't I?" Especially difficult to handle was the type of argument used by Mrs. Liang, a contentious neighbor. Mrs. Nevius explained at length to this old woman why it was wrong to revile people, and she exhorted her to calm her temper so she could go to heaven; Mrs. Liang replied that reviling people was the only earthly pleasure she had, and that she considered hell fair enough as a possible payment. [23]

Obviously, then, misunderstandings abounded in woman's work, and given the backgrounds of those involved this was perhaps inevitable. Still, many Shantung missionary women broke through all these difficulties to find lives of great satisfaction and much "usefulness." The process was gradual, complex, and very personal. Typically, it seems, the main thing required of the Western woman was that she stop viewing the natives simply as souls to be saved, and that she accept the Chinese environment as something more than heathenism. Usually this occurred in connection with individual relationships, while perceiving that Chinese women were sisters in ways other than metaphorical.

Martha Crawford is one impressive example of east Shantung adjustment. Nowhere more than in China, she wrote in 1887, did a nineteenth-century Western person face a civilization so totally foreign and at the same time so totally integrated in its own terms. "Owing to the nature of the people," she felt, "with their crystallized social, political, and religious institutions, any results will come only very slowly." Her husband's fundamentalism notwithstanding, Mrs. Crawford also felt that in China Christianity should be recast in indigenous terms. Even her own outlook on life, she believed, improved as she got more away from home and into contact with her "non-speculative and intensely practical" Chinese acquaintances.

Martha Crawford's personal talent for understanding began at home, where as a loyal wife she had many problems. She coped by treating T. P. Crawford lovingly, by talking literally behind his back in sign language, and by interpreting his demands as constructively as she could. When forced to give up her school she adopted Chinese dress and an itinerant professional style. To go with this she developed an evangelistic approach based on sociability, on winning friends through informal chats on subjects of universal female interest.[24]

To Mrs. Crawford the one great qualification for missionary work was a kind of everyday "living sympathy." Even for the most sympathetic woman's workers, however, it was never easy, as the saying went, to live among them. The woman's workers remained attached to many Western certitudes, and when they went native they did so instrumentally, because it seemed politic. Their friendships, when judged by standards of another century, often read rather patronizingly.

Shantung missionaries moreover led lives that contained much "loneliness, discomfort, and petty persecution," lives in which—as one way of coping—unmarried Western females tended to "go off like hot cakes" to the altar.[25] Considering the inhibitions that all these foreign women had, and how little they had in common with the only class of Chinese to which they had access, it would seem that many showed a great deal of realism and adaptability. Perhaps as they learned more about the Chinese they also understood themselves better. As Julia Mateer remarked, "Most questions have at least two sides . . . We say, 'Behold these filthy Chinese, who seldom bathe or wash their clothes,' and the Chinese say, 'Behold these filthy foreigners—what an amount of washing and scrubbing it takes to keep them clean!' "[26]

Indoctrination: Women's Classes and the Literary Work of Mrs. Nevius

Both personal relations and understanding of the Chinese scene were utilized in the instructional follow-up to initial contact. Sometimes the missionary would do her advanced teaching in the homes of Chinese acquaintances, a method which maximized exposure. Within a twenty-minute walk of the Chefoo Presbyterian establishment, for instance, were half a dozen villages of two hundred families each, and on a good day sessions could be held in at least one home in each. At other times the work would be done in the missionary's own dwelling, where a study group could be organized by capitalizing on "the variety it gives to the monotonous routine of their lives."[27]

In any case, the technique was to appeal first to curiosity, and then to build onto that a program of mental and spiritual uplift. The transition here was often difficult, because the Chinese women —at least as the foreigners saw them—were "so accustomed to be nothing and *know* nothing that they think it is impossible for them to learn." [28] The first requirement was to establish an atmosphere conducive to instruction. Also, as Martha Crawford wrote, "A firm determination *to be leader* in the conversation (always with suavity of manner) is necessary, and will save much of the time that would otherwise be spent in listening to useless chattering or in answering silly questions." [29]

Her ascendancy established, the missionary could if she wished go directly into explaining doctrine. Many, like Helen Nevius, proceeded indirectly. Mrs. Nevius would begin with a series of what she called "Things Worth Knowing" talks; here she would lecture and quiz her "big old children" on basic facts of world history, geography, natural science, religion, "and in fact all the general information I can crowd into such a short time." The talks would deal not only with the West but with China too. Usually an illiterate audience would be found to know only slightly more about Buddhist theology and Chinese geography than it did of foreign religions.[30]

The idea was both to educate the audience and to retain it. Other benefits included dissemination in the community of information about the West, plus confirming an image of the missionary as teacher. According to W. A. P. Martin, the noted Presbyterian educator, Helen Nevius had a special flair for impressing such gatherings—their response being typically, "How much you know and how little do we! We are cows and nothing more." [31] If things went well, Mrs. Nevius would warm to the association too: "They are a rough set surely, but I feel strongly drawn to them, and I think we feel mutually that we are the best of friends. They know that I desire their good and have their best interests at heart. I am conscious of an increasing influence over them." [32]

It was not considered wise, however, to prolong such preliminaries. The object was to deliver a religious message, and the longer this was put off the more difficult it tended to become. As Martha Crawford said, "We wish to be known as religious teachers. If we form their acquaintance on some other basis it may last longer, but it is questionable whether it will be profitable to either party. Few, except those who became Christians, form real friendships for us. Many like to come to our houses to see the pictures, the sewing machine, and other foreign articles, who will leave whenever

Christianity is mentioned. While it may be time well spent to entertain them to some extent with these things, they should never be allowed to crowd out the gospel." Sooner or later the heathen's "sneer of incredulity" had to be faced up to. Too much delay led to "presenting the truth in an apologetic manner, as if infringing upon the hearer's rights." [33]

Audience participation, properly handled, was by common agreement the best way to teach. Even if the participants were woefully ignorant—and their ideas on the Great Creator "always virtually Topsy's"—they could be taught something. Early lessons would involve repetition of a few lines of scripture, or answering questions on stories read aloud. Surprisingly, it was discovered that even the dullest people could learn to read such materials themselves, apparently to even greater spiritual benefits. Instruction had to be patient and repetitious, but coupling literacy with doctrine seemed to stimulate interest and foster pride in the students. [34]

A whole body of Christian literature in Chinese soon grew up to meet the special needs of woman's work, and in this process the contributions of Helen Nevius were of particular importance. Mrs. Nevius had come to Tengchow (1861) from a decade of language study at Ningpo, with the conviction that too often there was an inverse ratio between preaching done and impression made. She had determined to make sure at her new station "that they learned certain important things so well that they could never quite forget them." What was needed, as she saw it, was something simpler than the Westminster Shorter Catechism used by home Presbyterians— something that would transmit doctrine meaningfully, but at a level "comprehensible to the most ignorant." [35]

During the winter of 1861–62 Mrs. Nevius accordingly composed a new catechism in Mandarin Chinese. After testing it on her class of inquirers, she submitted it for publication the following year. Over the next fifty years it was reprinted many times and was reportedly used at one time or another by every Protestant mission in North China. In 1906 Timothy Richard called this little book "one of the two most influential tracts written by missionaries since Protestant missions opened" (the other being the Reverend W. C. Milne's much-imitated *Two Friends*).[36]

Helen Nevius's *Mandarin Catechism* (Yeh-su chiao [kuanhua] wen-ta) was not psychologically profound, nor did it promise or threaten overmuch. Better than most it simply did the job a catechism is supposed to do: it got its audience talking about the subject and saying the same thing. The questions are realistic ("Is Jesus not then just like Confucius?"), and the answers are intelligible in Chinese terms ("Jesus is a heavenly God; heaven and earth and the

10,000 things all come from Him").[37] In addition to being safe and understandable, it was a versatile teaching tool; for several decades it was much used, for example, as a kind of first reader in Shantung mission schools, where it was memorized and "backed" (recited) just like the Chinese classics.[38]

Besides doing the basic *Catechism*, Mrs. Nevius looked for ways to stimulate the spiritual lives of more advanced inquirers. Trying to teach her women to pray, she found them capable only of "vain repetitions," however simple she thought she made the prayers. She needed a lowest common spiritual denominator, and to get this she finally wrote a prayer geared to her densest pupil. This was a Mrs. Chou, wife of a church member who was considered "hardly sane." By community agreement Mrs. Chou herself was "stupid beyond any possibility of learning anything." Helen Nevius looked upon her as less stupid than simply blank ("I think I scarcely ever met anyone else who had so few ideas").

Helen Nevius taught Mrs. Chou first to repeat a prayer and then to read it and other simple materials. The Chou family and its neighbors were overwhelmed, and Mrs. Nevius was so encouraged as to have the successful devotional printed as a sheet tract. Going through many printings between the 1860s and 1900, this "Simple Prayer in Easy Mandarin" (*Ch'ien-pai tao-kao wen*) appealed to the longings that poor women were thought to feel for "a Father's care and love." Unfortunately it seems to have been widely misunderstood; travelers reported it pasted up in public places, for Buddhist merit, all over China.[39]

Mrs. Nevius wrote ten other works in Chinese, which varied greatly in length and subject matter. Three were schoolbooks, and two were polemics against footbinding and usury. She also did an expurgated version of a Confucian moral primer, which she admitted resulted in a "Hamlet with Hamlet left out." [40]

The most successful and interesting of her nondevotional books were two inspirational biographies. One of these was an account of the life of a fellow woman's worker, and the other was the "apparently true" story of a much-abused Swiss child. These pieces were written because it was felt that native Christians needed paradigm individuals, something on the order of the filial sons of Confucian lore. Since nothing suitable existed indigenously, Mrs. Nevius used Western models in hopes of creating a taste for the genre. Her two sketches afford interesting glimpses into Christianity as it was presented to nineteenth-century Chinese women.

Helen Nevius's first subject here was Rose MacMaster Mills, first wife of Charles Mills of Tengchow. Rose Mills, who died in 1874, represented the woman's worker ideal: her "beautiful life" was distinguished by virtue, duty, benevolence, and many misfortunes suffered for the sake of the Chinese. Having grown up the filial daughter of the chaste widow of a Buffalo Irishman, young Rose gave her final seventeen years to the uplift of China. She labored not only to save souls, but to learn the language and problems of the Chinese people. Stories involving teaching, nursing, and relief work display her wisdom and compassion.

Mrs. Mills's most distinctive feature, however (and the point of the tract), was the extent to which she suffered. Before her own death she lost both of her parents, four children, two nieces, a sister, and two brothers-in-law. A little son, her favorite child, was afflicted with deafness. Rose Mills herself was ill almost continuously, once for six years without relief. These misfortunes are used by Helen Nevius to emphasize her heroine's Job-like faith, which is put finally into focus by a dramatic deathbed scene. Here Mrs. Mills explains that she has remained a "virtuous churchwoman" so that in the end she might "fly up to heaven." [41]

Seppili the Swiss Boy (Hai-t'ung ku-shih), an old Western Sunday School story, is more exciting and also has a message actually attuned to the Chinese situation. Briefly, the *Swiss Boy* is about a Bible-reading thirteen-year-old who is compelled by famine to leave his native hsien (canton). He falls into the hands of a pair of sadistic atheists from Berne, who subject him to many cruelties and finally feed him to their savage dogs. Like Rose Mills, Seppili yet dies serenely, forgiving his tormentors as their beasts tear him apart.

In Helen Nevius's hands, this story has a distinctive woman's work slant. The setting is not so alien as it seems; depression and generally unsettled conditions were dislocating young men throughout her years in Shantung. Many wound up in Tengchow or Chefoo, where urban temptations threatened country boys. What Mrs. Nevius is saying is that it is mother's training that tells in times of social and economic stress—that gives a son moral strength when his father's material resources fail.

Every man who appears in the *Swiss Boy* is either weak or evil, while numerous women emerge as strong and good. Seppili's mother dominates the action completely, even after she dies, for it is her son's constant remembrance of her teachings that keeps him on a heavenly path. The ego of the female reader is flattered as she learns that she is a morally superior being, and that her son's salvation depends, after God, mostly on herself. She is further exhorted to prepare her children immediately for the trials they are sure to meet. [42]

Suffering Together: The Importance of Personal Relations

Helen Nevius believed that the chief conscious idea of her Chinese friends was that "life is full of sorrow, and that their burdens are greater than they can bear." [43] This was the general impression in woman's work, or that the native females lived in an unhappy vacuum "without aid in life or hope in death." [44] Shantung life was certainly hard, particularly for women. The woman's work emphasis, however—on this world as a vale of tears and on suffering as a high virtue—reflects the world view of the Western women at least as much as it reflects that of the people to whom they were bringing reassurance.

Christian pessimism, or otherworldliness, is involved here, but so are other factors. As has been suggested, many east Shantung missionary women came to their work from rather sad backgrounds. In the field they moreover spent their lives under "the tremendous pressure of heathen life," the feeling that "every surrounding influence is against us, we are on the devil's own camping ground." As late as 1890 not a single missionary mother in Shantung had lived to bring up her own children; as a Tengchow worker melodramatically wrote, "It is sad to see how tired and worn many of us are and sadder still to see how, one by one, our number is lessened by the death angel, coming for one after another of the young wives of Shantung." [45]

Helen Nevius, an outstanding example of the hardness of the life, seems to have been sick constantly. She was pronounced dead on several occasions, and the effect of her "thoroughly diseased" condition on her relationship with her famous evangelist husband—who spent his Shantung years largely intinerating away from her—elicited missionary comments so blunt, apparently, as to cause the Presbyterian Board of Foreign Missions to censor them out of its correspondence archives.[46] In the words of the Reverend Hunter Corbett, her husband's longtime colleague and rival, "For fifty-seven years in China she suffered as few servants of God have been called to suffer." [47]

Mrs. Nevius rose from more deathbeds than she wrote about, however, and often—as Martha Crawford demonstrates—missionary wives were healthier people than their husbands were. Indeed, many of the most successful adjustments were made by people who experienced unusual personal tragedy. Julia Mateer, her sister Maggie Brown Capp, and Mary Snodgrass all exhibited as Presbyterian missionaries at Tengchow a kind of idealism and good-humored endurance that seems directly tied to childhood deprivations. Nonetheless, given the "death angel" context in which these women worked, it seems small wonder that the message they delivered was often an emphatically otherworldly one. As Helen Nevius said (in one of her Chinese additions to the English *Swiss Boy* text): "Early or late you will surely die. After death where will you go? This is a very important matter, more important than anything else . . . If you want a serene and joyous death, you must believe in the Savior Jesus, love Him, and trust Him . . . If you can do this you need not fear the pain and sufferings of this life, for after death there will be no more evil. These sufferings will surely be changed to blessings." [48]

Not surprisingly, a high percentage of female converts were old or sick or mistreated people, those Chinese females to whom the idea of a happy death would be most attractive. It should also be remembered, however, that in nineteenth-century Shantung women tended to age rapidly, so there was a large group to draw from that still had the problems of this world very much on its hands.

A good illustration is the 1906 Christian Chinese Women's Conference at Wei-hsien, which climaxed the first four decades of Presbyterian woman's work in east Shantung. Arriving "like the Johnstown flood," delegates from one hundred and sixty churches discussed such this-worldly topics as the Christian mother-in-law, the Christian go-between, Christian restraint of children, and the need to "Beware of Long Ears and Soft Tongues." [49] The woman's worker and the women on whom she worked thus had an intensely lively relationship, where the Westerner found herself constantly called upon to devise Christian lubricants for the frictions of daily life in China.

Personal relations always constituted the real heart of successful woman's work. These individual associations typically combined the relation of teacher to pupil and mother to daughter with that of friend and friend. Out of this context would emerge the special cases, the old Mrs. Lis and Mrs. Chous whose troubles dominate the writings of female missionaries. Such cases were women whom the gospel message found in some particularly depressed situation, usually poverty-stricken widowhood. After being saved they adhered with special affection to their missionary ladies, frequently working for them as Bible women or servants.

The woman's workers sent home thousands of stories about these Chinese friends, to the extent that the woman's work literature is in a sense largely a collection of anecdotes. Such stories were important in sustaining the interest of home mission bands. They were also the missionary's proof to herself that, though many turned away, a few of God's chosen ones accepted her with love.

The American women in east Shantung apparently came like fairy godmothers into the lives of those who responded so enthusiastically to them. Some were scholars and story tellers, like Helen Nevius; some liked to be leaned on, like Martha Crawford; and some were beautiful to look at and sang with a lovely voice, like Mary Merrill Crossette. Usually, it would seem, those who were so accepted had, like Julia Mateer, a measure of all these qualities. Most of all they seem to have had the infinite and genuinely loving patience that such relationships demanded. As Mrs. Mateer once remarked while recuperating from an illness, "I have never before since I came to China been for one whole day out of the sight and hearing of the Chinese . . . I get clear tired of [them] and want to go home, but I have never kept that notion for more than one day."

To her half-dozen adherents it was Mrs. Mateer who made Christianity immediate and true. Or as one expressed it, "The Lord sent you to me instead of [sending me] a mother." [50]

Special Work: Education, Medicine, and Mrs. Mills's School

Whenever woman's workers defined their work by categories, as in the 1877 essays by Martha Crawford and Julia Mateer, the two chief ones were invariably evangelism and schools. In practice the two lines of work tended to be closely joined. Mission schools, especially when women conducted them, were evangelistic agencies; and evangelistic work, which reportedly dealt with big old children, involved a lot of educating.

Most of the women missionaries, unless they were physically disabled—most commonly by loss of voice—or preoccupied with children of their own, participated in both types of work. As Julia Mateer said, "We are all engaged more or less in schools," and more generally, "The whole missionary work, as far as the human agent is concerned, is teaching . . . it is just the monotony of school life, teaching the same things over and over to one class after another, year after year—the same lessons, but the class is ever varying and each individual learner brings new interest and new incentives to exertion." [51]

Mrs. Mateer illustrated by her own life, however, that some became educators more formally than did others. Teaching—despite greatly expanded concern for evangelistic work among adult females—remained a natural specialty for many women missionaries. This was tied partly simply to the staffing requirements of the increasing number of late nineteenth-century Protestant schools. It was also tied to the fact that teaching did not as a rule require the endurance and thick skin demanded by continuous evangelizing, especially itineration. Since the level at which women taught was usually fairly low, it moreover did not require any great amount of learning. Sufficient for the task, given Calvin Mateer's *Mandarin Lessons* and ample enthusiasm, were the counsel of veteran missionaries and Chinese assistants, who often spent much of their time educating the educators.

Early teachers like Mrs. Crawford and Mrs. Mateer frequently taught schools made up of boys, because boys were easier to get. As time went on, however, opportunities opened to acquire girls, and at the same time graduates of Christian schools were becoming available to teach the boys. With these developments women missionaries turned more and more to concentrating on young people of their own sex. This was more in keeping with what woman's work was supposed to be about—to take the unloved daughters of China from lives of "filth and wickedness," to save them and raise them up as wives, mothers, and teachers to Christian families.[52]

Such work still developed only slowly in east Shantung, because except from Christian families—and even in some of them—it was difficult to procure little girls. Despite reports that the heathen despised his daughters, missionaries in Tengchow and Chefoo found that for years parents would "rather they starve" or be sold to "miserable old men" than that their daughters go to a foreign school. When this attitude faded somewhat, the missionaries faced another problem firmly rooted in Chinese life: not only was the education of females considered by males to be a largely pointless enterprise, but "most amazing of all" the women largely agreed.[53]

Calvin Mateer's brother Robert, another Shantung Presbyterian, was an articulate and influential early champion of girls' schools in China. Their mother's training was more recent in Robert's memory than in Calvin's, and he often quoted, "The hand that rocks the cradle rules the world." In a paper read to the first Conference of Shantung Missionaries (1893) the younger Mr. Mateer dwelt on the need of Chinese women, especially converts, to be educated to the idea that they were human beings equal to their men. They were fully as intelligent and deserving of mental culture, he stressed, however unnecessary their cultivation might seem.[54]

Acquainting the native women with such human rights also fitted into the Christianization program. Chinese congregations, Robert Mateer said, would never be reliable until missionaries began seriously "lifting up into prominence the mother, the wife, and the school mistress." Female converts should be shown that such Christians as Martin Luther, the Wesleys, and George Washington owed their successes to saintly mothers. "Their minds must be awakened and stimulated and filled with beautiful hopes, dreams, ambitions, and aspirations," Mateer continued; "They must catch the spirit of self-sacrifice, which is the mind of the Lord Jesus." [55]

Even Robert Mateer conceded that the stunted egos of elderly converts limited their potential. The great hope, as with males, was capturing and awakening the young: "The girls must come young enough and be kept long enough under the personal influence of the foreign teacher to mould and fix reliable Christian character." [56] If this could be accomplished with even a modest number, great consequences would presumably follow.

The line of thought represented by Mateer emphasized brains and strong Christian homemakers. It also emphasized that girls should not be educated beyond the modest expectations of the typical Chinese Christian. So although Presbyterian girls in Tengchow were studying algebra, chemistry, and physics as early as 1879, they spent most of their time learning to cook, sew, and keep things clean. Julia Mateer remarked in connection with this that it did "not matter so much what they study, as that they study hard." Since Christian life in Shantung was full of problems, self-discipline and practical knowledge necessarily took precedence.[57]

The overall message is summed up well in Martha Crawford's *The Three Maidens* (San-ko kuei-nü). This book, which is a sort of Sunday school Three Little Pigs, says that Christianity and sending girls to school go together, bringing happiness and financial success in womanhood.[58] The young subjects are approached in chapter one by a Christian village teacher. Two accept his invitation to go to school, while the third heeds her heathen parents, who tell her it is all foolishness. At school the two scholars learn to read the New Testament and to be filial and industrious at home. Classroom lessons in doctrine fade into worship services, where the teacher (doubling as preacher) extends invitations to join the church.

In swiftly moving action the little girl who did not attend the Christian school grows up to a life of misery; her daughters are sold into concubinage, and her unfilial son runs off to become a bandit. The two little students grow up to be good Baptists. One of them finds what is presumably typical Christian happiness: her unique training enables her to marry a young Christian merchant, whose Protestant ethic brings them wealth and high position. Her classmate, however, is kept from similar happiness by her non-Christian mother, who allows a scheming go-between to match the girl to an opium eater. The daughter soon dies from an accumulation of abuses. But by her assurance of heaven her death comes as a joyous release; she tells her loyal schoolmate, "My body may rot in the ground, but my soul goes to Jesus." [59]

The school message is thus a double one: the confident suffering of the Swiss Boy and Rose Mills remains, but Christian education gives one a real chance for joy and security on earth.

Another natural line of work for woman's workers was ministering to health, first in the Western community and then among the Chinese. Native women, who often did not feel at ease with Western male physicians, were frequently willing to be treated by the doctor's wife, or for that matter by any Western woman present.[60] What this amounted to, in the words of Charles Mills of Tengchow, was that the Western women were "daily trying to prescribe in a bungling way for numbers of sick persons." [61]

Tending the sick and dosing schoolchildren came naturally to most of these good-hearted women. Real doctoring was something else again, and as a rule they did not like having to do it. Julia Mateer wrote, "I dislike to handle medicine, and as I rarely feel very sure I am doing the best thing, it worries me exceedingly . . . sometimes I wish that we had never the means of giving a single dose of medicine, because then I could turn away all such callers with a clear conscience." [62] Like it or not, the foreign women could not divest themselves of this work. In their hearts they were too vulnerable to the entreaties of the sick, especially those with whom they had established personal relationships in evangelistic work.[63]

The logical course was to secure female doctors, which was increasingly what happened. Some of these people—like the unfortunate Dr. Adeline Kelsey (see Chapter 9 below)—were tragically unfit for the sort of life and practice they found. Most of them worked out well, however, because in missionary work they were accorded an acceptance and professional freedom that they were denied at home. The Presbyterian Charles Mills, who had a certain gift for unhappy phrasing, made the point neatly: "If I were at home I would never employ a lady physician. And the very designation is repulsive to me. But giving ladies medical training for work on mission ground strikes me as different." [64]

The careerist impulse is not hard to spot in these nineteenth-century woman doctors, unable as many had felt to practice in their "man-monopolized" homeland. But they were doctors in the first place, presumably, largely because they had been generally idealistic girls, and in the context of their times there is little reason to think they were less committed spiritually than other missionaries were. The complexity of the type is suggested by an admiring evaluation: "They are not mere pretentious adventurers, but regular, well-educated physicians, actuated by the purest motives, immolating themselves upon the altar of humanity in order to lay the foundations for bestowing the blessings of a western medical knowledge upon the millions of their ignorant, downtrodden sisters in heathen lands." [65]

Occasionally an American woman would bring to China some talent or training which failed to fit within the conventional works but still met a real need. If successful, these "miscellaneous" works could take on a poignancy heightened by their very unconventionality. To the missionaries this would indicate a distinctive call, and no case better illustrates such a call than that of Annetta Thompson Mills and her Chefoo School for the Deaf.

Mrs. Mills's whole life appeared to have been a preparation for the work she was to do in China. Growing up an unhappy stepchild, she concentrated her affections on a deaf little half-brother. Her ability to communicate with him so impressed a Rochester specialist that he sent her to Boston for professional training, and in time she became head instructor in the Rochester school herself. In 1879 she met the recently widowed Charles Mills, who had brought his deaf son to the school from China. One thing led to another, and by 1884 she was in Tengchow as the second Mrs. Mills, trying to figure out ways to translate her Rochester skills into the Chinese she was learning. Letters in woman's work magazines had been calling attention to the need for such work since 1883.

Annetta Mills opened her first school (boys only) in 1887, and with the death of her husband she moved in 1895 to Chefoo. For almost forty years she worked on the books, charts, phonetic cards, and other appurtenances of her Chinese system, training assistants and several hundred pupils from nine provinces and Korea. She also traveled about China promoting her cause and trying to find jobs (typesetting, carpentry, tutoring) for the boys and— after 1907—girls. The school was supported by such people as Julia Ward Howe, Theodore Roosevelt, and Governor Yang Shih-hsiang of Shantung. Mostly it was maintained by contributions from some thirty associations for the deaf in the United States and Great Britain.

Mrs. Mills seems to have been a gifted improviser and an excellent businesswoman and promoter. She was also a sort of sentimental fatalist, or a person to whom the "worth of one soul" had a special meaning. On missionaries and Chinese generally, for example, she reflected that "We do not find ourselves angels nor the people among whom we labor angelic." She stayed in China, she said, because her own students had "so little to make them happy and it takes so little to bring a smile to their faces." Visiting Mrs. Mills at the time she was deciding to stay (1895), Lottie Moon remarked, "Two things struck me forcibly in witnessing the exercises of the pupils. One was the brightness of the boys, their eager response . . . Even more admirable was the beautiful sympathy that manifestly existed between teacher and pupil. I have never seen anything like it anywhere." [66]

Results in East Shantung, 1860–1912

By the close of the first half century of Protestant activity in Shantung, woman's work was an established institution throughout most China missions. It had its own mystique and traditions and a diversified programmatic approach. In some ways it looked as if the women were taking over. President Paul Bergen of Shantung Christian University (Arts College), for example, commented in 1910 on "a feature of missionary statistics of unusual interest and worthy of record," which was that "more women than men are engaged in missionary work in China."

The imbalance was actually much greater than Bergen's remark would suggest. By 1910 there were seventy-nine Presbyterian and Southern Baptist women in his own province, as compared to forty-six male missionaries. His colleague Calvin Mateer had observed thirty years previously that "The mission work seems to be going into the hands of the ladies not only at home but also on the foreign field . . . If not impertinent or ungallant I would suggest that men are needed just now in China a good deal more than women." [67]

In any case the women had come to stay, and they had built up an elaborate, separate-but-equal mission work. Techniques had been painfully wrought for meeting Chinese women, attracting and keeping their interest, nurturing them in mind and spirit, and shaping them for new lives as Christian mothers, wives, and community leaders. Teaching, doctoring, and "book-making" specialists worked at the various needs of these females, while a small but enthusiastic force of evangelistic regulars preached, comforted, and exhorted them to salvation and prideful womanhood.

Woman's work was in a sense a feminist movement, obviously, but its rationale and basic orientation were always evangelistic. The main goal was to save the souls of Chinese women, for their own sakes and because the men would theoretically follow. It is thus interesting that the great formative days of woman's work—the last quarter of the nineteenth century—is also precisely the period when China missions' emphasis as a whole began to shift from old-time religion to a combination of evangelism with good works, which had been rather downplayed since mid-century. The presence of the women missionaries seems to have pushed this along; at any rate the evolution that took place was in the direction of uplift—particularly through schools, which were always mostly in female hands. The movement seems moreover to have taken place in direct proportion to the womanpower available to implement it.

One important aspect of this development was that a certain confusion, or lack of visible results, befell evangelistic woman's work. This can be illustrated again by the case of Martha Crawford. Mrs. Crawford (who was known in her later life as a kind of woman's-worker's woman's worker) dressed like a native, practiced impeccable Chinese etiquette, and in one missionary's opinion "spoke the best Chinese I ever heard, the Chinese themselves not excepted." She was widely said to "combine in herself in a very unusual degree a large number of very beautiful and useful qualities." [68]

For at least the last thirty years of her life Martha Crawford felt quite close to Chinese women of the poorer classes. Their biggest human difference, she believed, was that she represented a prospering civilization while they were caught in one that was declining and demoralized. The Confucian family in her view provided many comforts in such times. What it and the Chinese lacked—what "they seem to have been waiting all their lives for"—was something to create "friends among strangers," a new social mortar. [69]

Mrs. Crawford believed her Christian faith offered this in its great principle of undiscriminating love. She accordingly devoted all her powers to demonstrating by her own life what this meant. As other woman's workers returned to teaching or took up similar adjuncts, Martha Crawford went to basic human relationships. She sought to involve her Chinese contacts in her faith by binding them personally to herself—spreading over them her own blanket of Christian love, concern, and assurance.

From many testimonies there seems little doubt that she made herself beloved. Something ironic, however, happened to her plan for winning souls. According to one of her most devoted missionary admirers, she became so successful at human relations that her religious purpose was largely lost on her friends. She would sit and hold an old woman's hand, it seems, and tell her of the love of

Jesus, while the old woman reflected on how good it was to have a loving friend like Mrs. Crawford. The missionary did her best to retain her identity as a religious teacher—to reduce "useless chattering"—but to her pupils she was known as "mother." Her influence, an associate reflected, was "less than it should have been." [70]

According to an obituary Martha Crawford was always sustained by memory of her 1849 call experience in Tuscaloosa. One gets the impression, however, that by her death in 1909 she was puzzled—how was it that she had learned to win the hearts of the Chinese for herself but not necessarily for Jesus? To most Shantung pioneers woman's work presented similar mysteries, and by the close of the period some had grave doubts about it. Helen Nevius, for example, came close before she died to saying that the whole concept was ill conceived. After much reflection she observed that none of the methods she had seen in fifty years had really worked. She also cited a letter from her old friend Mrs. Timothy Richard, who had decided that women simply had no influence in China. Mrs. Nevius remarked frequently on the fact that Mrs. Richard's Shantung English Baptists—who had no woman's work program—were more successful than most groups that did. [71]

A present-day reader gets several impressions from the record of pioneer Shantung woman's work. One of these is that it did produce a limited number of community leaders, or women converts who lived up to everything the theory envisioned. Among Presbyterians, for example, the three Chao sisters of Li-jen village (Chi-mo hsien) acquired semi-legendary status as schoolteachers and successful evangelists. [72] An even more striking case is that of an unnamed woman discussed by Martin Yang, in his sociological study of his own native village near Tsingtao. According to Dr. Yang, she was the area's first female convert and the only woman in fifty years who showed "a degree of leadership that affected the village as a whole." At the time of her conversion (apparently around 1910) local anti-Christianity was intense. She nonetheless attended a city Bible school, where she learned to read. By becoming the only literate woman of her village, its model housewife, and its most pleasant, unselfish personality, she won respect and—for a woman—uncommon eminence. She formed prayer groups, taught inquirers, and supervised the building of a village church. To local females her life was an eye-opener: "Her success in achieving her aims, despite their unconventionality and the discouragement of others, made her a stimulating and perhaps disturbing example to the other women of what women might do." [73]

Also existent are a number of accounts that are strikingly

suggestive of Martha Crawford's *Three Maidens*. Ning Lao T'ai-t'ai (Ida Pruitt's "Daughter of Han")—who was not Christian herself —describes two such cases from her years in Tengchow. A Mrs. Lan preached and taught for the Presbyterians while her husband, a strange character who looked like a "devil," tended the mission gate and itinerated with Charles Mills. The Lans lived fairly well, and their son got "a good place in a lace company in Chefoo." Mrs. Chang, the other case, was more successful still: "When Mrs. Chang and her husband and children came from the country they had nothing. She taught a little school for the missionaries and got three thousand cash a month, and he was a tutor to teach them language, and got six thousand cash a month. He had a good Chinese education, but she was a very intelligent woman. She knew how to plan and to contrive. Layer by layer she raised the level of the family, until now that she is old she lives in plenty on the rent of her land and her houses. Her daughters have married well, and her son has a high position with the railroad. Her husband was a professor in Cheeloo University before he retired. It was all due to her powers of managing. And she had a good heart too and was a good worker." [74]

The most famous of such stories in Shantung was undoubtedly that of the women of the "heavenly" Liu family. The women here were the wife and the mother of the Presbyterian Liu Shou-shan, a Tengchow College graduate (1884) who rose from poverty to "wealth like that of T'ao Chu." [75] Liu made his real fortune in Tsingtao after 1900, but he did so with capital raised earlier by the women. His widowed mother (Liu Wang-shih) had placed him under mission schooling as a child, and in the evenings he had transmitted to her his education in reading and "paper" arithmetic. With the Presbyterian Hunter Corbett's help she also secured work in Chefoo as an amah in Western homes.

Liu's wife (née Liu Mei-ch'ing) was known for "cleverness exceeding that of men." A product of mission schooling, she met Shou-shan through her brother, who was his college schoolmate. After marriage both husband and wife became Christian teachers in Chefoo. Mr. Liu opened a jewelry shop on the side, and Mrs. Liu learned foreign embroidery (*hua-pien*) from Fanny Corbett Hays, a Presbyterian woman's worker. She then converted their home, which included her girls' school, into a lace factory where she employed the schoolgirls as half-day workers. For some ten years the school-factory turned out up to 100,000 articles annually.

By 1894 Mr. and Mrs. Liu had raised their combined teaching income from 5000 to 12,000 cash per month. Mother Liu, by saving an English employer from a burning house, reportedly had her amah's pay raised by some 2000 percent. All three Lius lived frugally and invested in the lace business. While Liu Shou-shan's mother arranged export contracts among the "many foreigners she knew," his wife recruited Christian suppliers over an eight-hsien area. In 1901 Mr. Liu sold the enterprise for 10,000 yüan. With this and a thousand yüan left him by his mother, he moved to Tsingtao and to "celebrity" as a real estate and construction tycoon. As "crafty planners" and Christian philanthropists, Mr. and Mrs. Liu eventually won something approaching sainthood in the Shantung Presbyterian Church.[76]

Cases thus existed, including some rather spectacular ones, of remarkable achievement by Christian women in east Shantung. Only rarely, however, do these cases suggest a movement of the kind anticipated by missionary woman's-work theory. The impression conveyed is one of intelligent, ambitious women mixing native business skill, sect and family traditions, and timely Western help into individual Horatio Alger successes. This was, of course, one way of reading the *Three Maidens* message; and in the context of its times, it was an interpretation that both Chinese and Americans could endorse. But women like Liu Wang-shih were not—in the sense that their American friends intended—"Mothers of a Chinese Revolution."

The near-uniqueness of the woman described by Martin Yang (who says he never heard of anyone comparable) illustrates perhaps the main point here. The point is that she won genuine personal influence within a hostile family (as well as community) situation. By contrast, other heroines of the native church succeeded by operating through similarly disposed husbands, brothers, or occasionally sons. The fact that their cleverness exceeded their men's was not in itself very revolutionary.

This all underlines, perhaps, the apparent accuracy of the conclusion reached by Helen Nevius and Mrs. Richard: female conversion was meaningless (except in "worth of one soul" terms) without male family backing from the first. Under optimum conditions it seems moreover to have regenerated families without having much carryover effect on wider society. Woman's work, of course, operated on precisely the opposite assumptions.

The views of Ida Pruitt's Ning Lao T'ai-t'ai—who seems about as average a non-Christian Chinese woman as one can imagine—furnish another insight here. First, she seems to have looked upon the Christian heroines of Tengchow primarily as smart business-women and skillful husband-managers. As such she found them admirable largely by contrast to the great majority of local female converts. Most of the Bible women (as well as most American woman's workers) talked "such nonsense that I could reply to them"; for this reason she was unimpressed by their "always telling me to believe in Jesus." As an example she cites an encounter with old Kuo Ta-niang, a particularly obtuse Bible woman: "She was paid three thousand cash a month by the missionaries. She would say to me, 'You should believe and be grateful. See your arms and legs, good and strong, that the Good Lord gave you. Should you not be grateful?' And I answered, 'Before believing in Jesus, did you not have as good a pair of arms and legs as you now have?' . . . What could you do with such a woman?" [77]

An uneasiness on this very topic often came over the woman's workers themselves. The feeling is quite apparent, for example, in Mrs. Paul Bergen's report on the much publicized 1906 Christian Women's Conference at Wei-hsien. The 320 delegates, who were supposedly the "furthest advanced women" available in Shantung proved advanced mostly in age. Having taught these people to express enthusiasm by clapping, the American moderators were never able to bring the meeting really to order. Speakers who made themselves heard, according to Mrs. Bergen, displayed a disquieting confusion of Christian teachings with indigenous folkways. The woman who spoke on "Duties of a Christian Mother-in-Law," for instance, concluded by asking the delegates to pray for her son's unruly wife. The authority on "Christian Go-Betweens" similarly presented her address as a sales talk ("My sisters, let us follow Abraham's example, and get a wise go-between who will ask God's help").[78]

Such imperfections in female converts, who were always "mostly old women," constituted perhaps the greatest single stimulus to the program of education for girls. The illiterate and poverty-stricken aspects of the churchwomen also caused the missionaries to look wistfully toward the upper classes, for any token of acceptance or interest by those "like ourselves." By 1905 a Missions and High Life (progressive supper) program was underway in Teng-chow, involving woman's workers and some of the "richest women in the city." [79] Mostly, however, emphasis moved as Robert Mateer had wished, toward schools and the next generation. The effects of this Christian education on Chinese girls is an important question that remains to be answered; Liu Mei-ch'ing seems an early case study.

Classic woman's work seems to have been based on a series of flawed understandings of the nature and role of women in traditional Chinese society. Because many were clearly mistreated and emotionally starved—and because they sometimes sought solace in indigenous superstitions—it was assumed that these females would naturally appreciate and soon embrace the "pure religion of Jesus." Because women in general were largely out of public sight, they were at the same time presumed to be moving to subtle purposes and credited with entirely unrealistic powers. In a not unusual American style these views credited motherhood with occult effectiveness and Christianity with universal intelligibility. In a broader sense the whole program seems a religious and human-relations version of the contemporary commercial dream: the Chinese home and its secluded women exerted a fascination akin to that of the Chinese interior and its "limitless" market. All these dreams fell rather flat in nineteenth-century east Shantung.

As a rapid agent of Christian and feminine revolution, woman's work was thus perhaps ill conceived. Regarding Julia Mateer, a chief architect of the pure religion crusade, Ning Lao T'ai-t'ai recalled two incidents clearly. One was that Mrs. Mateer finished her thirty-four years in Tengchow in pain "so great that the doctor gave her too much medicine on purpose, and so she died." The other was a street scene of many years before: "One day when I was begging and feeling sad and sour in my heart I saw an old woman begging on the street. She was crawling on her hands and knees like a four-footed animal. My heart turned over and I was at peace. At least I still had my legs to walk upon . . . The old woman jumped over the edge of the Marble Bridge where the main street crosses the river inside the Water Gate. She wanted to die. I saw the old woman under the bridge, hunched up and suffering. The people went to see her as to a show. The foreign woman had mercy on her and took her home and cleaned her wound. She lived at the missionaries' home for many days and then she died and the missionary buried her. That was a good and brave deed. The old woman's scalp was full of worms." [80]

5

A Woman of Energy and Self-Respect

Charlotte (Lottie) Diggs Moon represents the pioneer days both of woman's work and of the Southern Baptist North China Mission. Her story also underscores in several ways the limitations of using individual biographies to make general points. As a woman's worker she was actually more archetypical than representative, and as a Baptist missionary she was quite different from T. P. Crawford, her Shantung colleague for some thirty years. A greater contrast than Miss Moon and Crawford would in fact be hard to imagine.

Properly speaking, Miss Moon's story is a very private but interesting one. A woman of unusual background, intelligence, and compassion, she pursued understanding of China with a truly remarkable intensity. In the 1880s—when such adventures were not undertaken by Western females—she lived alone in the Chinese interior, with the Chinese. This was only one stage in a forty-year career of such honest fortitude as to constitute a kind of spiritual and human-relations odyssey.

Another interesting reason for examining Miss Moon is that today, to millions of Southern Baptists, her name is "synonymous with missions" and in a way synonymous with China.[1] Where T. P. Crawford failed, in other words, Miss Moon succeeded; by a conjunction of circumstances, and by the quality of her life, she has won posthumously more Baptist glory than Crawford knew in all his dreams. She is an acknowledged saint to a church that suspects saints, and a symbol of interracial love in a section where hatred is supposed to have been peculiarly the rule. She has in fact become a genuine culture heroine, to a degree seemingly unapproached by any other missionary—or for that matter any American of any sort—who ever went to China.

To non-Southern Baptists Miss Moon's apotheosis may seem a little strange. This perhaps demonstrates only that Americans have tended to live in artificially different worlds. The idea that Miss

Moon most fundamentally represents is a wistful dream that lies somewhere, probably, in all of us.

Virginia and the Post-Bellum South, 1840–1873

Lottie Moon perhaps from the beginning needed only a cause to become a name to conjure with. Her birth in 1840 represented a confluence of "the best influences of Virginia." Her ancestry included English royal favorites, Quaker scholars, colonial governors, heroes of duels and of the American Revolution, and a Lady Gordon known as "The White Rose of Scotland."

Miss Moon's status was most compellingly that of her foster-grandfather, John Harris of Albemarle county. "Captain John" was a cotton merchant and a powerful figure in the early Memphis and New Orleans markets. His base of operations, however, consisted of eight estates and eight hundred slaves in the beautiful Charlottesville area. Lottie Moon grew up on the estate known as Viewmont, which had devolved upon her father, Edward Harris Moon. Until its destruction in 1958 Viewmont represented the oldest house still standing on the famous Road of Presidents. In Lottie's time it overlooked a five-thousand acre economic unit, where the inmates of thirty-nine slave cabins helped Edward Moon raise tobacco, wheat, corn, and cattle.[2]

The most important fact about Viewmont with regard to Lottie Moon was that it functioned as a matriarchy: There were numerous people to do all the work, but "the mistress of the home was the director of all that they did." The mistress's recreation and special joy was to communicate to her seven children her strong Baptist faith. Edward Moon, the master, was for some years "rather indifferent" in religion, as he appears to have been in most things. In 1852 Mr. Moon attempted to rescue a money trunk from a burning riverboat; he perished, and his wife Anna Maria assumed control as "mistress of Viewmont in every sense of the word."[3]

Under Mrs. Moon's influence her children grew into independent and very idealistic adults. Thomas, her eldest, became a physician, and like his father he died on a riverboat in the 1850s. More altruistically than Edward Moon, Thomas died of yellow fever contracted from boat passengers no other local doctor would treat. The second child, sister Orianna (Orie), was perhaps the most remarkable person in the family. A genuine rebel, she refused to attend any of the Virginia finishing schools and took her education in the north. There she became a Lucy Stone feminist, attended abolitionist gatherings, and emerged from the Female

Medical College of Pennsylvania as reputedly the first woman south of the Mason-Dixon line to earn an M.D. degree.[4]

Unhappy back home, Dr. Orianna studied in Paris and went in the late 1850s to the Holy Land, where as an unattached medical missionary she worked on ophthalmia among the Arabs. When the Civil War broke out she felt obliged to return to Virginia. There Orianna gave "all her splendid young womanhood," we are told, to service as a female captain (medical) in the Confederate army. After the war she practiced with her husband, who was also a doctor, and bore him twelve sons in several states.[5]

Lottie Moon was the third child and second of four daughters. In her youth she was not as serious-minded as Thomas or Orianna, nor did she evince much interest in her mother's religious instruction. Of superior but undisciplined intelligence, Lottie drifted through several female academies; she apparently absorbed little except a taste for romantic novels and for Thomas Paine, whose irreligion she found congenial. In 1857, however, Miss Moon enrolled at the Albemarle Female Institute, a sort of unofficial experimental extension of the all-male University of Virginia. In this more stimulating atmosphere she underwent a period of spiritual and intellectual maturation. At her graduation in 1861 she received a master's degree in classics, thereby acquiring (with four classmates) a reputation for being the first southern woman ever to earn the A.M. She also took from college a new religious faith—perhaps the one her adored mother had tried previously to instill—professed in a campus revival.[6]

As soon as she left school Miss Moon began to come under the pressures that would eventually send her to China. She arrived home to tend wounded from the first Battle of Bull Run, and to watch as Orianna and other family members "marched out to fight for the Stars and Bars." Male relatives rode with Mosby's Rangers (an elite guerrilla unit), with whom two in particular (cousins James and Jacob) became known as "The Dare-Devil Moons." Female relatives Cynthia and Virginia Moon, disguised as Irish washerwomen, went off to do "splendid service" as Confederate spies. Cousin Ginnie—a beautiful girl who by report smoked, drank, and generally "didn't give a damn"—cut such a swath among Yankee officers as to become "at once the toast of the Confederacy and the despair of the Union."[7]

With exciting careers thus opening for others, Lottie Moon was forced to sit out the war at home. Mrs. Moon required her help in running Viewmont and in tutoring Edmonia, the youngest of the Moon children. During the war years Lottie became deeply attached to Edmonia, or Eddie, and she spent her leisure time in language study with her sister. In addition to pursuing Greek and Latin, Lottie learned during the war to read books in French, Spanish, Italian, and German.

When the war ended the ex-slaves drifted away, and the outlook at Viewmont—now managed by Lottie's brother Isaac—dimmed considerably. It was a moment when everyone, including Lottie, had to reassess things. Though a Confederate chaplain had once "come a-wooing," she was not courted by many others. In southern terms Miss Moon was over-educated, not particularly good-looking, and no longer had compensations to offer. After several months' reflection she accordingly decided that teaching was the "primary need and the richest field of endeavor" available. She taught in the late 1860s in Alabama and Kentucky, where she formed a close friendship with a similarly dislocated Georgia girl named Anna Cunningham Safford. In 1871 they moved together to Cartersville, Georgia, where they established a female high school.[8]

The Cartersville school was successful, but Lottie Moon and "A. C." Safford were not satisfied. Both young women had become deeply religious while wandering about the postwar south; both had also become much involved in church work, particularly evangelistic and charitable visitation. Lottie was moreover greatly affected by the death of her mother in 1870 and by her sister Eddie's ensuing decision to go as a missionary to China. Her sister Orianna, who had retained an interest in the Arab world, encouraged Lottie to read her collection of books on "eastern lands." Among these books Lottie was drawn over a period of several years to those dealing specifically with China; they depicted, she felt, an interesting mixture of heathenism with "advanced culture and ethical teachings." In 1873 she startled her students' parents by announcing that she and A. C. Safford were giving up the school to become missionaries. Edmonia had left the year before.[9]

Lottie Moon's call thus came in a context of many converging influences. Her unusual family had provided her with ideals of piety and service and with an outstanding education. As doctors, executives, and spies its women had further demonstrated what determined females could do. Coupled with Lottie's own romantic bent, the cumulative effect undoubtedly made the Cartersville schoolhouse seem a narrow theater of operations.

Also, in all seriousness, it was "a serious world into which she stepped" from an antebellum childhood. A quarter of a million southern men had just perished, and in Lottie Moon's two states of Virginia and Georgia women outnumbered men in 1870 by more than 50,000. For women life in the south had been for a decade—as a recent study movingly recounts—a series of traumas, creating for many a kind of new "frontier where there were few precedents."[10] With the security of her background eliminated, Miss Moon traveled widely and thought deeply for eight years. When at thirty-two she finally put everything together, she found her life's work and a new inner satisfaction. A friend remarked that she left for China "as though she were going home."[11]

Tengchow: Adjustment and Finding One's Place

In China Miss Moon and A. C. Safford separated. Miss Safford went as a Presbyterian to Soochow, where she specialized in "bookmaking" and founded the periodical *Woman's Work in China*. In mission circles she won renown as a fierce businesswoman and something of a man-hater, and as a journalist who "never made a mistake and never forgot anything."[12]

As a Southern Baptist, Lottie Moon reported to Tengchow in December 1873. There she joined the North China Mission, which at the time consisted of Martha and T. P. Crawford, Sally Holmes, and Miss Moon's sister Edmonia. Crawford was embroiled with Kao Ku San and scholarly projects; the field was large, however, and missionaries were few, so each individual could go his or her own way. Miss Moon's first decade consequently amounted to a long period of personal adjustment, as she looked for a type of work to which she could fully commit herself.

For several years Lottie Moon remained physically and psychologically close to Tengchow city, and more particularly to her sister. While learning the language she served as a teacher; she had prior experience, and Edmonia was teaching too.[13] Very quickly the elder of the Moon sisters impressed her fellow missionaries as a "highly cultivated, very pious, self sacrificing woman . . . very systematic and industrious."[14]

Edmonia, however, constituted a different and—as Lottie soon discovered—highly problematic missionary case. Still only nineteen years old in 1873, Eddie had already alarmed her coworkers by doing, as J. B. Hartwell said, "queer and unreasonable things" and by having hysterical seizures in which she professed to be "crazy."[15] She also professed to be chronically ill with troubles of the throat, lungs, eyes, nerves, and other organs.

In Martha Crawford's opinion Eddie was a lazy hypochondriac who was rude, gossipy, and fault-finding to a "very burdensome" extent. She was also "so exacting and cross to the Chinese

[that]they do not like her." By 1875 the Moon school had devolved entirely upon Lottie, whose time was otherwise occupied in
nursing Eddie and expressing embarrassment over her sister's
"good for nothing" conduct.[16]

In 1877 Edmonia Moon gave up her romantic notions of
missionary service and went back to Virginia, where she carried on
feebly for another thirty years. Her departure released Lottie, after
three years in China, to come seriously to grips with the local scene.
From this point Lottie Moon spent as much time as she could in
language study, and she formed a habit of closely observing her
surroundings. She did not find them particularly stimulating. Her
first year without Eddie was depressing; discouraged by the Tengchow station's isolation and poor prospects, she wrote the Foreign
Mission Board, "I especially am bored to death living alone. I don't
find my own society either agreeable or edifying . . . I really
think a few more winters like the one just past would put an end to
me. This is no joke, but dead earnest. *Verbum sat.*" [17]

Just at this point Miss Moon was presented with an opportunity to reconsider her call, or to soften its starker aspects. Her old
beau—the former Confederate chaplain—was also from a notable
Virginia family, and he did not give up easily. Professor Toy, as
he had now become, wrote reproposing marriage and suggesting
mission work together in Japan. Lonely and thinking very highly
of him, Lottie decided after talks with Martha Crawford to accept
his offer.

Crawford Howell Toy was at the time teaching at the
Southern Baptist Theological Seminary, Greenville, South Carolina.
He was known as a brilliant linguist and theologian. Following the
Civil War he had studied in Europe, where he was exposed to
Darwinian theory and to "the new ideas of the German scholars"
on Old Testament history and inspiration. Lottie Moon was not
unaware that his advanced views on these subjects were now causing
a great stir in Greenville. Unlike T. P. Crawford, Toy had not
"removed the embarrassment that increasing wisdom has produced,"
or satisfactorily demonstrated the superiority of fundamentalist
interpretation. His missionary interest, and second proposal to
Miss Moon, coincided with a feeling at the seminary that Professor
Toy should correct his views or leave.[18]

While C. H. Toy was professing himself into an unacceptable
position (1879), Lottie Moon was securing and reading "practically
all the notable works" dealing with evolutionary theory. Her conclusion was that Darwin was perhaps the "gentlest and wisest of
heathens," but that evolution was for her an "untenable position."

She and Professor Toy agreed to call off their marriage. Toy served briefly as literary editor of the New York *Independent*, and in 1880 he went to Harvard, where he became Hancock Professor of Hebrew and Other Oriental Languages. He joined the Unitarian Church and later wrote many works of exegesis and commentary. Miss Moon, as she wrote her sister Orianna, was left to "plod along in the same old way." [19]

There seems little doubt that the Toy crisis was a turning point in Lottie Moon's life. Her thoughts are of course not altogether evident, but one factor that certainly influenced her was loyalty to her church. She read carefully the advanced books C. H. Toy recommended, and the fact that she "studied the question from his viewpoint" is illustrated by her marginal notations. At the same time, however, she was reading the "many articles that appeared in the Baptist papers" regarding Darwin and Toy, who among Baptists was apparently considered Darwin's leading disciple. [20]

Probably even more important was Miss Moon's need to protect the faith and sense of personal mission around which her own life was now structured. To all the independent Moon girls life was not primarily a matter of pleasing men. Lottie's elder sister, as a faithful Lucy Stone follower, would be buried by her sons as "Orianna Moon, M.D." Lottie herself, as one facing "almost insurmountable problems" on a "frontier of the Kingdom," decided that she could not risk attenuating her faith if she wanted to stay a "good workman." Having coped in China for six years with "the peculiarities that come to one who lives much alone," she had also reportedly "adapted herself to the hard conditions of the life in a pioneer station, [and] come to rely upon God as revealed to her in His Word." Many years later, to a relative who asked if she had ever had a love affair, she answered, "Yes, but God had first claim on my life, and since the two conflicted, there could be no question about the result." [21]

So the real effects of this affair were to turn Miss Moon away from reflecting on her boredom and to confirm her conviction that she had " a trust from God which no personal consideration could abrogate." The break with Toy, together with Edmonia's departure, amounted to a severing of human ties with the past. From this point Lottie Moon indeed went her own way. At almost forty years of age, she embarked on a search for her proper identity in a mission-centered context.

This search took about five years and consisted of two stages. Before Miss Moon could know definitely about Lottie Moon in China, she had to establish the position of the Western Christian missionary as a type. Her letters and articles of 1879–82 accordingly reflect a close study of her Chinese environment. She did not doubt that missionaries in general and she in particular belonged, but beyond that she was unsure about a number of things.

An important event here was an 1879 country trip, apparently her first real itineration. Early in that year she went with Sally Holmes to a cluster of hamlets some twenty to thirty li (5 to 10 miles) from Tengchow city. A bitterly cold wind covered her with snow en route, and in the villages were discomforts of other kinds: "To speak in the open air, in a foreign tongue, from six to eleven times a day is no trifle . . . if anyone thinks all this is agreeable, then I wish to declare most emphatically that as a matter of taste, I differ." [22]

She reacted to the villagers, she felt, as would any "refined and high-strung nature," by finding them to be a "Great Unwashed." Particularly upsetting on this trip was an experience one morning in Wan-ssu-k'o village. As she and Mrs. Holmes were breakfasting in an inquirer's home, a crowd of some thirty youths assembled outside. To the anguish of hostess and missionaries, the boys tore away the house's paper windows, first to get a look and then to climb through. Soon four people were standing on the table among the dishes. Recalling her feelings, Miss Moon wrote, "O! the torture of human eyes upon you; scanning every feature, every look, every gesture! I felt it very keenly for a moment, and then went on chatting with an old lady. 'Do you know what I have been doing?' I asked her. 'I have been counting the number of persons in this room.' For a moment she looked disconcerted, and then she said apologetically, 'We have never seen any heavenly people before.' After such a magnificent compliment, what could one do, but redouble one's efforts to be gracious?" [23]

However "simply maddening" her work was, Miss Moon thus brought to it a certain aplomb. The same attitude informed her efforts to analyze the nature of Chinese peasant women, who were the specific objects of her evangelizing attention. Except for a minority who were "of intelligence, eager to learn," she found that most exhibited "minds utterly vacant." [24] This she decided was not congenital so much as culturally induced, particularly by husbands and fathers who told these women they were "too stupid to learn" from childhood on. On the other hand, she felt a certain sympathy for the males, or rather she felt that "the Shantung woman's tongue and temper constitute a pretty effectual safeguard of her rights." [25] She was also impressed, on her first major itineration, by the chief elder of Wan-ssu-k'o, who paid a call to see if she and Mrs. Holmes were spreading unsafe doctrines: "*Elder:* 'In your country, do the women rule?' *Mrs. H.:* 'In our country the women are educated, the men respect their opinions and consult with them; but if after consultation there is irreconcilable difference of opinion, the right of the final decision lies with the man.' *Elder:* 'Ah! Just as it is here. They consult together and the man decides.' " [26]

Miss Moon continued to teach in the city, but from the time of her Wan-ssu-k'o trip she went frequently into the countryside. She found much encouragement. In contrast to the "hatred and cold distrust" of the urban Chinese in Tengchow, it was often possible in the country to draw an "eager crowd of boys, girls, and women." Evangelistic prospects seemed definitely superior. In one village Mrs. Holmes ("catechising them in her usual vigorous style") elicited responses that "had been taught them more than two years before." [27] Also, Miss Moon had arrived at an age when she appreciated such rural comments as, "How white her hand is!" "She doesn't look more than seventeen or eighteen." "How pretty she is!" "The fact is, their water and earth (climate) is better than ours." [28]

Like so many missionary pioneers in Shantung, Lottie Moon thus formed a sentimental preference for country Chinese. She and most of her contemporaries had grown up in rural American settings, and they found the urban natives to be hostile and full of deceits. The other side of this was that the urban natives had had more experience dealing with foreigners. As a happy solution for all there were for years many Shantung villages where heavenly visitors had been rare, and where those first to arrive generally pressed on before becoming nuisances.

During the early 1880s Miss Moon rationalized all this in an intelligent if in some ways typical Western fashion. Interested by yin and yang interpretations, she decided that city and country symbolized the two dominant traits of Chinese society. The cities represented "timidity," typified by Tengchow's silted-up harbor, its crowds of hapless beggars, and its decaying walled homes that had no windows facing out. The countryside, while often poor, represented a spirit of local independence and family loyalty amounting to "virility." The Confucian principle of filiality, in her opinion, held the whole structure together. This began in the village home, passed through the officials in the towns, and ended in the person of the emperor.[29]

From her own standpoint, Miss Moon saw the future as largely a question of role playing. She was strongly drawn to identify with the virile country folk; they were friendly, and Western colleagues like Martha Crawford and Sally Holmes were able to communicate with them. As a city teacher, however, she also had to cope with people from whom it had taken two decades to extort an "unwilling acknowledgment that the missionaries are good people whose purpose is to benefit them." [30] She was torn between a desire to spend her time in the villages and a psychological need for Tengchow city and its American community.

The state of Lottie Moon's thinking at this point is illustrated by an 1881 article entitled "Advantages and Disadvantages of Wearing the Native Dress in Missionary Work." The subject was one of the burning issues of the day. The progressive viewpoint here was typified by the flourishing China Inland Mission, whose recruits were striking out with shaven heads and native garb in all interior directions. The other position was typified by a certain Tengchow American who was scandalized by information that Chinese women wore no underwear. [31]

Miss Moon's position was that this whole dispute put too much stress on appearances, and that the answer, insofar as one existed, lay somewhere between the eye of the Chinese beholder (for whom no missionary could speak) and the sense of inner direction on which the missionary's own stability depended. Most of all the answer was individual. For country work she thought native dress had definite advantages: it made the foreigner look a little less foreign, and it eliminated "being called to tell, for the ten thousandth time, what his clothes cost, where they were bought, and by whom they were made." On the other hand, she firmly believed that no one but a Chinese looked natural in Chinese clothing, and that the typical Westerner emerged as an awkward caricature. More important, the typical Westerner wore such garb fraudulently: he or she did not, that is, wear it as a peasant did until it "rotted away," because unlike the peasant the Westerner did not have to. The usual reaction to such efforts, in her experience, was an unexpressed but (by her) keenly felt "profound contempt." Miss Moon also detected a subtle change that sometimes came over Westerners who strove so assiduously to understand: "Striving to divest himself of Western prejudices that he may learn to view things from a Chinese viewpoint, he comes to condemn a thing not because it is wrong, but because it is Western. In striving to avoid Scylla, he falls into Charybdis." [32]

With the exception of the Presbyterian Gilbert Reid (a noted wearer of mandarin attire), no other Shantung Protestant missionary seems to have examined the clothing question as closely as

Lottie Moon did. To Miss Moon, with the peculiarities of her years and background, clothes represented many things. In a general sense she saw the current controversy as indicative of a certain friction within the missionary body—a growing discord between passionate "understanders" of China and people of equal passion who had emotionally never left America.[33]

Living much alone, Lottie Moon was more concerned with determining her own position. Her clothing article clearly depicts confusion along with much honesty and insight, and she comes to no final conclusion. Her strongest feeling regarding the Chinese is that they respect people who are themselves. This is also her feeling about herself. Having taught in American clothing for most of her adult life, she concluded that her own image should remain that of a foreign teacher, and her public apparel a modified form of the foreign dress.[34]

Miss Moon's life, following a similar style, worked out to a routine of city teaching, weekend country trips, and a new (1881) home of her own in town. She called this place *Hsiao shih-tzu ko*, House at the Little Crossroads. Martha Crawford was at this time on furlough, and Mrs. Holmes had left the field; at the Little Cross-roads Miss Moon entertained a small circle of Chinese women acquaintances and saw T. P. Crawford rarely. Receiving these special friends in Chinese dress, she put them up overnight in a separate house. Otherwise she read inspirational books and studied Chinese, and grew touch-me-nots with seed brought from Virginia.[35]

Going to the Country: P'ingtu

At the end of her first decade in China Miss Moon had thus in a sense adjusted. As in Cartersville, however, she was not altogether satisfied. For one thing, her students came mostly from impoverished homes and did not display much scholarly aptitude. An attempt to start a "select" (higher type) school failed when the higher social types proved uninterested. Then Sally Holmes's departure forced Miss Moon to take on an additional group of poor girls. By 1882 she was speaking of "petty schools" and saying, "I am beating my head against a stone wall."[36]

Two factors other than student dullness contributed to this feeling. First, Miss Moon could not reconcile her chosen image of city teaching with a continuing stronger attraction to rural work. As often as possible she went to various friendly villages, where she observed family life with great interest. She found some of the truisms of woman's work to be largely untrue. She saw little evidence of infanticide or wife torture, for instance, and with regard to Chinese daughters-in-law, who were prominent objects of woman's work sympathy, she thought many deserved worse treatment than they received; severe mothers-in-law were perhaps necessary, because wives often "by sheer force of will and bad temper rule their husbands."[37]

Mostly Miss Moon's observations stimulated her interest in village women as individual people. On the one hand, she found them ill tempered almost without exception. On the other, the same females could be hospitable, intelligent, and religiously inclined. She decided that the unattractive element—their "ingenuity in finding ways to revile each other"—stemmed from unhappinesses caused by no villains in particular. One problem was that the typical country male remained "fine-looking" at forty, whereas due to poor diet, confinement, and hard labor "most women of twenty-five have lost every trace of personal charm." More important, the women suffered from a reverse effect of the otherwise constructive practice of filial piety. By emphasizing the family and its males, this principle suppressed the individual family member, especially the female one. To Miss Moon individuality was identical with Christianity's "worth of one soul." She felt strongly called to bring these women uplift by convincing them of their spiritual worth.[38]

The other factor influencing Miss Moon was a growing feeling that her city teaching life was incommensurate with her own nature as a "woman of energy and self-respect." An interesting article in this vein ("The Woman's Question Again," 1883) suggests that her itinerating and private housekeeping have turned her from a "timid, self distrustful girl into a brave, self reliant woman."[39] Having realized herself to be such a person, Miss Moon confesses to a feeling of intense disappointment. To be a missionary she has given up her own thriving Cartersville institution for China, where she expected to "go out among the millions"; instead, she finds herself bound again to forty children, and unstudious ones at that. Speaking for single female missionaries generally, she calls such petty-school arrangements "the greatest folly of modern missions." Speaking for herself, she asks, "Can we wonder at the mortal weariness and disgust, the sense of wasted powers and the conviction that her life is a failure, that comes over a woman when, instead of the ever broadening activities she had planned, she finds herself tied down to the petty work of teaching a few girls?"

The need here, Lottie Moon suggests, is that she and her counterparts elsewhere be allowed some independent line of work. To prove that she is able "to take care of herself," she attaches a story (all parties mercifully nameless) revealing that two local woman's workers have recently rescued a lost gentleman itinerator, just as he was trading his umbrella for an innkeeper's hospitality.[40]

Miss Moon's 1883 article attracted wide attention among woman's workers. It especially aroused Mrs. Arthur H. Smith, a conventional Congregationalist lady at P'ang-chia-chuang in west Shantung. Mrs. Smith's famous and scholarly husband and his companion the Reverend Henry D. Porter, M.D. (author of "Listen my children/And you shall hear/The wonderful story/Of Li the Queer"), constituted perhaps the best-known comic team in China missions history.[41] Mrs. Smith sometimes achieved similar effects herself; in a *Woman's Work* article replying to Lottie Moon she begins by suggesting that Miss Moon's mind has been affected by the "gross immorality of the heathen" and by her school routine "in a hot, foul city, with restless Chinese maidens hanging about." Then she makes her main point. This is that Miss Moon has presented the "repulsive image" of a maiden lady feeling her oats, or craving "lawless prancing all over the mission lot." The female missionary's proper role is to attend "with a quivering lip" to her own children (a duty Miss Moon would not understand), to keep them out of "quiet graveyard nooks." Mrs. Smith suggests that Miss Moon either attend with "sleepless vigilance" to her schoolgirls' morals or go back to Virginia.[42]

Lottie Moon was not saying—as Mrs. Smith took her to say—that missionary wives were indolent. As an unmarried woman, Miss Moon was only more aware that "what women want who come out to China is free opportunity to do the largest possible work." As the other side of Robert Mateer's typical male demand ("Give a first class man some rope on the field"), she felt that "What women have a right to demand is perfect equality." [43]

Also, in the person of T. P. Crawford, Miss Moon had a special problem of which Mrs. Smith was unaware. Though Crawford had until recently been the only male member of the Tengchow Baptist group, he tended under vague mission voting rules to attempt complete control over all female activities. Miss Moon, who had sided with Crawford earlier against J. B. Hartwell, found him by 1883 to be enforcing "peculiar views." [44]

Miss Moon was thus frustrated by her school work, attracted to the country, and restless under Crawford's tutelage. On the one hand, she could return home, a thought she entertained early in 1884. On the other, she could leave Tengchow city and go alone into "the wide extended fields around." She decided that the first alternative would show insufficient faith. The second was full of difficulties: in addition to being "by every instinct and by all her years of training" a teacher, she questioned her capacity as a foreign gentlewoman to live convincingly with Chinese peasants.[45]

Against the advice of T. P. Crawford, Mrs. Smith, Baptist friends at home, and her own better judgment, Miss Moon went ahead with the second course. Just as many influences had brought her to China, many again made her the first American woman to attempt sustained independent life on a genuinely Chinese level. She found a number of things, including adventure and a certain glory.

Lottie Moon chose P'ing-tu chou (department) as the area for her new work. P'ingtu, as missionaries called it, was a relatively prosperous valley region about one hundred and fifteen miles west of Tengchow, a week's journey by *shan-tzu* (rope-bottomed mule litter). John Nevius and Calvin Mateer had attempted to win a Christian foothold there in the early 1870s. They had made a few converts and deputized a preacher, but services were terminated by "the frequent visits of mandarin underlings." The Presbyterian work had long since collapsed. Missionaries remembered P'ingtu, however, with persistent hope; the natives had been "accustomed to thinking and talking much on religious topics" and were presumed to remain "in an unusual degree prepared for the reception of the truth." [46]

From mid-1883 Miss Moon spent two and a half years itinerating in "ever-widening circles" south and west of Tengchow. On these travels she discussed doctrine with the women and gathered information on likely places. The P'ingtu people were variously reported to be Buddhist, Mohammedan, Nestorian, or independently vegetarian by inclination. All reports indicated such an "attitude of seeking, an eagerness to learn and a vague remnant of teaching about the future life," that Miss Moon could see no other logical location. Also, her situation in Tengchow had by the spring of 1885 become desperate: Crawford was making her life miserable locally, and simultaneously prophesying lurid fates if she carried through her plan to leave. To Crawford she maintained, "What is there for me to fear if God be with me?" To the Foreign Mission Board she suggested that few fates could be worse than life with "the Doctor": "Dr. Crawford insists that his plan of work would give perfect freedom to all parties. As the rest of us see it, it would make him, through the Board, dictator not only for life but after he had passed from earthly existence. His plan includes even the cash we should spend for mission work and extends even to regulation of mission salaries. If that be freedom, give me slavery!" [47]

After one preliminary visit Lottie Moon moved to P'ingtu chou in December 1885. She had decided to establish herself first in the departmental city and to try for at least two years to find a village locus from that base. Following a neighborhood conference, she secured a room near the city's west gate; her landlord was a man named Chao Teh Shin, who turned out to be an opium eater in need of money. Miss Moon set up housekeeping the day after Christmas, nine days after her forty-fifth birthday.

From the very first Lottie Moon set out in P'ingtu "diligently to make friends" and to "arouse as little suggestion of foreignism as possible." Laying aside Western indulgences except for a portable cookstove, a table, and two chairs, she made it a practice to eat, sleep, and dress as she saw the natives doing. She even angered an itinerating male missionary by refusing to shake hands with him, because the local people thought that a queer custom. In general, Miss Moon said, "I tried to bring down my style of living as nearly to the level of my respectable middle-class neighbors as possible." [48]

Making friends she refined to a high art. Careful to avoid seeming forward, she held herself aloof "from even the appearance of seeking to enter their homes." Her rule was instead "to wait always to be sought, and to receive with the utmost cordiality and kindness all who came to visit." Initial contacts were made by putting plates of cookies in her doorway; these attracted neighborhood children, and through the children she met a number of mothers. Cooking, sewing, washing clothes, drawing water, and other points on the daily routine furnished openings to more friendships. She asked advice constantly and followed by explaining how the particular task was done in America. [49]

In a few weeks she had become more or less accepted in her immediate neighborhood, though in other parts of town the process took longer. In 1890 she recalled: "As soon as I set foot on the street there would be a storm of cries, 'devil,' 'devil,' 'devil,' . . . To be followed by a rabble every time one went for a walk was not pleasant, but . . . the only thing to do was to go so steadily and persistently that my presence on the street would create no more excitement than that of any Chinese woman. Slowly and gradually even the small boys ceased to follow me about, and now for years I have come and gone without remark, but always with abundant cordial greetings from friends and acquaintances." [50]

As she established herself in the community, Miss Moon proceeded with a "definite plan of mission work":

"The missionary comes in and settles down among the natives. His first object is to convince them that he is human and that he is their sincere friend. By patience and gentleness and unwearied love, he wins upon them until there begins to be a diversion in sentiment. There are those who will hate him to the end, but others come to recognize that he is both wiser and better than themselves. Now begins the work of teaching with some hope of making a real impression." [51]

Lottie Moon's conviction that she was wiser and better was part of her faith in God. It was also part of her nature as a woman of energy and self-respect who was by every instinct a teacher. As a social person she led a life consisting of amenities, hers and theirs, to keep everything in its proper place. And even as she was trying to live just as her neighbors did, she cultivated "leavening" eccentricities, ways of subtly marking off her Christian distinctiveness. Most notably these amounted to blameless moral conduct and observance of the Sabbath and of special times for prayer. Once, for example, the departmental magistrate summoned her to his yamen on a Sunday, and she refused to go; since the government was employing foreigners at a nearby gold mine, the magistrate was tolerant, and the neighbors were reportedly very impressed. [52]

As a teacher Miss Moon was again a heavenly newcomer, so she spent considerable time satisfying curiosity. As soon as she could she formed women's classes and began to teach hymns and to give lessons in Christian doctrine. For the latter purpose she used two books in particular, beginning with one called *Hsün erh chen yen*. This was a translation of *Peep of Day*, a popular primer originally a "reward-book for poor children" in London slums. The translation Miss Moon used was credited to Sally Holmes; actually it was by "Professor" Chou Wen-yüan, a sometime convert who was at some time hired and fired by virtually every missionary in Tengchow. The *Peep*'s doomsday grimness is terribly depressing in English, and Chou's translation is faithfully sad. It is remembered as "the forerunner of all the Baptist literature for North China." [53]

The second book, Martha Crawford's *Hsiao wen-ta* (Scripture Catechism), was very different. This little work clearly reveals the storytelling skills of Mrs. Crawford. It also suggests why Baptist storytellers sometimes attracted official curiosity, and why they found it easier to draw audiences than to show Christianity's distinctiveness. The Prophet Daniel, for example, is presented as a *ta-kuan* (high official) who cleverly survives various rulership changes, and whose rivals (traitorous ministers, *chien-ch'en*) are eaten together with their families by lions. In the New Testament Jesus is greeted everywhere by shouts of *wan-sui* (banzai). His death is attributed to wicked literati (or scribes, *tu-shu jen*), who with their yamen runners (publicans) exercise a malign influence over the foreign dynasty's local governor-general. Romans, Jews, and Christian saints and traitors mingle a little confusingly with each other and with Chinese analogues, but the stories are colorfully written and genuinely exciting.

Following the lesson from Martha Crawford's book, Miss Moon would lead in a form of prayer: "(I) pray (the) Heavenly Father (to) pity me (and) forgive my sins. 'Ah! yes,' says one, 'pray to heaven and to father and mother!' Another who always associates heaven and earth as two gods says, 'Just so. That's what we do, pray to heaven and earth.' Still a third, caught by the similarity of sound between the Chinese words for 'father' and 'happiness' says, 'Yes, pray to heaven for happiness.' The missionary, undiscouraged, patiently teaches them." [54]

The general response of the P'ingtu women was highly gratifying, both in town and in the outlying countryside. In her first six months in this valley Miss Moon visited one hundred and twenty-two city homes and several hundred more homes in thirty-three different villages. Entering nowhere without an invitation, she made "more friends and acquaintances than in ten years in Teng-chow." Much of this, she felt, was probably only curiosity to see a foreign woman; but she had great hopes that "this very curiosity may be utilized for higher purposes." To her board she wrote, "I am more and more impressed by the belief that to win these people to God, we must first win them to ourselves. We need to go out and live among them, manifesting the gentle and loving spirit of our Lord . . . We need to make friends before we can make converts." [55]

At the same time Miss Moon experienced frustrations regarding both her work and herself. On the one hand, she felt "that all like to have me here, that there are none who are unwilling," and she was receiving "invitations to visit which I cannot accept for lack of time." On the other, no one seemed interested in making a Christian profession.[56] She gradually perceived that this was because—in line with woman's work theory—she was reaching audiences composed only of women and girls, whereas to get "any tangible, visible results" she felt "it was necessary in some way to reach the men of the community. How to do this was the problem." [57]

A deeper worry, perhaps, was the life style that Lottie Moon was affecting. She lived as she did to emphasize the universality of her faith, to make the happiness and compassion it gave to herself seem accessible to everyone.. She began to feel that her tactic might be a forced one: "I wished them to believe that I had no more command of money than they themselves. Yet modestly as I lived, I was sometimes mortified by a dear old lady's saying to me, 'You only eat good food and wear good clothes!' From a Western standpoint I was roughing it indeed; from the middle-class Chinese point of view, my style of living was far above theirs." [58]

Miss Moon was also frustrated by the fact that she remained lonely. She had won acceptance—or at least she ceased to be a "devil-old-woman"—by maintaining that "all people on earth are brothers and sisters." Having persuaded the natives that "If I am a person it is not right that you should call me such names," she had won many friends and was willing "gladly [to] give my life to working among such a people": "People talk vaguely about the heathen, picturing them as scarcely human, or at best as ignorant barbarians. If they could live among them as I do, they would find in the men much to respect and admire; in the women and girls they would see many sweet and lovable traits of character."[59]

But there was something forced even in this. As she wrote during the same period, "It is literally true that there is absolutely nothing to attract one but abundance of hard work . . . . The life here, as we Western people consider life, is exceedingly narrow and contracted. Constant contact with people of a low civilization and many disgusting habits is a trial to one of refined feelings and tastes." [60]

Miss Moon was thus caught between conflicting sensations. She described herself with her friends as "we natives," and at the same time she thought her friends' "spiritual darkness" meant chiefly that "there must be an immense increase in our mission force." [61] The facts of her situation were that the natives were friendly but were not becoming converts, and that she as an individual could take only a certain amount of native life. She had also not yet really established herself in a single village, certainly not to the extent that she had planned.

As Miss Moon carried on alone her life varied. She lived in P'ingtu chou for five years, through 1890; beginning with three months in her first summer, however, she periodically lived another existence at her home in Tengchow. There she gardened, did a little teaching, and subscribed to *Edinburgh Review, Atlantic Monthly, Littel's Magazine,* and other Western periodicals. In P'ingtu she took in a supposedly demented woman as a hired servant; the servant made Miss Moon's life somewhat easier, and she noticed that the old lady's "reputed stupidity seems to have disappeared." She wrote of P'ingtu, while there, as "roughing it," and when away as the place "where was my heart." [62]

6/
Lottie Moon at Sha-ling and in History

One of the consequences of Lottie Moon's P'ingtu life was that she contracted a number of illnesses just as she was entering middle age. Since she had not been home in ten years, she planned a furlough for the spring of 1888. By her own account, these plans diminished in importance after three strangers knocked at her door one day late in 1887. The men introduced themselves as natives of Sha-ling village, which was about ten miles outside P'ingtu city; they had come to town, they stated, to find the "new doctrine" woman who was reported to be operating locally. Although as a rule she did not work with males, Miss Moon went out to teach these people and their women.[1]

In Sha-ling Lottie Moon found a response that was totally new in Southern Baptist Shantung experience. She discovered, she wrote, "something I had never before seen in China. Such eagerness to learn! Such spiritual desires . . . Such moral earnestness and teachableness!" Beset with invitations to explain the new doctrine, she hurriedly summoned Martha Crawford from Tengchow. Miss Moon meanwhile moved in with a local family and slept with her hostess on the woman's mud-brick *k'ang*. After Mrs. Crawford arrived, both missionaries worked twelve-hour days for a week, instructing women primarily but also men from several community hamlets. Christianity became a neighborhood preoccupation as about half the area's fifty families arrived to take instruction.[2] Miss Moon quickly became established as local spiritual adviser, a role she cultivated for the next two years.

As she got to know the Sha-ling people, Lottie Moon discovered that they fell for her purposes into two groups. One group was oriented toward orthodox Confucian values. The other, from which most of her inquirers came, consisted of present or former members of the Lao-t'ien hui, or Venerable Heaven Sect. This was a vegetarian "truth-seeker" cult. Its origins were obscure, but locally its position was strong.

Miss Moon concentrated her persuasiveness on two men who

111

were leaders in the respective groups. The Confucianist was a young man named Li Shou Ting, who was Sha-ling's most literate person and the teacher in its school. Li listened briefly and accepted some tracts, but he was at bottom unwilling to take Christianity seriously. He stated that her doctrine was "not equal to that of Confucius, not so deep or complete." She was more successful with Dan Ho Bang, a man who for twenty years had led a personal band of about forty vegetarians. Although repudiated by most of his vegetarians, Dan became an enthusiastic inquirer and began evangelizing on his own in neighboring Li-tzu-yuan village. There and in several other places Christianity seemed welcome—"as if, when the earth is dry, rain is longed for"—and inquirers "multiplied in all directions." [3]

By coincidence Miss Moon's exuberant reports from Sha-ling came at a critical moment for Southern Baptist missions, and for woman's work particularly. Her own North China Mission had little to show for its twenty-five years. Its leader, T. P. Crawford, was moreover giving the Foreign Mission Board a great deal of poor publicity. The financial picture in Richmond was also poor. The only really bright side to things at home, apparently, was a greatly increased interest in the board's work by the women of the home churches. What was needed, it seemed, was for this interest to be steered in some productive direction; as one church paper put it, "The women love organization," and the need was "for our wise men to formulate some scheme." [4]

The Moon name was by this point well known among Baptist churchwomen. Richmond mite boxes had paid Edmonia's passage in 1872, and when Lottie joined her the Baptist women of Virginia and Georgia had "in pleasant rivalry" collected some $2400 to help the sisters find suitable housing. By 1887 Lottie Moon was receiving donations from Rome, Savannah, LaGrange, and Cartersville in Georgia alone. Her general reputation was no doubt enhanced by her Virginia status, which was represented as that of a "lady of fine intellect, of rare culture, and of splendid social gifts." [5]

Lottie Moon had also captured home attention with an exciting article written in January 1886 during her third week in P'ingtu. Taking the "practical working of polygamy" as her subject, she described this "disgustingly filthy" business as she had observed it during a visit to a P'ingtu mandarin's home. Her hostess on the occasion, the official's wife, had reportedly greeted Miss Moon in rags, and before withdrawing into "the faint, sweet odor of the burning opium" the woman gave Miss Moon a memorable tour. They encountered blind lute-players, the bestial mandarin husband,

and many women ruled by an alluring second wife, who was "living in luxury with servants to anticipate her every want." Summing up her disgust with the whole scene, Miss Moon spoke cogently to her hostess's American contemporaries: "Years ago this miserable creature was probably a happy wife and mother, living in comfort, with servants to wait on her. Now she is an outcast, ill-clad, in abject poverty . . . in the adjoining room, separated only by a curtain over the doorway, lives in luxury the woman who has supplanted her and the man who was the husband of her youth." [6]

During the 1886–88 period Miss Moon published dozens of these "Letters from P'ingtu." They appeared in the board's own *Foreign Mission Journal* and in Baptist state papers like the *Religious Herald* (Virginia) and the *Christian Index* (Georgia). After her first few reports she did not dwell so much on disgusting things, but rather on the friendliness of her new neighbors and the "wonderful progress" that could be made if she had missionary assistance. The emergent picture was one of a uniquely brave woman holding on in a uniquely isolated situation, awaiting help from the "slowly crystallizing purpose" of her home readers. [7]

The most catalytic of these letters proved to be one printed in the *Foreign Mission Journal* for December 1887. Here Miss Moon described the China work of the Southern Methodist Church; her point was that that work had been virtually in collapse until saved by timely "enlisting of the women." The Southern Baptist situation was equally desperate, she stressed, and could be saved only by a similar feminine response at home. The key needs were organization and donation. Miss Moon suggested a week of prayer and special giving at Christmas, to be handled solely by the church's women and for the exclusive benefit of mission work. [8]

Lottie Moon's idea struck a responsive chord with the home churchwomen and also with the hard-pressed Foreign Mission Board. By the time of the convention's annual meeting (Richmond, May 1888) it had been circulated widely in Baptist periodicals. At the May meeting the women organized and formulated goals, expressing these in words that "in a remarkable manner were like those Miss Moon had used." [9] This movement shortly became the Woman's Missionary Union, Auxiliary to the Southern Baptist Convention. The WMU has been a chief support of Baptist missions ever since.

Developments at home were accompanied by continuing encouragement at Sha-ling. Inquirers flocked to instruction in the spring of 1888, and in June Miss Moon made her strongest appeal yet for helpers who would "come down and live among the natives": "We do not ask people to come out to live in costly foreign houses, with comforts and luxuries around them, and a pleasant foreign community, in which they may live entirely apart from the natives, barely touching the heathen world with the tips of their fingers; but we ask them to come prepared to cast in their lot with the natives, making themselves part and parcel of the native society around them." [10]

This letter appeared in the *Foreign Mission Journal* in October. By that point a woman's work "clearing house" had been established in Baltimore under Annie Armstrong, first secretary of the WMU. Working with H. A. Tupper of the Foreign Mission Board, Miss Armstrong made Miss Moon's appeal the union's first definite undertaking, or the project around which its purpose crystalized. Following Lottie Moon's suggestion of the previous December, the WMU thus solicited a special 1888 Christmas offering. The money was to be used to send two new workers to live among the P'ingtu natives, and to bring Miss Moon home to rest and make addresses. The campaign exceeded its goal by a thousand dollars, enough to pay for three new ladies instead of two. [11]

Miss Moon aided the campaign by sending more requests for "vigorous, healthy women" willing to "live out in the villages with the natives." Writing from Pingtu on January 9, 1889, she thanked Miss Armstrong for her enthusiasm; she also advised the new workers to come "rejoicing to suffer" and with an "abundance of heavy flannel underclothing." In a letter written the day before to Dr. Tupper, Lottie Moon had outlined "the ultimate goal of our aspirations," which was perhaps the most ambitious woman's work vision yet put on paper: "What I hope to see is a band of ardent, enthusiastic, and experienced Christian women occupying a line of stations extending from P'ingtu on the north and from Chinkiang on the south, making a succession of stations uniting the two . . . a mighty wave of enthusiasm for Woman's Work for Woman must be stirred." [12]

This letter was published in April, and the WMU was successfully launched. Annie Armstrong, however, had reportedly been haunted by some of Miss Moon's words as she read her letters in H. A. Tupper's office. [13] The style of Miss Moon's correspondence at this time is unusually turgid, and visions are juxtaposed confusingly with personal statements of extreme depression. In a much-quoted letter of August 1888, for example, Miss Moon had written, "I confidently believe that we would have hundreds, yea thousands, of inquirers and converts. I think I know whereof I speak, for I have lived right down among the people and I *know* they can be won by loving self-sacrifice." [14] This August letter was written from Chinkiang, where Miss Moon had gone for a brief retreat with missionary friends. In the same message she speaks of how the Sha-ling people want their teacher to return to living among them; but her own feeling (deleted from some published versions) is dread, a questioning whether she has "strength of body and soul to plunge again into that burial alive."

Returning to P'ingtu chou, she was asked by the board to send a "bright little tract" to help Annie Armstrong's efforts. Miss Moon replied, "that little word 'bright' frightened me from the effort. You can not possibly conceive the dulness of my surroundings and the general mental stupidity that supervenes." [15]

Lottie Moon's success at Sha-ling thus brought her prominence but also more problems. After a two-year period of partial adjustment in P'ingtu city, she had arrived—more or less—at her original goal of independent work at village level. With the new American helpers delayed by distance and language, she felt compelled to forego furloughs and to spend her time with her rural followers. In this togetherness she continued to alternate between intense loneliness (accompanied by sickness) and euphoria, or conviction that "Surely there can be no deeper joy than that of saving souls!" [16]

Miss Moon's paramount conviction was that her Sha-ling work was in a critical stage. A steady cadre of thirty people held four services weekly and additionally studied and evangelized. But as "newly awakened" Christians, they needed "the moral support of the missionary's presence"; their faith and dullness, she felt, would eventually be severely tested by antiforeignism and family opposition. In this situation her personal duty was clear: "Now what these people need above everything—next to the grace of God in their hearts—is to see the life of Jesus Christ set before them in the concrete, in the holy life of the missionary. They must see him meek under reviling, if they are to learn to be meek. They must see him gentle and mild and kind under rude provocations. They must see him brave and firm and strong, where to yield would be to betray the truth. From him—comparing his life with the law laid down in the New Testament—they must learn to mould their lives." [17]

The undercurrent of opposition, Lottie Moon felt, had by midsummer 1889 greatly abated. In October she thus formally established at Sha-ling the first Christian church in P'ingtu chou, baptisms being administered by C. W. Pruitt.

Unexpectedly, a "storm of persecution" broke out at once.

Family heads and disgruntled vegetarians joined to administer beatings and other humiliations for the next six months. Worship services were broken up, girl inquirers were married to "disgusting" non-Christians, and the "foreign devils" were rudely told to go somewhere else. Though "unable to protect the disciples," Miss Moon determined at least to come and go so as to "encourage and comfort and build them up." [18]

A number of other unexpected things took place during this period. Although Miss Moon was frequently away, none of the converts recanted. Li Shou Ting, in an untimely decision, announced at the cost of his teaching job that he was joining the Christians; he credited his decision to reading *Chen tao chieh* (The Truth Manifested), a book written by John Nevius especially for Confucian scholars. Dan Ho Bang, the former vegetarian leader, remained steadfast under particularly severe treatment. Word of his troubles somehow reached Tengchow, over a hundred miles away, and an old man who had resisted Crawford's preachments for years came out to be persecuted too. He explained that he had known Dan in the latter's vegetarian days, and that a "doctrine which brought forth such fruit [endurance] must be true." [19]

Encouraged by the disciples' fortitude, Miss Moon paid a morale visit early in 1890. Arriving amid Chinese New Year festivities, she was threatened with death by an anti-Christian leader of "vicious disposition and wicked history." In the margin of her copy of *The Imitation of Christ* she noted that on this date she expected to die. The storm of persecution turned into a "reign of terror," and her followers after several days asked her to leave for the safety of everyone concerned. She did, and within a few weeks the situation had calmed considerably. By the end of the year the church's position was stronger than it had been when it was established. [20]

Miss Moon lived at this time in P'ingtu city. By late summer she was revisiting Sha-ling, and her reports were markedly different from any she had ever written previously. Her own example is not mentioned, but rather stories are related dealing with native courage and "bright, earnest, and faithful" leadership. Writing in October, she observed that the Sha-ling church "seems to have in itself the elements of steady growth." For the first time she spoke of days there that "slipped by in happy work," and she concluded, "I leave these dear Sa-ling Christians with a deeper love for them than before, with a clearer perception of their difficulties, and a warmer sympathy with their efforts to lead true and holy lives." [21]

During the following winter Lottie Moon suffered in P'ingtu

city from what she called an "almost fainting spirit." This anxiety is not explained, but she suddenly found it possible to take her long-delayed furlough. Summing up her P'ingtu valley experiences for *Woman's Work in the Far East,* she wrote that both she and the Sha-ling Christians wished henceforth "to keep the movement as free of foreign interference as possible, and as spontaneous in its growth and development as it was in its inception." [22] The same sentence, in a slightly modified form, appeared in a simultaneous *Foreign Mission Journal* article; here Miss Moon also asked, "God grant us faith and courage to keep hands off," and to allow the Gospel to "grow naturally in China, without forcing the process." [23]

Leaving for Virginia in mid-1891, Miss Moon did not return to China until early in 1894. During the final two decades of her life she lived again in Tengchow. Li Shou Ting, writing many years later, recalled that she never went back to P'ingtu chou, although when her old friends visited Tengchow she always joyfully received them. Miss Moon now felt drawn to her Little Crossroads house and to "the kind of work I like best, quiet teaching." By her death in 1912 Li Shou Ting, as Pastor Li, had baptized some fourteen hundred persons, and P'ingtu had emerged as "perhaps the greatest evangelistic center we [Southern Baptists] have in all China." [24]

Tengchow Again, 1894–1912

Neither the preserved writings of Lottie Moon nor any other accounts explain very clearly why she did not return to P'ingtu. Her health was not as good as formerly, and in Tengchow she could live perhaps more in keeping with her years. Possibly she had also found answers to some old personal questions. Among these could have been the ones raised in her 1881 native dress article, and in her attraction to the country at that time. As she had observed in 1882, the "noise, publicity, filth and confusion" of Chinese village life was "something neither to be imagined nor described; to understand it one must live among the people." [25]

Miss Moon had now lived among the people—or come closer to doing so than any Western woman before her—and she had proven herself as brave and faithful as any true pioneer of the mission effort. But her experiences, by one way of looking at them, would seem to have borne out the vague misgivings she had initially had about the whole project. A logical restructuring of events indicates that she had indeed miscalculated in P'ingtu at virtually every turn. Her leavening evoked no conversions in the city, and her austere life did not strike her neighbors as identical with their own.

Her success at Sha-ling was due not to woman's work but to local males with previous religious interest. As a Christ-like organizer she had precipitated persecution by formalizing this response, and she then made things worse by paying inspirational visits. As an honest person, which Lottie Moon seems clearly to have been, she could not have emerged feeling like a very good leader.[26]

In any case the most marked change in Miss Moon after P'ingtu, as indicated by her letters, was that she apparently ceased to think of herself as a wiser and better individual. She also made no more comments on Chinese stupidity and dullness. She seems generally to have lost her old preoccupation with analyzing people, herself and the Chinese too.

Miss Moon lived the rest of her life in an unadventurous fashion that does not really add up to much of a story. Up to around 1900 she did a certain amount of "aggressive country work," visitation in the villages near Tengchow.[27] After that she gave herself almost exclusively to primary school teaching, the same petty work she had once called "the greatest folly of modern missions." At the age of seventy-one, in the year preceding her death, she taught forty-six boys in one institution while teaching or supervising in six other schools for girls and women. She deprecated, in a sense, the quality of these schools, calling them "Sunday School every day" arrangements. But she no longer deprecated the pupils. Describing her boys' school in 1905, she wrote, "The school is the joy of my heart. It is a delight to see the boys growing in character. Each boy feels that I am his friend, and from the oldest to the youngest they come to me without hesitation . . . My boys are growing up to be gentlemen, I hope, and perhaps someday they will be Christian gentlemen." [28]

Lottie Moon's last two decades were the happiest in many ways that Tengchow's American community ever knew. Young missionaries had arrived with vigor, and most of the old hands felt that they could see results from their years of work. Everyone missed Martha Crawford, and some expressed regret when her husband was reported to be "creaking and rattling" at T'ai-an-fu. J. B. Hartwell, now white-bearded and unchallenged as Baptist chief, supervised numerous native assistants and impressed new Americans with his "magnetic and masterful" manner. Even Julia Mateer, who had known him in his less magnetic days, conceded that he now seemed "a truly good man—less *intensely* a Baptist than he used to be." [29]

Most important, however, as Lottie Moon noticed in 1894, a wonderful change seemed to have eliminated antiforeignism in the

Chinese community. Miss Moon sometimes viewed this ironically ("It is getting quite the fashion to wish to associate with foreigners"); but mostly she accepted it gratefully, thanking God "that He has given me work that I love so much amid scenes so beautiful." [30]

Miss Moon's position in her work, or among local Baptist missionaries, was now somewhat similar to that of the pioneer evangelist Hunter Corbett among Shantung Presbyterians; each enjoyed a special eminence that was a mixture of accomplishment and personality. To Miss Moon's associates, who were now much younger people, she embodied an enviable quality of adjustment to their common life. This was described in variations on two themes, one being that she knew who she was and the other that she had a "most remarkable attitude to the Chinese and to their 'way of life.' "

The first of these impressions involved a reputed ability to live in two worlds and seem at ease in each. One missionary defined Miss Moon as being like her Little Crossroads home, or Chinese in design and daily routine, but on the inside still furnished mostly in American style. All the new people knew her as the only local foreigner who now wore Chinese clothing under all circumstances. Her stated reasons were that foreign dresses had become too troublesome and too expensive whereas the native styles "cover a multitude of faults." [31]

Miss Moon's attitude toward the Chinese was also something of a puzzle. To some people it was difficult to reconcile her status as "one of the nobility," Virginia-wise, with her insistence that "every missionary must be willing to yield to the Chinese social conventions, and strive to understand their viewpoint and conform to it." Miss Moon's own explanation was that "I give the road if any is to be given, because I am a guest in their country." Somewhat confusingly, she was once observed on a local road in a nearly physical fight with a Chinese soldier, who she said had tried to run her down with his horse; and on another occasion she chastised with unusual severity a favorite pupil, who had cut off his queue hoping to please her. [32]

Everyone seemed to understand and admire her capacity for "putting love into action," or for "helping someone who needed help." She took in several orphans and a large number of dogs, and she fed "poor hungry people" to a number that "God only knows." At one time, according to Mrs. C. W. Pruitt, some of the Crawfordites attempted to put a stop to this, but Miss Moon paid them no attention. [33]

Mrs. Pruitt's husband, who shared Miss Moon's views and who next to Martha Crawford had known her longer and better than anyone else, observed that after her P'ingtu period she spent less time in foreign company. Her closest friend, by most accounts, was a middle-aged concubine in the house of a Tengchow official. With this woman and several others Miss Moon had "adopted sister" relationships, and she often entertained personal Chinese friends for days at a time. The conduct of these people in Miss Moon's home was seen by some Americans as "exasperatingly Chinese." Describing one such episode, Miss Moon wrote, "My guests are to leave tomorrow. She is a bright and pleasant woman whom I like very much, but the children rush in and out at all hours, turn my chairs about as they please, drop crumbs all about the floor, and cut up generally. When they stand in the chairs or spit on the carpet, I venture to mildly interfere! One has to be so careful not to give offense. Chinese children who live on dirt floors can't be expected, when admitted to one's best room, to act as if they had been taught that nice chairs are not made to stand in, nor carpets put down to be spit upon." [34]

When not thus socializing Miss Moon spent her free time alone. She continued to read Western magazines and to study Chinese, and one of her last articles dealt with maintaining one's commitment to "this most intricate language." Each July, in the rainy season, she locked her door and read French novels for two or three weeks. She read daily in her Testaments, which were in Hebrew and Greek respectively; Hebrew was her last linguistic acquisition, and she was not too good at it. She was an accomplished amateur musician, however, and her main nonliterary recreation was playing her parlor organ. [35]

Miss Moon also continued to write articles, including several of the "Chinese civilization" type. The theme here, from P'ingtu on, was that "China and the West have misunderstood each other": "We should remember that the Chinese are not a small community of savages who gape in astonishment at Western civilization. On the contrary, China had a respectable civilization when our own ancestors had not emerged from barbarism. Proud of her government, proud of her ancient civilization, proud of her literature, it is no wonder that China has striven to keep out influences from the West." [36]

From her earliest itinerations Miss Moon was also a close observer of village life, which she compared to life both in Chinese cities and in the old American rural south. The basic distinction between the Chinese and American rural models, from which social and political differences arose, was that the Chinese farmed from village homes rather than living scattered about on individual homesteads. Within China she thought the villages differed from the cities most strikingly by having a remarkable degree of local freedom. She attributed this to the fact that imperial controls generally stopped in the administrative townships, leaving rural communities to run themselves informally. She dwelt a good deal on the "law and order" which this system ("family life is the basis of everything") seemed to foster.[37]

Another comparison that interested Miss Moon, as it did T. P. Crawford and other southerners, was that between Chinese and black people. Her views here seem to have changed in her later years. In romanticizing her P'ingtu friends she had sometimes made her points at the expense of American blacks, or the reference that would come most quickly to her readers' minds. All the good qualities of the Chinese were thus contrasted with Negro defects, which included brutality, moral turpitude, and lack of civilization generally. The most important distinction was that Negroes, unlike Chinese, were "non-homogeneous."

Miss Moon had of course not seen many Negroes recently, and her last two furloughs proved informative. Arriving from Sha-ling in 1892, she felt sorry for the current generation of Virginia blacks. They were making laudable efforts to help themselves but were receiving little help from their former masters. Miss Moon spent her furlough Sundays—or part of them, at least—teaching classes of black children. "Some point of contact is needed between the races," she wrote. "In politics they are opposed. Where shall we find this point if not in the religion that is common to both races?"

Similar contacts on her last home visit further affected Miss Moon's thinking. She now saw the nonhomogenized blacks as unwilling "sojourners in the land," to whom the whites should "do their duty." What she meant by this sort of talk is never explained very clearly. Not long after her last return to China (1904), however, Miss Moon wrote an unusual letter to a relative of a college roommate. The young woman had apparently asked her advice about becoming a missionary, and Miss Moon's strongest advice was to stay at home: "We send missionaries to Africa, but don't go into the miserable homes in our towns and cities to try to uplift their inmates . . . there is plenty of mission work even in dear old Virginia."[38]

Personally, Miss Moon had elected to leave Virginia after a rather short final visit. Viewmont had long since been sold off, her family was widely scattered, and it seemed that America was the foreign land now.

From this point Miss Moon's health declined markedly, and while never a gloomy person, she was not the buoyant spirit she had once been. Julia Mateer noticed as early as 1896 that she was "not so vigorous as formerly," and that she had "lost her teeth and looks older than I." C. W. Pruitt observed a little cryptically that since P'ingtu her manner was one of "downright hopefulness," where formerly it was "characterized by faith." Miss Moon's hopefulness seems to have amounted chiefly to a willingness to accept smaller satisfactions; as she wrote after Julia Mateer's death (1898), "I have felt the uncertainty of life very keenly of late, on account of the death of a member of the community who was only a little older than myself. She had a very long and trying spell of illness, lasting nearly four months, and I nursed her part of the time. I never saw such suffering or such helplessness. It made me feel what I have long believed, that it is a great blessing to be cut off suddenly." [39]

Miss Moon's friends also noticed that her letters after 1904 were "filled with the sadness of the sights about her." She was apparently much influenced, on her last return from America, by the effects in Shantung of the Russo-Japanese War. The situation was that "Our region is dependent for the overflow of its population on Manchuria"; with the Manchurian outlet eliminated younger sons had no place to go, and their families ceased to receive needed remittances. Miss Moon wrote in detail of rising food and fuel prices, and of the human consequences: "As winter deepens [1904–05], the poverty and want around us grow more acute. One admires the people who meet these trials. They fall heavy on the respectable poor, who are half the time, I may say now at all times, on the verge of starvation." [40]

Between 1905 and 1909 the cost of living in Shantung rose another 50 percent, and plague and smallpox ravaged much of the province. Hunger was chronic and increased with revolutionary disorder in 1911–12. Miss Moon worked in a number of ways to alleviate some of this suffering. One such instance involved a revolutionary battle at Huang-hsien, west of Tengchow; the missionaries in that area having evacuated to Chefoo, Miss Moon went there with Chinese friends and organized a nonpartisan Red Cross unit. In the fall of 1911 she also organized a Woman's Missionary Union of North China (Fu-nü fu-chu hui). This was a binational Baptist group that "felt the need of united strength to better send succor to their famine-stricken brethren and sisters."

Since the Foreign Mission Board was suffering at this time

from financial difficulties, missionaries in the field had to do relief work largely on their own. Most of Miss Moon's was on an individual basis. She helped a number of people, both converts and non-Christians, and many of these opportunities gave her much pleasure: "I like to have the little fellow around. He came with his mother on Thursday. I had not seen her for twenty years and had not the remotest idea who she was. She said she had longed to see me and so had come. She used to be in my school when a girl about twelve years old. She was in school about two years and has forgotten some and remembers some that she had learned. About four years ago her husband had smallpox and lost his eyesight, so the burden of the family fell on her. I feel very sorry for her and am glad for her to have a rest from household and farm cares for a few days. She will be here about eight days longer." [41]

When alone, Miss Moon seems to have been depressed by personal losses and by a feeling of helplessness with regard to the local economic situation. She made a journey to Soochow to visit the grave of A. C. Safford, and she was much affected by the deaths of Martha Crawford and of her sister Edmonia in 1909. Otherwise her letters dealt largely with famine conditions in Shantung and various "poor sufferers" whom she knew. Some of these accounts read almost apocalyptically, as she dwells on the strange appearance of the drought-stricken sky, roads strewn with corpses, and mothers hanging themselves in country villages. She sent a number of "last appeals" to home churches; these are full of exclamation marks and pleas "for the sake of God and humanity." [42]

From about mid-1912 Miss Moon lapsed into a state described by others as uncontrollable sadness or a time of great depression. In August she withdrew her small savings from a Shanghai bank and gave the money to a famine fund. Under the last entry in her account book she wrote, "I pray that no missionary will ever be as lonely as I have been." Declining into abject melancholia, she developed a cranial abscess and began as had Julia Mateer to experience hallucinations.

In December a Baptist doctor discovered that she had resolved to eat no more, and had in fact not done so for some time. This was a decision made out of sympathy with the P'ingtu Christians, whom she believed to be starving. It was decided by her colleagues that she should be sent home. Accompanied by a nurse named Cynthia Miller, Miss Moon was thus placed on a ship that sailed December 20. She died four days later. According to Miss Miller, she passed away conversing with "Chinese friends long since gone on before her." [43]

The Lottie Moon Story

Lottie Moon died in Kobe harbor, and according to Japanese law her body was cremated. The ashes were then sent to Crewe, Virginia, where they were buried in her brother Isaac's plot in the Baptist cemetery. Crewe is a small railroad town about fifty miles west of Richmond.

To a present-day visitor Miss Moon's grave seems hard to find. It is located on the out-of-town side of the railroad tracks, at a considerable remove from the church itself. The site is a bare hilltop, and the marker is very plain. A better-known memorial, back in town, is more impressive. In the words of one visitor, "High over the gallery in the Baptist Church at Crewe . . . is a glowing, golden window. I saw it at evening time when the sun in the west was pouring through it a flood of blazing light. Down through a field of beautiful lilies there walks the figure of a woman, with graceful, flowing garments, clasping the Word of God to her heart, and holding high a blazing torch. Her face is uplifted, she is looking out beyond me, into a distance that I cannot see. She is beautiful. Underneath the figure is the brief record in golden letters:

MISS LOTTIE MOON

OUR BELOVED MISSIONARY

Born Dec. 17, 1840 — Died Dec. 24, 1912" [44]

The impressive window and the description of it are both aspects of a phenomenon called "The Lottie Moon Story." The Lottie Moon story is a unique kind of memorial that extends well beyond Crewe, and which has made Miss Moon probably the most discussed American ever to live forty years in China. Like the window in the Crewe church, the Lottie Moon story needs to be seen from inside to be appreciated, and it similarly depends, perhaps, on lighting effects, as demonstrated by the stage directions in a present-day Baptist play: "At this point the light of the special lamp will be turned on the figure of Miss Moon, seated at her desk writing the [1887] letter to Southern Baptists, and her lengthened shadow will be thrown on the wall at rear. Hold steadily until close . . . Make sure before performance that focus of light is right." [45]

If the focus is right Miss Moon's shadow will be long indeed, underscoring Emerson's observation (in "Essay on Self-Reliance") that "An Institution is the lengthened shadow of one man." Miss Moon's shadow is the Woman's Missionary Union, which in her name now collects more than $20,000,000 annually for Southern Baptist missionary work.

The Woman's Missionary Union, to be technical, has been Miss

Moon's shadow only since 1918, from the point when its annual appeal was named The Lottie Moon Christmas Offering for Foreign Missions. Previously Miss Moon had lived and died at a distance, and the WMU was the shadow of two incontrovertible facts at home. These facts, identified in 1894 by Secretary Annie Armstrong, were that "the boards need money" and that "general organizations secured more money."[46] Miss Moon's 1887 letter was a sort of punctuation mark here: it arrived at the end of the first two years of general organizing by female Baptists, and just as missions emerged as the "wholly committed" feminine interest. The Christmas appeal was maintained, but after 1891 it was not specifically connected to north China.[47]

Lottie Moon's only other significant contact with the WMU was her furlough of 1891–94. The story here is rather vague, because to a large extent no record of her own feelings seems to exist. She is known to have been greeted with many demands for speeches, from Baltimore and elsewhere, but considering the length of her furlough she does not seem to have done much speaking. She expressed a desire to rest from her years in P'ingtu and to keep quiet generally. In her first year at home she apparently spoke only in Atlanta at the 1892 convention; in this "first contact with the organized body of Southern Baptist women" she surprisingly emphasized not woman's work but medical missions, a particularly undeveloped aspect of her denomination's work. Dr. T. W. Ayers of Alabama answered her appeal and soon established a hospital at Huang-hsien.

Otherwise, except for limited appearances in Virginia, Miss Moon declined invitations on grounds of health ("I was disposed to go, but only thinking about it made my head hurt"). In the final six months of her leave, after much persuading at the 1893 convention in Nashville, she toured Tennessee and Georgia. At that point she at last spoke at a "mad pace" about the women of China, to whom she now felt "anxious to return."[48]

As Miss Moon returned Annie Armstrong wrote her article stressing general organization, which would not be as subject to "loss of novelty" as a Christmas offering. Some idea of the process that followed can be gathered from the example of what happened in Georgia. In that state local missionary societies (WMS's) had grown from three to seventy-six in the years between Miss Moon's departure from Cartersville and her 1887 letter. In the succeeding decade a state bureaucracy formed, involving local secretaries, associational vice-presidents, district superintendents, a central committee, and two monthly newspapers.

The next stage was rivalry between the central committee ("a self-perpetuating body of twenty or thirty Atlanta women") and its subordinates in smaller Georgia towns and rural areas. The second faction achieved reforms in 1901 and supplied vigorous direction. By a typical turn-of-century annual report, the two leading state organizers traveled two thousand miles, held one hundred and seventy-eight meetings, mailed two thousand pieces of literature, and collected $18,000, all at a reported total expense of $152.93. A "type" WMS volunteer was defined (white housewife without servants), and in many letters such local secretaries testified to the uplift their work brought to their lives. Lingering male opposition ("These women are going to break up our churches") was crushed, and the monthly *Mission Messenger* grew from eight to thirty-two pages (1895–1910).[49]

Lottie Moon thus had only a walk-on role in early WMU history. Her death in 1912, however, coincided with the beginning of a new WMU era, and she again became timely. This new stage was one of maturation, of growing beyond what T. P. Crawford had called organization craze. The organization had now formed, and its multitude of objects required more money and programming than ever. A Plan of Work study was accordingly conducted between 1913 and 1918 by the union's national executive committee. The resulting plan, which has remained essentially unaltered to the present, stressed four activities centering around stewardship and mission study. Under stewardship, the union changed its "entire set-up" financially to help raise money for a variety of denominational causes. While working for the convention's 75 Million [dollars] Campaign, a venture of unprecedented scope, the WMU "proclaimed the campaign from every angle" and collected some $15,000,000 in five years (1919–24).

One of the angles here was apparently to proclaim Miss Moon. The Christmas offering, renamed and promoted in her honor, grew from $44,110 in 1917 to $306,376 by 1925. The startling success of this once-yearly appeal, combined with the emergence of financial difficulties from other directions—unpaid 75 Million pledges, loss by defalcation of $103,000 in 1927, and the onset of the great depression—confirmed Miss Moon in her role as an indispensable Christmas presence.[50]

In a more roundabout fashion Lottie Moon also became an important part of the mission study program. The WMS's, which numbered 10,522 by 1920, were now stocked with many books, mostly devotional manuals and WMU histories. In 1918 it was decided in Baltimore that the time had come for a genuine course of mission study.[51] To fill out this course the WMU asked missionaries and other interested persons to write books and booklets in their individual mission fields. During the 1920s a number of such works appeared that dealt particularly with China, and these were incorporated into local study programs. Understanding was enhanced by wall maps, picture books, dramatic scripts, and similar aids.

In 1930 direction of mission study was assumed at convention level by Una Roberts Lawrence, a legendary WMU personality. As an individual student of missions, Mrs. Lawrence had been unusually fascinated by China, the "Yellow Empire," and by "Lottie Moon, Virginia's gifted daughter, God's precious gift to China." These interests went back inseparably for many years, to a time when Una Roberts, as a little girl, heard the name of Lottie Moon "spoken by my pastor in such a way that ever after to me it was as the name of a brilliant star in the sky, to which I looked in awe and wonder, scarcely understanding why." [52]

Thus inspired, Mrs. Lawrence had spent the years between 1919 and 1927 putting together a biography explaining Miss Moon's "reality." In her research she went through hundreds of documents and sought out "eye witness testimony" in Virginia; the latter, as Mrs. Lawrence says, sometimes turned out to be "priceless." The finished *Lottie Moon* conveyed "a picture that we have never had before," and it has been successful in many ways. Una Lawrence herself directed mission study for eighteen years, until just before China missions relocated on Taiwan. Her *Lottie Moon*, justifying Mrs. Lawrence's conviction ("such a life can never die!") has gone through twenty-three printings as it approaches its fiftieth birthday. Recorded sales are close to 50,000 copies. [53]

Evoked by a number of influences, many other Lottie Moon representations have appeared since 1927. For some years attention focused on eye witness testimony, and several "Miss Moon As We Knew Her" pamplets were contributed by the Pruitts, Dr. Ayers, Li Shou Ting, and similarly knowledgeable people.

By around 1950, however, such expertise had passed from the scene along with Una Lawrence and contact with north China. What happened next was the development of a very different type of Lottie Moon literature. This new type seems to be based on enthusiasm rather than on personal knowledge or new research; it amounts strictly to promotional material, advertised as "earnest endeavor to maintain absolute fidelity to the spirit and attitude of Miss Moon." [54]

The trend here has been mostly toward short, simple presentations with heightened sensuous impact, for radio narration or theatrical performance. Three recent playlets illustrate this at various levels. Two of these ("Make His Name Glorious," 1958, and "Faithful Unto Death," 1964) stress music, suffering, and racial dialect along with a certain amount of information about Miss Moon. Against a background of "Traumerei," "Silent Night," and Schubert's Eighth Symphony, Miss Moon thus enunciates impeccably through numerous crises. Accompanied "at times only by a simple but earnest Bible woman," she deals winningly with hostile Chinese ("Behold, the foreign devils are taking up abode in our city!") and admiring slaves at Viewmont ("Now ain't she a sight! The sweetes' chile on this place, I tells Miss Ann"). Chinese inquirers improve in diction as well as spiritual grace:

CHOIR: (*Speaking in rhythmic chorus as one voice*)
　　　　Show us the *way!*
　　　　Show us the *way!*
　　　　Is there *hope* for us?
　　　　Is there One who *cares?*
　　　　One who *loves us?*
　　　　Show us the way![55]

The third playlet ("Her Lengthened Shadow," 1964) deals specifically with "actual incidents that portray the signal contribution of Miss Moon to the cause of missions," such as, apparently, Miss Moon demonstrating how to sing "Jesus Loves Me" in Chinese. Also dealt with are some neglected contributions by Lottie Moon to the Confederacy, and her "entirely authentic" love affair with one Andrew Fleming (Professor Toy). She greets the Reverend Mr. Fleming/Toy, who is off to join "our boys in gray," with a rose in her hair and an appropriate song:

　　　　My homespun dress is plain, I know
　　　　　　My hat's palmetto, too
　　　　But it shows what southern girls
　　　　　　For southern rights will do.

Her suitor says, "That's the spirit," and taking Miss Moon's flower he recites, "O my luve's like a red, red rose." Hurt by her response ("Nothing dearer than friendship, Lottie?"), he departs Byronically:

　　　　Maid of Viewmont — 'ere we part
　　　　　　Give, oh give me back my heart!
　　　　Or, since that has left my breast,
　　　　　　Keep it now, and take the rest!
　　　　Hear my vow before I go
　　　　　　Zoe moy sas agapo.'

Miss Moon is touched by this display. Later, in China, heated letters arrive, and "The temptation is great." The professor, however, now espouses theories that "do not square with God's Word." Rejecting C. H. Toy, Harvard, and glory, Miss Moon says, "My cross is loneliness" and recites Bryant's "To a Waterfowl." [56]

Undoubtedly the most popular of current treatments is an exciting motion picture entitled "The Lottie Moon Story," filmed under the auspices of the Foreign Mission Board. The viewer sees Miss Moon actually at work here amid Chinese-looking surroundings. Martha and T. P. Crawford appear, looking very serene, along with groups of WMU ladies and a number of Asian-American actors who will be familiar to all devotees of old war movies. Miss Moon's part is played by an actress named Lurene Tuttle. Miss Tuttle, whose secular credits include "Tomorrow is Another Day" and "Sweet Smell of Success," seems at ease in the role. She plays Lottie Moon somewhere between Patient Griselda and Saint Joan.

Another visual aid is a booklet called *Lottie Moon in Pictures*. Actually only one picture is of Lottie Moon; taken "while Miss Moon was teaching in Cartersville," it shows her in bows and ringlets at what looks like about age sixteen. Otherwise the booklet focuses on Lurene Tuttle, or on nineteen stills from "The Lottie Moon Story." Also included are pictures of Miss Moon's tombstone, of her 1887 letter, of the old Viewmont site, and of Monticello and the Hardware Baptist Church (two nearby landmarks).[57]

For homemakers attracted to Miss Moon the "Cookie Lady," there is the *Lottie Moon Cook Book*. This work is somewhat on the order of *Lottie Moon in Pictures*; it is not really a cook book by Lottie Moon, that is, but a reprint of one found among Miss Moon's effects and written by a Mrs. Hill from Georgia. In any case, we have some three hundred recipes presumably used by Miss Moon and adding up, we are told, to an experience "as adventurous and nostalgic as roaming through an 1897 Sears catalog."[58]

Other Mooniana include two children's biographies (*Her Own Way: The Story of Lottie Moon*, 188 pages, and *Lottie Moon of China*, 62 pages); a Lottie Moon Christmas card; a forty-five minute Lottie Moon tape cassette; and two official 8½ x 11 inch portraits. One of the portraits consists of Miss Moon's head removed from a 1905 group photograph, with a superimposed facsimile signature ("Yours sincerely, L. Moon"). The other is a sketch made from the same original, minus the signature and about half Miss Moon's age at the time.[59]

As far as Southern Baptists are concerned, American missions in China seem clearly to have produced someone unique. To put all this in perspective, one sees first and most conspicuously a real promotional phenomenon. Miss Moon's missionary prominence has from the beginning been tied to making money for missions. The tie has been especially close since the mid-1950s, during the years when most of the materials described were being generated. The fabulous fifties, as a WMU history puts it, was a time when the idea was stressed that "promoting Christian missions was big business," a time when outside consultants were hired and efficiency increased in many ways.[60]

A few figures will quickly suggest what a remarkable success the Lottie Moon Christmas Offering has been. The offering had its first million-dollar Christmas in 1945, which was also the first Christmas free from the debt that had plagued the SBC as a whole since the 1920s. The offerings grew steadily to a 1959 figure of $7,786,847; then the 1960s brought a takeoff when ten Christmases netted almost $123,000,000, more than twice what all the preceding seventy-two solicitations had gathered. By 1973, to commemorate the one-hundredth anniversary of Miss Moon's arrival at Tengchow, a goal of $20,000,000 could be set. The campaign that year—featuring a new film strip, a set of twelve Lottie Moon note cards, and an extremely attractive centennial booklet—exceeded its goal by over $2,000,000, raising the all-time total to $259,677,461.[61]

This money has come from individual Southern Baptist congregations, which each year set their own goals and encourage members to give. Missionaries on furlough make December addresses, and the WMU periodically gets out new biographical sketches to show what the ideal missionary was like. The Foreign Mission Board supplies overall encouragement plus promotional pamphlets geared to specific Christmas messages—themes like "You, Too, Can Go" (1969), "The Lottie Moon Christmas Offering: Where Does the Money Go?" (1970), and "The Lottie Moon Christmas Offering: Praise and Thanksgiving!" (1973). The Lottie Moon money, which constitutes a little over half the total amount received by the FMB in a given year, goes to a number of ends connected with overseas work in seventy-seven countries. Most important are the support of evangelistic activities and of the board's more than 2500 foreign missionaries, some 700 of whom receive their basic salaries from the Lottie Moon Offering. A full allocations breakdown of the 1973 offering amounts to a "twenty-page, back and front, single-spaced listing of hundreds of items." [62]

More interesting than the money and where that goes, perhaps, is the question of Lottie Moon herself, her own role in all this. After all, as the *Lottie Moon Cook Book* challengingly asks, "Who was Lottie Moon?" [63] Why this particular individual as saint and symbol of Protestantism's most continuingly vital and financially successful missionary endeavor?

One has to begin any answer here by underlining the historical importance of the southern part of Miss Moon's Baptist connection. It is conceivable, maybe, that a Lottie Moon could have arisen in the United States somewhere other than in the south. But since none seems to have done so, one can reasonably assume that Miss Moon's status is due at least partly to influences that have been peculiar to her section, and that have made such an apotheosis more likely.

The most obvious of these peculiarities, the one that is brought most forcefully to the Lottie Moon reader's attention, is that she was "a Southern lady of the highest type." [64] This idea involves two elements. One is the Virginia's gifted daughter angle, or Miss Moon's attractiveness as a lady of "fine intellect, rare culture, and splendid social gifts." She always had this kind of appeal; the accolade just cited, for instance, was given her on her departure for China in 1873. Miss Moon was (and is) part of an old and very persistent regional concept of womanhood. This concept, which figures heavily in all the playlets discussed above, amounts to what one southerner has called "downright gyneolatry": "She was the South's Palladium, this Southern woman—the shield-bearing Athena gleaming whitely in the clouds, the standard for its rallying, the mystic symbol of its nationality in face of the foe. She was the lily-pure maid of Astolat and the hunting goddess of the Boeotian hill. And—she was the pitiful Mother of God." [65]

The second aspect of Miss Moon's southern-woman ideality is of more recent visibility and is related to her missionary status as a woman's worker. Putting this simply—as the mission-study literature has done—she succeeded, after a fashion, where the men had failed. She was "the greatest 'man' among the missionaries" of her field. Since her death some rather dubious tough-girl stories ("Don't worry, Jane, I'll attend to this fellow") have grown up, of which the most extravagant is an account by Una Lawrence of "vigorous use of her umbrella" on an official named Yüan Shih-k'ai.[66] But the main point is simply that without Miss Moon's personal faith, courage, imagination, and stamina the North China Mission would never have made it, just as the whole male-run Southern Baptist mission effort would not have made it if it had not been bailed out by the Woman's Missionary Union.

In the light of these two attributes it becomes more understandable, perhaps, why Miss Moon has been a star in the sky to many Southern Baptist women. She seems to combine the genteel intangibles of an old-fashioned girl with the competent self-reliance of an emancipated woman; or in other words she is Melanie and Scarlett in one package. In a region—and within that in a denomination—where women have been sentimentalized in myth and repressed in fact, this is a powerful combination. Indeed, Miss Moon's two coexisting images suggest the role in southern social history of female missionary activism generally: a stage, like WCTU and woman's club, when consciousness was definitely raised—when women "learned to think for themselves, organize programs, and assume leadership"—but without openly challenging "prevailing views of the community about ladylike behavior." [67]

As a mystic symbol in the face of various foes, Miss Moon moreover has had an appeal that (though necessarily feminine) transcends sexual distinctions. The Southern Baptist Convention, to give one illustration, has traditionally been a denomination of rural and small-town churches—70 percent of its 35,000 congregations still have fewer than 300 members—and it has had to endure much abuse from more "sophisticated" Christians for reputed social and intellectual inferiority.[68] Lottie Moon obviously represents a number of points in refutation of such charges.

Much more important, however, Miss Moon carries gracefully a load of baggage that has lain ecumenically in almost every white southern mind. Born to a "small empire of beauty and culture," she was dispossessed by outside forces and left to shift for herself. Her only chance for happy normality (Professor Toy) would have required acceptance of disquieting ideas, plus personal alienation from the people who meant most to her. Taking up her cross of loneliness, she thus bore faithful witness to correct ideas until she died, a sacrifice to more causes than the average reader can comfortably handle. The Lottie Moon story is very much the whole white south's traditional story of itself—full of grace, good intentions, and tragic luck, and somehow a little closer to God. One further notes that the years of greatest expansion in the Lottie Moon business—the fabulous fifties and sixties, with all their promoting of Miss Moon the southern lady—were also years of increasing civil rights activism, white resistance, and heightened (in some ways) sectional awareness in the south.

There are of course other interesting themes in the Lottie Moon story. One might consider, for example, the fact that in her rise as a literary heroine Miss Moon has been continuously cast as such an embodiment of all-embracing, Christlike love. The extreme heaviness of this emphasis ("After all isn't love the sweetest thing on earth?") [69]—and the way it is textually developed—strongly suggest the idealized love theme that has been made famous by the literary critic Leslie Fiedler. The kind of love involved here, which Fiedler has located in a number of classic and contemporary American novels, is interracial. It is idealized because it represents an "exploration of responsibility and failure," or vicarious atonement for white racial crimes at home; it is also idealized because "to develop it openly would unleash the twin taboos of homosexuality and miscegenation." Miss Moon—or Miss Moon the woman's worker, as she has been posthumously handled—compares most interestingly with the model lovers Fiedler finds in the novels of Herman Melville and Richard Henry Dana; all become wanderers, that is, and find love and forgiveness in some exotic place, with a nonwhite race more palatable than the people sinned against at home. Such lovers also choose partners of their own sex and love them chastely, thereby conveying an impression more acceptable than the thought of any kind of interracial male-female affection.[70]

A more specific connection of this type is made in the writings of the late Lillian Smith, the Georgia novelist and social critic. Like Fiedler (who uses Carson McCullers to make much the same point), Miss Smith stresses racial guilt and sees it tied to "genital immaturity." In her southern context she sees females as historically the genital victims and racial expiators. She sees the traditional religious activism of southern Protestant white women in terms of race-associated sexual frustrations. Their missionary enthusiasm she views as an escape from facing wrongs nearer at hand, and as a perversion on several levels of what she thinks love ought to be.[71]

Anyone who wants to can find abundant atonement, and a certain amount of sex frustration, in the purplish prose of Una Lawrence's *Lottie Moon*. By reproducing an apparently unique "love letter" to a young female missionary, for instance—and by identifying it with the "tender, loving, confiding Lottie Moon whom few people ever knew"—she creates in a non-Southern Baptist mind the impression that Miss Moon's "innermost feelings" were homosexual.[72] Whether Mrs. Lawrence fits Leslie Fiedler's "true Magnolia Blossom or Southern Homosexual style" is a moot question; her book seems pseudo-magical and maybe even pseudo-religious enough, though her style and overall message are not exactly those of a Carson McCullers.[73]

On a broader and less bizarre level, the Lottie Moon story may just reflect our over-organized and emotionally undernourished times. As Anne Firor Scott has observed, the whole Lillian Smith historical approach ("everybody's psyche was out of joint") gives the south and southern women credit for too much uniqueness.[74] In many countries—certainly in the United States and China—manufactured celebrities have become a sort of modern commonplace; made possible by gains in public communication and losses in private comprehension, these paradigms are extremely useful for inspiring corporate participation. Miss Moon, who appeals so strongly to Southern Baptist hearts, is personally hard to criticize as a choice for such canonization. The alternative—or certainly a candidate antithetical to everything represented both by Lottie Moon and by her story—might have been T. P. Crawford.

The only thing really objectionable is that something seems to have happened to Miss Moon herself somewhere in the movies and cook books, that some of the best Lottie Moon stories seem to have been incompatible with the needed message. The Dear Old Southland—so traditionally talented at helping people like Lottie Moon receive calls elsewhere—has represented her as a personification of its traditional norms. None of the lessons that the "best educated woman in Virginia" learned at such painful cost over so many years in China, lessons about humility and sympathy and imitating Christ, emerge at all. Her whole P'ingtu experience and her mature idea of human community—her conviction that she, the Chinese, and the folks back home were equally brothers and sisters—have been discussed mostly in terms of her own sufferings, of a gifted daughter dying in some faraway place. And very little has been said about what she was taught by those dull people whose Christ-like example she aspired to be.

It should be brought out here that some changes may be taking place even now in how Miss Moon's story is handled. A new dramatic presentation ("It Cannot End at Kobe: How Lottie Moon Lives in Missions in the 1970's"), for instance, takes the position that "there was nothing traditional about Lottie Moon" and builds her up as a radical who "dared to do new things in new places because she knew they were right." This playlet further suggests that if Miss Moon were alive today she would be fighting racial and sexist prejudice and doing good works, as well as evangelizing, and doing these things perhaps not overseas but in a nearby ghetto or even country club. Her sufferings and tragic death are specifically downplayed, and her message is said to amount to "a few truths which she understood from God." [75]

These breaks with the literature of the 1950s and 1960s are part of a certain identity change in the Southern Baptist Convention, which is expanding geographically into urban, nonsouthern home areas, and whose younger membership is becoming attuned to social messages more widely relevant than Old South nostalgia. One of the most publicized American religious stories of the 1970s has in fact been the SBC's plan to transcend regionalism, to become a national church rather than "the Confederacy at prayer." Intensive missionary work—based on computerized demographic studies and a multimillion-dollar home mission budget—is being done in New England and other pioneer areas.[76] There has also been talk by some of increasing fellowship with evangelically inclined black Christians. Even the historic Woman's Missionary Societies have been abolished, by a 1970 WMU overhaul, in favor of Baptist Women groups tailored to fit the ages, interests, and time schedules of a more diverse membership.[77]

None of this, however, seems to have effected much change in the fundamentally promotional character of the Lottie Moon story. There is great stress, for instance, in "It Cannot End at Kobe" on the need for more personnel ("Send on the missionaries") to handle an ever more complex missionary operation—now including coffeehouses, drug programs, teen-age youth centers, and other expensive activities which Miss Moon would presumably endorse. Also not much changed is the superior and indispensable role of the missionary; identified with "living out love" and with God Himself ("The people who have learned to trust us are learning to trust Jesus"), the missionary corps brings "adult leadership" to people apparently incapable of leading themselves. Part of an 1888 Lottie Moon letter from "Sah-ling" (actually from Chinkiang) is presented, misconstrued, as evidence that such relationships can be happy ones.[78]

So Lottie Moon as a story seems quite amenable to shifts of emphasis, for relevance appeal, while Lottie Moon as a recruiting and fund-raising institution rolls along ever larger. The point is again not to imply, as one way of putting it, that T. P. Crawford was absolutely correct in his long-ago judgments on "money makes the mare go" trends in his and Miss Moon's church. It is probably "only natural," as a recent study of Southern Baptists says, that "with so large a denomination their work takes on the aspect of being spectacular in its immensity."[79]

To be fair to Southern Baptists we should note that the historical Lottie Moon represents a kind of story that Americans in general, perhaps, are not accustomed to handling. She was "beautiful" really in an existential sense, like the denationalized heroes of *Man's Fate;* like Malraux's revolutionaries, Miss Moon was a person who spent her life trying to put abstract ideals into action—qualities like love and brotherhood—and she, too, found that her pursuit paradoxically increased her consciousness of individual aloneness.[80] Since this pursuit was also not very successful professionally (as a female she is not officially credited with a single convert), and since it technically ended in something like lunacy and attempted suicide, it makes an unconstructive and rather un-American message. So she has been reconstructed mostly as a martyr, which so often seems to be the American understanding of tragedy.

Miss Moon's death does make a logical stopping place, and maybe the most important point about Lottie Moon and her story. The food Miss Moon did not eat was perhaps in a sense like the cyanide that Malraux's Katov gave away: nothing was changed—she was dying anyway—but by dying precisely as gruesomely as did the friends she was unable to save, she could make death itself a means of achieving closeness to them.

The Lottie Moon story, however, seems to need a death *for* them, not with them. It also apparently needs a situation with a handle, a public lesson rather than a private pilgrimage. Miss Moon and her Shantung friends thus starved because "Southern Baptists had failed over here." How the home Baptists had failed, other than by not giving enough money to feed as well as to evangelize a Chinese province, is not entirely clear; the important thing is that Miss Moon—God and Virginia's lonely gift to China—atoned for their failure by becoming "herself a Christmas gift to heaven, for 'twas Christmas Eve!" Both God and the Chinese forgave the Southern Baptists; or at least everyone "from Tengchow all the way out to P'ingtu" was overcome by sorrow. With Miss Moon's love permeating the north China field "from generation to generation," later missionaries—more numerous and better financed—would find a "glad light of welcome."[81]

Now available in a variety of mass-circulation forms, the love of Lottie Moon redeems us still. Christians will yet "multiply in the land to which she gave herself," and "in the great corridors of time" the Chinese will love us as they love our God. Assessing just this kind of "final vision" ("In each generation we *play out* the impossible mythos"), Leslie Fiedler quotes Mark Twain—or rather Nigger Jim, who says to Huck, "It's too good to be true, Honey. It's too good to be true." [82]

III / Calvin Wilson Mateer

*"My spiritual grandfathers," Henry [Robinson] Luce
once said, thinking back on his youth in China,
"were all strong, bearded men like Calvin Mateer"—
who baptized Luce and here looms above the boy.*
———LIFE, *March 10, 1967*

*His [Luce's] continually searching, constantly
dissatisfied mind, geared to an incessant will to get
things done (he sometimes said he was lazy: that was
his kind of humor), was his formula, remorseless as
arithmetic, for success. He had no relaxations; he
had no hobbies; he never stopped working. Pauses for
sleep and food were only the necessary pull-ins at
the mechanics' pit; even then he was thinking of how to
drive the next lap.*
———*T. S. Matthews, ". . . tall,
balding, dead Henry R. Luce . . . ,"*
Esquire, *September 1967*

7 / A Call and the Struggle to Interpret It

To students of modern Chinese history the Presbyterian Calvin Mateer is already a well-known figure. This is because Mateer was one of the first people to teach the skills of the modern West in China, to an appreciable number of people and in a setting at once Christian, scientific, and Chinese.[1] Those who know of Calvin Mateer also usually know that teaching was only one of his interests. If not a genius, he was an all-round man in the finest American style, an omnicompetent success story somewhere between one's images of Benjamin Franklin and of the typical Eagle Scout. Busy all his life at "an amount of work that would have killed most men," he distinguished himself in literary work as well as in teaching. More modestly he was a scientist, an inventor, and a kind of backyard industrialist.

Among Presbyterians Mateer has been eulogized as one of the "Three Founders" or "Three Great Pioneers" (the other two being Hunter Corbett and John Nevius) of that church's Shantung mission field, which at the end of the nineteenth century constituted reputedly the biggest Protestant field operation in the world.[2] He also had great influence on China missions generally. As W. A. P. Martin observed in 1908, Calvin Mateer's influence permeated at that time the life and work of practically every young Protestant missionary north of Shanghai, from the day the individual began language study in Mateer's *Mandarin Lessons*.[3] If the newcomer became an evangelist, it would perhaps be with the help of Mateer scripture translations. If he engaged in educational work, he would probably use texts written by Mateer and have as colleagues a Chinese graduate or two of Mateer's Tengchow College. Whatever the missionary did, he would likely join associations, attend conferences, and otherwise participate in an organized style of endeavor that Mateer had personally done much to establish.

Calvin Mateer made his greatest mark, however, by founding

and developing what was debatably the first—but almost certainly was the best—of the nineteenth-century China Christian colleges. In this work he was unique in his time in his emphasis on and success with the teaching of natural science. He also had only scant company in his lifelong insistence that the larger purposes of such teaching would be defeated if it were not conducted exclusively in the Chinese language. What he proved by this, so his friend Dr. Martin believed, was that the language was "capable of adaptation to all the demands of modern science," and that the rawest of Chinese talent could be educated to anybody's standards.[4]

As a combined educational and evangelistic enterprise Mateer's college had a remarkable record. All its graduates were Christians, and according to one of them, the school's founder "personally molded more than a thousand men in virtue." [5] Over half the graduates became teachers themselves in Christian schools or government institutions, and a large number became Christian ministers. Otherwise the college's products spanned a broad geographical and occupational spectrum during the last three decades of the Ch'ing dynasty. Among these men could be found doctors and scientists, journalists and mathematicians, yamen advisers and compradores, reform officials and revolutionary activists.

The present study indicates fairly fully just why and how the Tengchow College developed, and evaluations are also made of other aspects of Mateer's work. The subject, however, is Calvin Mateer himself. He was a remarkable individual, and the story of his personal development is one kind of commentary on the whole Protestant enterprise in late imperial China.

Christian Nurture: Childhood and Missionary Call, 1836–1863

Calvin Wilson Mateer was born on a farm in Cumberland County, Pennsylvania, in January 1836, and he spent his boyhood on a succession of farms in the Harrisburg area. His father, John Mateer, was a restless man; between Calvin's birth and the father's death in 1875 the Mateers moved approximately once every ten years. By the time Calvin was old enough for school they were settled on a place outside Gettysburg, at a farm so secluded that the family called it the Hermitage. They stayed long enough for Calvin to do most of his growing up, and this was the spot he remembered as home.[6]

Calvin's father, like most American farmers of his day, saw life as a strongly familial affair—himself and his wife and their seven children, all thrifty and hard working, and all making tangible contributions. Perhaps more than most, John Mateer clung to a classic pioneer image of the family, the *Snow-Bound* idea of the autarchic farm unit. Calvin's sister Jennie remembered the Hermitage as a "hive of industry, making most of the implements used both indoors and out, and accomplishing many tasks long since relegated to the factory and the shop." [7]

As the eldest of the Mateer children, Calvin grew up quickly to a responsible position. From picking up chips of slate he soon graduated to plowing fields, and from building water wheels to helping his father fashion the tools the family used. It was a highly organized sort of life for everyone involved. John Mateer, however, communicated something more than a consciousness of chores to be done; he had a strong measure of what his children recalled as "ideality," which seems chiefly to mean that he genuinely loved his land as well as living off it. [8]

Although all the Mateer children grew up to do something other than farm, they remained much affected by these years at the isolated Hermitage. Like many nostalgic ex-farmboys, Calvin tended later to sentimentalize this; but the discontinuity between his youth and his adult career was more apparent than real, and he quite correctly believed that the one was tied to the other by way of direct preparation. In 1861, while confirming in his mind his missionary call, he wrote: "I have lived in the country nearly all my life, and I much prefer its quiet beauty. I love to wander at this season over the green fields, and listen to the winds roaring through the young leaves, and to sit down in the young sunshine of spring under the lee of some sheltering bank or moss-covered rock. I love to think of the past and future and, thus meditating, to gather up courage for the stern realities of life." [9]

So Calvin apparently inherited a measure of his father's ideality. His appreciation for stern realities, however, came from his mother, Mary Diven Mateer, and the ideals he explicitly followed in life were hers. This was one of those things which he felt especially deeply in later years, and which, according to his friend Watson Hayes, he expressed best in Chinese, to an audience specially attuned to the idea of "a whole lifetime of great filiality." [10]

According to Calvin's and other accounts, his mother's primary occupation was to lead a life of great personal piety and to involve her children in it as early and as closely as possible. She saw to it that family worship was held twice daily, with prayers, hymns, and readings from scripture. After church and pastor's class on Sunday Mrs. Mateer instructed at home from the *Sunday*

School Union Question Book. Other religious books were borrowed from the pastor's library, and beginning with Calvin, each child memorized Christian selections as part of growing up—catechizing each other, for example, as they helped in the field. Their mother expected no mistakes in such recitation, not even "so much as an article or preposition."

The atmosphere was not unlike the descriptions one reads of Calvin's later school at Tengchow. The Mateer children all grew up very religious; and as people who never knew themselves as anything but Christians, they never needed to be saved, revived, or otherwise hastened to grace. Because of his parents, Calvin wrote, "I cannot tell when my religious impressions began. They grew up with me." [11]

The only thing that needed clarifying in the lives of the Mateers was what "channel to service" each should take. Here we reach the heart of the mother's influence: of five sons and two daughters, all but one entered one of what she called the consecrated professions—teaching, the ministry, or, most emphatically, foreign missions. This was not precisely what John Mateer, the father, had had in mind, "to have his boys one after another leave him, depriving him of their help on the farm." But his wife, having "counted the cost of what she was doing," had worked specifically to bring it about.

Mary Mateer taught her children that piety is the first of virtues and that dutifulness is piety's ethical expression. In her judgment their particular duty was to go to the ends of the earth as Christian missionaries. As a child she herself had been fascinated by her church's mission to the Sandwich Islands; as an adult she remained an avid reader of missionary biographies and periodicals, and as a mother she read these aloud. She also built a missionary mite-box from sticks and wallpaper, to be the "shrine of the children's devotion." In this whole program "one aim was kept steadily in view, that of fitting them either to carry the gospel to some heathen land, or to do the Lord's work in their own." She lived to see four of her children in China. [12]

Something else that Mary Mateer impressed on her children was the value of learning. She did not have much learning herself, and this was her life's great regret, which she expressed in various ways. Sometimes she would go back in dreams to her girlhood, matriculating at Mount Holyoke rather than settling so soon on John Mateer's farms. Mostly, however, she compensated in a classic American fashion, by doing everything she could to secure for her children the education she had missed. She taught them to read and to value books and, later on, to stick with school when their father had neither the money nor the desire to keep them there.

As in other things, Mary Mateer's greatest success was with Calvin, and he always gave her full credit. She was helped, however, by two other people, men who embodied to Calvin what his mother had in mind and who became his personal models. The first of these was his grandfather William Diven, Mrs. Mateer's father. Mr. Diven could quote Shakespeare and Burns and, as Calvin described him to his own Chinese pupils, "discourse on great affairs ancient and modern, and on methods of cultivating virtue."

After Grandfather Diven came a young man named James Duffield, a teacher at Calvin's first school. Duffield must have been a remarkable person, and Calvin was perhaps a little unusual for being able to appreciate him. The teacher was homely, awkward, and shy, and his school was a shabby place. But to young Mateer he was a genius who made "every subject alive with interest." Duffield adopted Calvin as a special project and undertook to teach him algebra, which was not in the regular curriculum. Calvin stayed after school for two years, and during this time Duffield communicated two things to him which he kept from that time on—a fascination with mathematics and a consciousness of the power of teachers to shape lives.[13]

Calvin's career as a scholar could still have ended at seventeen, when he left James Duffield's school. His father felt that he should come back to the farm, and "the question whether he ought not to have fallen in with the paternal wish caused him serious thought." But supported by his mother, he managed to split his time for several years between work at the Hermitage and study at various higher academies. He also did his first teaching, at eighteen, in a country school where many of the pupils were older than he. The school's dominant tone was "rowdyism," but Calvin managed to cope because he needed the money to go on to college. Writing about this in 1897, he recalled that "I held my own . . . and finished with credit, and grew in experience more than in any other period of my life." [14]

In 1855 he entered Jefferson College, today's Washington and Jefferson, at Canonsburg, Pennsylvania. It was a hard school ("These were the palmy days of Jefferson College"), and Calvin remembered himself as arriving "very green and bashful . . . an unsophisticated farmer's boy." Somehow he persuaded the administration to admit him as a member of the junior class, and taking extra work along the way, he graduated in 1857 as covaledictorian.

The general impression at Jefferson was that Calvin was not exactly the smartest student in school, but smart enough, and with an unlimited capacity for "hard, constant work." This was also Calvin's opinion of himself.[15]

On graduation he was invited to join the faculty at the fashionable Lawrenceville School in New Jersey. Instead he went to Beaver, Pennsylvania, and bought the local academy, a ramshackle affair "run down almost to nothing." He wanted something, he wrote, that would put him more on his mettle. He taught and recruited, and in three terms he built up the Beaver school from twenty boys to ninety. This accomplished, he was ready to accept the higher type of challenge for which his mother had prepared him. Putting it simply in later life, Calvin remembered, "I could easily have gone on and made money, but I felt that I was called to preach the gospel, and so I sold out my school and went to Allegheny [Western Theological Seminary], entering when the first year was half over." [16]

Calvin's decision here came as no surprise to those who knew him. It did not so much even come to him, really, as grow up with him in his sense of duty. His spirituality deepened as he matured in the 1850s, a development encouraged by his mother's frequent letters. When he finally arrived at seminary, a classmate recalled, his dedication was "head and shoulders above his fellows around him." By the time he graduated in the spring of 1861 he had already been preaching for over a year, off and on, and he had also applied for work of "greater usefulness" as a foreign missionary.

In later years Calvin Mateer thought that he was atypical as a missionary in that he had wanted to go to the foreign field even before he wanted to be a minister: "From my youth I had the missionary work before me as a dim vision. A half-formed resolution was all the while in my mind, though I spoke of it to no one. But for this it is questionable whether I would have given up teaching to go to the Seminary." This is probably true, but it is not the whole story. He had actually spoken a good deal in letters to his mother, and Mary Mateer's sympathy was again an important factor in her son's final decision. Late in 1860 he wrote her, "I have about concluded that so far as I am myself concerned it is my duty to be a missionary . . . I have not come to such a conclusion hastily. It has cost me very considerable effort to give up the prospects which I might have had at home." [17]

All this questioning was part of Calvin Mateer's spiritual maturation, of reaching the point where he could affirm, "I must go; I am glad to go; I will go," even while feeling he was still "not as willing to go as I should be." In 1856 he had begun to keep a journal, to understand "the history of my own life, and the motives which impelled me." The journal's entries reflect a series of depressions and exaltations, not a lifelong vision coming smoothly to fruition. Increasingly, he was separated from home by time as well as by distance. He had achieved much to be proud of; but he had never stayed long in any one place, and his struggles seem to have been lonely ones.[18]

Given such considerations, it was probably quite significant that he became acquainted with Julia Ann Brown in 1860, while on a preaching assignment in Ohio. Julia Brown was a quiet, thoughtful girl who shared Calvin's values and, in her own way, his missionary impulse. She was also very pretty. In a broader sense she was a beautiful person—she had a strength fully equal to Calvin's, but from a very different background of much sadness and little assurance. And where Calvin had the ability to command respect from people, Julia seems to have moved them to love. She meant a great deal to him from the first, and her quick response, her trust in him and his half-formed resolution, were all immeasurable comforts to him.

They were married late in 1862, and almost immediately the Presbyterian Board of Foreign Missions confirmed Calvin's appointment. He and Julia discussed their assignment for "less than three minutes." As he wrote in his journal, "Her first exclamation after hearing the letter I shall not forget: 'Oh, I am glad!' That was the right ring . . . I shall remember that time, that look, that expression." [19]

Because life to Calvin Mateer was a matter of selecting between duties, he really did need someone like Julia with whom to share it. She loved him and admired him greatly, but she understood him well enough to know when not to take him too seriously. At the last moment, for example, he became highly conscious of his duties in America—his younger brothers and sisters, the pastorate he had been filling in Ohio, and President Lincoln's Union Army, which he thought of joining. Julia settled these doubts by simply packing up everything they owned. They sailed for China on July 3, 1863, on the same afternoon that Calvin's own country's future was being determined within earshot of his boyhood home.

Pistol and Cane: Evangelistic and Pastoral Work, 1864–1874

Calvin Mateer succeeded in China, but not all at once. The board had sent him to his last choice among mission fields, and for a long time he was not very happy with it. Life was a struggle—on the one hand to establish a boys' Christian school, which was where his experience lay, and on the other to deal with adults, for whose evangelization he felt primarily called. Concentrating on the latter task, he had a rather dismal first ten years.

To begin with, he barely reached China alive, after having tried repeatedly to be assigned elsewhere. The board had posted him first to Canton, which he refused to accept. He had heard that the Chinese language would be "exceedingly difficult" for a twenty-eight-year-old foreigner, and evangelizing "peculiarly discouraging." He had also heard that he would be "entrammeled by rules and rigid instructions." He appealed for reassignment to India, Africa, or Japan, before finally compromising on Tengchow. It was still Chinese, but at least there would be few entrammelments. The Presbyterian mission was only three years old, and only one missionary couple (Charles Mills and his first wife) remained alive and at work there.

Calvin and Julia Mateer took passage to China on the same ship with Hunter and Lizzie Corbett. It was perhaps a minor miracle that any of them made it; the two wives never completely recovered physically from this initial six months' voyage; when not sick or being chased by Confederate marauders, all the missionaries were bullied by the ship's captain, a sadistic type who starved his crew and hated religious people on principle. After a stop in Shanghai for an abortive lawsuit against the captain, the Mateers and Corbetts took another vessel for Chefoo. This one ran aground, and the journey was finished in a lifeboat. Another series of misfortunes followed ashore, before the missionaries finally reached Tengchow on January 15, 1864.[20]

Mateer found his new home even freer of entrammelments than he had expected. In fact there were hardly any rules at all, which he quickly discovered to be a mixed blessing. There was some doubt, for instance, as to his legal right to be in Tengchow, since it was in the process of being replaced by Chefoo as the official Shantung treaty port. He had to find a home, learn the language, and somehow begin work in a virtual vacuum. The Chinese, particularly the officials and local gentry, were not disposed to make any of this easier.

His first difficulty was finding a place to live. The Mateers had come to Tengchow presuming that the recent treaties at Tientsin and Peking entitled them to buy, lease, or build a residence on arrival. Like the Crawfords before them, however, the Mateers found that by the mid-1860s the inhospitable Chinese seemed better versed in treaty rights than Americans were. For almost a year the Presbyterian housing situation was up in the air. The

P'eng-lai district magistrate, his superior the circuit taotai (intendant), the Tsungli Yamen in Peking, and a local gentry leader named Yüan T'ing-chen all took turns interpreting the property sections of the relevant treaties to the foreigners' disadvantage. Even American and British diplomats seemed often to be on the side of the Chinese authorities. While all this boiled on, the Mateers and Corbetts continued to bump into the Mills family in the latter's four-room bungalow. Calvin, who with Julia was allotted the dining room, wrote, "I can only call this staying, and very poor staying at that." [21]

Eventually Hunter Corbett gave up and moved to Chefoo, and Charles Mills got another house outside the city. The Mateers remained in the old Mills place, which was actually a broken-down Buddhist temple. The Kuan-yin T'ang, as it was called—the Temple of the Goddess of Mercy—proved adequate for the little school which Julia opened, and it served as the physical nucleus from which the Tengchow College grew later on. But by American living standards it was most unsatisfactory. It was cold and damp and generally suggestive of its haunted house reputation. Calvin had colds, Julia developed rheumatic symptoms, and their few neighbors were unfriendly.[22]

In these depressing circumstances Calvin set about learning the Chinese language. He did not like either his tutors or the available Western textbooks, and in general he found the whole task as painful as he had feared. His opinion of Chinese culture, already low from the housing situation, dropped further: "I do not wonder that the Chinese have never made great advances in learning. It is such a herculean task to get the language that a man's best energies are gone by the time he has himself prepared to work. It is as if a mechanic should spend half his life, or more, in getting his tools ready." At the end of the first year Mateer nonetheless gave his first lecture to his wife's schoolboys, a job previously handled mostly by a Chinese assistant. By March 1865 he was able to converse successfully with Confucian examination candidates, and shortly after that to preach in the streets.[23]

As he learned the language Mateer also learned his way around. At the 1867 Chinese New Year, when he knew money was tight, he managed to buy a little land adjoining the Kuan-yin T'ang. This gave him the whole temple area for the school's use; more immediately important, he could build a healthier home for his wife and himself. By Thanksgiving the new house was finished —the first foreign-style dwelling to be built in Shantung—and they lived in it comfortably for the next thirty-seven years.

Calvin Mateer's early struggles with housing and the language seem most importantly to indicate something about him as a person. Both were tough problems which he not only overcame, but, as it turned out, thrived on. As a student in America he had never shown much aptitude for languages like Greek and Latin. Chinese was harder still; but he accepted it as something he had to master, a sort of personal character test. He began taking notes on things he read and heard, trying to impose an inductive grammatical order on what seemed to be complete confusion. After a few years he was a fluent speaker. In time, as his notes grew and took shape, he became an expert.

The house that he built, like those of his colleagues John Nevius and Hunter Corbett in Chefoo, was the kind that globetrotters would cite in later years to illustrate missionary luxury and cultural arrogance. Although not as extensive as the Crawford establishment, Mateer's place was indeed larger than most of the native homes and built more impressively. It was also two-storied, thus violating Chinese sentiments against unpropitious shadows and against looking down into neighbors' courtyards. It was surrounded by rosebushes and manicured trees, and inside, after a few years, were things like electric fly-whisks and musical fountains.

Appraising the situation in his own way, Mateer built his house big because he was building a headquarters, a place from which he meant to carry on numerous activities. If it was impressive, he had at least built it largely with his own hands—including the fly-whisks and fountains—from carpentry and masonry manuals brought from America. Building things, like language study, was something that was important to him for its own sake in these early years; frustrated in other areas, he could wrestle comforting results out of bricks and Chinese characters.[24]

The other side of these years was Mateer's failure in the preaching and pastoral work he had come to China to do. Finding Tengchow city uncongenial, he spent his professional time largely in the countryside, trying to get something started evangelistically. Between 1864 and 1873 he covered fifteen thousand miles by foot and donkey, all over Shantung. His home became a sort of command post, where supplies were stored and expeditions mounted, and he improved his language skills in more than twelve thousand "addresses to the heathen." Long afterwards another missionary called these Mateer's "pistol and cane" years, when he went out full of pious pugnaciousness and got something out of his system. To Mateer himself they were years of torment that at the time seemed to lead nowhere.[25]

By his own account, Calvin Mateer itinerated in those days

with only an iron spoon, a saltshaker, a navy revolver, and all the religious literature his donkeys could bear. He visited hundreds of villages and apparently every city of any size in Shantung. His trips kept him in the interior for three to four months at a time. He kept elaborate records; his progress, for example, was measured in miles (one thousand per tour as the goal, two hundred and fifty a month the norm), human settlements (one hundred to two hundred preaching stops), and even streams crossed (twenty per day not unusual). Sometimes he estimated his success by pages distributed (277,000 in 1865), and sometimes by gross weight (twenty-eight seventy-pound boxes in 1866). He always counted the crowds and how long it took to collect them.

All this method, however, failed to bring evangelistic success or even predictability. Mateer would present himself in a village, spread out his books, and give the natives a half hour to gather. If, as often happened, no one was interested, he would pack up and move on. In the next place he might find several hundred people eager to mob him. The mob could be inspired by murderous rage, curiosity, or even religious interest; he rarely knew which to expect. He faithfully recorded it all, as once when in two days "at least ten thousand mouths" called him a foreign devil.

This sort of life was quite adventurous, and men like Nevius and Corbett loved it. Mateer, however, was less temperamentally suited for it than they. This was his misfortune, because he believed it was what he was supposed to be doing. He was committed to itineration as a "very excellent" idea; but he disliked being away from Julia, and he tired of having to exercise his "moral right to protect himself from assault." He did not understand why people would assume he was a devil simply because he was foreign ("It is strange how such a term could have gotten such universal currency"), nor why he continually had to demonstrate the "futility of such interruptions." He won only a handful of converts.

As time passed, he found it all simply much too confusing, too full of variables and things "for which in most cases we have no means of accounting." He became involved in other tasks, and after 1873 he rarely went into the countryside at all.[26]

During these same years Mateer was also an active pastoral worker. He always liked formal preaching much better than evangelizing, because pulpit messages were much less subject to "all sorts of interruptions and irrelevancies." He felt freer to speak in his preferred style, in sermons that were "logical, direct, a unit in thought." He also enjoyed the administrative aspects, presiding over meetings and counseling people in Christian growth.

Rather quickly, however, he found this work very depressing

too. The little Tengchow church really belonged to Charles Mills, his senior in the field. There were not enough members (usually around thirty in the 1860s) for two pastors, and Mills got along with them better than Mateer did. To Mills they were "very interesting characters," even when "crazed with religion" or, as was more usual, simply "a little startling to those who from childhood had known . . . what might be termed the conventionalities of religion." To Mateer these people were mostly just sources of "a great deal of anxiety and sorrow of heart." He was discouraged by their residual vices, which emerged in cases of lying, stealing, fighting, forgery, idolatry, opium usage, and adultery.[27]

The pastoral work, like evangelism and Christian activity generally, was also disturbed by unfriendly interference from outside. Many of the church members lived in villages outlying Tengchow city, and on occasion they had to contend with some local headman's "schedule of penalties"—reactions such as Lottie Moon's Sha-ling Baptists encountered later in P'ingtu. In the city of Tengchow itself the day-by-day attitude was a cool indifference, but from time to time the inhabitants would join with the country folk to threaten Christians in some way.[28]

Calvin Mateer was of course, like T. P. Crawford, one of the early foreigners to attempt residence in Shantung, and he responded to the local antiforeignism with a feisty self-righteousness at least equal to Crawford's—so much so in fact that for some years such struggling was virtually a profession for him in itself. One has to understand that to Mateer and Crawford and their pioneering associates this sort of trouble was not just an occupational hazard. It seemed to be the proximate cause of all their frustrations, something that had to be understood and extirpated at its source before they could expect to do any effective work at all.

Like their contemporaries elsewhere in China, the Tengchow pioneers also tended to blame even the most patently spontaneous resistance on the "ruling and literary classes"—or as Mateer called them, the wealthy and unprincipled men. By the time the Mateers came in 1864, the little foreign community already saw itself as locked in mortal combat with a twenty-man clique (referred to as the *kung-chü* or *yueh-hui*) of influential natives. With Calvin Mateer making important contributions, this struggle with the local Vigilance Committee went on for about a decade.[29]

Mateer's first brush with the opposition had occurred when he arrived and tried to secure a residence. The next such encounter, which took place in the summer of 1866, was briefer in duration but a good bit more spectacular. Elated at that time by T. P.

Crawford's April victory in occupying the house rented by Chao Ting Ching, Mateer used the same underhanded tactic to rent a chapel for himself, to gain a personal base separate from Charles Mills's church. The landlord here, mindful of what had just happened with Crawford and Chao, specifically required his lessees —three Chinese middlemen secretly acting for Mateer—to promise in their contract that they would not sublet to any other party. The middlemen claimed they wanted the house only for themselves, to open a "general grocery and shop." Immediately, however, they forged a significantly different document and turned the place over to Mateer.[30]

The response that greeted Mateer's attempt to use his chapel was predictably intense. In addition to angry demonstrations at the chapel site, there was a fresh outbreak of desecrations at the missionary cemetery, a development which seems to have outraged all foreigners in the area.[31] In an effort to compel local officials to protect this graveyard and to stop such "terrorism" as that experienced by Crawford and Mateer, the Tengchow missionaries took a forceful tack themselves. Helped by Chefoo Consul E. T. Sandford, Mateer and others persuaded Commander Robert Townsend of the *U.S.S. Wachusett*—which had put into Tengchow on a supposedly peaceful call—to bring his crew ashore and stage an armed demonstration. On July 14, 1866, this landing party muscled its way into the yamen of the Tengchow prefect. There a group consisting of Commander Townsend, E. T. Sandford, Calvin Mateer, and various other people presented the prefect with a list of demands. The two chief items were an indemnity of 200 taels for tombstone repairs and immediate arrest of Yüan T'ing-chen and five other *kung-chü* leaders ("bad characters who have excited the people"). Afterwards, at least by Chinese accounts, the *Wachusett* sailors were turned loose on the town, where they committed thieveries, beatings, and other indiscretions.[32]

The Tengchow missionaries apparently got nothing from all this except more frustration. The Tsungli Yamen, acting on reports from a number of Shantung officials, skillfully turned the whole incident into a great embarrassment to United States diplomatic representatives in Peking. Prince Kung sent them statements, for instance, contrasting the "artful plans" of the "violent" Mr. Mateer with the property-rights language of the Tientsin Treaty ("each party shall conduct itself with justice and moderation"). He also asked, "Let the reckless conduct of Commander Townsend's men . . . be set over against the worth of the tombstones," especially considering the "terrible fright" given the citizens of Tengchow.

In the end Consul Sandford received one of his numerous reprimands, and Commander Townsend escaped similar action, apparently, only by suddenly dying. Calvin Mateer had to give up his chapel; and he and his Tengchow friends found in general that "since the departure of the *Wachusett* . . . our position has been tenfold more embarrassing than it was before." [33]

More embarrassment followed in 1867 and 1868, as T. P. Crawford and Matthew G. Holmes drew Vigilance Committee attention for shady business activities in the countryside.[34] Then in the summer of 1870 Sino-foreign relations in Tengchow came to a sort of historic head. The situation was that the Tientsin Massacre in June of that year had terrified missionaries all over China, and in east Shantung—as Helen Nevius put it—not a day passed without some new rumor of similar bloodbaths locally. Substantiating the rumors was an inflammatory and seemingly widespread anti-Christian literature.

By July the Shantung missionaries were in a state of near panic. They wrote frightened letters to *The North China Herald* (Shanghai), and John Nevius got up a petition asking for a U.S. Navy gunboat. Mateer and Hartwell, perhaps helped by Nevius, also began doing a translation of the *Pi-hsieh shih-lu* (translated as *Death Blow to Corrupt Doctrines*), the most popular of the anti-Christian tracts. Convinced that the Tengchow Vigilance Committee was locally responsible for this scurrilous document, they meant to circulate it broadside among concerned foreigners. This, it was hoped, would provide a true insight into the Chinese mind and prove the need for a "proper adjustment of relations between this nation and foreign countries." [35]

On August 18 the *Death Blow* translation was completed, and on the twenty-ninth Nevius sent a last appeal for naval help to Samuel A. Holmes, Mr. Sandford's replacement at the Chefoo consulate. On September 1 two warships arrived at Tengchow, making a "most wholesome impression" and evacuating the missionaries to Chefoo. A delegation went to Shanghai to get the *Death Blow* printed, and late in October the whole group returned to Tengchow aboard the *U.S.S. Benicia*. Commander Kimberley of the *Benicia*—perhaps mindful of Commander Townsend before him—declined a missionary request to "walk about the city with the officers of his ship in full uniform." Still, reported Martha Crawford, the missionaries' withdrawal and their impressive transportation seemed to have accomplished something psychologically. The natives seemed "more friendly than for a long time." [36]

Calvin Mateer, however, felt more confused than gratified

by this 1870 experience. Commander Kimberley and several American and British diplomats, including Ministers F. F. Low and T. F. Wade in Peking, had accused the Tengchow missionaries of exaggerating the danger of their position. Mateer himself had been reluctant at the last to leave his station; he had evacuated late and returned early, on horseback, sending Julia with the naval parties. He was not as sure as were some of his "emotionally less stable" fellows that they really had been in such peril as they thought. He also wondered if the 1870 warships had really accomplished anything very different psychologically from the *Wachusett* affair of 1866. All he knew for certain was that "I will not fly from Tungchow again unless there is a great deal more imminent danger." [37]

In the years immediately following Mateer had more new thoughts on relations between missionaries, Chinese, and Western power. Before the end of 1870 he expressed doubts in his journal about the whole idea of depending on treaties and gunboats. On a related subject he wrote in 1872, "In general I am more and more satisfied that bad results come from our efforts to assist the [Chinese] Christians, and from their appeals to us." Near T'ai-an-fu in March 1873 he was stoned and roughed up worse than on any occasion since he had begun itinerating. He sought no redress for this. The incident seems instead simply to have helped him make his decision to give up itinerating work. [38]

Of all Calvin Mateer's experiences during these years, however, there was one in particular that affected him most profoundly and drew together his thoughts on both missionary method and Sino-foreign relations. The story here centered around a man named Miao Hua-yü, a Christian leader for whom Mateer had a special affection. Mateer first met Miao Hua-yü while itinerating early in 1869 in Ch'i-hsia, Miao's home district in the southern part of Tengchow prefecture. As a generally unsuccessful evangelist, Mateer was touched when this man made a dramatic Christian profession. He was even more impressed when Miao's testifying motivated his whole village, plus a number of relatives from outside, to attend an all-night preaching session. By the beginning of summer, with strong encouragement from Mateer, Miao Hua-yü was a full-time evangelist. [39]

Around the first of July 1869 Miao moved from Ch'i-hsia hsien to Chao-yüan, about fifty miles southwest of Tengchow. The new location seemed an ideal spot for his dynamic style of witness: the natives were friendly, and J. B. Hartwell's people had already established a Baptist work there. For several weeks Miao's preaching drew small but enthusiastic crowds. Then on July 22 Calvin Mateer came to visit. With him were Julia and a delegation of Tengchow Presbyterians. The group stayed for two weeks while Mateer rented a chapel for Miao, preached with him, and helped stage Christian feasts and a highly publicized chapel opening. Mateer also called on the local magistrate to tell him that Miao was the missionary's special friend, and he arranged for two of the Tengchow Christians to stay permanently in Chao-yüan as Miao's assistants.

The Mateers went back to Tengchow on August 6, and within a week Miao Hua-yü was in trouble. On the twelfth he was arrested, together with the chapel's landlord, and brought before the magistrate. The landlord was charged with illegal renting. Miao was accused of "secret and unauthorized communications with invisible beings" and of preaching "strange words which caused men to wonder." Both men, by "introducing foreigners into the city," were also suspected of trying to "form combinations dangerous to the state." [40]

The landlord, a man named Hsiu Chi, received two hundred blows with the bamboo. Miao Hua-yü was offered pardon if he would confess and give up his corrupt activities; when he refused, he too was beaten and sent back in chains to his native Ch'i-hsia. There his home magistrate subjected him to a second trial that proved even more painful. Miao not only still refused to recant, but by singing hymns, praying on his knees, and disrespectful talking, he so enraged the Ch'i-hsia official as to be given some five hundred more blows during a two-day examination.

As soon as Calvin Mateer heard of what was happening he rushed to Ch'i-hsia. Arriving just as Miao was collapsing on the second day, Mateer was overcome by his friend's condition: "I shall not soon forget my feelings when I saw this Christian brother with a chain around his neck and his body disfigured for the gospel's sake. I could not restrain the tears as I looked him in the face. It is one thing to talk of persecution a thousand miles away, and another to see it face to face. I assured him . . . that I would do my utmost to rescue him." [41] Mateer immediately contacted Samuel Holmes at the Chefoo consulate, and by August 22—less than a week later—Holmes had pressured the Chefoo taotai into ordering Miao released at Ch'i-hsia.

This did not satisfy Mateer. He also wanted the Chao-yüan chapel returned to Miao, and he wanted the Chao-yüan and Ch'i-hsia magistrates brought to trial together with all others who had falsely accused his associate. Here he found Holmes's diplomacy to be of only limited help. For one thing, the Chefoo taotai—conducting investigations of his own—produced a good deal of information contradictory to Mateer's conspiracy charge. Hsiu Chi, the chapel landlord, was found to have a criminal record and to have indeed rented illegally to Mateer; the chapel, formerly Hsiu's pawnshop, had been officially closed for extortion, and Hsiu had rented it without securing official approval. Regarding Miao Hua-yü, a number of acquaintances saw him simply as a well-known showman—a "reckless boaster and deceiver"—rather than as a reborn soul. There were also numerous witnesses who had interpreted his strange preaching ("at present all is quiet, but it is difficult to predict security for the eighth month") exactly as did the Chao-yüan magistrate—that it was "the design of Mateer and Miao in the eighth month to kill the officers and raise an insurrection." [42]

The taotai promised to reprimand the two magistrates for punishing Miao Hua-yü so severely without securing higher approval, but he categorically refused to summon them to any trial. He also refused to order the chapel restored to the Presbyterians. S. Wells Williams, writing for the U.S. Legation in Peking, agreed that such a trial would contravene Chinese custom, and that it furthermore was not a right conferred by any Sino-American treaty. Williams also reminded Mateer that he had no legal right to rent property outside an established treaty port. [43]

To Calvin Mateer the taotai's claims were all fabrications. He was moreover infuriated by the whole tone of his own government's response. In November he accordingly went alone to Chao-yüan, where the trouble had started; he was determined somehow to reopen Miao's chapel, expose and punish the opposition, and generally to show "what a determined man who has right on his side may accomplish." Unable to get the old chapel building back, he found a middleman who rented him a new one from an eccentric old woman. This landlady turned out to be even less reputable than Hsiu Chi, and Mateer found himself in a hornet's nest of "chicanery, brutality, deceit, low cunning, and petty meanness running over several months." The landlady and the middleman, after beatings by both the magistrate and the old woman's family, tried to evict Mateer; amid much cursing the missionary threw them bodily out of the house. For some five months he also struggled with the magistrate and against a gentry member named Yang, whom he identified as the local anti-Christian ringleader. Two out-of-town missionaries came to help Mateer, and all three went about the city displaying their pistols and determination.

Finally Mateer won, in a manner of speaking. A new district magistrate took over, and by threatening him with prosecution "on up to Peking" Mateer secured clear lease to a third chapel building. Preacher Miao returned as a legitimate member of the community. Ringleader Yang, after much protesting from the magistrate, was "required to knock head to me and . . . own up to his sin." Calvin Mateer returned to Tengchow in March 1870, stating that the settlement was "quite an advantageous one," which would "put us on a good footing in Chow Yuan for the future." [44]

Succeeding events, however, took an unexpected course. Most significant—and to make a long story short—Miao Hua-yü proved to be a great disappointment. As Julia Mateer put it, "His religion endured persecution much better than quiet study. He neglected his books, by and by ceased coming to church, and after a year or two had to be excluded." Calvin Mateer further discovered that Miao "presumed on his relationship with foreigners, and tried to assume the standing and privileges . . . of the highest literary rank." Such preaching as he did was unfruitful. Sporadic efforts were made to sustain the work at Chao-yüan, but in 1881 it was given up as a total failure.[45]

It would be difficult, from all indications, to overestimate the effects of all this on Calvin Mateer. For over five years—from 1869 through 1874—he devoted "page upon page, folio size" in his journal to the Miao Hua-yü story, and instead of a victory he wound up with a "most baffling experience." [46] He had invested quite an emotional stake in Miao; not only did the man demonstrate phenomenal Christian courage, but he was a valued friend and Mateer's greatest pastoral project in a decade of few successes. In the end, however, Miao emerged as precisely the opportunistic deceiver that the Chinese authorities had always maintained him to be. To look at it another way, he perhaps succumbed to the same worldly weaknesses that J. B. Hartwell's Chao-yüan Baptists were simultaneously displaying in their struggle with T. P. Crawford. To Calvin Mateer, who rarely in his life gave unqualified endorsements, Miao's later performance was in any case a great blow.

Judging from Mateer's subsequent career, he drew two important lessons from the Miao Hua-yü story. First, he made it an explicit principle not to be drawn into disputes with hostile Chinese, particularly the power structure. At Chao-yüan in 1869—as at Tengchow in 1864 and 1866—he was basically outmaneuvered by the Chinese authorities; their "fabrications" actually seemed informed by a superior understanding both of treaty rights and of human nature. Mateer, on the other hand, found himself time after time involved with dishonest associates, and with no recourse except force or bluff. The only lasting effect of his success at Chao-yüan was apparently to encourage his protégé Miao in some very harmful ideas. With only scattered exceptions Mateer henceforth stayed out of Chinese yamens and American consulates, and he did not make further appeals to treaty rights.

Calvin Mateer's Chao-yüan experience also fed into a philosophy he was developing on anti-Christian resistance in general. The term foreign devil, for instance, he decided "expresses not so much hatred to the gospel as it does the national enmity of the Chinese to foreigners." In his 1870 *Death Blow* translation he again found not so much anti-Christianity as antiforeignism, expressed as rejection of ideological heterodoxy. Christianity was only "the point of attack, because religion in the minds of the Chinese is essentially political and national." Persecution of converts, he wrote in 1872, should be understood in the same context: "It is the reliance which the Christians place in us that makes them hated by the people." [47]

By 1872 Mateer had thus had an experience somewhat like the one Lottie Moon would have at Sha-ling. Having played a part in launching an exciting Christian awakening, he had seen it painfully persecuted after he injected himself too conspicuously into the picture. In his case there was also the fact—as a friend of Mateer observed—that from the moment Miao was released at Ch'i-hsia the case was no longer one of "a mere struggle to right the wrongs of an individual convert." [48] Calvin Mateer was struggling to prove himself personally smarter and tougher than the native leadership, and the more he struggled the more embarrassing his position became. He had been carried away by his emotions, and to a lesser extent he was similarly affected by the succeeding Tientsin Massacre scare. It did not happen again.

The second important lesson of this period was tied to what has just been discussed, and also to Miao's failure to grow after such a promising start. The only conclusion Calvin Mateer could ever admit concerning Miao Hua-yü personally was that Miao had lacked something important from the first, despite his obvious bravery. His failure in more routine witnessing indicated an absence of depth, an incomplete understanding of what being a Christian was all about. He was in that sense not so different from Charles Mills's "crazed" characters or from J. B. Hartwell's corrupt followers, or for that matter from the Chinese who persecuted him. The common denominator of all these people—and to Mateer this was the important thing—was that they seemed to lack the spiritual and intellectual background to be capable of more than a kind of occasional fanaticism. The Chinese as a people, Mateer reasoned, did not really know what religion was.[49]

This judgment was borne out by another experience of the same time. In an effort to get evangelizing more into Chinese hands, Mateer and three other missionaries operated a peripatetic theological school at Chefoo and Tengchow between 1872 and 1874. Twelve promising converts enrolled. One disappeared in course, five failed to pass the work, and the remaining six were eventually licensed to preach. Of the six, only two persisted to ordination as ministers. One of these two then had to be severed from the church for adultery, as did one of the licentiates. The other minister settled purposefully at P'ingtu, but he never got a church organized.[50]

As a result of all these things, Calvin Mateer also stayed away after 1874 from routine evangelism and from doing much work with adult converts. He was not embittered; he still saw such tasks as the conventional, proper work of missionary enterprises anywhere. He had simply been unsuccessful at them himself, and henceforth he left them to people like Nevius and Corbett and Charles Mills, who all seemed better able to cope with the frustrations involved.

8 / *The Tengchow School*

The work to which Calvin Mateer now turned his attention had been a side interest for many years. On April 2, 1864, less than three months after he and Julia arrived at Tengchow, he had written in his journal, "We have it in prospect to establish a school." [1] The Tengchow Boys' School opened in the Kuan-yin T'ang on September 25, and Mateer served as its principal continuously thereafter. One gathers, however, that for a long time his mind was mostly elsewhere, and for about a decade the school was in the hands of Julia and a succession of Chinese assistants.

Mateer always confessed that the school had been his wife's idea and not his own. His tendency in later years to monopolize the credit for its success led other missionaries to underline this fact. Julia is variously reported to have run the school alone (virtually) and to have done fully two-thirds of the work up to 1873. The real picture, said one later associate, was that Julia perceived early that she would be childless and chose an obvious foster mother role; Calvin, on the other hand, "at twenty-eight wanted to preach and itinerate, and they got along by not intruding on each other's work, tho each helped the other." [2] This should not be overinterpreted, but it does suggest something about the Tengchow College's background.

The situation in Tengchow itself was another motivating factor. Mission work was new in all aspects and not much of a success in any. Helen Nevius had operated a small girls' school in 1862, briefly but with some encouragement from student response. The missionaries accordingly thought another school, for boys, might be worth trying. A conservative, out of the way place like Tengchow might by its very perversities be vulnerable to this particular approach—its main pretension, after all, was that as a prefectural

159

examination center it was academically oriented. Second, having apparently won its case against being a treaty port, Tengchow was free not only from foreign money but from the China-coast riffraff and sundry temptations that bedeviled mission schools in other places. Bookish pride, economic depression, and the missionary monopoly of foreign contact, so it was reasoned, ought to make the natives responsive to an efficient, inexpensive, and discreetly managed Christian school.[3]

The first class convened in the fall of 1864, oriented around Confucian primers and free of charge except to the Mateers, who personally assumed all expenses. The initial response was about as expected. The people at large were apathetic or fearful, and the upper classes declared the project presumptuous. Calvin and Julia Mateer, the two foreign teachers, were not yet competent enough linguistically to do much real teaching. Chang Kan-ch'en, their Chinese assistant and stand-in, had mixed credentials. He was a Christian, and as station copyist and tutor perhaps a "good enough scholar for beginners." Chang's other qualifications, wrote Mr. Mateer, were his willingness to work for low wages and the unavailability of anyone better.[4]

The first students were "six little heathen boys" enrolled as boarders from around Chai-li, a Ch'i-hsia market village thirty miles southeast of Tengchow. The boys were of varying ages up to eleven, came from extremely poor farming families, and with one exception were totally illiterate.

Teacher Chang opened each day with prayers and scripture. He then took the pupils through reading lessons in the *San-tzu ching*, the Three Character Classic. From its opening lines ("Men at their birth are by nature radically good") the *San-tzu ching* varied considerably—to cite one missionary's American comparison —from such analogues as the *New England Primer* ("In Adam's fall / We sinned all").[5] By mid-year Calvin Mateer was searching for new texts and a replacement for Chang Kan-ch'en, who seemed unable to cope with the contradictions in his job. Julia took over much of the instructing, using Helen Nevius's *Mandarin Catechism*.

The first year was disappointing. Two of the six students were withdrawn by suspicious fathers, and the Mateers dismissed a third for excessive dullness. Three new boys were enrolled in course, bringing the total back to six, but none of the group seemed much affected by the school's offerings. The only child able to read at all at year's end was a boy named Wang Ch'un-ling, who was also the only one with prior native schooling. There were no Christian conversions.

The Mateers were nonetheless optimistic in reports to the Board of Foreign Missions. This was perhaps partly because they needed the board's sanction (financial support) to increase enrollment, which they had decided was a prerequisite to success. Julia in particular believed the experiment should be continued. Writing for his wife, Calvin declared, "Our boys are getting along very well," all things considered, and "If it is worthwhile to have a school at all, it is worthwhile to have a good one." The board gave its approval and enough money to double the enrollment to twelve.[6]

The school thus continued and gradually expanded into the early 1870s, with the Mateers adding from their own pockets to the board's allowance. Calvin conducted devotionals and taught when available, and he did recruiting on his country trips. Julia immersed herself in the school as a combined head teacher and housemother. Pupils were paired off in the Kuan-yin T'ang dormitory by age, behavior, and other factors, and Christian "molding" became a serious program.

The school's problems, however, also expanded and tended to dominate the operation. The first of these, and certainly one of the thorniest, was recruiting and managing Chinese teaching assistants. The students' families sent their sons to the foreigners primarily because they promised to educate them in the Confucian classics. Without such training the boys stood little chance of being accepted as educated men in Chinese society. The built-in contradiction between the requisite teachers and the school's Christian intention is obvious, and it kept the Mateers in continuing anxiety.

Chang Kan-ch'en was apparently incompetent on many counts, and he was quickly released. In his place Mateer hired Chou Wen-yüan, who was a Christian of J. B. Hartwell's Baptist group and, it will be recalled, the *Peep of Day* translator. Chou was also a respected local scholar. In 1866 he passed the official examinations to become a *fu-sheng* (lowest grade) licentiate; but the Mateer's appreciation of him faded somewhat from that point, as he renounced his Christianity out of respect for his new Chinese status. He indulged in Confucian rites and taught "heresy" to the boys, but because his services were needed he was retained for five years. Before Chou left in 1871, Julia discovered that he was denouncing the school not only off campus but in his courses too.[7]

To counteract Chou Wen-yüan's influence, Julia would close his classes by leading in prayer for the teacher's soul. In addition, Calvin engaged a second scholar late in 1866 to teach younger pupils. This man was Li Kuang-nai, who was also a professed local Christian. As a man of learning his credentials were imposing: he was a *lin-sheng* (senior) licentiate, and thus stood two notches above Chou in the local scholarly community. Unfortunately, Li was so old and set in his ways that his religious beliefs turned out to be "in Christianity in addition to Confucianism, rather than in Christ alone." He died rather quickly (1868), but his "influence in the school had been bad, and was felt long after the poor old man had gone to his reward account."[8]

Disenchanted with such elderly degree holders, Calvin Mateer began hiring younger men whom he met on his travels. Li Hung-chung, of Huang-hsien, succeeded Li Kuang-nai early in 1869. He was an immediate "hopeful convert" and seemed a modest person of strong character. Best of all, Li Hung-chung was popular with the boys and very effective as a teacher and disciplinarian. This made it all the harder to get rid of him when "evil reports" regarding his character followed him from Huang-hsien and were confirmed in Tengchow by his off-campus behavior. Li Yün-lu, a young man who succeeded Chou Wen-yüan with the older boys, was recalled as the only real (*yüan-ya*) scholar of this whole aggregation. As a Christian, Li Yün-lu at best "did less to oppose our efforts but did no more to help." [9]

Given such a faculty, it was difficult to do much molding or anything else. Of a total of eighty-five students (excluding the first six) between 1864 and 1872, "fourteen accepted Jesus, and by 1872 five had already renounced Him." [10] Paralleling this was an even greater lack of success in imparting secular learning.

The Chinese teachers could not be held solely responsible for any of this. A much bigger problem was the student body, which Calvin Mateer recruited very indiscriminately, and which neither he nor Julia knew quite how to handle. What Calvin Mateer did here was to send his wife a steady stream of all the ragged youths he could secure, from virtual toddlers to large farmboys of nineteen and twenty, generally untutored and from backgrounds highly prejudicial to scholarly success.

Up to 1870 all the students came from Ch'i-hsia hsien, particularly from around Chai-li, where the school was advertised by Shantung's most flourishing Presbyterian community.[11] There (and later elsewhere) Calvin would be introduced to prospective patrons by a local Christian. He would discuss the school with a father or elder brother, and if things went favorably both parties would sign one of the Mateers' contracts (*ting-yüeh*). As school *chien-tu*, or principal, Mateer here promised to educate the child in "confucian books" and to furnish room and board, clothing, and medical care, and not to take the boy away from Tengchow for any reason. The parent agreed that his son "will not return home or enter a trade or profession until successful completion of the prescribed course of study. If he leaves without [approved] cause, the school will be repaid the entire amount spent on him while enrolled. If the student runs away, he must be searched for and sent back. Only with the approval of the *chien-tu* will the student become betrothed, or marry, before graduation. The *chien-tu* may furthermore dismiss the student to his home if he is unmanageable (*yü-wan*) or unable to complete the work." [12]

These contracts (really indentures) thus delivered boys to the school's keeping for as long as the prescribed course might run. Many parents refused to sign, or argued later, on this point. But the Mateers, thinking in terms of six-year molding courses and up, admitted no one without such an agreement. The alternative was familiar to Americans like Calvin Mateer from personal experience; as an English teaching friend wrote, "The difficulty was a real one . . . the parents really needing the lad's strong body in the field, while we want his developing mind in the school." [13]

Practically as well as legally, these contracts were unenforceable. Mateer expended much nervous energy in dozens of squabbles before finally dropping the practice, and of twenty students who withdrew without approval through 1872, only five reimbursed the school.[14]

Contracts were just one aspect of continuing difficulties with pupils' families. Another practice that led to trouble was that for some years the school did not as a rule take as boarders the sons of native Christians. There were several reasons for this rule, which seems rather perverse considering the school's reliance on Chai-li Christians for help in recruiting the non-Christians it did accept. It was felt, however, that the important thing was to maximize evangelistic contact. Another purpose was to stimulate the Chai-li believers to patronize the local school operated by their own leader. But mostly the idea was to keep a parent from converting simply to get schooling for his son; the Mateers seem never greatly to have trusted the Chai-li Presbyterians, and the church there did in fact collapse in 1871.[15]

In any case the non-Christian rule failed dismally in practice. The non-Christian parents broke agreements, countermanded regulations, ordered their sons home at will, and generally sabotaged the school's Christian purpose. As late as 1874 Julia Mateer noted, "So far, we have not known one individual instance of the friends or relatives of the boys being brought under the influence of the gospel by the school. Instead of carrying home the good they get, as we naturally supposed they would, they only get it laughed out of them, and their frequent visits home tend to harden them against Christian influences." [16]

Caught between claims of parents and foreign teachers, many of the more conscientious boys fell into depressions, occasionally to the point of attempted suicide. The great majority simply took the whole program with a large dose of salt, despite numerous conferences, thrashings, and expulsions. With Calvin Mateer away and Julia out of sight, bullies like the long-remembered Li brothers (Li Yüan-t'ung and Li Yüan-k'ai) dominated the dormitory, terrorizing would-be converts and small boys generally. Thievery and petty racketeering flourished around the kitchen, where successive cooks either collaborated or were themselves denounced for student crimes. A usury ring arose at one point, with much speculating and buying of notes from young creditors. Opium addiction, drunkenness, and even sodomy appeared along with routine vices like laziness, gluttony, and lying to teachers.[17]

With unmoldable boys coming and going, and without reliable teachers, books, or a consistent course of study, the school's hopes failed to materialize. In its tenth year the Mateers counted up and found that only seven of their ninety-one enrollees had completed the theoretical six-year program. Twenty-two others had transferred to an alternate arrangement called *i-yeh*, or vocational training, with mostly unsatisfactory results. The accomplishments of the remaining sixty-two boys were visible only in "the pains of those who had tried to teach them"; seventeen of this number had been dropped for academic reasons, eleven were expelled on unmanageability charges, another eleven disappeared, and so on. Of the fourteen hopeful conversions, only one boy had proved "useful to the church." [18]

Success Is Granted, 1873–1877

The point of all this, as everyone more or less recognized, was that the school was a failure. Julia Mateer's voice and nervous system were breaking down, and still none of her boys "excepting two or three" seemed "at all convinced that our system of education was of any value." Whatever she or her husband accomplished was wiped out by people like teacher Chou, who "constantly told them these things were all of no use." [19] That the Mateers persisted with the school seems a little odd in itself; that the school survived, and suddenly showed results, seems quite remarkable.

Basically, three things happened to change the picture. The

school altered its enrollment policy, settled on better books and courses, and achieved a sort of three-way communications breakthrough between its students and biracial faculty. The last of these things appears the most important, and the key throughout was Calvin Mateer himself. Now in his mid-thirties, he was finally led by his experiences to the school as the place to put his life together.

Calvin Mateer's heightened interest in the school actually had a roundabout beginning, during the period following the 1870 missionary evacuation of Tengchow. The school was closed for the last half of that year, and early in 1871 Mateer went to Shanghai to take temporary charge of the American Presbyterian Mission Press. The press was an old and valued institution, but it had shifted about often and had recently fallen into administrative confusion. Calvin Mateer became its superintendent in a complicated follow-up to his involvement with translating the *Death Blow*—but only very reluctantly, under pressure, and largely because the job meant his wife could get Western medical attention. The boys' school reopened under Maggie Brown, Julia's sister, who was a recent addition to the Tengchow station.

Julia had to go back to help Maggie, but Calvin stayed in Shanghai for the better part of two years. As things turned out, this was important in a number of ways. First, the press survived under him and emerged as one of the leading foreign-style printing establishments in China. The effects of the experience on Calvin Mateer himself were immediate: editing gave him a taste for personal literary work that he indulged with zest for the rest of his life, and he also had opportunity to develop further his considerable mechanical talents. Perhaps even more important, he had to come to grips with running a biracial, multilingual concern of some size, which bought equipment in Europe and America and handled orders all over East Asia.[20]

The executive aspect was the part of the job that was most unfamiliar to Mateer, and because he was so successful at it, the most stimulating. He started with the firm's machinery and record keeping, both of which were in disrepair. He studied and improved both and moved the whole operation to better Shanghai quarters. There he reorganized his personnel, put men of his choosing in charge, and took on more work. By late 1872 the press was a "well-organized business, running regularly and smoothly, and doing its work about as efficiently as was possible under the conditions."[21]

Despite his success in Shanghai, Mateer remained eager, somewhat like a good soldier, to get back "into the field." He worked to finish the job at hand, he said, "with an assiduity that I have rarely given to anything in my life." He also persuaded his brother John to come from America, work with him, and take charge when he left. He similarly brought in Wang Ch'un-ling from the six-year course at Tengchow; Wang learned metallurgy and other things and was installed as John's assistant and guide. The two became a successful team on this job and later at Peking, where they operated the (American Board) North China Press.[22]

Calvin Mateer returned to Tengchow in time for a fall itineration in 1872. Early in 1873 he went out again; this was the point, previously noted, when he was stoned and when to all effects he gave up such work. In its place he became involved in educational tasks such as theology classes and reorganization of his wife's school. In the second job he found himself fitting his entrepreneurial experience to a challenging field project—one whose organization, supervision, and logistics now seemed, much like the press, to constitute "in reality a large miscellaneous business."

At the boys' school the Mateers made what amounted to a new start. Studying the record, they were struck especially by the fact that almost half their pupils had either run away or been expelled. They decided that their recruiting had stressed quantity at the expense of quality, perhaps partly explaining the dropout rate of about 30 percent annually. After 1873 admissions were definitely selective. New enrollees were generally older, better prepared, and very important, from Christian homes. As Calvin described it, "We sifted out some good ones," on the theory that "a school to be a healthy one should *grow* up from a small beginning." [23]

Enrollment of Christians, a reversal of earlier practice, was found necessary largely because only "beggar class" non-Christians seemed otherwise to appear. Results recommended against such Pygmalion projects. Christian influences were a little more widespread now; but mainly students were secured among brothers and cousins of the "hopeful conversions" already in hand. Certain families were particularly cultivated by Mrs. Mateer, who visited and corresponded with them and displayed her mastery of the complex family relationships involved.[24]

This core group in time expanded, while procurement of new non-Christians proceeded on a less numerous but healthier basis. In 1873 Mateer pushed Chou Li-wen, a convert and outstanding student, into the P'eng-lai *hsien-k'ao*, or initial qualifying examination for the lowest academic degree. This was a risk, Mateer felt, but he thought it was necessary to counteract former teacher Chou Wen-yüan's public maligning of the school's classical program.

Chou Li-wen passed, while at the same time Chou Wen-yüan's own two sons did not. The combination of events reportedly gained more favorable local publicity than any other single incident in the school's history.[25]

Over the next ten years sixteen of seventeen other boys put forward by the school similarly passed the *hsien-k'ao*, bringing an attendant rise in respectable non-Christian applications. The Mateers accepted such boys if they looked particularly promising, or if their families would otherwise sign indentures of up to twelve years. Both Christian and non-Christian indentures were in fact gradually obviated by requiring parents to pay for at least something each year; this began with clothing in 1874, and it extended in time to bedding, Confucian books, school supplies, and other items.[26]

The Mateers also read the early record to mean that something had been wrong with the school itself. Curriculum and courses were accordingly overhauled and improved. As the *hsien-k'ao* story would suggest, this began with the Chinese classics and faculty. By 1874 unreliable Christian teachers like Li Yün-lu and Li Hung-chung were gone. From experiences with Chang P'ei-ling, Li Yün-lu's replacement, the missionaries decided—in contrast to their decision regarding students—that "heathen teachers are far less hindrance spiritually than inconsistent Christians."[27] A few of the later literati faculty members eventually converted, but their jobs no longer depended on it.

The Mateers also gave these teachers a much freer hand in class. Formerly Calvin or Julia had observed their teachers, imposed Westernized routines on the classes, and tried to restrict *pei*-ing (rote "backing"), which was traditional but which was so loud and monotonous as to give Mrs. Mateer headaches. Now the teachers were put on their own, told only to supplement the recitational shouting with appropriate explanations. Otherwise they could pursue the idea that "Chinese method was best for Chinese children," with results evaluated in composition tests each Friday. Digressions that were heretical from a Christian standpoint apparently ceased, and certainly education improved.[28]

Chinese studies had always been considered one third of the curriculum, though taking up half each student's time. The other parts were religious instruction and Western science. Christian molding was now expedited by an increased body of literature in Chinese and, more pointedly, by Calvin Mateer's vigorous presence. Science was still mostly an aspiration, but real progress was made there too.[29]

Mateer had been irregularly teaching arithemetic for some years, and since 1868 he had been slowly putting together written lessons. When he returned from Shanghai he issued these in class in a lithographed format. From the time the finished book (*Pi-suan shu-hsüeh,* in three volumes) appeared in 1877, the Mateer method was picked up by other mission schools. Reflecting Calvin's blackboard technique, the idea was to ease the student's transition to Arabic numerals and other aspects of modern life. Illustrative figuring was done in several different fashions, for clarity; and problems dealt with useful matters like taxation, partnership, customs duties, and banking charges, all cast in terms of Chinese currency, weights and measures, and similar usages.[30]

Convinced of the need for more "brain-energizing subjects," Mateer began teaching algebra in 1873. In an interesting parallel to his own experience with James Duffield, he took a selected group through an ad hoc course lasting several years. Mrs. Mateer reported in 1874 that his success with these algebra tutees was as significant as was Chou Li-wen's passing the *hsien-k'ao*; it indicated, in effect, that the school was making progress in two worlds, both of which were important to it.

By 1876 Mr. Mateer was conducting similar courses in geometry, trigonometry, astronomy, and chemistry. The courses were unprogramed and restricted in scope, and it was all the teacher could do to stay a day ahead of his class. The courses were very gratifying, however, because they were entirely his own, and because of the effect they seemed to have on the boys involved. In the school's report for 1876, Julia said the students were "thoroughly convinced that our system of education is of use—They see its advantages, and know that not only is their wun-le [*wen-li,* classical Chinese] not hindered, but that the mental training they get is of immense advantage to their wun-le. The school enjoys . . . the confidence of all the native Christians, and quite an extended reputation." [31]

By cultivating contacts and scholarship the school also increased its enrollment again, from twenty-two in 1874 to thirty-four in 1876 and forty-five by 1880. This presented the Mateers with new problems. Calvin's select courses tended both to take up his time and to make the student body more academically disparate than ever. At the same time the non-Christian Chinese faculty put the whole molding burden explicitly on Julia and himself.

The academic challenge was met by physical expansion—a room or so a year—and by complicated scheduling, which kept both teachers and students working long days in class. That molding succeeded must be attributed partly to less resistant students, but mostly to the Mateers' own hard work and improved understanding.

In 1872 Calvin Mateer wrote that "All depends on the direct personal conduct of the superintendent with the scholars, and the personal influence that is gained over them." This was a lesson he had learned by default, largely, and out of a sense of futility over thrashings of boys he scarcely knew.[32] As he spent more of his time with the school he could see his theory working. In constancy of contact he established himself as a sort of powerful moral presence, or as a student put it, as an official (*kuan-fu*) who truly taught as well as judged.[33]

Calvin Mateer thus taught all science except mental arithmetic, as well as classes in religion (moral science) for the older boys. According to the school's *Alumni History*, his classroom performances soon inspired "god-like awe . . . for his mental faculties, his intense activity, and his good judgment." More comprehensively, "They loved him like a father. When someone transgressed a rule, he punished severely; but once past, he forgot it at once and did not remember it. When someone was in difficulties, he would find a way [to help] generously, appropriately, and without partiality. There was nothing that he did not thoroughly investigate—the difficulty or simplicity of lessons, the diligence or laziness of teachers, the fitness or unfitness of students—down to the smallest affairs of school. Whenever he promulgated a regulation, he was very strict in carrying it out, and there was no exception without important cause. *Hsien-sheng* [teacher] was in fact a good teacher of [how to] supervise a school."[34]

He was known on campus as *Lao Hu*, or Old Tiger, especially among younger pupils. He was not a permissive person, and discipline was indeed strict. Given the traditional father-son relationship in China, this was perhaps not necessarily detrimental to the love his boys bore him. From the mid-1870s he certainly organized their lives, but toward seemingly worthwhile achievements and with a minimum of written *t'iao-kuei* (regulations) and *chin-ling* (prohibitions).

It was all rather more informally—by daily classes, dormitory visits, and devotional messages—that the principal indicated how to "follow the mean between liberality and strictness, and to perceive what was work properly done." When occasion warranted, he did not hesitate to "render judgment, separating the crooked from the straight." He was always available for appeals and frequent conferences, and from around 1876 the boys mostly regulated themselves, through a system of weekly student monitors (*chih-jih-sheng*).[35]

Calvin's work enabled Julia Mateer to give most of her time to the younger boys. She taught them geography and music, on which she wrote a book, and handled their religious training. Her extracurricular relationship to her pupils was even more intense than her husband's. As befitted a substitute mother to little boys, it was by report "like a hen brooding over her chicks." [36] One of the pupils recalled in 1912 that she seemed always "tirelessly walking about," checking food and drink, the dormitory thermometer, and many other things: "If a student's clothing were dirty, she had it cleaned; if the clothing were torn, she had it mended. If the place were very dirty, she would supervise a cleanup. If there were sickness, she would supply medicines. When the weather was muggy, she would caution [the students] to avoid drafts and to shun raw fruits. When it was damp, she had them sun the bedclothes. When they were dirty, she told them how they must wash; if their hair were unkempt, she told them how they must comb it. In every coming and going, in every look of distress or joy, there was nothing she did not notice and rectify." [37]

Mrs. Mateer apparently managed all this fairly well. As one of "those whom she delighted to call her sons" wrote, "If ever she failed or did wrong in the compassion of her nurturing, we never knew it"; and the result, we are told, was that "hundreds of students loved her as a kind mother, [even while they] respected her as a strict teacher." [38]

The way Julia Mateer succeeded in getting what she called a hold on the boys seems particularly interesting. As the students saw it, she punished wrongdoers according to well-understood principles (*li*), causing each "clearly to understand his error." She also presented lessons in religion "as if these were worldly stories," arousing laughter and interest.

Mostly, however, she strove to create a personal bond between herself and each young pupil. In the first week of the school year she would learn the multiple new names and kinfolk connections. At daily sick call, or more often in dormitory room visits, she would then go on gradually drawing them out, gently and with good humor. She had a large stock of stories about Western heroes who had been homesick boys, and about native customs in her own Chi-lieh hsien (Mount Gilead, Ohio). The visitations paid off, as she saw it, when a boy began to talk more than she did, asking questions and giving opinions on whatever was on his mind.[39]

The *Alumni History* remembered Julia Mateer as "unique

among women," as did many of her missionary acquaintances. Although ill for much of her later life, she is said to have remained a person "whose simple presence [was] a stimulus and an elevation." One alumnus's way of explaining this was that "*Fu-jen's* [Mrs. Mateer's] teaching was accomplished through graciousness (*i hui*), and without the anxiety of constraints she transformed all the students . . . Her loving sincerity flowed out in the way she spoke, and in the expression on her face." As an American put it, "The impression made was this—if ever I were in great trouble I should like to have Mrs. Mateer with me." [40]

One is sometimes inclined to go along with the standard missionary explanation that the Mateers were born teachers. But Julia's efforts did not come to much before Calvin's interest picked up, and Calvin did not succeed with many boys who had not first been drawn out by his wife. Perhaps the truest picture is that suggested by Calvin's brother Robert Mateer, who thought Julia and Calvin brought out the best in each other, and lacking children of their own, that their school ultimately brought out what was best in both. [41]

The impression reported of the Mateers as a team was in any case that they "personally attended to all matters of educating and nurturing, [to a degree] unsurpassed even by the care given by parents to their own children." With much truth Mrs. Mateer could write, as she did in the early 1880s, that the pupils were "entirely under our control." She qualified this, however, by adding "while in school." Both she and her husband had learned to avoid the appearance of alienating boys from their real parents; the lesson here was that their program had little chance where a patron family was opposed, suspicious, or not fully informed. This was why fathers were invited for discussions of up to six hours in length, and why Julia believed "a visit to the mother gives me a hold on the boy such as nothing else can." [42]

The Mateers were able to make all this work, one gathers, largely because they enjoyed what they were doing, enough to spend a great deal of time cultivating a few not very imposing people. They enjoyed it more, of course, as the students responded, fertilizing their proposition "that every child [has] something good, and should have a fair opportunity to develop the best possible." [43]

The key to molding was again to show the boys that they were cared for, as individuals and on more than a transitory basis. For some thirty years the Mateers devoted themselves to backing this up. They educated the students and helped them to marry, find jobs, and move on to better ones. In smaller ways, as by visits, emotional speeches by Calvin, and birthday presents from Julia, they expressed their gratitude for what the boys meant to them.

The teacher-student relationship was thus one of growing mutual appreciation, both of achievement and of personal worth. Growing with this was a very subjective kind of loyalty on each side. To Calvin Mateer his senior students were by definition "choice men." To them, one gathers from the *Alumni History*, he was not just an Old Tiger but also the sort of person suggested by his *tzu* (Chinese style name), which was Tung-ming (Light-in-the-East). Mrs. Mateer similarly changed qualitatively at some point in a boy's experience. The difference here is suggested by the contrast between the mother hen picture and a *pien*, or tablet, presented on her sixtieth birthday (1898). The alumni at that point honored her as *yü ying shou mu*, translated as Aged Mother Who Nurtures Eminent Sons—but meaning specifically that "she could recognize talent in the bud and bring it to maturity." [44]

This sort of relationship obviously took many years to develop fully. The requisite good feeling, however, was already clearly apparent by 1877.

To inculcate vital religious consciousness, a Christian school in China also had to convince its students that its positive sort of spirituality comprised a better and truer value system than what prevailed in the surrounding society. This was facilitated to an extent by the semi-isolation of the Tengchow School, but mostly it depended on the character and general impressiveness of those in charge—or as Chinese say, on the ability of the Christian teachers to unify theory with action, and by moral influence to draw others to identify with them. This is what the Mateers were essentially trying to accomplish, and from available evidence it seems they succeeded. In only three years from 1874, wrote Julia ("a little like boasting"), almost the entire student body had been drawn to accept their system as a whole. [45]

The system's indoctrination aspects had been significantly reorganized. In 1874 the student body was pruned, partly by attrition and partly on purpose, so that for the first time a majority (fourteen out of twenty-two) of the boys on hand were at least baptized. The Confucian teachers were separated from their traditional function of moral guidance; instead they were paradoxically reduced to resident specialists in a type of knowledge that was useful, but foreign to the school's real orientation. Moral science was taught entirely by the two Westerners. These classes were all by lecture and question-and-answer, maximizing the teachers' personalities and thoughtful relation to individual students. The students also met with them at least once daily, twice on Wednesday, and four times on Sunday, for worship, addresses, and further religious discussion.[46]

The ultimate step, as with dormitory discipline, was when religious motivation was developed enough to be institutionalized downward, into the hands of the students themselves. This had several effects. It established religious activism as a prestige area complementary to scholarship, and it put comformist pressure on non-Christian outsiders. It also led some young men into Christian activism as a life work. This program became established in 1876— long before the YMCA era—with the school's Evangelization Society (Ch'uan-tao hui). The society was voluntary (*tzu-yüan*) and reportedly student-organized, "out of gratitude for the illumination of the gospel, and for solid learning from the West." Members evangelized nonmembers in the dormitory, worked off campus on Sundays, and pledged to continue contributing "propagation money" in later life. According to the Ch'uan-tao hui's records, all the students soon joined, although Mrs. Mateer reported early in 1877 that ten of thirty-one boarders were still not professed Christians. She was delighted nonetheless, because the society made "the whole moral tone of the school . . . higher than ever before." [47]

At the end of 1876 the Mateers discovered somewhat to their surprise that they had been overtaken by success. Their corrective measures had not followed from any master plan, but had been piecemeal responses to lessons learned both inside the school and out. It was already apparent, however, that at least three young men had mastered everything Calvin Mateer could presently offer. Each had also been under Christian molding for over ten years, and all seemed ready "for the Master's use, and to trust Him to appoint them to their places." [48]

Calvin Mateer accordingly made plans to hold the school's first graduation exercises. Students, parents, and local foreigners were invited to attend a two-day commencement in February 1877. On the first evening ten outstanding students waged a literary contest; dividing into two teams, they orated, debated, and read essays composed in Mandarin and *wen-li*. The second evening was devoted to speeches by the three graduates, plus one by the principal.

To those in attendance this whole event was very impressive. The student body reportedly "saw distinctly that there is a definite goal before them, and their ambition was stirred." Charles Mills said

Chou Li-wen's address on "Progress the True Law of Living" was the "most scholarly speech I ever heard in the Chinese language." Martha Crawford wrote that Calvin Mateer excelled himself in his own speech, and even T. P. Crawford felt "peculiarly gratified." Crawford's gratification seems to have been peculiarly tied to the superiority, in his view, of the Mateer debates to a similar event just staged in Pastor Wu Tswun Chao's school.[49]

From this point the three graduates went on to reasonably successful careers. As the school's first fruits, however, they remained all their lives especially important to the Mateers. All three wanted to be ministers, for example, but Calvin Mateer guided them in another direction because he believed the church had "more call for teachers than for preachers at present." Li Ping-i, the valedictorian, thus went to teach mathematics at Martha Crawford's Baptist school, and then at village day schools in P'ingtu chou. He did not take theological training until the late 1880s, after which he served as a pastor in Shou-kuang, Lo-an, and Ch'ang-lo districts. Sometime after 1900 he retired to organize a family merchant firm, remaining active as a lay Christian.

Li Shan-ch'ing, the second graduate, similarly began with a small day school and later evangelized. With Mateer's help he then studied Western medicine with various missionary doctors. He practiced in a number of places, most notably as a surgeon in a Tsingtao hospital; but more often he did his operating in country apothecaries owned by himself. When last heard from around 1910, Li Shan-ch'ing was village doctor and druggist at Lan-ti, in P'ingtu.

Mateer kept his favorite, Chou Li-wen, for himself. Chou taught chemistry for a while at Martha Crawford's, but mostly he instructed for the Mateers and helped Mr. Mateer write books. It was Chou who finally got the Mateer *Arithmetic* to press, and who also did much of the later *Mandarin Lessons* and an algebra text. Eventually he became a ministerial student and for a short time pastor at Lu-chia-ch'iu, P'ingtu. As preacher, teacher, and scholar in two worlds, he was a man after Calvin Mateer's own heart.[50]

Apart from the promise they envisioned in the graduates, both Mateers took pride at the end of 1876 in another young man named Hsing Tao-ming. Hsing had been one of the original six little boys of 1864, and one of three from that group to complete the original six-year curriculum. His father had then taken him back to Chai-li, to work on the family farm and to get rid of his Christian inclinations. Tao-ming's filiality "sorely grieved" the Mateers, but Julia wrote that she was continuing to pray for him. After six and a half years he suddenly reappeared at Tengchow, the first boy ever to run away toward the school. Hsing graduated in 1881 and spent the rest of his life on "hardtack and turnips" as an itinerant evangelist in central Shantung.[51]

To Julia Mateer Hsing Tao-ming's return was a particularly gratifying conclusion to the first chapter in the school's story. She had done her first and hardest work on him and his six-year class-mate Li Shih-kuang, who was another of the original Chai-li boys. They had followed parallel courses of apostasy under parental pressure, and Li Shih-kuang had long since "gone dreadfully to the bad." By her kind of arithmetic, Hsing and Wang Ch'un-ling at the Presbyterian Press added up to some kind of vindication of all the 1864 fumbling.

As part of graduation the school adopted the rather fancy Chinese name Wen hui-kuan (Literary Guild Hall). More prosaically, the institution's Western status improved too, from a boys' boarding school to Tengchow High School. In typical style Charles Mills added that it was really a college, and that "all other missionaries in China" agreed it was "decidedly the best school in China." Less effusively, Julia wrote that after "a long and wearisome road . . . success has been granted to us." [52]

The 1877 Conference: Success Defended

The first General Conference of Protestant Missionaries, held at Shanghai in May 1877 has already been noted as an organizational milestone in the China missions story. It was also an important event in individual missionary lives such as those of T. P. Crawford and, even more significantly, Calvin Mateer. The idea of holding such a conference grew up in the mid-1870s, simultaneously with Mateer's work at Tengchow. The two developments were in fact connected, and they influenced each other in an important way.

The relationship here was partly coincidental. Because of denominational and regional jealousies, Protestant work implying union had to begin casually, as in chats at a joint gathering place. In the late 1860s the Chefoo–Tengchow area bloomed as a summer watering spot for missionaries, and as resident hosts the local Presbyterians were in a strategic position. Sooner than most of their contemporaries, they seem to have perceived the usefulness of cooperation. Two of the local group—Mateer and John Nevius— took the lead in creating a structure for it.

Nevius always had a proclivity for mobilizing things. He brought up the conference idea as host to his church's China Synod of 1874, just as he had proposed forming the synod itself in 1869. Chefoo vacationers from other denominations were sounded out and tentatively enlisted. Two more summers, numerous circulars, and three planning committees followed. Nevius led things for a year and then brought in Calvin Mateer in his place. Mateer was also an organizing type, and he pushed the project vigorously at a lengthy planning session in 1875. He then served on a total of six conference committees and had a hand in everything from steamer arrangements to speaker selection. Afterwards, his Presbyterian Press contacts made him a natural coeditorial choice for the conference's published *Records*.[53]

Reading the corpus of Calvin Mateer's 1877 General Conference statements, one is struck by his sensitivity to what was going on. He came to Shanghai fresh from his school's first graduation, whose timing, like his whole relation to the conference, does not seem accidental. The speech he made in Shanghai, which has been described as part of a valiant defense of educational work generally, was really a defense of the Tengchow School.[54] By the time the conference met, he needed the conference—or something like it— to save the school, and in a sense to save himself as well.

Mateer's feelings about his school added up at this point to more than mere satisfaction. In 1876 he gave up his personal journal, which he had been painstakingly keeping for over twenty years. He said he was too busy for it. More accurately, one suspects, he no longer needed it. The journal had been part of a long effort to understand himself and his work, and he had found the answers he was looking for. In his particular game Mateer had touched all the bases: he had done "more itinerating than any man in the [Shantung] mission," he thought, and he had worked with all the conventional convert types. After years of frustration he was pleased in a very personal way by his first success; or as he said years afterwards about his 1877 graduates, "However others may regard them, they are very precious to Mrs. Mateer and myself."[55]

This was the point, then, where calling and experience came together for Calvin Mateer. It had taken him forty years, including thirteen in China, to reach it.

Paradoxically, however, Mateer's kind of work was being specifically disavowed by almost everyone else. For many years in China—or from 1838, the year W. H. Medhurst wrote a special plea for schoolmaster missionaries—there had been significant opposition to missionary schoolmastering. In part, it has been suggested, this had social roots in America and Europe, where a great change had occurred in public attitudes toward education; it had become a responsibility of the state, that is, and was secular work.[56] In China, particularly after 1860, missionaries were also preoccupied with schemes for evangelizing the interior. In this context schools appeared to be a diversion, or an adjunct of doubtful utility.

The general attitude toward education was reflected by the lack of attention given to it in the *Chinese Recorder*, the professional journal of Protestant missionaries to China. In this most important forum "Only two articles on education appeared . . . between its first publication (May, 1868) and the General Conference . . . and both of these were in the first volume. The series of reports of the development of mission work appearing in each issue of the *Chinese Recorder* in 1876–1877 invariably fell into three divisions: evangelistic, literary, and medical. When education was mentioned at all, it was usually in connection with evangelistic work." [57]

Such schools as still survived, insofar as boys and men were concerned, were mostly training schools for missionary assistants. For girls there were "Sunday School every day" institutions. D. Z. Sheffield, a pioneer Congregationalist educator, summed up his denomination's attitude in a typical 1877 comment: "The American Board after an experience of fifty years, had considerably modified its position in regard to educational work, now making but sparing appropriations for the support of secular schools . . . It had been found that men simply taught in Western science were harder to be reached by the Gospel than the heathen." [58]

Mateer and the Tengchow School were thus caught by a sort of undertow just as they got their heads above water. As early as 1874 he was protesting against his own home board's disparaging of schools and defending his station's competence to assign its work priorities on a local basis. For three years he argued the case in letters, petitions, and talks with visiting board officials. He emphasized his and his wife's "great labor and pains," their thrift, and the promise they saw in individual boys. By 1877 he could claim, with Charles Mills's backing, that the school was the strong point of their mission work. Not only was it *"in some important particulars* different from any other boarding schools," but its "relative importance . . . to our work is greater than in any other of the stations in China." [59]

In the matter of finances, the nub of the issue, Calvin Mateer did all he could to reduce his school's burden—and dependence— on the Board of Foreign Missions. By initiating partial charges he was able to keep annual per-pupil maintenance within a fifty-dollar limitation for over twenty years. More important, he collected a considerable sum in America outside board channels. He did this by using what he called the mainspring of Christian benevolence, which was "sympathy excited by knowledge—most of all by particular and special knowledge." He communicated knowledge of the Tengchow School to former seminary classmates, now home pastors, and to similar friends of Charles Mills and of the Reverend Edward Capp, a new missionary who had married Maggie Brown. By 1876 some fifty American churches were receiving annual letters, either in Mateer's hand or off a small lithographic press he had brought from Shanghai.[60]

Response to these appeals came in the form of subscriptions by Sunday school classes. The program was especially successful in attracting support for individual pupils, whose needs could be documented with names and poignant anecdotes—"poor little heathen Sam" stories, as Martha Crawford once called them. In Calvin Mateer's first graduating class only Li Ping-i was maintained by the home board; Chou Li-wen and Li Shan-ch'ing were "owned and supported" by Sunday schools in Buffalo and Philadelphia respectively.[61]

This system had several limitations. At Tengchow, Mateer noted, "So many boys necessarily fail in one way or another, that it is rather a dangerous plan to give them to a particular church." Open scholarships, while wiser investments, were less emotionally compelling. Also, it was not so much for individual boys as for the institution itself that money was now needed—for new equipment and buildings—and here further difficulties arose. As school principal, Mateer wanted money that he could spend at his own discretion; but in soliciting for particular schools rather than particular boys, he was in a sense soliciting for himself, or for a personal project whose merit was not as fully established in other people's eyes as in his own. As early as 1873 certain more conventional missionaries began to complain, as they heard of his promoting, while discretionary contributions were disappointingly small.[62]

The school thus remained dependent on the board. The BFM was sympathetic; but considering Mateer's extra income from private sources, it declined to exempt him from its policy of uniform educational reductions. These reductions culminated in a 25 percent cut in 1876, despite pleas by Mateer that "this school be made an exception." By 1877 the Tengchow School had reached a financial impasse, just as it appeared otherwise ready for a takeoff. It had, Mateer thought, been made a "scapegoat for reduction," when "to go backward now is to throw away the labor of years." To keep open the kind of school he wanted would "compel the sending away of half the scholars," and rather than that "it would be better for some of us [missionaries] to go home." He did not exclude himself here. Speaking of his own future, he had written, "The work cannot afford to lose the individual enthusiasm which a man only feels when he is doing his work in his own way." [63]

The Shanghai Conference was Calvin Mateer's opportunity to get a hearing, to explain his work to his colleagues and enlist support. He thus prepared an address on "The Relation of Protestant Missions to Education," to demonstrate that there were actually strong natural affinities. He intended "not to exalt education as *the one* great means of christianizing China, but simply to show its great importance, and claim for it its legitimate place." [64]

In the first of this speech's three sections Mateer sought to justify schools on general grounds. Among a number of analogies, mission work was compared most pointedly with military strategy of the type recently successful in the American Civil War. The point was that numbers were not really decisive. The key was to cut the enemy off from his resources, while organizing one's own to best advantage. Preaching might be the infantry of mission work, but education was its human commissariat, and a necessity for what was seen by Mateer as a war of attrition on the traditional Chinese establishment. Schools were needed to erode the opposition's morale and to provide a competent native officer corps.

The standard objections to education—that it was unscriptural and diversionary—Mateer believed to be ill founded. If the apostles did not teach science, neither did they run Sunday schools nor seminaries. Since they had miraculous powers, they "used the means which God put in their hands, and were governed by the times and circumstances in which they lived." Modern missionaries could not work miracles, but in the "reconstructed science of the nineteenth century" they had a workable substitute.

More important, missionaries should simply take a broader view of their job. They were already engaged in "planning and consulting for the temporalities of their converts." This should be extended to planning "great good both physically and socially" by using "all the means which are in any way either directly or indirectly adapted." Putting this another way, "In a word it means to give to the whole world all the blessings which Christianity has to bestow . . . I argue hence that Protestant missionaries are not only authorized to open schools for the teaching of science, but that Providence calls them to do so."

In the second section of Mateer's speech these arguments were applied to the specific case of China. No matter what missionaries might do, contact with the West would cause the Chinese Empire to undergo a great transformation. In part this could be "a good thing in itself"; but Christian schools were again essential, not just to expedite modernizing, but to identify Christianity with the process. If the church did not take the lead here, Mateer believed, it would be menaced by "attacks of educated skepticism." These Chinese attacks would be harder to handle than the present superstitions, because Chinese veneration for learning was deeper than superstition and would prove more enduring. A new anti-Christianity would emanate from new schools, in fact from *"all schools which are not expressly Christian schools."* Chinese Humes, Voltaires, and Renans would "certainly be reproduced" in these institutions, and on a day "not so distant as might be supposed."

Christian schools, on the other hand, could make the native Church self-reliant and prepare it intellectually for all challenges. All children of Christian families should receive schooling; the imperative, however, was to train leaders, particularly "an effective and reliable native ministry." Only thorough educating could produce such people and give them the resources and prestige to confront both future skeptics and present "Confucian magnates."

The final part of the speech was a description of the best kinds of Christian schools. Best of all was the kind with the most comprehensive curriculum, including religion, Western science, and Chinese studies. Schools "whose prime aim is to give Christian instruction" were in Mateer's opinion defective in principle. Christian instruction should be communicated by moral influence, in the missionary teacher's relation with individual students. It followed from this that the long-term boarding school was the kind most needed. The program described here was one aimed primarily at producing adult leaders; if properly molded, such individuals would have an impact "impossible to tabulate in the form of statistics." This was Mateer's idea of where Chinese Protestantism was most deficient. It was also his personal line of work, and the remedy he prescribed was his own Tengchow program. To those who questioned his limited number of products, he maintained that "the men who are needed cannot be made to order, nor raised up in a day. Educating is a gradual process, and time must be given to work it out." [65]

The conference's reaction to Mateer's message, judging from the *Records,* was negative. Of six missionaries who offered judgments only two approved, and one of these did so with qualifications. Other commentators were not very enthusiastic or professed to have "long since lost all faith in science as a converting power." One man believed that the "convictions of this body of missionaries" differed greatly from Mateer's, and another reaffirmed that "the missionary as such has something better to do." [66]

Off the conference floor, however, a small undercurrent moved in another direction. Five men with educational interests, reportedly encouraged by Mateer, joined him in securing approval for a permanent School and Textbook Series Committee. As explained by Mateer, many reputed educational failures stemmed from the available teaching materials, which amounted to a "careless hash." [67] Suitable books—described in terms suggestive of his own *Arithmetic*—could turn secular learning into a revolutionary tool, and "which way it cuts depends entirely on who has hold of the hilt." Since the committee's members would do most of this work, raising funds "the best way they could," books were also an inoffensive approach to the controversial larger issue. [68]

As things turned out, the textbook committee was one of the conference's most important achievements. Between 1877 and 1890 it published over a hundred books, maps, and charts, with sales (30,000 volumes) dispelling financial shakiness. The committee's activities, in one modern writer's opinion, "successfully turned the tide for Christian education in China." [69] In any case students in mission schools tripled, from around six thousand to almost seventeen thousand by 1890; and the textbook committee became sufficiently established to be succeeded by an "Educational Association of China." The EAC, organized in 1890, consisted of teaching missionaries who wanted to "expand and widen" the textbook committee's work considerably. [70]

The textbook committee also institutionalized Calvin Mateer's prominence at the 1877 conference. He did not do as much work for the committee as did its editor, John Fryer, or its permanent secretary, Alexander Williamson. He did write several of its most successful books; and equally important, his committee connection turned him into a publicist and stimulated him to write educational articles in Chinese as well as English. [71] As for the Tengchow School and its financial difficulties, its principal's conference and committee work—perhaps helped by the "specially noted" sympathies of American Sunday schools—apparently won the school an exceptional status after all. The Presbyterian Board of Foreign Missions gave the Tengchow program enough money to go forward, and after 1877 to expand.

Displaying shrewdness, energy, and tact, Mateer thus helped himself while contributing to an important wider development.

The Protestant missionary community in China by no means embraced schoolwork unanimously in the 1880s, and "educationalists" remained a minority. Such people grew rapidly in numbers and influence, however, as did the missionary community generally. For them schoolwork was a convenience at least as much as it was a cause; schools were places where they could serve apprenticeships, learn the language, and often—particularly with regard to women missionaries—do work they had done at home. As more people shared in educational experiences, many found as Mateer had that these were two-way propositions, and more holds like Mateer's were formed, or emotional links between schools and students and individual missionaries. Educational organization, initiated by Calvin Mateer really in self-defense, was simply the step that began bringing these commitments together. Implicit in this was a kind of specialization in China missions work, the germ of a new teaching profession within the old one of full-time evangelism.

The extent to which Calvin Mateer (or anyone else specifically) led all this is hard to measure and could easily be exaggerated. It seems accurate to say that Mateer was a working, organizing prototype for a new movement. More than any of his contemporaries, he was also its prophet. The points underscored in his conference speech—the importance of an informed native ministry, of liberal Christian education, of giving China "all the blessings which Christianity has to bestow"—became basic concerns of the next two missionary generations. His address was the first significant public expression of such ideas. Rejected by the evangelical temper of the moment, it took the lid off, in a sense, for a much larger group of people who a few years later would be speaking and working for the same things.

Life at the Wen hui-kuan, 1881–1904: The Mateer Program

Two years after the 1877 conference the Mateers came home, their first furlough in sixteen years in China. Julia needed rest physically, and Calvin had work to do in America. He traveled extensively, speaking to his supporting churches and studying developments in the academic subjects he taught. When not otherwise busy, he did a good deal of trading on the reputation he had established. His new literary work, and the growth of the school (temporarily entrusted to a friend from Peking) meant he needed a full-time assistant. Helped by his first honorary doctorate and by testimonials from Charles Mills, Hunter Corbett, W. A. P. Martin, and others, he also suggested that the BFM promote the school to college status.[72]

These requests were resubmitted as a mission petition when the Mateers returned to Tengchow in January 1881. The next year both requests were granted; the Reverend Watson Hayes arrived for training as Calvin Mateer's helper, and the Boys' High School became officially Tengchow College. It would be a year or two before Hayes was fully qualified, but the name change had immediate uses. "This is an age of pretentious titles," Dr. Mateer observed, "and if any enterprise is to succeed it must at least claim to be all that it is." He believed Tengchow's balanced curriculum, particularly the science courses, gave it a "higher standard of scholarship than any similar [Christian] school in China." The new title reinforced the claim. More to the point, it gave him leverage in asking for money from the board and from "christian men of wealth" cultivated on furlough.[73]

In a number of respects the takeoff anticipated for the school in 1877 took place now, in the two years following Calvin Mateer's return to China. He was in effect president of the first Christian college in that country, and in Watson Hayes he had a man who became, as the students put it, his left and right hands.[74] In addition he had extensive new plans and increased security, which together enabled him to expand and further rationalize his operation. The most important specific innovation was the institution of a regular course of study, or uniform curriculum, in 1881. Specific courses did not change significantly; but by adding more teachers (three Tengchow graduates) it became possible for the first time to offer each course every year. The result, Mrs. Mateer wrote, was a program equivalent to the ordinary college curriculum in America. Within a year Calvin Mateer also saw higher student motivation due to the new element of predictability.[75]

The uniform curriculum was further useful in securing "the largest and best class" of students. Mateer ran off Chinese copies on his lithograph machine, with short explanations of what science and college had to offer. Missionaries and Chinese Christians distributed these over a wide area. Combined with the reputation the school already had, and its increased Christian constituency, the new promoting ended recruiting problems. By the spring of 1882 enrollment was up to seventy. At that point the Mateers cut it off, perceiving that "more are likely to want to come than we can possibly receive." [76]

To handle admissions Mateer devised a series of entrance examinations based on the school's courses. The tests took a month to take, including placement interviews. The six-year college course was actually the Higher Department (*cheng-chai*) of what were administratively two schools, the lower being Julia Mateer's five-year preparatory department (*pei-chai*). Promising boys who were younger or academically deficient could enter any preparatory grade; except in special cases, however, everyone was supposed to take the full upper course, which was defined as a three-year middle school followed by higher school (*kao-teng hsüeh-t'ang*). In modern American terms it meant something like high school followed by junior college.[77]

By the end of 1882 Calvin Mateer could see a "distinct advance all along the line." The students, who now came mostly from the west—meaning Wei-hsien, in the central part of the province—had almost doubled in two years. In quality and motivation Mateer thought them the best he had ever had, for which he credited a tightened grading system as well as the uniform curriculum. Eight more young men had graduated, making a total of fourteen, and all but one were teaching in Christian schools. Alumni were in fact teaching all but the highest branches of Western studies at Tengchow too. Two neighboring houses had been purchased for school use, and a third was about to be added.[78]

All these improvements put the school on a much stronger footing for carrying out its mission. As advertised in recruiting, this was to train human talent completely (*tsao-chiu jen-ts'ai*), and to cultivate "morality and scholarship, in that order."[79] In English Mateer expressed it more precisely, in line with his position at the 1877 conference: the college existed to train choice men for Christian leadership. Its program for achieving this, summarized in a celebrated 1890 formula, remained substantially unchanged from 1881 on—"first, by educating thoroughly; second, by educating in the Chinese language; and third, by educating under strong religious influences."[80]

By thoroughness Mateer meant the opposite of the "entirely vicious" approach of schools that were "too exclusively religious." His position was that "it takes more than religious teaching" to raise Christians able to "outshine" those who would oppose them. He stressed, for example, the need for geography, with its "enlightening and liberalizing effect," and for history of all kinds. The idea was to show citizens of China "what has been and is now her real position," in a framework of "moral lessons and interesting episodes."[81]

The Wen hui-kuan offered four such courses. Mrs. Mateer taught introductory geography to preparatory boys. College students took a year each of Chinese history and world history, and finally, for graduating seniors, there was a course in political economy (*fu-kuo ts'e,* literally "plan for enriching the nation").

Otherwise students debated and wrote papers on these subjects, as the library accumulated helpful books. In terms of the total curriculum, formal instruction in social science was clearly rather limited.

Calvin Mateer blamed this deficiency on the unavailability of suitable textbooks. But in mathematics and science he considered the college second to no school in China, and it was in these fields that its reputation was primarily made. All graduates after the mid-eighties had at least a year in algebra, geometry ·(two years), trigonometry, and calculus, plus surveying and navigation. In the sciences they took chemistry, physiology, astronomy, geology, and three years of physics. Lack of texts here was offset by Mateer's, and later Watson Hayes's, ability to write or improvise their own.[82]

The heavy load of mathematics and science, like all courses at Tengchow, was required for everyone. Unusual—and for some years unique—in a missionary school, this program was a keystone of the Mateer strategy. It produced some men who could be called scientists, and others who used scientific training as a springboard into other professions. Calvin Mateer spoke often of careers of general usefulness. These were by-products, however, not primary objects of his program. What he most wanted were Christian community developers—ministers and schoolmasters—who would use science as he did, as a tool for making an impression, gaining face, and "witnessing" to more important truths.[83]

The fact that he required so much science went with his maxim "The only thing that commands respect is thorough scholarship." There was also another, more important, reason. Like most of his Western contemporaries, Mateer observed around him a "mental and moral stupor, which holds the Chinese mind in its embrace." But as a teacher he was also impressed by the way his own boys had taken to brain-energizing courses. He attributed the disparity between the Chinese mind and theirs to the Confucian educational tradition, a "wretched system" that was "as destitute of ideas as a jellyfish is of bones." On account of Confucianism the typical Chinese remained "like a donkey, with eyes hooded and head tied fast to the centre of the mill he is compelled to turn . . . as he stupidly and patiently trudges round and round the same old track." Mathematics and science, in large doses, were devices to lift the donkey's hood, to "develop the mental faculties symmetrically and stimulate men to think and act for themselves."[84]

Science was thus taught in a comprehensive framework. Geology field trips, astronomical observations, physics experiments, and lessons in watch repair were various approaches to fostering "faculties of reasoning and analysis." Along the way, in the early 1880s, Mateer and the students also put together what he called the largest and best assorted collection in China of laboratory apparatus.[85] He loved this kind of work in an applied, hobbyist sense, and he was good at it. He never gave it his primary allegiance, however, and he did not mean for his students to do so.

The Tengchow application of Calvin Mateer's second guiding principle, education in the Chinese language, was first of all an old-fashioned classical course. Graduates had memorized the canonical Four Books and Five Classics in their entirety, and additionally they had studied the appropriate commentaries, written expositions, and composed odes according to the traditional Chinese methods.[86]

Since all this was very time-consuming, Chinese studies actually dominated the curriculum in terms of hours. There seems to be a paradox here, in view of Mateer's opinion of what the classics had to say. He thought they were at best "a sort of moral-political economy"; otherwise they were "a mighty aggregation of trifles . . . an elaborate collection of rhetorical old saws woven into a labyrinth of transcendental nonsense." [87] Nor was he interested in producing government officials or even degree holders. Of his first eighteen graduates, all but one had passed the qualifying *hsien-k'ao* "with much credit" by 1885. Julia Mateer noted approvingly, however, that "No one has, after leaving school, followed up the course of study necessary to get a government degree. They have little relish for it, and they all say 'Classical composition loses all its relish to one who knows science and the true religion.' " [88]

Her husband's first point here, as with science, was simply that if something were worth doing it should be done thoroughly. Within limits, namely the *hsien-k'ao,* a classical program was worthwhile as advertising. More important, the whole Chinese atmosphere demanded that his graduates be knowledgeable in the literature that had shaped their civilization. Mateer often compared this with the heavy dosage of Greek and Latin at his own Jefferson College. He had not liked those texts either, and he remembered them as "incomparably more heathen than the Chinese classics." He had applied himself to them because he would not otherwise have become, or been recognized as, an educated man. To him the Chinese analogy was obvious and much more compelling.[89]

He further saw some real benefits in the Chinese study technique. He believed strongly in memorizing as a self-disciplinary device. He also believed that ability to read and write well was the foundation of all education, and only people who had "familiarity with the best models" seemed to possess such ability anywhere. In this sense the Confucianists were correct again, in thinking that the people most familiar were those who knew the models by heart.[90]

Literary ability was itself important because there was a pressing need for literate Chinese Christians. Calvin Mateer learned at first hand that translations and writings by foreigners, or through interpreters, "always result in the loss of much . . . original vigor and vividness." The writers required were educated natives, with a true feeling for style in their own language.

At the Wen hui-kuan it was believed that Christian Chinese writers had a unique historical role to play. Mateer saw mass literacy ahead as part of modernizing, and with it a new, utilitarian literature based on Mandarin. "It scarcely needs a prophet's vision," he wrote in 1896, "to foresee that it will ultimately displace the Wen-li, being itself greatly enriched and elevated in the process."[91] Versed on the one hand in "express[ing] inanities elegantly," the college's graduates would be trained on the other to "stress having something to express." By 1896 students at the school had been paraphrasing, composing, and debating in Mandarin, in conjunction with their classical studies, for more than twenty years.

Education in the Chinese language, like science, was thus very thorough at Tengchow. Conceptually, Mateer attributed an indivisible strategic importance to the two curricula. Western learning would change China, but it would have to be filtered through the Chinese language, and in the process both would assume new shapes. His aim was to give to Christianity men who fully understood both and who could consequently help shape the encounter. In their learning process the men themselves would be molded for the task, by balanced emphasis on analytical thought and mental discipline.

Calvin Mateer never doubted that such people could be evangelically Christian. His program was designed not only to eliminate relish for Confucianism, but to show that rationalism by no means had to follow from scientific knowledge. His personal example at the top embodied the idea that science, like history, was "in fact but an exposition of the unwritten laws of God." If properly taught in a godly context science would be so assimilated and used to God's service in China.[92]

The program thus rested, when all was said and done, on its third ingredient, strong religious influences. The school never existed "simply to bring about conversion"; but neither was its aim ever "simply to teach so many things." Its main goals were character development and "the inspiring of a high and generous purpose." There was nothing particularly inspirational, Mateer felt, in scholarly thoroughness; it had to be complemented by a strong spiritual message, to make the point that scholarship, while essential, was not all-sufficient.[93]

Formal Christian indoctrination—the most obvious means to this end—took place chiefly in the preparatory department, a practice facilitated by the fact that after 1880 most entrants came from Christian homes. In the college only six of fifty-six courses were specifically religious, and all were interpretive. Numerous religious regulations (*li-pai t'iao-kuei*), however, supported proper intellectual apprehension. From the mid-1870s to 1900 Calvin Mateer conducted daily devotionals and preached on Wednesday nights and Sundays; students were additionally required to attend three different Sunday school classes and nightly prayer meetings led by student monitors.[94]

Several voluntary religious organizations, which all grew out of the 1876 Evangelization Society, were also important Christianizing devices. Christian Endeavor (Mien-li hui), founded in 1883, held weekly meetings for Bible study, hymn singing, and exchanging of Christian experiences (*hsiang-yü kuan-mo*). A Foreign Missionary Society (Tsan-yang fu-yin hui) was organized in 1885 to plan evangelization of other Chinese provinces; one early campaign raised some sixty dollars to support such activity. The YMCA (Ch'ing-nien hui), arriving in 1895, absorbed these older groups, added new projects, and put members in touch with Christian students elsewhere.[95]

Of at least equal importance in building character and high purpose were the college's austere atmosphere and demand for sheer hard work. Plain food and clothing, earthen floors, and mud-brick *k'ang* were school rules. Each of a student's courses featured daily "catechizing" or written tests, plus monthly and final exams. Mathematics and laboratory work in particular were presented as struggles for survival; the Tengchow boy who got help from others here, as Watson Hayes put it, would in later years "fail or break down in the presence of danger or money." Emphasis throughout was on doing things *hsün-hsü* (step by step), punctuated by relentless testing and very minimal time off. For many years students had only a month's vacation in the summer, a few days between terms (Chinese New Year), and Christmas Day, with a maximum of an hour and a half's free time on weekdays and two hours on Saturday.[96]

The purpose of all this was to establish a "controlling moral force" that would develop "strong, manly, self-reliant Christian Chinamen." To additionally develop "pushing along" qualities—

aggressiveness, efficiency, and general executive ability—the school had what amounted to a leadership training program.[97] The monitor system, where each monitor submitted a weekly log (*ts'e-pu*) of his activities, was one element. Mostly, however, leadership was cultivated in student organizations. The school's three debating societies (Pien-lun hui) were by far the most important of these. Beginning in 1867, the Saturday debates had by the early eighties become the high point of the school week, and commencement contests, set off by singing, chanting, and red-silk diplomas, were the peak of excitement for the whole year. Teachers sometimes made "suggestions from the side"; but student voting determined debate winners, and the whole operation was run according to parliamentary procedure by elected student officers. The *Alumni History* describes the debate as a *pu k'o pu li* (indispensable) part of the college program—popular, exciting, and a "solid testing ground" for nurturing a "spirit of self-government and independence." [98]

Because the debating societies "trained in republican characteristics," the alumni thought, meetings were occasionally enlivened by official visits. The first of these apparently occurred in 1885, from Tengchow's chief military mandarin.[99] Although the debates and other activities were consistently cleared as "advantageous to learning and morality," a certain tension always existed because of Calvin Mateer's misgivings regarding both the imperial government and foreign secular designs on China. In a context of "evolution, not revolution" the college increasingly encouraged students to think about their country and "her real position," and to develop "managerial talents for the nation's future position of independence." The eventual result, according to a 1904 graduate, was something approaching the ferment of ideas (*feng-ch'ao*) that visiting officials seemed to fear.[100]

This kind of atmosphere is first noticeable around 1895, when various stimulants coincided. In that year, following the war with Japan, Watson Hayes established a Current Events Club (Hsin-wen hui); this activity stressed library research and analytical thinking to complement the rather abstract and sophistic skills developed in debating.[101] National consciousness was further strengthened by Calvin Mateer's stress on Mandarin use and, surprisingly, by Julia's musical work. Her Introduction to Music course (*Yueh-fa ch'i-meng*) was aimed chiefly at enlarging "the joy of childhood," but students both in and out of the course were also involved in gathering songs for a projected Mandarin collection. The Chinese needed such indigenous anthems, she wrote in

1896, for their inevitable future wars; and in any event "so great a people is entitled to its own style of music, if only it has in it the spirit of life and growth." [102]

The extent to which the Tengchow College may have been a revolutionary institution should not be exaggerated. It did, however, produce graduates like Wang I-ch'eng ('99), who died in battle for the 1911 revolution, and Feng Chih-ch'ien ('98), who contributed to the *Alumni History* a 1908 song advocating "shaking the Western [nations'] heavens and turning their world into an endless bloody sea." [103] Even the Christian educational and ministerial work into which most of the graduates went were seen by Calvin Mateer and by the graduates themselves as instruments of radical change in China; just as these men learned from Mateer to reject the ethos of "being, not doing" of the Chinese literati, they absorbed his injunctions against the new temptation of becoming "lackeys of the foreigners" in the treaty-port business world.[104] In its stated purpose of producing idealistic, self-sacrificing individuals who would give their lives to building a progressive Christian China the Tengchow program was a considerable success; its flaw, perhaps, was that it could not anticipate how quickly China's needs would outgrow its stated "evolution, not revolution" approach, and how puny its limited number of graduates would seem in the confusion of twentieth-century events.

9 / *The Missionary as Entrepreneur*

Despite the proliferation of molding devices, Calvin Mateer always felt that the school's success depended ultimately on himself. The devices were extensions, not alternatives, to the individual "ministerial character" in charge of things, and only "faithful and able preaching" could keep these lines open. Furthermore, it was up to him to establish a proper image of the "temperature of Christian life."[1] Christianity in action, the harmonizing of heart and mind, had to be visibly embodied in the man at the top.

During the Tengchow College years, from 1881 to 1904, Mateer embodied dynamic action in quite a few directions. All his activities originated at the school or in daily life at Tengchow, but some of them took him rather far afield. As he told the 1877 conference, expansion of a missionary's roles was one index to how well he was doing. Combining his experiences with his abundant energy, he expanded into scientific, literary, and organizational roles. From age forty-five to his death at seventy-one, he operated as a sort of many-sided virtuoso. The effect of all this, his friend Hunter Corbett said, was to impress himself not only on his students, but on nearly everyone who came into his orbit.[2]

Science, Literature, and Pushing the Organization

As a scientist Mateer was really a master mechanic. He grew up with a talent for tinkering, and life in China led him to capitalize on it. "Philosophical apparatus," or laboratory equipment for the college's science courses, was either unavailable or too expensive. Presuming he could "teach himself anything from books and working at it," he made an air pump in the early 1870s. This was quickly followed by devices to demonstrate gases and electricity. By 1897 he could claim "more than twice as much [apparatus] as Jefferson had when we graduated, two thirds of it made on the ground at my own expense."[3]

191

Mateer's laboratory machines are enumerated in five pages in the *Alumni History*.[4] Things he could not make he secured by promoting, which became a sizable activity in itself. Cyrus Field, for instance—whom he met by chance on his first furlough—gave the school its electric generator. An observatory, traditional prestige item of the denominational college, was furnished by patrons in New York and Philadelphia. Mateer always handled such "peculiar associations" aggressively but with great discretion, a little like seductions ("They must be cultivated, and their interest worked up"). In return his "Uncle Johns" facilitated expansions, paid overdue bills, and made possible a bigger budget than the Board of Foreign Missions could ever have afforded.[5]

Apart from major items he was "ready to do anything" on his own. Life in Tengchow gave him plenty of opportunities. In the early years, in addition to his own house, Mateer built everything from false teeth to coffins for fellow missionaries. By 1886 he had "quite a complete workshop," consisting of several side houses organized into a *chih-tsao so,* or manufactory. On the bottom floor of the main building were his personal laboratory and the shop proper, which included machinery for "turning, blacksmithing, plumbing, screw-cutting, burnishing, electroplating, casting, and so forth." Above were painting and storage rooms, and all around were sheds where "every conceivable amount of space" was organized and used.[6]

The workshop was a kind of microcosm of Calvin Mateer's personality; it harnessed his energy, or his abhorrence for inactivity, to his mind, which thought "naturally in terms of logic and mathematics." [7] It was his way of resting, and it was also a continuing education of much practical use. Furloughs were extensions of the same attitude. On his first two he toured locomotive factories, sketched industrial exhibits, and took cram courses in medicine and dentistry. He spent a month, for example, in Machinery Hall at the 1893 Chicago World's Fair. Hunter Corbett found him there "making drawings, measurements, and so forth, of the most complex machinery. He seemed to understand everything as though this had been the work of his life." [8] Books, notes, and drawings were filed for teaching or writing, or for periods (which were frequent) when the station lacked a doctor. On his last furlough, in Siberia in 1902, he was finally called upon to fix a locomotive.[9]

Most of Mateer's projects had as much to do with human relations as with physical necessity. He continued to run *i-yeh* programs to give vocational training to selected older converts and college dropouts, the idea being "to get the Chinese Christians started" by teaching them "such arts and trades as are connected with modern science." [10] Mateer and his shop foremen produced an unknown number of blacksmiths, machinists, and electricians, plus men trained in brass and ironwork, electrotyping and plating, watchmaking, telegraphy and photography. He reportedly "had no patience with that kind of education that simply trained the Chinese to become 'lackeys of the foreigners.' How his lips would curl as he muttered that phrase! He would waste money often in trying to help some one to assertive, manly work in independent lines, rather than as an employee." [11] He thus would not train carpenters but would help machinist trainees secure lathes, textile looms and presses, and once "an outfit for a flouring mill." [12]

Calvin Mateer also had a definite flair for "demonstration effect," which was combining advertising with good works. He used this in various ways on many people. Letters to "practical minded" benefactors were loaded with impressive scientific jargon. He swapped physics problems with W. A. P. Martin, and they reviewed each other's textbooks in the *Chinese Recorder*. The noted reform advocate Timothy Richard credited his own unusual career largely to working with Mateer as a young man; Richard became interested in an educational approach to the Chinese higher classes, he said, while assisting Mateer in the 1870s in scientific demonstrations before Tengchow officials and examination candidates.

Once Mateer pumped out a flooded coal mine, and after 1900 he made apparatus on commission for the Chinese government's provincial college. For the lower classes he fixed eyeglasses and bicycles and treated toothaches, burns, broken legs, and cholera. With Cyrus Field's generator the Tengchow School got the city's first electric lights, and with money made from his *Mandarin Lessons*, the missionary established a "wonders of science" museum. The museum's stuffed animals, model railroad, and "shocking machine" survived him and reportedly drew twelve thousand visitors in 1909. [13]

Outside his college connection, however, Calvin Mateer made his greatest mark in literary work. In some ways this seems anomalous. He never really relished writing as much as he did mechanics, and he was neither a linguist nor an artist by inclination, at least not in the usual sense. His chief talents were that he could write as he thought—with clarity, organization, and a pithy succinctness—and that he developed a number of ideas worth writing about. Beyond that he simply worked hard.

Mateer's writings reflect his growth, from itinerating to teaching to an immense variety of projects. His first effort was a sheet tract in 1870, called *Yeh-su wei shei* ("Who Is Jesus?"). While running the Presbyterian Press he did more tracts and a pamphlet on infant baptism *(Hai-tzu shou-hsi li lun)*. Back in Tengchow he finished his first real book in 1875, a catechetical Genesis *(Ch'uang-shih-chi wen-ta)* in one hundred and ninety-one leaves. The *Nevius-Mateer Hymnal*, first published in 1877, was the only one of these early religious writings that was very successful or even widely circulated. It was also mostly John Nevius's work, and by the time it appeared Mateer was engrossed with his school.[14]

His educational books document his increasing experience and ambitions as a teacher. The *Arithmetic*, published concurrently with the *Hymnal*, was reviewed in 1879 by W. A. P. Martin as a real advance in its field, and as in most respects a model for the new textbook committee.[15] This no doubt gratified Mateer, because furnishing a model was one of his intentions. In a separate *Chinese Recorder* article he had already discussed and recommended his book's approach. Whatever success it would have, he felt, stemmed primarily from his own working contact with the subject. He had learned that "in China as elsewhere the majority of students are mediocre," and that missionary teachers tended to "refute" rather than teach. To close the gap here he stressed precise terminology and presentations oriented to Chinese usages. Texts should be comprehensive but plainly written, as a rule in Mandarin, and they should make some attempt to be interesting. To this end he endorsed pictures, contrasting type styles, and "puzzles and curious questions, or remarkable facts and phenomena in nature."[16]

The *Arithmetic* met these criteria, or at least it sold by "tens of thousands" for over forty years. Mateer became a specialist in mathematics texts, eventually doing three more that won usage. He chose this field because it was basic and because he had an aptitude for figuring. He also disliked the prevailing texts. Such books were mostly translations credited to Alexander Wylie, the great missionary linguist, and to John Fryer, who translated for the Chinese government at Shanghai. Dr. Wylie, or so W. A. P. Martin once said, had been a fine sinologue but not much of a mathematician; and Fryer's idea of an algebra book, Julia Mateer observed, was to translate an article from the *Encyclopedia Britannica*. Calvin Mateer thought both men's math books "too elaborate and got up in too expensive a style," all about methods and principles "but having no practical problems, and neither intended nor fitted" for school use.[17]

Mateer's *New Geometry in Chinese*, published in 1885, lived up to its title, although it was neither as original nor as chattily Chinese as his *Arithmetic*. Like Alexander Wylie, he based the *Geometry* on Euclid. But where Wylie's comparable book simply continued an earlier translation from the Greek, Mateer added algebraic shortcuts, simplified examples, and modifications to Euclid from three modern texts. He also wrote in a plainer style. The term he introduced for geometry (*hsing-hsüeh,* form study) was greeted enthusiastically by Martin and his colleagues at the government's T'ung-wen school in Peking.[18] Mateer's last two books, an elementary and an advanced *Algebra,* were likewise based on current Western texts. The second of these two works did not appear in print until 1908, after many revisions in draft over a twenty-year period.[19]

As he worked through the higher branches Mateer's handling of mathematics thus changed somewhat. He moved away from the *Arithmetic*'s repetitious style, and from its lowest-common-denominator orientation to China. His concept of the purpose of his series (plus the nature of geometry and algebra as subjects) led him to increased imitation of foreign works, condensed to outline (*pei-chih*) format. Having started the student with everyday problems in Chinese life, Mateer aimed to draw him into the broader world suggested by symbolic mathematics. The technique's efficacy, he felt, was attested to by his own students. They had not only mastered this "species of universal language," but they advised him not to "change or garble" it in his books. Anything else, they said, would be patronizing and fraudulent.[20]

Mateer's approach to higher math, and his insistence on Mandarin, led him into other fields by way of arguments with fellow text writers. John Fryer, for one, advocated Chinese numerals instead of Arabic, and Chinese expressions (including a number invented by Alexander Wylie and himself) for fractions, signs and symbols, and other items Mateer thought universal.[21] W. A. P. Martin, speaking for a sizable group, objected to Calvin Mateer's "low kind of Mandarin" as an offense to "the taste of the educated classes." [22] Fryer's position started Mateer on a twenty-year search for a usable scientific vocabulary in Chinese. Hostility to the use of Mandarin stung him first into issuing a *wen-li* edition of his *Arithmetic,* and then to a general campaign on behalf of colloquial Chinese.

Both nomenclature and Mandarin became large projects. Mateer worked on terminology with Watson Hayes, D. Z. Sheffield, and a few others at first, and from 1893 to 1908 under auspices of the Educational Association of China. The pertinent committees divided and changed names several times, Mateer supervising all along and receiving chief credit for the final product. Whether the terms became standard ones, as was confidently expected in 1910, is a project-size question itself. *Technical Terms in English and Chinese* did, however, gather together and systematically label twelve thousand items, or "briefly the whole range of scientific and general terminology." [23]

The other side of this effort, or making China intelligible to Westerners, is represented by the *Mandarin Lessons*. Like the *Technical Terms,* the *Lessons* took twenty years to write and drew on contributions from many people. More than the *Technical Terms,* the Mandarin book was also a uniquely personal lifetime work. It began, really, with Calvin Mateer's initial difficulties with spoken Chinese, which he solved only by years of itinerant preaching. To help his sister-in-law he got together "three lessons for Maggie" in 1867. As he learned more himself, and at the urging of Charles Mills and others, he drew up other lessons, and by 1873 he had "quite an extensive plan." [24]

From 1873 the book was a fixed goal, and after 1881 a large project. Chou Li-wen spent four years entirely occupied with it, and Julia and various others helped considerably.[25] Published in 1892, the *Lessons* was an immediate success. For some thirty years it remained the starting point for most English-speaking arrivals in north China. To Calvin Mateer personally it brought a measure of both fame and fortune.

Apart from longevity and bulk (six pounds), Mateer's language book was also a notable scholarly achievement. Like science texts, its writing demanded continuous defining, in this case of the subject itself. He was first struck in the early 1870s, while working at the Presbyterian Press, by the *kuan-hua* commonalities in spoken Chinese from the Yangtze north. This was the rather vague basis on which he began trying to figure out for himself what Mandarin was. His main problem throughout, as he wrote in 1873, was classifying—or distinguishing widespread colloquialisms from localisms, and then steering a middle course between "the Scylla of *Wen-li* . . . and the Charybdis of *Su-hwa* [low colloquial]." He was consistently patronized, if not exactly opposed, by the best missionary linguists and by classically oriented Chinese tutors. As one of his Chinese assistants describes it, "Westerners who saw him so worn and wearied would laugh with derision. But when the book was completed and printed, and circulating like the very winds, both foreigners and Chinese were surprised. *Hsien-sheng* took a quiet satisfaction [in that]." [26]

The product here was an interesting combination of bi-cultural labor, largely by correspondence, with personal editing and on-the-spot research. Except for Julia Mateer and two old friends, John Wherry and Chauncey Goodrich, Western assistance came from younger missionaries scattered all over north China. It apparently took most of the 1880s to assemble a network, with Chinese counterparts, that had adequate competence and enthusiasm. Dr. and Mrs. Mateer took the *Lessons* draft down the Grand Canal, and then up the Yangtze River, in 1889, making final checks themselves. The book was reviewed before publication—separately and several times each—by Chinese and Western informants in Peking, Nanking, Kiukiang, and Tsinan. The final draft incorporated extensive revisions, variations, and Sound Tables for areas as far west as Chungking.[27]

Mateer had two main teaching goals in the *Lessons*. The first was to provide a true conversational approach to the Chinese language, to give "even ladies whose time is limited" a good spoken command. To this end each of the 200 lessons was organized around one or a few common idioms. Vocabulary included folk maxims, "pithy book expressions" (from *wen-li*), and such exclamations, insults, and witticisms "as are presentable in print." It was assumed that an individual tutor would guide each student's pronunciation, and that the student would commence conversing "as soon as you can put two words together." [28]

The course could thus be strictly oral, but it was assumed again that most students would try to become literate. Here Mateer aimed at a second and more ambitious goal, which was to sell "enriched, corrected, and dignified" colloquial Chinese to new missionaries as a literary medium. To this end he himself "scarcely composed a single sentence" of the thousands in the last one hundred and seventy lessons. The sentences were models chosen from "all extant Mandarin literature," or made to order by Chinese teachers. To ensure that examples were "truly Chinese in thought, style, and idiom," he left the teachers "to their own spontaneous judgment, *never in any case controlling or overruling them.*" Chou Li-wen added a separate Chinese introduction asking tutors to cooperate.[29]

One large reason for the book's success was undoubtedly its timeliness. Between 1890 and 1898 the Protestant missionary body in China almost doubled (1296 to 2458), and it increased another 65 percent, to 4059, by 1908.[30] At the same time the tempo of events in China quickened considerably. The *Lessons*'s conversational, idiomatic, and thoroughly organized approach made it an expeditious device to get the new foreigners communicating. Second, the text came from life itself, from "as wide a range as possible of words and ideas . . . of domestic, social, literary, and official life; of art, science, commerce, business, history and religion." In this sense, as Calvin Mateer hoped, it served as a primer in "useful information about China and the Chinese people." [31]

In retrospect the *Mandarin Lessons* seems to have been a middle stage, between the old haphazard method of Chinese language study and the streamlined institute approach. After numerous revisions and abridgments the book died of old age in the 1920s, left behind by the new literary style it had tried to anticipate, and by changes in the social and political scene on which its readings were based. As an influence on a generation of Westerners in China, and as a linguistic adventure, the *Lessons* remains a remarkable document.

Calvin Mateer's last big effort, his New Testament translation work, kept him busy from the end of the *Mandarin Lessons* until just before his death in 1908. Elected head of this project by the 1890 General Conference, he felt providentially called to it, and that all his earlier work had been intended as preparation. In typical style he spent several years orienting himself to the job, recruiting coworkers, and trying various approaches to overall goals. By his estimate he gave the translation an aggregate seven years before its completion in 1906. Work was divided among a number of participants, who concentrated on their own areas and also checked the translations of all others; of sixteen revision committee members, however, only Mateer and Chauncey Goodrich served throughout, and the finished work was primarily theirs.[32]

According to Wang Yüan-te, his chief assistant, Mateer had two main goals in doing the Testament. One of these, "agreement with original texts," is obvious and traditional—to convey the Bible with integrity, or as Calvin Mateer put it, not as "what the writers would have said if they had been Chinese, but [as] what they actually did say." The second goal, which Wang calls *kuanhua chih t'ung-hsing*, meant not only to make the Bible intelligible in Mandarin but to spread everywhere (among Chinese Christians) a literary model, just as Mateer was doing among missionaries with the *Mandarin Lessons*.[33] Linguistic, cultural, and denominational differences made it very difficult to achieve even integrity and intelligibility. Given the literacy level of the contemporary Chinese church, the educational additive was ambitious indeed.

In working on the Testament Mateer fused principles drawn from his other experiences. As in the *Lessons*, he searched for the most telling phrases, colloquial rather than formal. The test of each colloquialism, or "how far a given phrase does prevail," was supplied by his heterogeneous collection of assistants. In translating emotions, qualities, and difficult key terms, he operated by a method rather different from the one he had used in scientific nomenclature. This was to go back to the "very highest and rarest *wen-li*," for dignity and precision, in place of ambiguous or overly colorful compounds. Five common compounds expressing "love," for instance, were rejected for the single character *ai*—just as *chi-ho* and *kou-ku hsüeh* had been thrown out in favor of *hsing-hsüeh* as terms for geometry. Finally, the whole work was rationalized on the concept developed in the mathematics series. The time had come, Mateer thought, to write the Bible in plain but not patronizing language; as he quoted a Christian acquaintance, "Do you suppose that we Chinese cannot understand and appreciate a metaphor?" [34]

Mateer translated from the Greek, but his model was obviously the King James Version. The Bible, that is, should be in the people's language, but if properly translated it would set them an ideal in beauty as well as truth. With so many ambitions the Mandarin Revision, like all other Chinese Bibles, failed to satisfy everyone, and by 1920 it had already been re-revised. It remained, so Kenneth Latourette wrote in 1929, the most noteworthy achievement of all the post-1890 union revision efforts. The tone achieved, and devotion involved, is poignantly suggested by Wang Yüan-te's epitaph to Calvin Mateer in the *Alumni History*: even better than the King James Version, the citation here (II Timothy 4:7–8) evokes the end of "the good fight" (*pi mei hao chih chan-cheng*) that Wang and Mateer had fought together.[35]

Calvin Mateer's literary career seems more impressive than his mechanical work for several reasons. Not only was its reach much wider, but the labor involved—given his aptitudes—was much greater. The final balance of this work, which sometimes in retrospect seems almost blueprinted, came from his ability to learn and grow from one level to another. Moreover, in a somewhat more difficult area, he was still able to apply his craftsman's knack for economy, of making even waste or failure useful. A total of nine unfinished books, including texts in calculus, electricity, electroplating, mechanical drawing, experimental chemistry and physics, and homiletics, were copied and carried off as teaching guides by Tengchow College graduates.[36] A "colossal" Goodrich-Mateer dictionary project similarly died, on Mateer's part, as a cubic foot of manuscript. But from this came much of the *Mandarin Lessons* vocabulary and a primer, *Analysis of 2118 Characters (Fen tzu lüeh chieh)*. Dr. Goodrich's by-product, his famous *Pocket Dictionary*, is still in print.[37]

Also, Mateer eventually achieved an unusual appreciation not only of Chinese, but of the subtlety of language and of language's influence on thought. Language to him was communication—action, not theorizing or study for its own sake—just as science boiled down to building machines. His enthusiasm for the colloquial, and all his scholarship, were accordingly pragmatic. At the same time all his work was clearly idealistic, almost painfully so. Each stage—from the math books through the New Testament translation—represents an effort to get across some personal vision of the author, as teacher, preacher, or democratic observer. Working all these concerns into Chinese, he found, raised questions almost as fast as it solved them.

An interesting example of this is his nomenclature method, which was largely modeled on the Linnaean system used in biology. Mateer's idea was to fix unchanging facts—in faith as well as science—in a sort of one-character Chinese amber, classical or invented, above transient vernacularisms. This worked beautifully in chemistry, where known elements could be tagged without regard to anything but logic and clarity. His system for matching elemental compounds with linguistic ones was called (by a fellow Westerner) "without doubt the most rational and consistent that has yet been devised . . . in Chinese."

When he applied this to Bible translation, however, Mateer discovered something like the development that according to legend drove the original Linnaeus insane. In struggling for matching expressions of spiritual truth he experienced, as Linnaeus did in botany, the intimation that when species (or cultures) are crossed the result suggests mutability and formlessness rather than fixity and precision. Unlike Linnaeus, Calvin Mateer could believe in his own case that "the peculiarly Chinese methods of presenting the truth" would someday be discovered by Chinese Christian linguists. His last word on the subject, in a posthumously published article, was that "There are limitations to every man's knowledge of truth and language. Every man's vision is distorted in some of its aspects. This is a lesson we have been learning day by day, and are still learning. If any man wishes to find out his limitations in these respects, let him join a translating committee."[38]

Finally, it should be mentioned that Mateer's language work seems to have put him at the center of the development of Mandarin as a respectable field of Western scholarship. The prevailing missionary language approach, formed on the China coast, had always stressed good *wen-li* Bibles complemented by secondary translations in regional vernaculars. As the Yangtze valley, and north China after 1860, opened to evangelism, a literature developed in Mandarin. By the 1870s a community of talented missionary linguists had emerged, centered on Peking and Shanghai. Its members undertook numerous roles, still in a framework of *wen-li* for respectability and colloquial language for tracts and popular Bibles.

As he got into language work Calvin Mateer ran head on into this group of famous names, which Paul Cohen aptly calls the "scholar-elite of the Protestant missionary body in nineteenth-century China." [39] Mateer viewed it rather as a scholar establishment. The members' best literature in Chinese—their efforts in *wen-li*—seemed to him to follow the classical style mostly by stressing form at the expense of content. Thus W. H. Medhurst's Bible (Delegates' Version) was "an approximate success as a literary production" but "a failure as a translation." [40] Scientific and mathematic renditions, whether in *wen-li* or Mandarin, Mateer found typically poorly chosen, too "high," or technically inaccurate. [41]

Mateer's preference for straight presentation in accurate and idiomatic Mandarin brought disagreements with Martin, Fryer, Joseph Edkins, Ernst Faber, John Chalmers, Gilbert Reid, and others of such stature. Rationally, he objected to their style of "apologetic adaptations" in language, science, and theology, or "what I regard as too great a desire to harmonize Chinese with Western ideas." At bottom his position seems largely one of visceral distaste, both for such Westerners and for the specific class of Chinese to which they adapted themselves. They preferred, he felt, to "cater to the pride of Chinese scholars" rather than to live among and deal with "the class of people [God] gives us." [42]

Mateer's literature, like his educational work, was thus tied to some strong personal biases, but its effects were again wider than himself. Finding *wen-li* initially repugnant (and difficult), he "early formed the purpose of becoming an adept in the spoken language." This led him to see the need of a text book. By 1874, with the *Mandarin Lessons* mapped out, he was defining his work—and himself—as distinct from the "literary missionaries" model. In the same year, and again at the 1877 conference, he associated himself with Chauncey Goodrich to promote Mandarin. Shortly thereafter he began corresponding with Frederick William Baller, whose *Mandarin Primer* first appeared in 1878. The group sought out in the 1880s for help with the *Lessons* continued, on the whole, as the successive membership of the New Testament Revision Committee, with Goodrich and Baller repeating as Mateer's chief collaborators.[43]

The post-1890 missionary generation learned its Chinese largely from books by these men. The *Mandarin Lessons* and Goodrich's *Pocket Dictionary* (along with Herbert Giles's massive dictionary) appeared in 1891–92—just in time to be very useful, but obviously based on years of work. The Mandarin Revision Committee, forming at that point, was the first such body to be dominated by proven Mandarin specialists rather than by classicists or "easy *wen-li*" practitioners. The specialists moreover spent sixteen years at the task, which must have made earlier attempts by Medhurst and the Reverend Griffith John, and by the "Peking Committee" of the 1860s, seem like comparative rush jobs.

A very modern pride, or perhaps *ressentiment,* is easily discernible in revision committee statements. Calvin Mateer liked to stress that his group was writing for the people, in *"their own spoken* language," thus honoring a "cardinal principle of Protestantism." Mateer himself, wrote one member, was proof that a great linguist need not be a great classicist. The committee's work was widely publicized and debated among missionaries, and gradually it was accepted as a more difficult and substantial piece of work than any of the *wen-li* versions. Its completion interestingly coincided with China's abolition of the official examination system, which had been the last prop to *wen-li* as a living language.[44]

Mateer's Bible revising, which involved diplomacy almost as much as translation, suggests a third major area of activity. His mechanical and literary careers, as described above, began as personal avocations and grew to enterprises involving many people. His theories on writing and education were moreover advanced against significant opposition. Given his independence, multiple ambitions, and limitation to a seventeen-hour working day, his biggest job— as he put it—was "pushing the organization." He was able to do this with remarkable success, to the extent that he stands out in retrospect as more an executive than anything else. Or to be more accurate, it is only when one sees him as a kind of entrepreneur that he appears as the sum of his preaching, teaching, writing, and machine-making parts.

Calvin Mateer's organization consisted of anyone, Western or Chinese, who crossed his path, seemed useful, and allowed himself to be drawn in. Like all his work this began at Tengchow, where his missionary associates and perhaps (at any given time) a hundred Chinese formed a captive cadre. Applying what Chauncey Goodrich called his "facile princeps" touch, Mateer spent twenty-five years mobilizing things locally, followed by twenty more operating on a broader scale. The first period was spent getting his ideas straight, initiating lines of work, and training others to take over in each. In the last two decades the local enterprise largely ran itself, leaving him free to write and promote.

Most of this structure, and the projects involved, have been discussed. By the mid-1880s Watson Hayes, assisted by Julia Mateer, was carrying the greatest load at the school. Calvin Mateer continued to teach moral science and some physics, but otherwise his role was reduced to key molding areas—preaching, counseling, and job hunting for seniors. The manufactory was run for many years by Ting Li-huang, a talented machinist and *i-yeh* graduate. Chou Li-wen, and later Wang Yüan-te, supervised literary helpers, who were drawn from diverse backgrounds and tended to turn over frequently.

Both manufacturing and literary research broke down into smaller project groups. Chemical apparatus, for example, was considered a special work, as was Mandarin Bible revision. The idea, however, was to do as many things as possible simultaneously, and this led inevitably to doubling (or more) the work of key people. This is strongly apparent first in the 1880s, when the manufactory got into full operation, and as the *Mandarin Lessons*, the dictionary, and a half dozen textbooks proceeded concurrently. To all appearances the pace never slackened, and both Julia Mateer and Chou Li-wen are said to have worked themselves literally to death at it.[45]

As had been planned, teaching at the college passed largely into Chinese hands. This had of course always been true in *Han-wen*, or Chinese classical studies. Of seventeen such teachers between 1877 and 1904, thirteen held degrees, including one *chü-jen* (provincial degree) scholar from Huang-hsien. Only two of the seventeen were Wen Hui-kuan graduates, and only one other was a Christian. That man, Yü Hsi-chin, was a *fu-sheng* licentiate from Lai-chou and apparently functioned as a sort of *Han-wen* dean. One of the two Tengchow College graduates, Chung Wei-i ('85), seems also to have been the only Tengchow alumnus ever to get beyond the *hsien-k'ao* and achieve full *hsiu-ts'ai* (first degree) status.[46]

The Western studies *(Hsi-hsüeh)* faculty was entirely different. Of twenty instructors (1877-1904) all were Wen hui-kuan graduates. Judging from their subsequent careers, they were prize prospects of successive classes. Chou Li-wen was the first, and except for a brief ministerial tour he never left Tengchow. Chu Feng-tan ('86) similarly stayed, to do research and teaching in chemistry. All the others served limited tenures and moved on, mostly to colleges elsewhere. Seven taught after 1900 at the government college in Tsinan, and one each went to St. John's College and to Peking and Shansi Universities. Wang Hsi-en ('93) was for many years a noted mathematics teacher at Cheeloo University, and Yüan Yüeh-chün ('90) became a leader in the Shantung church. Ting Li-mei ('92), as the most famous Chinese evangelist of the twentieth century, achieved an almost mystic stature among Christians.[47]

The faculty as a whole was not large. There were never more than ten teachers, including Calvin Mateer, at any one time, and administration consisted of a bursar and a janitor. Faculty turnover was rapid partly for reasons of health. Several *Hsi-hsüeh* teachers died prematurely, and those in *Han-wen* were specifically hired as needy local scholars of advanced age. All but four of the classicists were listed as deceased in 1912.[48]

The Western studies instructors, however, turned over chiefly by design, their appointments being rather like teaching assistantships. Mateer typically retained one outstanding graduate per class for two or three years each. The individual would teach and do advanced study in science, or else join a literary project. Those with inspirational qualities, like Chou Li-wen and Ting Li-mei, also worked extensively with student organizations. By the time each man left, Mateer had usually found him a strategic position elsewhere.

Placement was of course crucial to the whole Tengchow College scheme, and to some extent every graduate received career guidance. Calvin Mateer's personal ties were closest to members of the earlier classes who had gone into teaching and preaching. He followed and helped a number of these men for more than twenty years; the alumni in turn scouted out positions to which Mateer guided later graduates. Alumni contacts—family, teaching, and ministerial—also helped supply the college with promising new students.

Chiefly because of Calvin Mateer's relative interests and influence, he guided the teaching graduates most closely. His strategy here from around 1895 was first to work as many people as possible into the new intellectual life developing in government schools. If enough staunch Christians could be so implanted, he felt, Christianity could "control China, socially, politically, and religiously." [49] At the time of this rather extravagant statement (1899),

Mateer was convinced that China was changing overnight, from "dead and stagnant" to "life and motion"; he had twelve men at the imperial universities in Peking and Nanking, and (according to one report) an offer repeated from year to year from Viceroy Li Hung-chang for all the teachers he could produce. This was also shortly before Watson Hayes left, at Governor Yüan Shih-k'ai's invitation, to become first president of the Shantung government college at Tsinan.

Parallel to this Mateer pursued his longtime policy of building up separate Christian schools. He sent teachers to all the Protestant colleges and to most of the better known mission middle schools in north China. Almost all teaching graduates, and many in ministerial or other work, taught at some point in community Christian primary schools. As the Chinese government put its own educational reform programs into effect after 1900, the attentions of Mateer and other missionary educators were further drawn from hopes of general control to building and protecting Christian schools.[50]

The present point is that among late nineteenth-century missionary educators, Mateer had a large jump on the field. As the demand increased in the 1880s and 1890s for teachers, particularly in science, he controlled a limited but well-known source. His teaching graduates were both advertisements and an intelligence system, supplying information on government as well as missionary school developments. No graduate of any other college, it might be noted, ever taught for Calvin Mateer.[51]

His school's eminence and his personal pushing proclivities had a continued broadening effect on Mateer's educational and other organizational activities. Against still significant opposition, he was instrumental in founding the Educational Association of China in 1890. He was elected its first president and chairman of the publication committee, which carried on the association's most important activity. He also served a term as vice-president and continued on numerous committees until his death.[52]

Apart from his EAC work, Mateer served on a total of nine committees at the 1890 and 1907 general conferences. During this period he also pushed a variety of cooperative projects in Shantung and headed the New Testament revision. He seems to have been a sort of pioneer organizer of cooperative programs—playing things mostly by ear, but with an instinctive feel for making his own interests seem identical with those which any reasonable person would choose.

Insofar as he developed techniques here, these are most apparent in his EAC work on scientific nomenclature and in Testament revision. Everyone with an interest was invited to join these efforts. For efficiency's sake, policy and the bulk of the labor were then entrusted to various committees. Mateer controlled all terminology and Mandarin revision as general chairman of each; on higher levels, as at the 1890 Conference and in the EAC, he had an influence on election of key officers. One or another Shantung Presbyterian missionary served regularly, for example, on the EAC's nominating committee, and Mateer was its chairman while Hayes was moving up to the presidency.

The Testament revision story illustrates how Calvin Mateer pushed in areas of special interest. The 1890 General Conference, which established the project, had not even invited him to the relevant preconference discussions. He intruded himself anyway, and at closing time volunteered to write up a report. He describes the next step in a letter of May 26: "As I walked home from the meeting, and revolved in my mind the difficulty of the situation, the idea of an executive committee, to whom the whole work should be entrusted, came across my mind. When I reached my room I sat down, and in a few minutes and without consultation with anyone, wrote out the plan, which without essential modification was subsequently adopted. It seemed to strike all parties very favorably. On the second day of the conference two large, representative committees were appointed by the conference, one on Mandarin and one on Wen-li. I was a member of both these committees." [53] Elected chairman of the Mandarin group, he quickly resigned from the *Wen-li* body. Writing John Nevius, a fellow committeeman, he said, "I never even dreamed . . . that I should take any prominent part in the matter of Bible translation." To the American Bible Society (which would publish the product), he wrote, "I have never done anything in which I felt more the guiding hand of God than in drawing up and carrying through this plan." [54]

All this indicates is that Mateer could believe several things at once. Despite contrary protestations, he clearly wanted from the first to head what he thought would be the Chinese King James Version, just as he clearly aspired to be a kind of Chinese Linnaeus. His executive committees, for which he became rather famous in missionary circles, always turned over rapidly and boiled down to himself and two or three friends. His rivals—like John Fryer in scientific terminology—tended to assume "uncooperative" stances and eliminate themselves. Mateer thus received credit— as well as supplying probably the most work and best ideas—for two projects of unprecedented labor and sophistication. [55]

Viewed as a whole, Calvin Mateer's organization can be seen as a loose corporation, a military unit (his own sometime analogy), or even as a game played on several levels. His many interests and activities developed independently over long periods of time, each project leading into several others, with the whole visibly joined only by himself at the top. By the 1890s several hundred people were working with or under him, in a very rational Christian enterprise involving the leader's prestige, promotion of his ideas and protégés, and a considerable amount of money.

The money part should be appreciated but not misinterpreted. Mateer was always a personification of the Protestant ethic idea, living austerely and reinvesting everything in people or projects. To operate as he did, however, he needed and made a good deal by missionary standards. Put simply, he earned enough from his manufactory, textbooks, and private supporters in America to make up for losses at the school, to pay for a variety of nonprofit interests, and generally to live and work as he pleased. Though no real records seem to exist on this, there are numerous remarks about a sizable (or "modest," "substantial," "large," etc.) income coming in from patrons in America, from apparatus sales, and from the *Arithmetic* and *Mandarin Lessons*. Out of this he personally paid employees, constructed buildings, supported lower schools ("feeders"), underwrote Chinese Christian conferences and business ventures, and on occasion paid back or went without his annual salary from the BFM.[56]

His Tengchow base, as ought to be obvious, supplied him with human as well as financial resources. Apart from Julia Mateer, Watson Hayes, and a handful of transients, the base was entirely Chinese. In modern parlance Mateer dealt paternalistically with these people, and perhaps in modern terms he qualifies as an exploiter. His Wen hui-kuan professors earned a maximum of nine dollars monthly in the early 1890s, and craftsmen in the shop about six dollars (25¢ per diem). On the other hand the organization had lifted almost all from farm labor, where, as Julia Mateer computed in east Shantung, each could count on clearing no more than fifteen dollars annually.[57] Calvin Mateer stressed to all that he operated not by "cheap sentiment" but by "carefully-planned schemes for their benefit."[58] The college and the manufactory trained them to do various things, and anyone could leave whenever he wished after graduation. Mateer also went to extensive trouble to help former students and employees set up elsewhere. Individuals like Chou Li-wen and Wang Yüan-te clearly stayed on for reasons other than money.

Apart from appeals to duty, loyalty, or self-interest, Calvin

Mateer made rather an art out of keeping the people he needed satisfied. With Chinese this consisted largely of flattery, public demonstrations of concern, and an almost ritualized working etiquette. At the college, for example, there were five rules for management of Chinese teachers. As detailed by Hayes in 1893, these included frequent consultation, avoidance of interference and radical innovation, use of "good and healthful" native techniques, and frequent displays of confidence.[59] Mateer encouraged his literary assistants to write tracts and books on their own, and pushed these through sometimes reluctant mission presses.[60] His renowned memory for biographical minutiae was useful, too, for personal relations as well as in promotional articles for the home church.

His relations with fellow Westerners were not so smooth. Here he had to deal with people who were not as dependent on him as his Chinese associates were, and whose missionary stature was frequently equal or superior to his own. His instinct, as Wang Yüan-te says, was moreover to avoid "debasing" his ideas by compromising them with those of others. To some of these associates—people like Chauncey Goodrich and Hunter Corbett—he was a "royal friend." Watson Hayes, in an overworked sort of way, was the "own dear son" he had never had. At the other extreme were men like Nevius, Fryer, and Gilbert Reid, who were dealt with as threats or abominations of various kinds, and who must have seen him rather differently. In between were most of the non-Chinese people—educators and literary missionaries—with whom Calvin Mateer worked. The impression here seems to have been that he was a reasonable if strong-willed person who returned favors, supplied trained teachers, and knew how to get things done. His ability to execute, and to be tactful when it counted, seems attested to by all his chairmanships.[61]

As a virtuoso, or entrepreneur, Calvin Mateer seems finally to personify the heart-mind unity he preached about. As Dr. Goodrich once observed, Mateer's mathematical mind in a sense endowed him with an artistic approach to life. He had a scientist's instinct for patterns in nature, and an even stronger Calvinist faith that everything he did had some meaning in terms of a pattern for himself. Within this overview he operated wherever his curiosity took him, at the very limits of the possible, but totally pragmatically.

His organization was similarly a many-sided extension of himself, involving all his work and evolving out of years of constant self-education and self-expansion. It was intensely idealistic in its missionary purpose, its promotion of Mandarin among Westerners and Christian Chinese, and its efforts to help people in a variety of ways. The practical aspects, and the ties to Calvin Mateer's personal urges and needs, are equally apparent. His ability to put all these things together indicates a strong psychic balance, or sense of direction, plus a considerable talent for influencing other people.

Three Faces of Ti K'ao-wen

Despite his leadership qualities—perhaps as one of them—Calvin Mateer was always something of an enigma even to those who knew him well. His personality seems simple at times, until one reflects on all the roles he played. As Chauncey Goodrich said, he was "at once conservative, progressive, and original," and the various judgments on him add up to a complicated individual.[62] He seems a very angular person, one who struck everyone strongly but in a manner affected by the type of relationship involved.

Having established himself as an educator, he continued to his death to identify himself primarily with teaching and molding. With much justification he regarded all his other activities as expansions on this base. In this sense his relationship to his students and graduates was the most important he had and an appropriate starting point from which to appraise him.

The story here includes a number of elements. F. W. Baller, a frequent visitor in Tengchow, was impressed by the fear in Mateer's students as they struggled to meet his standards and avoid censure.[63] The school's *Alumni History* attests to his disciplinary vigor, which ranged from "considerable displeasure" to dismissal "without the slightest mercy." [64] The written record, dealing as it does with successful relationships, leaves out the views of failures and "vicious and unmanageable" boys.

On balance, Goodrich thought, Mateer's students "loved him more than they feared him." The dominant theme is that of a strict headmaster and helpful counselor, and the students, like his American acquaintances, seem to have accepted him almost as a combination of two people. One was a brusque, sarcastic Puritan, "such a matter-of-fact man that his best friends often wished that he were less so." The other wept regularly in his weekly sermons and when talking of his mother or deceased former pupils. This was the person who, according to the *Alumni History*, quietly assisted "an incalculable number of church members . . . and unemployed graduates in distress." [65]

Calvin Mateer's Chinese biography puts him together quite comprehensively from the graduates' viewpoint. The reminiscences came from many people and were woven into a narrative by Wang Yüan-te of the class of 1904. Wang, says Goodrich, had been one of the college's best students, a Mandarin specialist with a "keen, incisive, logical mind" and several lucrative offers of postgraduate employment. Drawn largely by Mateer's personality, he stayed as Mateer's literary assistant until the latter's death. Wang adds, "I received *Hsien-sheng*'s nurture from my youth . . . and worked together with him for a long time. I knew *Hsien-sheng*'s conduct (*hsing*) rather fully."[66]

Wang Yüan-te's account is an interesting variation on the traditional Chinese *lieh-chuan* (biographical) form, describing its subject under topical headings in an overall moral context. Some of Mateer's roles, or his distinctively foreign ones, thus come across a little strangely. His workshop efforts, for example, make him from a Tengchow viewpoint "one of the great manufacturers (*chih-tsao chia*) of the modern world." As school principal and entrepreneur he emerges as a *kuan-fu*, or official, and as a teacher of administration. As a preacher he expounded on "vast, deep theories and wonderful ideas," with a voice "as strong and clear as the blowing of the wind, or as the bubbling of a spring." Students and others listened "as though obtaining tokens of rare jade, earnestly giving attention and retaining [his words] throughout their lives." As a Christian missionary he was the Meritorious Founder *(Yüan-hsün)* of the Shantung Presbyterian Church.[67]

From some aspects one would not recognize him as foreign at all. Like many noted scholar-officials, he managed "within the limits of annoying affairs public and private" to write "a pile of books as high as his head (*chu-tso teng-shen*)." Like any good Confucian teacher, he "properly managed" and "constantly cultivated" his disciples*(ti-tzu)*, maintaining personal bonds as the graduates went their separate ways. He was moreover perfectly filial, transmitting his grandfather's wisdom to many adoptive sons and returning to his native place to visit his aged mother (Mateer's explanation to his students of his 1892-93 furlough). His great tragedy was that he was without sons. He did, however, have a wife who "within the home was amenable and attentive, and outside the family unfailingly practiced the four virtues [proper behavior, speech, demeanor, and employment]."[68]

All these elements were complementary parts of a virtue *(te)* transcending cultural distinctions. In becoming a missionary Mateer followed the *tao* (way) of Jesus (and Mencius), by "placing heaven's nobility before that of men." In his scholarly pursuits he exemplified two separate log-cabin myths: he rose from a village school to advanced degrees (a doctorate of divinity and two L.L.D.'s), and to what "one might call a pinnacle of earthly glory." His key trait of *yin-ch'in, erh tzu,* to which Wang Yüan-te mainly attributes his success, translates as identical to the "quality of perseverance" singled out in him by Chauncey Goodrich.

His diligence was properly rewarded by financial success; but as a Christian and upright scholar, says Wang, Calvin Mateer was "stingy with himself and liberal toward others." The "strength of his spirit and learning" would survive in his books, but even more in the "footprints" of his former students at the Wen hui-kuan. "From this," Wang feels, "one can see what sort of teacher *Hsien-sheng* was . . . How could this have been attained if they had not been [so] constantly cultivated?" [69]

Despite a bit of exaggerating, Wang Yüan-te's picture seems more sensitive and sensible than some of Mateer's eulogies in the *Chinese Recorder.* Except for Hayes, Baller, and Goodrich, none of Calvin Mateer's Western associates bothers to explain how, or why, he did so many things; he is rather a kind of supermanager, unique and irreplaceable "in what is getting to be more and more an age of specialists." [70] His daily routine, proceeding from 5:30 prayer to swimming in the sea to manufactory, classroom, and study, emerges mostly as a marvelous ability to cover ground. But to Wang all this is something like *hsiu-shen,* the superior man's ability to cultivate himself comprehensively. As a quality it is both divine and very human: "The painstaking way *Hsien-sheng* did things was a characteristic bestowed by heaven . . . During the day he worked without stopping, and used change of work as his way of resting. For example, he had a time for teaching, a time for translating books, and a time for making [apparatus]. When he was on his way from this to that, he would frequently talk to himself, oblivious to all about him. When I questioned him [about this], he said, 'I am about to undertake a certain thing, and I must prepare myself in advance, to avoid temporary confusion.' In everything he did, *Hsien-sheng* concentrated all his energies. His ears heard nothing else around him, and his eyes noticed nothing else. The dinner bell might ring, but he would not hear. When his niece [Margaret Grier] was in Tengchow, she usually had charge of the bell; but she had to seek him out and pull his beard, or flap his ears. *Hsien-sheng* would then laugh heartily, and they would go arm-in-arm into the dining room." [71]

Personally, Wang Yüan-te saw Mateer from two viewpoints. As a former student, he remembered him as intensely interesting. This was "because he prepared lessons with such detail, and always checked the main points with numerous reference works, back and forth," and because "his voice was moreover loud and clear, and the words he spoke like pearls." As one of a small group of continuing assistants, Wang was also impressed by Mateer's leadership qualities. Included here are his sense of duty, both to his *tao* and to his disciples; his ability to smooth out quarrels; and his looks, which "while imposing, exuded friendliness." Perhaps most important, he "cherished his *tao* with self-respect" but at the same time made his Chinese colleagues (*t'ung-jen*) fellow interpreters of "our *tao*." "Those who have criticized *Hsien-sheng* have called him obstinate (*chih-yao*) and headstrong (*chüeh-chiang*). But when *Hsien-sheng*'s view proved correct he did not put on a pleased look; and when the view of another proved correct he accepted it open-mindedly, his face beaming with a smile. Thus one could not describe *Hsien-sheng* as obstinate or headstrong."[72]

What this seems to illustrate is that to some Chinese associates Calvin Mateer was indeed an attractive exemplar, and that he enjoyed very much playing his *hsien-sheng* role. Our picture of his relationship to non-Christian educated Chinese is quite different. To a degree unusual among scholarly missionaries, his remarks on the ruling and literary classes convey from beginning to end a notable loathing. Consistent with his examination essays ("the mere shell and shadow of learning"), the typical Confucian literatus appears here as a sham, a man "ignorant of the first principles of useful knowledge, yet filled with insufferable conceit in that he knows how to write and define so many of these empirical characters, and can quote glibly the apothegms of the Sages . . . that he knows everything worth knowing when in fact he knows little or nothing, and what he does know is worth little or nothing."[73]

From such long schooling in the art of deception, Mateer tells us, the Confucian "magnate" has a life style amounting to an artistic lie. As local gentry leader, and as head of the affluent extended family, he exemplifies "laziness and vice" plus imbecility. As public official he tends to avarice, inefficiency, and uninstructibility; in fact he basically lacks "public conscience . . . the *sine qua non* of the effective prosecution of any great scheme." [74] With these people Mateer wanted (and received) minimal physical contact.

Calvin Mateer's attitude here suggests several things. For one, it denotes his confinement as an observer to his own particular time and place. More important, probably, one sees a tension always implicit between missionaries and mandarins; and in the intensity of the feelings—the resistance to understanding—one has the other

side of the relationship described by Wang Yüan-te. As rival claim-
ants to moral authority, missionaries and Confucian magnates were
natural competitors. As one specifically a teacher, molding disciples
—and as an organizing *kuan-fu*—Mateer epitomizes the conflicts
involved. His successes with students and other followers, achieved
largely in Chinese terms, in this sense heightened his distinctiveness,
and perhaps his animosity toward his native opposites.

Involved too is a conflict between the ideals of two civiliza-
tions. The Chinese literati life style seems to be what Mateer despises
most; what Max Weber calls their beau geste ideal is to Mateer the
"being, not doing" ethos of a type who "plumes himself on knowing everything worth knowing, while in fact he knows almost
nothing." [75] By Mateer's lights such people can do almost nothing.
Their way of life is a lie because to him its justifying omnicompetence is fraudulent. By contrast he is the Faustian Westerner *par
excellence,* in a nineteenth-century Protestant American manifesta-
tion. Against the Confucian superior man model he poses an acti-
vist, expansive individualism, based on personal faith in another set
of patterns.

The rub here was particularly abrasive on Mateer because in
one important way he was much like the magnates. He identified
personal virtue with comprehensive self-cultivation, just as they
did, and he interpreted personal success as confirmation of his own
world view.[76] By contrast to his own practical-minded versatility
Confucian values were thus a persistent frustration. Despite scientific demonstrations, Mandarin expertise, and *hsien-k'ao* successes by
his students, the Tengchow Vigilance Committee establishment
kept a "compact" against him—or so he believed— for over thirty
years, and not a single boy from an official or really upper-class
home enrolled at his school during that time.[77]

Given the peculiar directness of their competition, it seems
a credit to both Calvin Mateer and the local powers that he did
not, during his final thirty years, get into official trouble. The story
here appears to turn on the Miao Hua-yü affair, but also on another incident that occurred a few years after that. At Chao-yüan,
it will be recalled, he had learned to avoid precipitate action and
confrontations in general; and it was from that period that he
began downplaying more conventional missionary work to concentrate on the school. Before long, however, he was faced with an
official challenge on his new ground. This amounted to the most
serious such encounter in the Tengchow School's history, and Mateer's conduct compares interestingly with his behavior in earlier
times.

214 / *Calvin Wilson Mateer*

The story here, which takes place in 1876, originated in the sort of passionate confusion that one suspects lay behind many anti-Christian incidents. For more than a year bad feelings had been building up out of the 1875 murder of A. R. Margary, an Englishman, in distant Yunnan province, and from the Anglo-Chinese Chefoo Convention of September 1876, which was the murder's diplomatic consequence. Then, in the third week of November, three soldiers of the Tengchow garrison came one day to a house close by the Mateer school. The soldiers thought they were coming to the establishment of one Ho the Pearl, a well-known local madam. Actually, the house had passed into the hands of a respectable family named Li; Mrs. Li was Julia Mateer's amah, and Li Fu-tze, her fifteen-year-old daughter, was a student at Maggie Brown Capp's school for girls.[78]

Undiscouraged by their mistake, the soldiers began chasing young Li Fu-tze around the neighborhood. Jumping over several walls, she fled to the Wen hui-kuan and sought help. What happened next, as described by Ida Pruitt's Ning Lao T'ai-t'ai—another nearby resident—was that "When the students in the boys' school heard the story they went to the Li house and beat the three soldiers and dragged them to the Kuan Yin T'ang by their queues. It was the place of the students in the boys' school to defend the pupils in the girls' school. They were school brothers and sisters for they studied under one master; in one society, the church; and the customs governing family relationships are very binding on those who study under one master and belong to one society."[79]

Calvin Mateer acted as *shuo-ho-ti* (peacemaker), and the soldiers soon got away from the students. One soldier, however, had been tied briefly to a mission tree by his queue, and afterwards he became "so angry that he died of heat in the intestines." His garrison mates, reacting just as loyally as had the students, decided to avenge his death. On the following Sunday afternoon a mob of soldiers—variously estimated from twenty or thirty to one or two hundred—accordingly descended on the Kuan-yin T'ang. Calvin Mateer had gone to a meeting in Chefoo, as it turned out, and in fact nobody at all except "one of the students, to keep watch, and one or two women" was present. The frustrated soldiers beat up the unfortunate watchboy, smashed windows, broke down doors, and generally took the place apart. Then they went to the Li home, where they chased off father Lao Li and beat Mrs. Li over the head until she was unconscious.[80]

When the soldiers had gone T. P. Crawford came over, to protect Julia Mateer and initiate official protests. The Tengchow officials as a group seem actually to have regretted the whole incident; by the time Calvin Mateer returned a few days later, they had already voluntarily paid reparations and punished a number of soldiers.[81] At about the same time, however, the chief officer *(tsung-chen,* brigadier) of the military garrison returned from duties that had kept him, too, out of town recently. The commander was enraged to learn that Christians had "used violence" on his troops, and that the troops were the ones who had wound up being punished. Determined to change things around, he sent messages ordering both Crawford and Mateer to come to his yamen for further questioning.[82]

According to the Tengchow College *Alumni History,* the brigadier had by this point told a number of people that he intended to execute Calvin Mateer. Most of the Presbyterian community urged Mateer not to go near the garrison area, but *"Hsien-sheng* said, 'The right is with us, the wrong in them. I am not afraid to die. [Otherwise] I would be unfaithful to the church.' " So together with Crawford he went at the appointed time, 3:00 P.M. on December 7, 1876.[83]

At the yamen the missionaries found themselves surrounded by many armed soldiers. The brigadier "displayed his awesomeness" by speaking contemptuously to the foreigners from a raised platform, a position signifying that he was interviewing inferiors. To Mateer he said, "So Ti K'ao-wen has come after all!" (*Ti* was Calvin Mateer's Chinese surname, *K'ao-wen* his *ming* or personal name.) To T. P. Crawford he said, *Ni hsing shen-ma,* which under the circumstances roughly translated, "And who are you?" Crawford reacted hotly to this and to a following lecture by the brigadier on *li* or "principles of right." He told the officer that "it was not necessary for him to teach them on that point, [that] they were themselves teachers of *li.*" Then, he later recounted to his wife, he said, "I don't acknowledge the platform on which you sit or your jurisdiction over us—Come down here." [84]

Calvin Mateer, responding somewhat differently, said to the brigadier, "As civilized as your great country is, still you call out to a visitor from afar by his *ming.*" Then, regarding both the salutation and the subsequent lecture on *li,* he said—quoting the *Li chi* (Book of Rites)—"This is not the *tao* of 'treating strangers kindly in order to win their hearts,' " and "You send for us to insult us— why did you not invite us onto your platform?" The brigadier was reportedly so nonplussed, or lost so much face, by Mateer's knowledge of the classics and of Chinese etiquette that he "had to submit." The Tengchow perfect—the highest-ranking official in town—had also now arrived on the scene, and by report he apologized for the brigadier's rudeness and escorted the missionaries out. The whole incident soon blew over, with no consequence except (says the *Alumni History*) "From this time on, [because of Mateer's] reputation for bravery, no one dared trouble the school. Ah! *Hsien-sheng* was a good shepherd." [85]

Various aspects of this story differ according to the teller, and the *Alumni History* account, written many years later, sounds a little legendary. The technique displayed here, however—reticence, Chinese etiquette, and an appropriate classical maxim—unquestionably typifies an approach that kept Calvin Mateer and the Tengchow School out of further trouble and helped win establishment respect, finally, for both.

Mainly Mateer abided by certain general rules for official dealings, developed from observation of how Chinese officials seemed to operate. He gradually became an authority, or at least he headed a committee on the subject ("The Missionary and Public Questions") for the 1907 Centenary Conference of Protestant Missionaries. His 1907 speech and resolutions, and a similar statement of 1893, can be condensed to two basic rules. First, he stressed circumspection, meaning restraint by missionaries and Chinese Christians. Missionary interposition, except to save a life, he found practically useless, and "about the worst thing for the progress of the Gospel is to have a persecution case taken up successfully." The missionary's energy should go into emphasizing the apolitical, moral nature of Christianity, and the importance of loyalty to the Chinese empire.

Second, he stressed the *suaviter in modo* type of contact. The missionary should maintain friendly relations by expressing his "deep sense of obligation" for Chinese official protection, and congratulations on any official reforms. In case of trouble he should deal directly with his district magistrate, not with Western consuls (which arouses the magistrate's antiforeignism) or with the magistrate's Chinese superiors (which insults him professionally). Appeals should be directed to the magistrate's sense of justice, in abstract Chinese terms, rather than to treaty rights; the official usually knows the latter "all too well" anyway. Finally, use all contact to point out the industry and national loyalty of local Christians, and the essential unfairness of certain Chinese legalisms (the term *chiao-min*, for instance, which implies that "Christian Chinese are not *min* [people] in the same sense as other Chinese").[86]

Mateer's circumspection, aided by historical developments, paid off locally in gradual erosion of higher-class hostility. In 1885, following the chief military mandarin visit, the Chefoo taotai gave the Tengchow school a gift of money for commencement prizes.[87] Then in 1895 a young man with a literary degree enrolled as a day student. Mateer attributed this particular event mostly to the recent Sino-Japanese War, which had increased the desire for foreign learning. But the gentry compact was breached nonetheless; he took the case as a sign "that we are going to reach some of the educated people," and several men of literary standing sent sons to the college subsequently.[88]

Mateer's interest in nationwide, or imperial, educational reform has been discussed. His first steps are represented by an 1881 *Wan-kuo kung-pao* article entitled "On Advancing Schools" ("Chen-hsing hsüeh-hsiao lun"); the message is basically the same as in his English-language pronouncements on Chinese education, but the diplomatic tone is much different.[89] In articles and through the EAC he advocated new public (*kung-hsüeh*) and vocational (*t'e-hsüeh*) schools; a new scheme for *hsiu-ts'ai* examination degrees; and a "comprehensive plan of educational reform which may be engrafted on the system of examination."[90] From the 1896 EAC triennial to his death in 1908, he was active in a number of projects, mostly educational, aimed at proving missionaries *"true friends"* of China. "The material, moral, and spiritual good of the Chinese people," he comprehensively stated in 1907, "is our supreme aim. For this we came; for this we labor."[91]

It should be noted, however, that Calvin Mateer's labors of this type consisted exclusively of promotional work within and from the missionary community. His advice came from a position totally outside higher Chinese circles, where missionaries like W. A. P. Martin, Timothy Richard, and Y. J. Allen tried to cultivate contacts and push for modernizing reforms. As a pioneer exponent of science and mass literacy, Mateer did actively endorse the more liberal views of higher officials toward education.[92] But from his provincial location, he was impressed by the illiberality of many lower imperial functionaries, by the failure of educational reforms to diffuse downward, and by the residual "social ostracism that prevents a small official or a private gentleman from employing a Christian teacher."[93]

Mateer hoped and anticipated that educational changes in China would eventually destroy the kind of literati mentality he so disliked. In the meantime he never lost his desire to keep a certain distance between the "magnates" and himself. In August and December 1898 he was offered positions at the new imperial universities in Peking and Nanking (Dean of Science and headmaster respectively). In each case he declined a salary "much greater than a missionary gets," he said, because he "felt that my obligations to the missionary work were more imperative." [94] To his disciples, says Wang Yüan-te, he commented, "Even if there were time, I would be unwilling. How can our *tao* be advanced in the official circles of China? They court me today, but tomorrow they will oppose me." [95]

This distrust was confirmed by Watson Hayes's experience in 1901 at the Shantung Provincial University: less than a month after Hayes arrived Yüan Shih-k'ai was transferred to Chihli, and under the new governor a dispute ensued over compulsory "Confucian worship." By mid-1903 President Hayes and six Christian teachers (all Wen hui-kuan graduates) had resigned. [96]

Mateer's relation to the Chinese establishment was thus rather complex. He never learned to like the higher classes, nor to write about them in English without references to their heathenism, antiforeignism, corruption, inefficiency, and so on. He dealt with them on a *quid pro quo* basis; and the understandings reached appear procedural rather than substantive, or appreciations of problems and techniques rather than of people.

Viewed against Calvin Mateer's own ego, however—which was clearly of a size matching his energies—his achievements still seem noteworthy. Mateer's Western, or Christian, inner-directedness was about as strong as one can imagine, and the directness of his competition with Confucianism likewise. In a personal sense, his achievement was to use this competition as an additional stimulus. The literati and their values—or his idea of them—became less a frustration than a foil, against which he maximized his own development as something different. At the same time, he learned to communicate his distinctiveness not by treaty-right stances, as his instincts impelled him to do in his early years, but by Chinese rules—arguing from principles rather than laws, and with great attention to matters of face. This is the point of the story about the Tengchow brigadier and, in a more developed way, of the 1907 general rules. Putting the personal and diplomatic elements together, he matured to a relationship where he and the Chinese establishment could use each other, with no loss in self-esteem to either.

In addition to dealing with students and literati, Mateer of course had to relate to fellow missionaries. His general reputation here, which was based on books, projects, and "force of personality," was quite high. At his death the *Chinese Recorder* summed up, "It is not infrequently remarked that God removes his workers, but the work goes on. It is difficult to conceive, however, how all the work that was being done by the late Dr. C. W. Mateer can still go on, or at least with anything like the vigor and efficiency he was wont to impart to it." [97] Foreign mission sympathizers recognized him with honorary degrees (Hanover 1880, Wooster 1888, Washington and Jefferson 1902), and with comments like that of an English observer at the 1890 General Conference, who found him "the most striking personality there." [98]

On what he was, as distinct from what he did, the reports vary considerably. Chauncey Goodrich's view is the predominant one among longtime project associates: "Dr. Mateer possessed a rugged strength of character. He was almost Spartan in his ability to endure hardships, and in his careless scorn for the amenities and 'elegant superfluities' of modern life. Yet 'beneath a rugged and somewhat austere exterior' he had a heart of remarkable tenderness. He was a block of granite with the heart of a woman." [99] Like T. P. Crawford, he was known for his jokes and table talk, which in Mateer's case could cover practically anything. Missionaries who knew him as children remember riding piggyback, playing ball, and seeing a beautiful, mirthful smile when with him. Julia once told a friend her "heart thrilled as she heard her husband's steps," and Hunter Corbett thought "this world will ever seem more lonely without him." [100]

Such eulogies aside, an unattractive Calvin Mateer most definitely existed, and particularly to people who had to live with him. One element in this was no doubt simply his physical presence. To children—whom he supposedly loved on principle—he sometimes seemed an Old Tiger indeed, with his long, gaunt figure, booming voice, and pale gray eyes. Ning Lao T'ai-t'ai, who remembered him as the first foreigner she ever saw, was "so frightened that I fell to the ground and hid my face in my arms"; she was especially frightened by "the eyes, so far back and sunken into the face." [101] His "big voice," which Wang Yüan-te associated with hearty laughter, reportedly also served rather often for shouting down contrary opinions. To Ida Pruitt he was "certainly a giant among men," and also "not a lovable man." [102]

Most people, like Ning Lao T'ai-t'ai, learned to live with his bark. His bite was something else, and those who got close enough to experience it often found it unnerving. The problem with Mateer, wrote one missionary (for himself and three 1885 associates), was that he was "impossible for anyone to live long in the house with," or for most people even to live close to. [103] There was a certain high tone of commitment, that is, about the Mateer household and influence, which dominated Presbyterian work in Teng-chow. Looked at from outside, Calvin and Julia Mateer symbolized a "rare oneness of spirit"; [104] to some on the inside, this came across in a "very disgusting and often painful" personal way: "Instead of trying to make our work pleasant, they seemed to us to try to make it as hard and unpleasant as possible. They possessed a relish for keen and unjust criticism which was cultivated by constant practice. In fact there are few in Shantung who escaped, while the Board and others got their full share. All faults and defects—and who are without them—must be discussed and criticized, some more and others less, as suited their fancy and the occasion. They were fully conscious of others' faults, but failed to see their own, while all must bend to their will . . . If people suited their fancy and followed their dictum, very well; if not they were, as one who has passed through the experience said recently [1899], 'weighed in the balance, found wanting, and passed on.' A little reflection on the past record of Tungchow will suffice to recall . . . several such cases." [105]

The record does make for interesting reflecting. In Calvin Mateer's forty years at Tengchow he had some sixty-eight American Presbyterian associates. Forty-four departed in three years or less, and only the Mills and Hayes families—plus Miss Mary Snodgrass, a remarkable woman—stayed more than ten.[106] To a certain extent this mobility stemmed from deaths, from the general hardness of the place, and from the station's position in an expanding mission field: it served as a training base for newcomers, who learned the language and became acclimatized for later interior work. The training program, however, was not altogether intentional, and there is abundant evidence that the atmosphere described above was a major incentive to move on. For missionaries who had to stay—single females, college teaching assistants, and a succession of doctors—the situation sometimes became desperate.

For one thing, Calvin Mateer could not resist organizing everybody into his own projects. A few people were willing and able. In 1900, for example, two years after Julia's death, he found an ideal new wife in Ada Haven of the Peking ABCFM mission. Miss Haven had a reputation of her own as a writer and as an expert on Greek, Mandarin, and survival under Boxer siege conditions. She quickly became an assistant Testament translator, as well as chief reviser and abridger of the *Mandarin Lessons*. Watson Hayes joined himself to Calvin Mateer equally closely. According to his son Ernest, Hayes took Mateer as mentor and model for all his own sixty years in China. Even this powerful bond, however, was strained at times. In 1893, for instance, Mateer denied a furlough request by Hayes with laziness accusations that outraged the younger man. He wrote the board that he had never had a furlough, and that in fact Mateer had given him only three days off in ten years in China. That, he recalled, had been on the understanding that he would visit a remote lighthouse and get up a lecture on it for a physics class.[107]

No other Tengchow Americans were as committed to Mateer personally as his wives and Watson Hayes were. Medical missionaries, who felt called to work in a special way, ran head on into the Mateer stress on omnicompetence. The first of these men went home in less than a year, having "mistaken his calling." Another left as one of the group calling Mateer impossible to live with. A third was transferred after Mateer, with Hayes and Charles Mills also signing, wrote the home board that the physician was frivolous, slothful, a heavy drinker, and generally an undesirable influence on the Christian schoolchildren of Tengchow.[108]

Four other medical doctors also left abruptly, although Mateer complained regularly about the intervals when medical care was unavailable. As he saw it, writing in the early 1880s, "The Dr's we have had in Shantung thus far do not seem to be made of the same stuff as the clerical missionaries. Their difficulties are in no respect greater than those of other missionaries, yet they have thus far made a very poor show in the matter of endurance."[109] Another view, of a physician on hand in 1893, was that Mateer's own unkind and unjust—in fact shameful—attitude toward them was the problem.[110]

Both the Mateers were also rather hard on the station's young female missionaries. Calvin tended to regard them as silly adventuresses, "*bent on* getting married" rather than working, until they proved otherwise.[111] As Julia put it, there were too many cases of inconsiderate haste and "failure to appreciate the work to be done, and trials to be borne."[112]

A striking example here was Calvin's own sister Lillian, who came to Tengchow in 1881. Lillian lasted two years before leaving as a "bald failure," Calvin wrote, "of whom I am thoroughly ashamed." Against her brother's wishes she married a Southern Baptist and moved to Shanghai; there her husband went insane, and she gave up missionary work to take him back to America. Calvin's response, according to their embarrassed brother Robert Mateer, was to send the Southern Baptists a bill for Lillian's passage. On Lillian's missionary career Calvin wrote, "Certainly it has not been very creditable either to herself or to her friends. She is my sister however and I feel a great deal of sympathy for her in this great trial." Robert, who was a rugged sort himself, agreed that it was all humiliating; but he felt it was God's will, and in any case he was "very far from entertaining the views and feelings of my bro. and wife at Tungchow." [113]

The most spectacular of these unfortunate incidents was the case of Adeline de H. Kelsey, M.D. Dr. Kelsey, who arrived at the end of 1878, was to outward appearances a superlative candidate for pioneer woman's work. She was a bright, idealistic girl, generously supported by the Steuben Presbyterial Society (sixteen member bands) of New York. Being both female and a physician, she was an object of special pride at home and of special interest at Tengchow. Her early reports were optimistic. She had been warned, she wrote, that she might find her associates demanding; but Mrs. Mateer had been very kind, and Dr. Mateer thought she promised well. She was favorably impressed with how hard everyone worked.

More quickly than she seems to have expected, Dr. Kelsey was working hard, too. Maggie Capp took her on an interior itineration of almost a hundred miles, at the end of which she found inedible food, repellent sleeping arrangements, and village Chinese who were as "uncouth, dirty, ragged and odorous a crowd as you can possibly imagine." As a doctor she was consoled by "some very interesting and some hopeless cases"; but even this satisfaction palled when at one stop she had to treat one hundred and twenty-five people in four days. Both in the country and at Tengchow, Dr. Kelsey wrote in 1880, she got no rest, quiet, or privacy. Lower-class Chinese women bedeviled her with questions, petty thievery, and complaints that kept her exhausted in body and spirit.

By early 1881, when Calvin and Julia Mateer returned from furlough, Dr. Kelsey was nearing a breakdown. She had already requested transfer away from the repulsiveness of village work and the "dead and dreary" life in Tengchow city. In addition, as Mateer put it, she had engaged herself to an Anglican missionary. Pending further developments she apparently expected sympathy from the Mateers. Instead she got an onslaught, she wrote, of savage criticism and indeed "overt acts of tyranny and oppression." When she complained of being overworked the Mateers told her she was lazy, and that work was what they understood she had come to do. Mateer's medical opinions, based on his recent cram course in Philadelphia, were an additional insult. Especially galling was his attitude toward her sensitivities about the Chinese; she found his sarcasms "deeply culpable," particularly his harping on her inability, after two years in the field, to communicate without an interpreter. As for her marriage and transfer plans, he made it clear that he considered them confessions of moral weakness.

Dr. Kelsey's final year at Tengchow, before her departure in 1882, was an unmitigated nightmare. Her fiancé, like Lillian Mateer's husband, lost his mental stability and went back to England. The marriage apparently fell through, and her transfer approval dragged agonizingly. She fell into a depression that crushed her and a lingering illness diagnosed as due to miasma and Calvin Mateer. Finally Dr. Kelsey left and went to Japan, attributing her withdrawal to "a *general line* of conduct which I have had to endure ever since I came here. The gentlemen here *act* as though they hold as a *principle* the idea that a lady and *most especially* a *single* lady has no right which a *white* man or a *yellow* man either is bound to respect . . . I do most urgently appeal to you [the BFM] to never again send an unprotected lady to this place. Gentlemen will have a rough enough time of it . . . Very few would ever venture to write to the Board a statement of what they had to endure. They endure in silence till they break down or get married!" [114]

The case of Adeline Kelsey was unfortunately not all that unusual at Tengchow. With regard to Calvin Mateer, perhaps he was less than human in some ways, just as in others he is described as seemingly a bit more. This is what Dr. Kelsey thought, and it brings to mind—among possible comments—David Riesman's theory that "it is better when the saints are celibate." From days as a student volunteer at the Grenfell Mission in Labrador, Riesman advises a certain skepticism toward "most people who devote all their lives to the service of others in an alien milieu." Somebody, he believes, has to pay in suffering or neglect for what such saints achieve, and typically the sufferers are those who by choice or chance are closest to them, and from whom most is expected.[115]

Calvin Mateer's attitude on missionary work thus contrasts interestingly with that of Riesman, who feels that "it should be recognized that most people's motives are mixed and that it is all right not to be wholly committed either to doing good or to doing well." [116] Mateer achieved a great deal because he was smart and energetic, and because he had quite a bit of time and freedom to figure out where he was going. Many younger associates felt he denied them both these elements that had been so important to his own development.

It would be unfair on the other hand to put Mateer down as some stereotypical Puritan. He laughed often, we are told, and he had a variety of interests and certainly he enjoyed life. People who voluntarily stayed on with him, like Hayes and Wang Yüan-te, found him more inspiring than intimidating. His troubles with women and doctors, it might be argued, stemmed as much from a personally confirmed broad view of human potential as from male chauvinism or professional narrow-mindedness.

It seems also worth noting that the people whom Calvin Mateer did like—the ones he called choice—he liked without reservation, for qualities like endurance, resourcefulness, and sangfroid. Among medical missionaries, for instance, he was a great admirer of Dr. J. B. Neal, who broke in at Tengchow before founding what later became Cheeloo Medical College at Tsinan. "Cold Grey Eye" Neal was a fabulous personality known for majestic handsomeness, toughness of fiber, and incessant hard work.[117] Among female workers, Mary Snodgrass was a person whom Mateer called "beyond praise." She more than met his two requirements of women missionaries: she learned the language, and among Chinese she became—by dint of sympathy, generosity, and a renowned sense of humor—probably the most popular foreigner ever to live in Tengchow.[118]

It would thus appear on balance that Mateer had a certain hardness that was magnified by missionaries of short, intense acquaintance. Interestingly, many changed their views on him after transferring away from Tengchow. The man who felt weighed in the balance was one who did this; ten years after being found wanting by Calvin Mateer, he asked to preach, and gave a touching eulogy, at Mateer's funeral.[119]

Again, it seems certain that at least some of Mateer's mental cruelty was self-inflicted by the victims. The biggest problem was that he came too soon in some careers. Having been called by God, these idealistic young people found Mateer doing the choosing. He was not a fanatic, any more than were the rest of his choice American men; rather—as Robert Mateer liked to style them— they were all rustlers, tough people with a tested capacity for survival and freewheeling enterprise. In Calvin Mateer's case an associate found himself with a man who lived forty-two years in China, to 1905, without a single specific illness; who got his rest from taking on more work; and who, Hunter Corbett once said, was universally regarded as a man who never failed at anything.[120] The potential tensions seem obvious.

For perspective on Calvin Mateer one finally has to see him against what he was trying to do. To different Chinese and American elements he presented contrasting faces, depending on how each related to his many-sided personal operation. As a kind of cross-cultural empire builder he had adherents and opponents, plus colleagues who did not show him the "stuff" he wanted. In keeping with his own role (and by his own testimony) he considered himself an all-round, self-made man who, if he did not have all the answers, had a few more than most people he knew. A "man of this sort," as a nonmissionary said about Mateer, "travels a road with serious perils along its line. A loss of balance may make of him a bigot or a dangerous fanatic." [121]

The same observer, however—speaking for others who knew Mateer well—thought the "defects of his qualities . . . were not serious enough greatly to mar his usefulness or to spoil the beauty of his character." Others who credit him with good balance stress his broad interests, which broadened his tolerances, along with his forgiving spirit and essential humility, which one gathers often took long acquaintance to perceive. As a person who rarely disagreed with him on matters of right and wrong, Watson Hayes says, "Being a man of decided views, and disapproving of what did not seem to him wise and good, he did not always approve of the course taken by his colleagues; yet if convinced that a man was working with a single heart for the interest of Christ's kingdom, he was ready to forgive, and to hope for the best. He loved the Lord who had forgiven him, and so loved those who had offended against himself. This extended both to those with whom he labored, and to those for whom he labored. One of his marked characteristics was not to give over any man who had fallen away, and he was always ready to give him another chance." [122]

On his humility, Chauncey Goodrich remembered him as "a sort of prince among men . . . He was born to lead, not to follow. Having worked out his own conclusions, he was so sure of them that he expected, almost demanded, their acceptance by others. Yet he was not arrogant and was truly humble. Moreover, he could ask forgiveness for words that he felt had been too hasty or too harsh, feeling much broken by giving pain to a friend. In this he showed his greatness." [123]

Calvin Mateer's humility, according to Hunter Corbett's daughter May, was simply that of a man "quite sure of his standing." After his death he was a legend of much interest and some puzzlement to young Americans teaching at Cheeloo, a successor institution to Tengchow College. By the 1920s, when Sino-foreign understanding was an urgent problem at all Christian colleges, he was being interpreted by Wang Yüan-te, Wang Hsi-en, and other Chinese professors formerly Mateer disciples. In situations calling for foreign humility, the story goes, these men delighted in recommending Ti K'ao-wen's stock response when stumped by student questions—*Lien wo, yeh pu chih-tao* ("Even I do not know").[124]

Conclusion

In the last decade of his life (1898–1908) Calvin Mateer was confronted by difficulties that are perhaps best called contradictions. At the college, for instance, his many outside activities greatly curtailed the time he could give to student molding, a situation that gave him much anxiety. His insistence on running a "first class" liberal arts institution—coupled with his insistence on *not* teaching the English language—also brought the school up against financial difficulties, and against a missionary educational trend toward more specialized curricula. After 1895 Watson Hayes, and later the Reverend Paul Bergen, served as presidents of the Wen hui-kuan, though by most testimony (including that of the *Alumni History*) Mateer's personality dominated the school at least until 1904.[1]

In literary work Mateer's unresolved problems are suggested in a long series of articles (1901–02) on the Chinese character *shen*. This series, which was never completed—and which was marked by a very uncharacteristic lack of both plan and logic—represented an attempt on Mateer's part to maintain that *shen* (rather than the compound *shang-ti*) is the proper Chinese term for God. Most missionaries (or 91.4 percent of usage in Christian literature in 1892) had long since resolved the so-called term question in favor of *shang-ti,* and Calvin Mateer's belated efforts were not very convincing. After giving him space for fourteen issues, the *Chinese Recorder* yielded to reader complaints and dropped his series.[2]

In 1904 the college moved to the city of Wei-hsien, where it became bidenominational with the English Baptists and received a new name (Shantung Union College). In 1917 it moved again, to the provincial capital at Tsinan, where it was thenceforth the nucleus of Shantung Christian University (Cheeloo). The first of these moves, the only one that need concern us here, took place basically for three reasons. First, because of a large influx of new missionaries into John Nevius's old itinerating field, the center of gravity in Presbyterian work shifted west in the 1890s to the area around Wei-hsien. Second, a railroad was built (1899–1904) by German interests from Kiaochow, about 130 miles south of Teng-chow, west through Wei-hsien and Tsinan. From a mission viewpoint this changed the whole situation in Shantung; it underlined Tengchow's isolation and greatly increased the desirability of a site closer to the largest number of Chinese Presbyterians.[3] Third, the Reverend Henry Winters Luce arrived to join the Tengchow College faculty in 1897, simultaneously with the beginning of Germany's takeover in Kiaochow.

Henry W. Luce, like the German railroad, embodied what seemed to be a new era in Shantung—in Luce's case a new era for American Presbyterian educational work. Luce was perhaps the perfect second-generation man: smooth and progressive as an executive (and later a gifted moneyraiser), he made Mateer's college the first step in a long personal career of distinguished service to Christian education. With Mateer and Watson Hayes occupied with other work, Henry Luce and his friend Paul Bergen campaigned quietly to move the college physically and then to alter its program. They succeeded, more or less, in both efforts. Programmatically, much of the old molding emphasis was dropped at Wei-hsien, and the English language and a more diversified teaching approach entered the curriculum. Luce's aim was "to attract the intellectual, social, and cultural elite," to work on Chinese society "from the top down." The Mateer theory, of course, had been to work "from the bottom out," by much molding and by an all-Chinese linguistic approach.[4]

Calvin Mateer never personally accepted the ideas of Luce and Bergen, and to a certain extent he fought both the ideas and their proponents. Moving the college and teaching English, to Mateer's way of thinking, were entirely consistent with Henry Luce's bourgeois-elitist approach.[5] But such changes obviously cut against what Mateer himself had been trying for forty years to do, which was to take peasant boys and raise them—in a geographically and culturally isolated situation—into self-sacrificing leaders of lower-class Chinese Christians.

Innovations that seemed logical and humane to Luce and Bergen thus seemed merely opportunistic to Mateer. The academic "understanding of the natives" that such younger missionaries brought to the field was to him of a piece with their fondness for short-cut administrative and educational techniques, and he saw his work as passing into the hands of a softer, lazier missionary generation.[6] Understanding of China, to Calvin Mateer, was something to be acquired by long and painful personal search. Teaching English to Christian Chinese students (however much they wanted it) simply corrupted the students and undermined the missionary's proper language job, which was to learn Chinese himself, thoroughly, and to put into the native language such things from English as were worth Chinese knowing.

Emphasis on Mandarin proficiency remained as one of the distinctive features of the successor institutions to Tengchow College. Logic, however—in the form of geography, financial considerations, and wider educational developments (including the abolition of the traditional Chinese examination system)—seemed to dictate a number of changes after 1900. Not very gracefully, Calvin Mateer acquiesced. He moved the school to Wei-hsien, where his local alumni received him "headed by mounted soldiery, with banners flying and flags waving, and the air filled with the noise of cannon and firecracker."[7]

His final years were spent in typical energetic fashion. When not translating he busied himself building up the new physical plant; and in 1907, following a student strike against the new administration, he even returned briefly to the college presidency.[8] Then in September 1908 Calvin Mateer suddenly died of peritonitis in Tsingtao. A delegation of his old Tengchow graduates waited all day, in a rainstorm, at the Chefoo jetty for the steamer bringing his body. Honoring one of his last requests, they had brought Julia's remains from the Tengchow cemetery, and both were buried with great ceremony beside John Nevius.[9]

Mateer's work survived him chiefly in his *Mandarin Lessons* and in the "footprints" of the Wen hui-kuan's one hundred and seventy graduates (1876–1904). Of the 145 of these men still living in 1912, 87 were teaching, 26 were in religious vocations, and 32 were engaged in a variety of other work. The teachers were by far the college's most important product: by 1912 Tengchow graduates had held a reported 380 teaching jobs in eleven provinces and Manchuria. Three hundred and four of these positions represented mission or other Christian employment, including 103 at rural schools in Shantung. Among the 76 government positions were professorships at Peking Imperial (National) University, plus jobs at a variety of Chinese provincial colleges and primary, middle, higher, normal, agricultural, and military schools. A total of 26 positions, or the largest concentration, had been at Ch'ing reform-era institutions in Tsinan and Tientsin. The 32 alumni who went into other work (not teaching or preaching) concentrated in medicine, business, and literary work, including journalism.[10]

The Tengchow College graduates, like the school's founder, encountered new problems in the twentieth century. To a large extent their difficulties stemmed from the spread in China of scientific and national consciousness, two ideas that the college itself, in its own way, had stressed. The *Alumni History,* for example—written in 1912—expresses an attitude quite similar to that of Mateer himself in his last years. On the one hand, the alumni writers display great pride in the achievements of their various *t'ung-hsüeh* (schoolmates) and patriotic faith regarding China's Christian and republican future. The same optimism appears in one of Mateer's last letters: "The dark and discouraging days are over and the future is bright with promise. As I look back over the first twenty-five years of my missionary life, it seems like a troubled dream. The last fifteen years have wrought wonders in China. Old customs and prejudices are giving way. The bright dawn of better things is upon us. The most conservative and immovable people in the world, persistently wedded to the old ways, are getting used to new things . . . I often wish I were young again, just ready to start in on the bright opening campaign. In a large sense the future of the church and of the world lies wrapped up in this great people. Why in the providence of God the gospel of salvation has not long ere this reached this oldest and greatest nation is an unexplained mystery. These unconverted millions of the Mongolian race will presently come into their inheritance of truth and grace, and then who shall say what they will become, and do? Their fecundity, their physical stamina, their patient persistence and intellectual vigor, are factors that will count in the world's future history." [11]

On the other hand (and concluding the same article), Mateer noted that "the opportunity [for Christianity] is passing," and that "the changes of many years are now crowded into one." Wang Yüan-te, in the *Alumni History,* similarly remarks on the rush of "circumstances before our eyes"; and the book's dominant theme as a record of the past is that it is an attempt to explain circumstances and achievements that already seem dated. [12]

The careers and problems of the college's graduates constitute a topic in themselves, one that requires considerably more development than the present study can undertake. The same can be said about the weaknesses, with respect to a changed Chinese situation, of Calvin Mateer's educational and stylistic approach. For present purposes the last decade of Mateer's life can accurately be called not one of failure but of success. For a moment in history—the moment Mateer said he had "waited all my life for"—a number of his former students held modestly influential positions, and his literary work helped educate both Westerners in China and an unknown number of Chinese schoolchildren. [13] Even Henry W. Luce's organizational maneuvering, which in effect took Mateer's school away from him, was an ironic application of techniques that Mateer himself had long used to much advantage.[14] If any China mission-ary ever opened and closed his campaigning at precisely the right moments, it was Calvin Mateer.

To sum up Mateer, beginning with the influences that he represented, is no easy job. Most obviously, some would now say, he was an American pioneer type, a frontiersman displaying in East Asia some of the faiths and talents that were simultaneously winning the American West. One recent summary of such charac-teristics, by an American historian, sounds like a description of Mateer himself: the traits include self-confident optimism and faith in progress; practicality and an inclination to experiment; and a feeling that "there is so much work to be done, and so few people to do it, that the idea of labor is apt to absorb the entire area of the mind."[15] Mateer's rugged individualism, his physical toughness, and his willingness (indeed desire) to live in semi-isolation abroad were basic to his personal pioneer style. If he had stayed at home—or as a discerning friend said, if he had "set down in China at some such place as Shanghai"—he would probably not have been stimulated to develop his talents so extensively.[16] The variety of his enterpreneuring, at any rate, would almost certainly have been considerably reduced.

Calvin Mateer's status as a Protestant Christian, it should also be said—and specifically as an American one—was at least equal in importance to his pioneer attributes. His view of the Protestantism of his literary work, of writing "in *their own spoken* language," has been noted. He became a teacher, he also once professed, because he believed education to be "the especial crown and glory of Protestantism."[17] In both these areas Mateer furthermore directly reflected American interpretations of Protestantism.

In his literary work the last point is epitomized by his life-long insistence on *shen,* a "people's" word, as the Chinese character for God—and gods generally—and on *ni* (you) as the proper form of divine address in prayer. The more erudite literary mission-aries (the majority of whom were English) thought *ni* was too familiar, too vulgar, and they saw nothing disqualifying (as Mateer did) in the fact that the term *shang-ti* was historically identified with the civil religion of the Chinese empire. In Mateer's curious obstinacy on these matters one sees the famous term ques-tion for what it probably always at least partially was: rival nine-teenth-century understandings—British imperial and American democratic (or "young republican")—of the nature of God Him-self. Was God, that is, simply the eternally all-powerful being—which was the idea that *shang-ti* basically conveyed—or was He, as *shen* implied to many missionaries, rather the proven true one of a multitude of historical spirits, and perhaps identical with the individual human soul? The lack of understanding by many turn-of-the-century American missionaries of Mateer's 1901–02 *shen* series ("Where is the other *end*?") suggests, perhaps, how imperial their own nation had become since the pre-Civil War years of Calvin Mateer's memory.[18]

As a Presbyterian teacher Mateer represented not the Calvinism of Geneva—or of the *New England Primer*, for that matter— but something close to the famous Christian nurture theology of Horace Bushnell of Connecticut. Bushnell's basic idea had been that "there was no caprice in the divine selection of candidates for redemption; God fixed on those whose families reared them to recognize Him in their actions. Correct Christian nurture that trained people in good behavior would open a way to salvation that could comprehend all." [19]

This was the idea behind Calvin Mateer's own upbringing, and it was the idea behind the Wen hui-kuan. Every boy had something good in him, that is, which could be brought out by a devoted teacher's living example. The Wen hui-kuan, with its "esprit de corps," was a preparatory school version of Bushnell's organic Christian family; and Mateer's anxiety, as school *chien-tu*, to project personally the temperature of Christian life was identical with what Bushnell had called the only true teaching—the teacher's struggle to raise each child to "love the truth afterwards for the teacher's sake." [20]

As an educationalist scholar Mateer was no less an American type. In contrast to the literary missionaries—whom he specifically likened to medieval monks—he valued no work scholarly or otherwise that did not have some application in "real life." He thus wrote textbooks in Mandarin (and called treatises and *wen-li* writings impractical), and apart from mathematics he made physics his teaching specialty. The most basic of the sciences, physics is of course also the one most closely related to everyday life and to the problems of technologically undeveloped societies. And it is the one whose laws could in Mateer's time be seen as most demonstrative of an unchanging universal design.

The purposiveness of all his work—and the downright anti-intellectualism of his attitude toward nonpurposive scholarship— sometimes make one wonder if Calvin Mateer was really a scholar, as distinct from a promoter, at all. In his teaching style he also sometimes reminds one not so much of Horace Bushnell as of a much more famous clerical teacher who, like Mateer himself, found his destiny as a surrogate father in a foreign land: "There can be no doubt that the Cardinal's affection . . . was genuine. Yet somewhere in Mazarin's ceaseless and sensible admonition one senses the promptings of that most terrible of all ambitions: the urge to fashion the character of another human being in the shape of one's own design." [21]

The *Mandarin Lessons* and the *Alumni History* suggest two thoughts that seem worth mentioning on these points. One is that the best kind of scholarly research is always the kind that involves some deep personal feeling of the researcher, and that also broadens him in the course of his study—enabling him to say something, finally, that is both worthwhile and unique. The other idea is that the best teacher is the one who teaches not only by what he can verbalize, but by what he has become in the process of educating himself.[22] This is exactly how Mateer is described by Wang Yüante and other disciples. Like Christian nurture, the whole notion is not unlike some Confucian ideas that Mateer never professed to appreciate.

As a total personality, Calvin Mateer seems finally to exemplify the development that one historian has called the "subtle process by which the central body of American religious thought assimilated [by 1860] the concepts of progress and perfectibility." The new faith that this process produced was one that "demanded action," that "required men actively to ameliorate the conditions of humanity." Wrapped up in this was the fact that "In arriving at this faith in man's ability to perfect himself, the Americans had come a long way from the time when they had conceived themselves helpless sinners in the hands of an angry God. Indeed, faith in the essential goodness of man and in his capacity to progress toward perfectibility rested squarely upon American experience." [23]

Not all religious Americans, of course, belonged to the central body, and some had not come as far from an angry God as others had. T. P. Crawford, for instance—certainly a second pioneer type—embodied a theology that Horace Bushnell had specifically criticized as the antithesis of the Christian nurture approach. Most American Baptists, Bushnell wrote in 1847, believed not in nurture and growth but in "adult conversions, revivals, angular experiences, hard and violent demonstrations, painful exhaustions," and other sudden encounters with grace, all adding up to "extreme individualism." [24] Such nurture as Crawford personally received moreover came largely from that Tennessee Baptist aberration called Landmarkism. Originating in Crawford's student days at Union University and in the Big Hatchie Association, Landmarkism stressed not only angular experiences, but much the same kind of near-paranoid church independence that Crawfordism later championed.[25]

From Tennessee Crawford went on to a missionary career that paralleled and contrasted with Mateer's as strikingly as did his theological background. Neither of the two men did well in early evangelistic and pastoral work, and both turned during traumatic experiences (Kao Ku San and Miao Hua-yü) to personal scholarship and to an interest in schools that their wives had started. The depth of their scholarly and educational interests proved very different. By 1877 each had developed a personal philosophy; as enunciated and commented upon at the General Conference in Shanghai, the philosophies were progressive (or even radical) in Mateer's case and reactionary in Crawford's.

As one looks at these two lives diverging sharply in the 1870s, one sees a case study, perhaps, in something besides personality differences. Out of two sets of personal experiences—each involving money worries, professional pride, and relations with associates from two races—one also sees two classic American life orientations evolving to articulation. In Calvin Mateer, from work at the Tengchow School, a faith in long-term progress and in human goodness in unexpected places is clearly assimilated. From experience both at the school and with Miao Hua-yü comes also the lesson that, although we must accept people as sincere when they tell us they have changed radically from an established pattern, we must also be prepared to deal with them if they backtrack or veer off equally radically. In T. P. Crawford one sees exactly opposite conclusions: the great majority of human beings, if given the chance, will always follow their worst instincts, and the way to keep them in line is through fear and discipline administered by God's chosen white few. If the majority cannot be persuaded to accept such domination, then by Crawford's philosophy the few simply wash their hands of them.

What one sees is again not simply one man who is smarter or bigger than another. In religious terms we have, as one student has described it, "this Christian view of man, which is both pessimistic and optimistic about life," and apart from which "it is impossible fully to understand or appreciate the nineteenth century missionary movement." [26] Applying another label, we have a case of the tough and tender strains that have formed the dialectic of American social thought for at least the last hundred years.

The Christian, American presence in China could thus be a two-edged sword, and which way it cut—as Calvin Mateer said about science in 1877—depended on who held the handle. In the hands of both Mateer and Crawford the sword was forcefully wielded, because both men were ruling spirits—meaning, by missionary parlance of the time, that both were persons driven to "make their presence felt on all sides, for power to be or do is exactly their line." [27] The difference in how such spirits could make themselves felt seems epitomized in the closest relationship that each of these two had, which was to his wife. T. P. Crawford, from jealousy and from a terrible kind of dependence, forced his wife to exchange work that she loved for a life of practicing what he preached; she became certainly a better and more useful person than he, but only at what her best friends described as great psychic cost and disappointing concrete achievement. Calvin Mateer, by contrast, decided that Julia's choice of work was a better bet than his own, and by working truly together they achieved measurable success and great personal fulfillment.

How these two men viewed life and the people around them was obviously closely connected to their individual health, happiness, and professional influence. As Calvin Mateer expanded in many directions in the 1880s, T. P. Crawford withdrew into a progressively more distorted view of himself and his fellow man. In 1893, as the *Mandarin Lessons* began to circulate and as Mateer began his New Testament work, Crawford led the Gospel Mission west to T'ai-an-fu. At his death Mateer left books and former students that were spread out, as Wang Yüan-te put it, " like men on a chessboard, or like the stars." [28] Other than some strong negative impressions, Crawford left nothing.

Lottie Moon, as an unmarried woman missionary, faced difficult problems that Crawford and Mateer did not have to confront. In her own way she was fully as tough and aggressive as they were. She also underwent, as the two men did, a lengthy and at times traumatic period of missionary apprenticeship—one that totaled some seventeen years, as compared to thirteen in Mateer's case and over twenty in Crawford's. The style and attitude that came out of Miss Moon's experiences, however, contrast quite strongly with those of both her male contemporaries. Like Calvin Mateer, and unlike T. P. Crawford—whose theology she technically shared— she kept her balance and her optimism, and she made her formative years in China a period of constructive self-education. But where Mateer learned ways to maximize his own talents, with a view to changing China and the Chinese, Lottie Moon seems to have learned to accept things (herself included) more for what they were than for what she hoped to turn them into.

The differences between Miss Moon and Calvin Mateer are underlined by the fact that each was by every instinct a teacher. Also, in religious terms, life in China was for each a process of achieving personally an idealized Christian life. The contrast between the idealizations is suggested by that between their favorite inspirational books, which were respectively *The Imitation of Christ* and *Pilgrim's Progress*. As a teacher and as a person, Miss Moon perhaps differed most from Mateer as well as from Crawford in that she was not—or learned not to be—a ruling spirit. She neither directed nor hurt other people as regularly as did each of the two men.

The differences between the three people are summed up by their activities during the late 1880s. Lottie Moon was in P'ingtu, and T. P. Crawford was traveling back and forth across the Pacific, working out his revolution. Calvin Mateer was busy organizing numerous worthwhile projects. Each found in his or her work a sort of microcosm that taught ultimate lessons. One of the lessons that Miss Moon learned in P'ingtu was to appreciate her own limitations. The lessons absorbed by the two male missionaries amounted to individual appreciations (very different, of course) of how to rationalize their limitations away.

Out of all this Mateer and Miss Moon emerge as two Americans who achieved understandings of China that for their time and place and purpose in life made good sense. Mateer's variety, which saw his Chinese associates in terms of "carefully-planned schemes for their benefit," seems as dated now as does, perhaps, his molding pedagogy. In his own day he was a true success story, acknowledged at the end by flags and cannon and lavish ceremony. To a present-day observer there is something unsettling about his compulsions, however sublimated, to conquer and to direct and to achieve so much; the whole impressive style reminds one of a recent epitaph on Joseph W. Stilwell, as one of those American heroes who "all seem to have lived a long time ago, in a past age when heroism was sufficient unto itself." [29] It also reminds one of what has been called the oldest American faith—the conviction shared by General Stilwell and Calvin Mateer that, in the end, "if you want anything done right you will have to see to it for yourself every time." [30]

Lottie Moon's kind of understanding of the Chinese, which emphasized "a clearer perception of their difficulties and a warmer sympathy for their [own] efforts," seems perhaps more appropriate to our own time. By home background she brought to China more of a basis for putting on airs than did any of her Western associates; partly because of that, some of her most intense struggles were with herself, over matters that seem specifically not to have worried most missionaries so greatly—things like personal clothing, style of life, and work—but which added up to her whole pose as a bringer of enlightenment to racially and socially different people. Her background also included an unusual (for an American) amount of direct experience with defeat, loss, and loneliness. The eventual product was a consistent tolerance and assured humility that made her very different not only from Calvin Mateer, but also from, say, her sister Edmonia. Without detracting in any way from Mateer's achievements, one cannot help noticing the many faces of his kind of tolerance and humility, and how his compassion sometimes seems like that of an engineer for the parts of his locomotive.

The results of these lives, as they appear to us today, are expressive of the irony that has been so pronounced in Chinese-American relations generally. Calvin Mateer's name and accomplishments have faded away together with his Chinese disciples, who embodied his hopes and made all his work possible. The historical significance of men such as those from the Wen hui-kuan—whose work was always scattered "like the stars"—remains really to be determined; scarcity of individual documentation, plus the "message" attraction of viewing people by groups, will make evaluation difficult. With official China, by one way of putting it, it has of course been as Mateer complained: "They court me today, but tomorrow they will oppose me."

Lottie Moon, on the other hand, who statistically achieved very little worth either commemorating or opposing, is at least in the American south more famous than ever. The many paradoxes here remind us of how truly difficult it is to know what, if anything, in our lives may seem decisive to people who live after us, or what such people may find it necessary to turn us into. One is especially struck by how the life story of this woman—who can justly be said to represent the finest traits of her country and her faith—has been turned into an institution that seems fair game for the kind of criticism developed, out of the smallest and meanest of motives, by her long-forgotten associate Crawford.

The Chinese adjustments of all three of these nineteenth-century Americans do seem to confirm that there are some understandings of an alien culture, at any historical moment, that are both more logical than others and also more helpful to everyone concerned—that better express what has been called constructive empathy.[31] The three stories also suggest that the road to such understanding is not an easy one; hard work and genuine openness to disquieting lessons seem a required part of the trip. Most importantly—and painfully—they underline "the great lesson of modern Western art and thought" that at least a few Westerners have more recently found in Southeast Asia, the fact "that one discovers in the object of one's creative and reflective attention only what one has found or constructed in oneself." [32]

Notes

Bibliography

Glossary

Index

Abbreviations Used in the Notes

APMP | Manuscript papers, American Presbyterian Mission, (East) Shantung province, China. Document numbering refers to volume and number of document within that volume. See bibliography for additional information.

Conference Records 1877 | *Records of the General Conference of the Protestant Missionaries of China, Held at Shanghai, May 10–24, 1877* (Shanghai, 1878).

Conference Records 1890 | *Records of the General Conference of the Protestant Missionaries of China, Held at Shanghai, May 7–20, 1890* (Shanghai, 1890).

Conference Records 1907 | *Records, China Centenary Missionary Conference, Held at Shanghai, April 25 to May 8, 1907* (New York, n.d.).

CR | *The Chinese Recorder and Missionary Journal.* Foochow, 1868–1872; Shanghai, 1874 et seq.

EMMV | Tarleton Perry Crawford, *Evolution in My Mission Views, or Growth of Gospel Mission Principles in My Own Mind* (Fulton, Ky., 1903).

FMJ | *The Foreign Mission Journal.* Organ of the Foreign Mission Board of the Southern Baptist Convention; Richmond, Va., 1851–1916.

MFCD | Diaries of Martha Foster Crawford. Seven ms. volumes, covering period 1847–81.

OMF | *Our Mission Field.* Organ of Women's Foreign Mission Societies, Presbyterian Church in the U.S.A.; New York, 1871–85.

SBCP | Manuscript papers, Southern Baptist North China Mission; cited by numbered folders assigned to individual missionaries. See bibliography for additional information.

241

	tion. Published yearly since 1845.
WHKC	Wang Yüan-te and Liu Yü-feng, eds. *Wen hui-kuan chih* (Alumni history of Tengchow College; Wei-hsien, 1913).
WWC	*Woman's Work in China.* Interdenominational organ of Protestant woman's workers; Shanghai, 1877–1889.
- *WWFE*	*Woman's Work in the Far East.* Successor (1890–1921) to *WWC.*
WWW	*Woman's Work for Woman.* Organ of Women's Foreign Mission Societies, Presbyterian Church in the U.S.A.; New York, 1886–1924. Successor to OMF.
WWW-OMF	*Woman's Work for Woman and Our Mission Field.* A transition title used in 1885–1886, as OMF was succeeded by *WWW.*
SBC Proceedings	*Proceedings of the Southern Baptist Convention.* Records, reports, etc., of the annual Southern Baptist Conven-

Notes

Preface

1. Ida Pruitt, *A Daughter of Han: The Autobiography of a Chinese Working Woman* (originally published 1945; reprinted Stanford, 1967), p. 5.

2. As an established location P'eng-lai seems typically traced to the visit by Ch'in Shih Huang-ti, as in ibid., pp. 5–6. In the late nineteenth century, however, residents of the city commonly spoke of it as having been *built* around 100 B.C. by Han Wu Ti. See Lottie Moon, "Sketch of Tungchow," *WWC*, 6.2:141–148 (May 1883). Rather confusingly, the city expanded so greatly during the brief Sui dynasty (589–618 A.D.) that it was sometimes said to have been founded also at that time; and although its name was officially changed to Tengchow (or Teng-chou-fu) during the reign of Ming Hung-wu (1368–98), many local people were still calling it P'eng-lai five hundred years later. That the place was extremely old and unusually conservative is certain in any case—still prevailing, for example, was the ancient practice of regularly closing gates across key streets, dividing the city into sections for security purposes. See ibid., pp. 141–142; and Ida Pruitt, pp. 15, 39–40.

3. Ibid., pp. 5–6, 18–19; *Su Tung-p'o: Selections from a Sung Dynasty Poet*, tr. and introduced by Burton Watson (New York, 1965), pp. 104–106; and Liu T'ieh-yün, *The Travels of Lao Ts'an*, tr. and annotated by Harold Shadick (Ithaca, 1952), pp. 3–11, 237n1, 238n13. For excellent and beautifully written background information on nineteenth-century P'eng-lai/Tengchow and on life in premodern China generally, one should read Ida Pruitt's whole book.

4. Alexander Armstrong, *Shantung (China): A General Outline of the Geography and History of the Province; a Sketch of its Missions; and Notes of a Journey to the Tomb of Confucius* (Shanghai, 1891), p. 43; also Lottie Moon, "Sketch of Tungchow," pp. 141–143.

5. See ibid., pp. 144–148.

6. Ibid., pp. 147–148.

7. Armstrong, p. 43.

1. Battering Satan's Ramparts

1. Marshall Frady, "Growing Up a Baptist," *Mademoiselle*, 70.5:156, 225–229 (March 1970).

2. Statistical information from Eugene L. Hill, "Administering Southern Baptist Foreign Missions," and J. Winston Crawley, "East Asia,"

both in Baker J. Cauthen, ed., *Advance: A History of Southern Baptist Foreign Missions* (Nashville, 1970), pp. 25–118; James A. Field, Jr., "Near East Notes and Far East Queries," in John K. Fairbank, ed., *The Missionary Enterprise in China and America* (Cambridge, Mass., 1974), pp. 23–55. S. C. Clopton was of course the first SBC China missionary only in a technical sense; Issachar J. Roberts and J. Lewis Shuck, two veteran China hands, changed their affiliations to the SBC's board shortly after Clopton was appointed as a new recruit.

3. Crawley, "East Asia," p. 79.

4. See William Barnes, *The Southern Baptist Convention, 1845–1953* (Nashville, 1954), p. 113; and preface by G. P. Bostick to L. S. Foster, *Fifty Years in China: An Eventful Memoir of the Life of Tarleton Perry Crawford, D.D.* (Nashville, 1909), p. *v.*

5. *EMMV*, p. 153.

6. Henry Allen Tupper, *The Foreign Missions of the Southern Baptist Convention* (Philadelphia, 1880), p. 202; and *EMMV*, p. 9. Typical of Crawford's rather strange upbringing and sense of humor was the delight he took in telling the story of how he got his given name. He claimed to have grown to a fairly advanced age with no name at all. Then one day his father bought a Bible, and, finding a page for the entry of family vital statistics, realized his fourth son had no designation, apparently, but "you." Brought in from play, the boy was asked if he had any preference. "With impartial admiration of friend and foe," the story goes, "he selected the name of a famous British general, who had served during the American Revolution, and the name of a distinguished American commodore, who was engaged in the war of 1812–1814." See Foster, p. 22; and Robert Coventry Forsyth, ed., *Shantung: The Sacred Province of China in Some of Its Aspects* (Shanghai, 1912), p. 178.

7. Foster, p. 24; also *EMMV*, p. 10.

8. Tupper, *The Foreign Missions of the Southern Baptist Convention*, p. 203. Union University, operated by Tennessee Baptists from 1848 to 1861, had a brief success as spiritual headquarters and training ground of the Landmark Movement, theological predecessor to Crawford's Gospel Mission of the 1890s. See *Encyclopedia of Southern Baptists*, 2 vols. (Nashville, 1958), II, 1435.

9. All Crawford citations in these two paragraphs are from T. P. Crawford to J. B. Taylor, Corresponding Secretary, FMB, dated Murfreesboro, Tenn., April 20 and May 25, 1850, SBCP (T. P. Crawford Folder No. 2).

10. A note on the Big Hatchie Association is in order here, as Crawford's connection with it is tied to his subsequent Gospel Mission theology. The Landmarkers, dedicated to the primacy of local churches over the Southern Baptist Convention and its denominational boards, organized at the Big Hatchie annual meeting of 1851; the next year Crawford was selected as the association's own missionary. James Madison Pendleton, leader (or "prophet") of the group, was Union University's leading professor and very likely Crawford's sponsor before the Big

Hatchie membership. In the congeniality of his views Crawford proved more than faithful to the association's trust. See Barnes, pp. 100–105, 114; and Tupper, *The Foreign Missions of the Southern Baptist Convention,* p. 204.

11. MFCD I: March 8, 1864.

12. MFCD I: Oct. 13 and Nov. 20, 1849, and II: Nov. 14, 1850. See also Foster, pp. 29–33.

13. MFCD I: Nov. 20, 1849.

14. MFCD I: Dec. 24, 1847. See also many other entries, especially (1846) March 16, 21, and 23, May 4 and 21, June 8, Jul. 28, Oct. 17; (1847) May 12, Sept. 13 and 27, Nov. 8; (1848) May 12 and 13; (1849) Jan. 6, July 25, Aug. 18, Oct. 18, Nov. 20; (1850) July 13.

15. MFCD I: Dec. 24, 1847. See also entries for Jan. 22, May 12, 13, and 15, and Oct. 3, 1848; and July 25, 1849.

16. See Foster, pp. 30–31.

17. MFCD I: May 25, 1849.

18. MFCD II: Feb. 14, 1851. See also entries for Nov. 2 and 14, 1850, and Jan. 23, 1851; also MFCD I: entry for August 1851.

19. See MFCD II: Jan. 23, Feb. 14, 18, and 19, March 11, and Nov. 4, 1851; Tupper, *The Foreign Missions of the Southern Baptist Convention,* p. 203; and Foster, pp. 37–47. One of the Fosters later commented, "Their minds were cast in entirely dissimilar molds and were very differently trained . . . She was taking a step purely, simply, in faith, and believed without the shadow of a doubt that she was guided by the divine hand." Ibid., pp. 44, 46.

20. Ibid., pp. 55, 99. See also pp. 47–51.

21. MFCD II: Jan. 15, 1853, with later marginal additions in pencil.

22. MFCD II: June 6, 1852. See also Aug. 20 and Nov. 28, 1852, and Feb. 12, 1853.

23. MFCD II: June 6, 1852 (penciled marginal addition).

24. Foster, p. 353; MFCD II: Sept. 24 and Dec. 8, 1852, and Jan. 14, 1853; and *CR,* 16.10:438 (November 1885). Several Shanghai missionaries and Christian Chinese learned Crawford's system, and both T. P. and Martha Crawford and two other missionaries (the Reverend A. B. and Mrs. Cabaniss) wrote books in it during the 1850s. Alexander Wylie commented more or less approvingly on Crawford's script, which seems to have been limited mainly by the fact that only about a thousand characters could be expressed. Crawford tinkered with his system off and on for another thirty years, increasing the character range and devising a Tengchow Mandarin replacement of the original "Shanghai script." He always resented the fact that there had not been more missionaries who "took the trouble to learn it." See Alexander Wylie, *Memorials of Protestant Missionaries to the Chinese: Giving a List of Their Publications, and Obituary Notices of the Deceased, with Copious Indexes* (Shanghai, 1867), p. *iii;* also *CR,* 16.9:398 (October 1885), and T. P. Crawford, "A System of Phonetic Symbols for Writing the Dialects of China," *CR,* 19.3:101–110 (March 1888).

25. All information and citations on Crawford and the Gützlaff case are from *EMMV*, pp. 26–29. See also Foster, pp. 213–214.

26. MFCD V: entry dated 1864. See also Foster, pp. 85–86.

27. Ibid., pp. 62–67, 82, 87.

28. *EMMV*, p. 30; and comment by Miss Lottie Moore (read Lottie Moon) in Forsyth, p. 179.

29. Foster, pp. 75, 82, 88.

30. See ibid., pp. 70, 109–120; and MFCD III, IV, and V. Volume III of MFCD, which has the most abundant and interesting observations on Roberts (whom Martha Crawford loathed) and the Taipings, is available in typescript as Virginia M. Thompson, "Extracts from the Diary of Martha E. Foster Crawford, 1852–1854. Edited, With Notes, An Introduction, and Some Historical Comments on the Role of Mrs. Crawford as a Christian Emissary from the United States to China" (M. A. thesis, Duke University, 1952). Ms. Thompson's opinion of Mrs. Crawford, based on a brief and early slice of her subject's fifty-eight-year missionary career, is misleading.

Issachar Roberts has of course already attracted attention from historians of modern China. For a good short treatment of his activities in the 1850s see Yuan Chung Teng, "Reverend Issachar Jacox Roberts and the Taiping Rebellion," *Journal of Asian Studies*, 23.1:55–67 (November 1963). A much more detailed and recent study is Margaret M. Coughlin, "Strangers in the House: The First Baptist Missionaries from America to China, J. Lewis Shuck and Issachar Roberts" (Ph.D. dissertation, University of Virginia, 1972).

31. Financial information on Crawford is from Barnes, p. 114; Foster, pp. 76, 130–133; and MFCD V: entry dated 1864. At Crawford's death in 1902 his friend G. P. Bostick called his business acumen brilliant and said his Shanghai properties had grown into extremely valuable holdings. "It is perfectly apparent," Bostick wrote, "that if he wished to make money, he could with very little trouble have easily doubled his estate." See Bostick, "In Memoriam. The Late T. P. Crawford, D.D.," *CR*, 33.9:456–458 (September 1902). For an idea of how land values rose see Rhoads Murphey, *Shanghai, Key to Modern China* (Cambridge, Mass., 1953), p. 10.

32. Foster, pp. 133–136; and MFCD V: entry dated 1864.

33. See letter from J. B. Taylor to T. P. Crawford, March, 1861, cited in Foster, pp. 126–127. Also MFCD V: entry dated 1864.

34. Foster, p. 138.

35. Anna B. Hartwell (J. B.'s daughter) in Forsyth, p. 181. I am unable to identify the eight members added by Crawford in 1864–65, or to ascertain how he added them. The first named Shantung convert claimed by Crawford was Mrs. Liu (actually Martha Crawford's "addition"), who was not baptized until 1866. See Foster, pp. 140–141, 147.

36. MFCD V: Dec. 28, 1865, and Feb. 11, 1868. See also J. B. Hartwell to H. A. Tupper, Corresponding Secretary, FMB, Chefoo, March 30, 1874, SBCP (J. B. Hartwell Folder No. 1).

37. Letter from T. P. Crawford to unidentified FMB addressee, SBCP (T. P. Crawford Folder No. 3). This letter consists of five ms. pages; upper part of page 1, including date, is missing, but internal evidence places it during 1876. Addressee was probably H. A. Tupper. See also MFCD V: May 30 and Dec. 28, 1865, and Feb. 11, 1868.

38. Sandford to S. Wells Williams, Chefoo, Aug. 11, 1866, in "Chefoo-Tientsin Counsular Records, 1863–1869" (bound ms. correspondence, National Archives, Washington, D.C.), pp. 161–167. Also Foster, p. 144.

39. T. P. Crawford to Samuel A. Holmes, Tengchow, Dec. 18, 1868, "Chefoo-Tientsin Consular Records, 1863–1869," pp. 359–366; also E. T. Sandford to S. Wells Williams, Chefoo, April 30, 1866, pp. 115–118.

40. Foster, pp. 145–146. See also Martha Crawford letter dated Tengchow, May 4, 1874, *FMJ*, 7.2:7 (August 1874); Martha Crawford, "History of Missions in Tungchow for the First Thirteen Years," as condensed by H. A. Tupper, *The Foreign Missions of the Southern Baptist Convention*, pp. 229–230; Martha Crawford, "A Call to North China," in H. A. Tupper, *A Decade of Foreign Missions, 1880–1890* (Richmond, 1891), pp. 667–675; E. T. Sandford to S. Wells Williams, Chefoo, April 30, 1866, "Chefoo-Tientsin Consular Records, 1863–1869," pp. 115–118.

41. Floor plan and description in MFCD VI: Jan. 28, 1876.

42. See Foster, p. 147. For the deGrew story see MFCD IV: entry dated July 1862, and V: Dec. 23, 1866. In Shanghai both T. P. and Martha Crawford took a vigorous interest in performing Christian marital rites over "harem" situations involving Western men and their Chinese paramours. The legality of these marriages seems to have been somewhat debatable. See also triangular "insatiable desire" story, MFCD IV: entry dated April 1863.

43. T. P. Crawford letter dated Tengchow, May 25, 1883, *FMJ*, 15.1:3 (August 1883).

44. See Foster, pp. 142, 147; Martha Crawford (Tupper condensation), "History of Missions in Tungchow for the First Thirteen Years," p. 227; MFCD V: Dec. 16, 1867, and VI: March 20, 1868.

45. See Foster, pp. 150–151, 156–160; *SBC Proceedings, 1868*, p. 44; and MFCD VI: March 20, 1868.

46. *Tsao yang-fan shu* (Shanghai, 1866), esp. English preface (unpaginated) and Chinese text, pp. 1 and 24b–25. According to Foster, p. 318, this book went through many editions and was still in treaty-port demand as late as 1909.

47. Martha Crawford, "My School," *WWC*, 3.1:7–10 (November 1879). See also *EMMV*, pp. 35–37; and [Cicero Washington Pruitt], "Some Recollections of Dr. T. P. Crawford and Wife," dated Philadelphia, Dec. 22, 1917, SBCP (Martha Crawford Folder), p. 4. This eleven-page ms. is unsigned, but handwriting and many other features identify it unmistakably as Pruitt's.

48. Martha Crawford, "My School," p. 8. See also T. P. Crawford

letter, Tengchow, April 25, 1870, *FMJ*, 3.1:25 (June 1870); and T. P. Crawford to H. A. Tupper, Tengchow, June 25, 1876, SBCP (T. P. Crawford Folder No. 2).

49. *SBC Proceedings, 1869*, p. 45.

50. MFCD VI: Nov. 1, 1869.

51. All citations and information on this episode are from "Chefoo-Tientsin Consular Records, 1863–1869." See in order T. P. Crawford to Samuel A. Holmes, Tengchow, Dec. 11, 1868, pp. 387–389; T. P. Crawford to Samuel A. Holmes, Tengchow, Dec. 18, 1868, pp. 359–366; James Wilson to T. P. Crawford, Chefoo, Dec. 23, 1868, p. 385; Chinese original and English translation (by J. B. Hartwell) of "Perpetual Prohibition" *(yung-yüan shih-chin)* monument dated Aug. 4, 1868, pp. 397–399; T. P. Crawford to Samuel A. Holmes, Chefoo, Dec. 26, 1868, pp. 379–384; T. P. Crawford to Samuel A. Holmes, Tengchow, Dec. 31, 1868, pp. 367–377; J. Ross Browne to Samuel A. Holmes, Peking, Feb. 3, 1869, pp. 409–411; T. P. Crawford to Samuel A. Holmes, Tengchow, March 8, 1869, pp. 415–418. For further commentary see MFCD VI: March 24, 1869, and VII: Feb. 11, 1878.

52. MFCD VI: April 7 and Oct. 5, 1868.

53. MFCD VI: Oct. 5 and Nov. 3, 1868; March 24 and Nov. 1, 1869.

54. MFCD VI: Nov. 3, 1868.

55. See MFCD V: Feb. 11, 1868, and VI: March 20 and 24, 1868.

56. Martha Crawford (Tupper condensation), "History of Missions in Tungchow for the First Thirteen Years," pp. 225–226.

57. Hartwell describes Wu Tswun Chao and his qualifications in *SBC Proceedings, 1871*, p. 43. For Crawford's feelings see especially his letter to H. A. Tupper, Tengchow, Nov. 1, 1875, SBCP (T. P. Crawford Folder No. 2). The ordination is described by Hartwell in *CR*, 3.9:257 (February 1871). On Eliza Hartwell's ungracious death and the evacuation to Chefoo, see MFCD VI: June 9 and Nov. 12, 1870.

58. See T. P. Crawford to H. A. Tupper, Tenghow, Nov. 1, 1875, SBCP (T. P. Crawford Folder No. 2).

59. Copy of Mills to J. B. Taylor, Tengchow, Feb. 17, 1872, in pocket inside front cover to MFCD III. See also Tupper, *The Foreign Missions of the Southern Baptist Convention*, p. 234; and MFCD VI: Jan. 16 and February, 1872.

60. See E. E. Davault, "First Impressions," dated Tengchow, Jan. 30, 1885, *FMJ*, 16.9:2 (April 1885); and *SBC Proceedings, 1875*, p. 60.

61. C. W. Pruitt, "Some Recollections," p. 4. See also Foster, pp. 91, 277–279.

62. Cited in Tupper, *The Foreign Missions of the Southern Baptist Convention*, p, 237. For Crawford's views on Christian Chinese see especially his letter to H. A. Tupper, Tengchow, Nov. 1, 1875, SBCP (T. P. Crawford Folder No. 2).

63. T. P. Crawford, "Hui-t'ang li ti kuei-chü," in *Lüeh lun tsa-chi* (n. p., 1870), pp. 4b–5.

64. T. P. Crawford, "Ch'in-mu chih chun-sheng," in *Lüeh lun tsa-chi,* p. 3; and *Conference Records 1877,* p. 396.

65. Foster, p. 158.

66. See Martha Crawford, *Discouragements and Encouragements of the Missionary Situation in China* (n. p., 1883), pp. 7, 12.

67. T. P. Crawford, *Lüeh lun tsa-chi,* pp. 4–5b, 11–18b. See also *Conference Records 1877,* pp. 396–397.

68. C. W. Pruitt, "Some Recollections," p. 3. See also T. P. Crawford, "What Caused the Sudden Death of Christ?" in *CR,* 5.4:199–204 (July-August 1874); and review by E. C. Lord in *CR, 5.5:279–286* (September-October 1874).

69. See *Ku kuo chien lüeh* (Tengchow, 1873), pp. 73–81b.

70. Impressions of the Crawfords are from C. W. Pruitt, "Some Recollections," pp. 1, 10; W. D. King in Foster, p. 295; Tupper, *The Foreign Missions of the Southern Baptist Convention,* p. 237; MFCD VI: Jan. 29, 1870; and T. P. Crawford letter, Tengchow, May 15, 1874, *FMJ,* 7.3:11 (September 1874). The description of his appearance comes from a conversation with Ida Pruitt. The comment on Hartwell's lovable nature is by his daughter Anna in Forsyth, p. 183.

2. A Stranger in a Strange Land

1. See *SBC Proceedings,* 1871, p. 42; and M. T. Yates to J. B. Hartwell, Shanghai, March 28, 1876, SBCP (J. B. Hartwell Folder No. 1).

2. See T. P. Crawford to H. A. Tupper, Tengchow, date missing (*ca* 1876), SBCP (T. P. Crawford Folder No. 3); and J. B. Hartwell to H. A. Tupper, Chefoo, Dec. 4, 1874, SBCP (J. B. Hartwell Folder No. 1). On Matthew G. Holmes's departure see his letters to Assistant Secretary of State J. C. B. Davis, dated Uniontown, Pa., March 14, 1872, and to Secretary of State Hamilton Fish, dated West Union, W. Va., Oct. 30, 1872, both in "Despatches from United States Consuls in Chefoo, 1863–1906" (National Archives Microfilm Publications, Record Group 59, Microcopy No. 102; Washington, D.C., 1965), Vol. II. For some of M. G. Holmes's past scrapes with the law see Prince Kung to S. Wells Williams, two letters dated Peking, Dec. 3, 1867, and Jan. 5, 1868, in "Chefoo-Tientsin Consular Records, 1863–1869," pp. 307–309, 319–321.

3. See *SBC Proceedings, 1871,* p. 42; *1873,* p. 41; and *1876,* p. 36. For a breakdown on Wu Tswun Chao's congregation see Lottie Moon to H. A. Tupper, March 24, 1876, SBCP (Lottie Moon Folder No. 1).

4. On Wu's salary see report of North Street Church for 1872 in Tupper, *The Foreign Missions of the Southern Baptist Convention,* p. 238; and *SBC Proceedings, 1875,* p. 58. On how the money was used, see Martha Crawford (Tupper condensation), "History of Missions in Tungchow for the First Thirteen Years," pp. 226–227; and Lottie Moon to H. A. Tupper, Tengchow, July 8, 1878, SBCP (Lottie Moon Folder No. 1).

5. T. P. Crawford to H. A. Tupper, Tengchow, April 4, 1876, SBCP (T. P. Crawford Folder No. 2).

6. My account of events between 1872 and Crawford's break with Wu Tswun Chao has been pieced together from lengthy accounts by several people. For J. B. Hartwell's version see Hartwell to H. A. Tupper, Chefoo, Dec. 4, 1874, SBCP (J. B. Hartwell Folder No. 1); Hartwell's letter amounts to 34 ms. pages, in which T. P. Crawford is accused of crimes ranging from dishonesty to boorish manners, with numerous remarks on his lack of mental competence. Hartwell's unselfconscious viciousness seems surprising, to say the least, in a Christian minister. For Crawford's side see especially his letter to H. A. Tupper, Tengchow (date missing, *ca* 1876), SBCP (T. P. Crawford No. 3), and MFCD VI: Jan. 28, 1876, and VII: Jan. 26, 1877. The first of Mrs. Crawford's diary entries totals 55 ms. pages and is very informative. For information on Li Chin-yü and M. G. Holmes—Kao Ku San's side of the story, in a sense—see the following documents in "Chefoo Consular Records, 1868–1874" (bound ms. correspondence, National Archives, Washington, D.C.): James Wilson to F. F. Low, Chefoo, Nov. 18, 1871, pp. 843–845; James Wilson to F. F. Low, two letters, both dated Chefoo, Dec. 14, 1871, pp. 849–857; English translation, W. S. Wadman to Kung Taotai, two letters, April 25 and May 2, 1871, pp. 859–864; "Memo of Accounts Drawn Up by Mr. Holmes," p. 865; English translation, James Wilson to Kung Taotai, Chefoo, July 14, 1871, pp. 867–871; three miscellaneous documents, pp. 875–886. For additional information see Lottie Moon to H. A. Tupper, Tengchow, Oct. 23, 1876, SBCP (Lottie Moon Folder No. 1); and *SBC Proceedings, 1874*, p. 33.

7. J. B. Hartwell to H. A. Tupper, Chefoo, Dec. 4, 1874, SBCP (J. B. Hartwell Folder No. 1).

8. See Tupper, *The Foreign Missions of the Southern Baptist Convention*, pp. 239–243; J. B. Hartwell to H. A. Tupper, Wake Forest, N.C., Oct. 7, 1878, SBCP (J. B. Hartwell Folder No. 1); MFCD VI: undated entry (date removed along with several ms. pages) between entries for June 14, 1872, and Jan. 28, 1876; and VII: March 25, 1876.

9. T. P. Crawford to H. A. Tupper, Tengchow, Nov. 1, 1875, SBCP (T. P. Crawford Folder No. 2); and date missing (*ca* 1876), SBCP (T. P. Crawford Folder No. 3).

10. J. B. Hartwell to H. A. Tupper, Chefoo, March 30 and Dec. 4, 1874, both in SBCP (J. B. Hartwell Folder No. 1).

11. J. B. Hartwell to H. A. Tupper, Chefoo, March 30 and Dec. 4, 1874, both in SBCP (J. B. Hartwell Folder No. 1).

12. T. P. Crawford to H. A. Tupper, date missing (*ca* 1876), SBCP (T. P. Crawford Folder No. 3). Crawford's first allusion to his difficulties with Hartwell comes in his letter of Nov. 1, 1875, in response to a request by the FMB that he expedite an "amalgamation" of his church with that of Wu Tswun Chao. By this time the board had been receiving Hartwell's complaints for almost two years (plus an 1875 personal visit by him and Mrs. Hartwell), and the Crawfords had been informed that the FMB was

"alarmed" about the state of things in Tengchow. See MFCD VI: Jan. 28, 1876.

13. Lottie Moon to H. A. Tupper, Viewmont, Va., Jan. 20, 1877, SBCP (Lottie Moon Folder No. 1). See also J. B. Hartwell to H. A. Tupper, Dec. 4, 1874, and April 7, 1875, both in SBCP (J. B. Hartwell Folder No. 1).

14. See M. T. Yates to J. B. Hartwell, Shanghai, March 28, 1876, SBCP (copy in J. B. Hartwell Folder No. 1); also J. B. Hartwell to H. A. Tupper, Petersburg, Va., Dec. 4, 1875, and Columbus, Ga., Feb. 13, 1877, both in SBCP (J. B. Hartwell Folder No. 1). Yates's investigation at Tengchow was the FMB's response to Hartwell's own solicitations for help against Crawford, which obviously backfired. See MFCD VI: Jan. 28, 1876.

15. T. P. Crawford to H. A. Tupper, Nov. 1, 1875, SBCP (T. P. Crawford Folder No. 2); also MFCD VI: Jan. 28, 1876.

16. See Martha Crawford (Tupper condensation), "History of Missions in Tungchow for the First Thirteen Years," pp. 227–228; and MFCD VI: entry dated February 1872. On the long and stormy career of Mrs. Liu see MFCD VI: Oct. 5, 1868; March 28, April 1, June 26, and Sept. 13, 1869; Jan. 29 and Nov. 12, 1870; Jan. 16, 1872; and Jan. 28, 1876.

17. T. P. Crawford to H. A. Tupper, Tengchow, 1874 (rest of date missing), and Nov. 1, 1875, both in SBCP (T. P. Crawford Folder No. 2). See also J. B. Hartwell to H. A. Tupper, Chefoo, Dec. 4, 1874, SBCP (J. B. Hartwell Folder No. 1); and MFCD VI: Jan. 28, 1876.

18. MFCD VI: Jan. 29, 1870; also T. P. Crawford letter in *FMJ*, 10.12:3 (March 1879).

19. MFCD VII: May 4, 1876. See also MFCD VI: Jan. 28, 1876.

20. See MFCD VII: Jan. 18, 1877, and Feb. 11, 1878.

21. MFCD VII: June 26, 1876.

22. MFCD VII: Feb. 28, 1876, and Jan. 11, 1877. Also Foster, pp. 167–171; Tupper, *The Foreign Missions of the Southern Baptist Convention,* p. 234; and Martha Crawford (Tupper condensation), "History of Missions in Tungchow for the First Thirteen Years," pp. 227–228.

23. Martha Crawford, "My School," pp. 9–10.

24. MFCD VII: March 9, 1876. See also 1876 entries for May 4, 5, 17, 22, and 23; June 20 and 26; July 3 and 13.

25. See MFCD VII: Aug. 9, 1879. According to Ida Pruitt, Mary Kiang had been adopted by the Hartwells and was known among foreigners as Mary Hartwell (letter to this writer, Feb. 11, 1974).

26. T. P. Crawford, *The Patriarchal Dynasties from Adam to Abraham, Shown to Cover 10,500 Years, and the Highest Human Life Only 187* (Richmond, 1877), pp. 5, 7–8, 54–55. See also "The Ancient Dynasties of Berosus and China Compared with Those of Genesis," *CR,* 11.6:411–429 (November-December 1880); and "A Compendium of History in Thirty Volumes. By Wong Shi-ching, an Eminent Scholar of the Ming Dynasty, A.D. 1526–1590," *CR,* 12.2:77–86 (March-April

1881). For a startled Baptist review of *Patriarchal Dynasties* ("while it may not convince, it cannot fail to interest"), see FMJ, 9.8:1 (November 1877).

27. See E. C. Lord in *CR*, 5.5:279–286 (September-October 1874). It should be noted that Edward C. Lord, a Northern Baptist at Ningpo, was himself a notoriously difficult and opinionated individual. Unfortunately for T. P. Crawford's scholarly reputation, Lord seems to have been writing this review just as Crawford was separately attracting attention by an original poem lamenting the death of the Reverend M. J. Knowlton, Lord's "great enemy" for almost twenty years. See Foster, pp. 313–314; and MFCD VI: Jan. 28, 1876.

28. See H. T. Cook in *EMMV*, p. 21; and T. P. Crawford, *The Patriarchal Dynasties*, p. 8.

29. See Foster, p. 176; and MFCD VII: July 24 and Nov. 15, 1876, and Jan. 26 and March 21, 1877. Also T. P. Crawford to H. A. Tupper, date missing (*ca* 1876), SBCP (T. P. Crawford Folder No. 3); this letter, incidentally, is dated by its closing reference to the recent expiration of Kao Ku San's two-year grace period, with an allusion to Crawford's attendant maneuvers against Kao.

30. MFCD VII: Jan. 26 and March 20, 1877, and Dec. 31, 1880.

31. MFCD VII: July 24 and Nov. 15, 1876; also Foster, p. 320; and T. P. Crawford letter in *FMJ*, 10.12:3 (March 1879).

32. MFCD VII: March 20 and Sept. 6, 1877.

33. See MFCD VII: Jan. 18, 1877; and T. P. Crawford letter, Nov. 8, 1877, *FMJ*, 9.11:2–3 (February 1878).

34. Ibid., pp. 2–3. Also MFCD VII: Feb. 17, 1876, and Jan. 18 and March 6, 1877; *SBC Proceedings, 1879*, p. 58; and Martha Crawford, "My School," p. 10.

35. See Lottie Moon to H. A. Tupper, Tengchow, March 24, 1876, SBCP (Lottie Moon Folder No. 1); M. T. Yates to J. B. Hartwell, Shanghai, March 28, 1876, SBCP (copy in J. B. Hartwell Folder No. 1); H. A. Tupper to J. B. Hartwell, Richmond, Jan. 15, 1877, SBCP (copy in J. B. Hartwell Folder No. 1); J. B. Hartwell to H. A. Tupper, Columbus, Ga., Feb. 13, 1877, SBCP (J. B. Hartwell Folder No. 1); T. P. Crawford to H. A. Tupper, Tengchow, July 16, 1877, SBCP (T. P. Crawford Folder No. 3). Also MFCD VII: Sept. 6, 1877, and July 30 and Aug. 30, 1878; *SBC Proceedings, 1880*, p. 45, and *1878*, p. 49.

36. See *Conference Records 1877*, pp. iii, 4–22, plus articles by Martha and T. P. Crawford, pp. 147–152, 323–328. All four papers by females were read before the conference by male missionaries, presumably for propriety's sake (p. 23). For the same reason, one supposes, Martha Crawford's name does not appear as author on any of her Chinese-language writings; this was *not* the case with most other literarily active female missionaries in Shantung. What one most pertinently sees in all this is one of the ways in which T. P. Crawford exploited his wife. Her 1877 conference paper was clearly written at her husband's urging, as part of his effort to get her away from her school and into other work; then in

Shanghai he felt it necessary to read her paper himself, doing so in a fashion that created misunderstanding and adverse comment (ibid., p. 159; MFCD VII: Feb. 9 and Sept. 6, 1877). In the 1880s and 1890s, as T. P. Crawford came into conflict with his home board, one sees a marked increase in public statements under Martha Crawford's name, espousing her husband's views (and often his phraseology) on matters she herself had never thought much about. One cannot help remarking on this use of a woman whose own reputation for character and sound judgment had grown as her embattled husband's declined.

37. T. P. Crawford to H. A. Tupper, Shanghai, May 28, 1877, SBCP (T. P. Crawford Folder No. 3); and MFCD VII: Feb. 11, 1878.

38. *Conference Records 1877*, p. 295.

39. T. P. Crawford, "Advantages and Disadvantages of the Employment of Native Assistants," ibid., pp. 323–328.

40. *Conference Records 1877*, pp. 324–325; and comments on pp. 75, 252.

41. See ibid., pp. 334–336; and MFCD VII: Sept. 6, 1877. Actually the disclaimer was printed immediately under a speech following and similar to Crawford's by the Methodist Nathan Sites of Foochow. The concern was that among readers of the *Records* it might "be inferred from the fact that both of the essayists took the same side of the subject, that the majority of the Conference holds the same views. By order of the Conference." See pp. 329–333.

42. Answering a request from Secretary Tupper for information on Hartwell's loose talk, one correspondent commented, "For I could but think, that if the public knows what I learned, how much more money would be given for F. Missions in this country? Rest easy . . . no publicity shall be given by me of this unhappy state of affairs." See Thomas E. Skinner to H. A. Tupper, Macon, Ga., June 23, 1877, SBCP (J. B. Hartwell Folder No. 1).

43. J. B. Hartwell to H. A. Tupper, Colerain, N.C., Feb. 13, 1878, and Wake Forest, N.C., Aug. 13, 1878, both in SBCP (J. B. Hartwell Folder No. 1). See also MFCD VII: Feb. 11, 1878, and Jan. 28, 1880.

44. J. B. Hartwell to H. A. Tupper, Rockford, N.C., Sept. 26, 1878, and Wake Forest, N.C., Oct. 7, 1878, both in SBCP (J. B. Hartwell Folder No. 1). Latter letter includes original and Hartwell translation of correspondence from Chinese members of North Street Church. See also MFCD VII: Feb. 11, March 2, and July 30–August 30, 1878; and Jan. 28, 1880.

45. Lottie Moon to H. A. Tupper, Tengchow, July 8 and 27, 1878, both in SBCP (Lottie Moon Folder No. 1); Martha Crawford letter dated April 5, 1879, FMJ, 11.4:4 (July 1879); and MFCD VII: May 25, 1878.

46. MFCD VII: Jan. 11, 12, and 30, March 20, and Sept. 6, 1877; May 25, 1878.

47. MFCD VI: Jan. 28, 1876; and VII: Sept. 6, 1877, and Feb. 11, May 31, and July 30–August 30, 1878.

48. MFCD VII: Feb. 11 and March 2, 1878.

49. MFCD VII: Jan. 18 and March 21, 1877.

50. On Crawford's health problems and furlough decision see Lottie Moon letter dated Tengchow, March 9, 1874, *FMJ*, 7.1:3 (July 1874); T. P. Crawford letters in *FMJ*, 7.7:26 (January 1875) and 10.12:3 (March 1879); MFCD VII: July 24, 1876, and May 25 and June 22, 1878; Lottie Moon to H. A. Tupper, Tengchow, Dec. 24, 1877, SBCP (Lottie Moon Folder No. 1); T. P. Crawford letter dated San Francisco, Nov. 3, 1878, *FMJ*, 10.9:4 (December 1878); T. P. Crawford to H. A. Tupper, Richmond, Feb. 12, 1879, SBCP (T. P. Crawford Folder No. 3).

3. *Blowing the Gospel Trumpet*

1. T. P. Crawford letter, *FMJ*, 10.12:3 (March 1879).

2. T. P. Crawford letter dated San Francisco, Nov. 3, 1878, *FMJ*, 10.9:4 (December 1878).

3. Martha Crawford to T. P. Crawford, Tengchow, Dec. 9, 1878, cited in *FMJ*, 10.12:3 (March 1879).

4. Ibid., p. 3; Foster, pp. 181, 310–311.

5. Ibid., pp. 310–311. See also T. P. Crawford, *The Patriarchal Dynasties*, p. 137; "The Ancient Dynasties of Berosus and China Compared with Those of Genesis," p. 419; and letter dated Tengchow, Feb. 5, 1866, "Chefoo-Tientsin Consular Records, 1863–1869," pp. 107–109.

6. See Foster, p. 181; and *EMMV*, pp. 46–47.

7. MFCD II: penciled addition (undated but written years later, obviously) to final entry dated Jan. 15, 1853.

8. T. P. Crawford letters dated Tengchow, May 15, 1874, *FMJ*, 7.3:11 (September 1874), and Sept 27, 1880, *FMJ*, 12.11:3 (February 1881).

9. MFCD VII: Aug. 9, 1879; and Foster, pp. 182–183.

10. MFCD VII: Dec. 31, 1880.

11. MFCD VII: Aug. 9, 1879. Also Tupper, *A Decade of Foreign Missions, 1880–1890*, p. 124; and C. W. Pruitt, "Some Recollections," p. 7.

12. Ibid., p. 3. Also *EMMV*, p. 38 and MFCD VII: Aug. 9, 1879.

13. MFCD VII: Jan. 12 and Dec. 29, 1880.

14. On Martha Crawford's early affection see especially MFCD II: Nov. 28 and Dec. 31, 1852; and III: Feb. 12, 1853. On "hooks of steel" see C. W. Pruitt, "Some Recollections," p. 7.

15. On the horrifying situation in the Roberts family see MFCD III: Aug. 25, Sept 13, 15, and 17, 1853; and May 10, 1854.

16. MFCD VII: March 2, 1878; May 7, 1879; Jan. 12 and Dec. 29, 1880; July 12, 25, and Nov. 11, 1881. Also C. W. Pruitt, "Some Recollections," p. 8; and Foster, p. 186.

17. Ibid., p. 187.

18. C. W. Pruitt, "Some Recollections," p. 9.

19. Ibid., pp. 7–9; *SBC Proceedings, 1882*, p. 62; Tupper, *A Decade of Foreign Missions, 1880–1890*, p. 219; and Foster, p. 189.

20. See N. W. Halcomb letter dated Tengchow, March 26, 1883, *FMJ*, 14.11:3 (June 1883); Martha Crawford to H. A. Tupper, Tengchow, March 19, 1884, SBCP (Martha Crawford Folder); C. W. Pruitt, "Some Recollections," p. 9; and compound floor plan under MFCD VI: Jan. 28, 1876.

21. C. W. Pruitt, "Some Recollections," p. 3.

22. Ibid., pp. 3, 9–10; *EMMV*, p. 38; MFCD VII: Nov. 11, 1881; N. W. Halcomb letter dated Tengchow, March 26, 1883, *FMJ*, 14.11:3 (June 1883); T. P. Crawford letter dated Tengchow, May 25, 1883, and Lottie Moon letter dated Tengchow, May 21, 1883, both in *FMJ*, 15.1:3 (August 1883); Martha Crawford to H. A. Tupper, Tengchow, March 19, 1884, SBCP (Martha Crawford Folder); and *SBC Proceedings, 1884*, App. B, p. *ix*.

23. Chu Yuen Hsun, quoted by T. W. Ayers in Fannie E. S. Heck, *In Royal Service: The Mission Work of Southern Baptist Women* (Richmond, 1913), p. 250. Ayers also reports here on the careers of four other former students of Mrs. Crawford. Kwo Yu Yoong married Mary Kiang/Hartwell, moved to Manchuria, and became a "prosperous business man." Information on Kwo from C. W. Pruitt, "Some Recollections," p. 8; and from a note to me from Ida Pruitt, Feb. 11, 1974.

24. Lottie Moon to H. A. Tupper, Tengchow, June 27, 1885, SBCP (Lottie Moon Folder No. 2).

25. *EMMV*, pp. 38–40.

26. Ibid., pp. 36–37; and C. W. Pruitt, "Some Recollections," p. 2.

27. *EMMV*, p. 38. See also Martha Crawford to H. A. Tupper, Tengchow, March 19, 1884, SBCP (Martha Crawford Folder).

28. Lottie Moon letter dated P'ingtu, March 12, 1886, *FMJ*, 17.11:4 (June 1886).

29. C. W. Pruitt, "Some Recollections," pp. 5, 10–11.

30. Foster, p. 234; Tupper, *A Decade of Foreign Missions, 1880–1890*, p. 390; *SBC Proceedings, 1885*, App. A, p. *xvii*; and Anna S. Pruitt, *The Day of Small Things* (Richmond, 1929), pp. 27–28.

31. Foster, pp. 193–194.

32. T. P. Crawford letter dated Tengchow, Sept. 27, 1880, *FMJ* 12.11:3 (February 1881).

33. Descriptions of Southern Baptist life in east Shantung during the 1880s generally read like years passed on Devil's Island. See *SBC Proceedings, 1888*, App. B, p. *xxxviii*; Tupper, *A Decade of Foreign Missions, 1880–1890*, pp. 268, 392, 404, 589; *A Century for Christ in China* (Richmond, 1936), p. 51; and Anna S. Pruitt, *Up from Zero* (Nashville, 1939), pp. 54–55.

34. T. P. Crawford letter dated Tengchow, Sept. 27, 1880, *FMJ*, 12.11:3 (February 1881).

35. See Lottie Moon letter dated April, 1885, cited in Una R. Lawrence, *Lottie Moon* (Nashville, 1927), p. 133; Lottie Moon to H. A.

Tupper, Tengchow, June 27, 1885, SBCP (Lottie Moon Folder No. 2);
and Foster, p. 210.

36. Lottie Moon to H. A. Tupper, Tengchow, June 27, 1885, SBCP
(Lottie Moon Folder No. 2).

37. See Foster, p. 205; *SBC Proceedings, 1885*, App. A, p. *xvii*; and
1887, App. A, p. *ix*; and Lottie Moon letter dated P'ingtu, March 12,
1886, *FMJ*, 17.11:4 (June 1886).

38. Lottie Moon to H. A. Tupper, Tengchow, June 27, 1885, SBCP
(Lottie Moon Folder No. 2).

39. See ibid.; C. W. Pruitt, "Some Recollections," p. 1; and Tupper,
A Decade of Foreign Missions, 1880–1890, p. 389. Crawford did at this
time turn over his authority as mission treasurer to Pruitt and, by his
own account, his pastorate as well. See Foster, pp. 204–205.

40. C. W. Pruitt cited in ibid., p. 225.

41. The book was C. H. Carpenter, *Self-Support, Illustrated in the
History of the Bassein Karen Mission, from 1840 to 1880* (Boston, 1883).

42. *EMMV*, pp. 40–41, 50–52.

43. *EMMV*, pp. 40–41.

44. Lottie Moon to H. A. Tupper, Tengchow, June 27, 1885, SBCP
(Lottie Moon Folder No. 2).

45. T. P. Crawford to H. A. Tupper, Tengchow, June 24, 1884,
SBCP (T. P. Crawford Folder No. 3).

46. Lottie Moon to H. A. Tupper, Tengchow, June 27, 1885, SBCP
(Lottie Moon Folder No. 2).

47. See *EMMV*, pp. 48–55.

48. *EMMV*, pp. 57–58, 60–62; and Tupper, *A Decade of Foreign
Missions, 1880–1890*, p. 453.

49. See *EMMV*, pp. 64–75, 115; and Tupper, *A Decade of Foreign
Missions, 1880–1890*, pp. 451–454.

50. *EMMV*, pp. 75–77. In the most interesting letter E. Z. Simmons
compared expenses and results, based on reports in the annual *SBC Proceedings*, of Crawford's self-supporting Tengchow mission with those of
his own "subsidizing" one at Canton. During an eleven-year period prior
to 1885, Crawford's mission had received $78,000 from the FMB, while
Canton had received less than $70,000; yet during the same period
Crawford had reported only 90 baptisms while Canton had baptized 323.
Simmons concluded, "I hope Dr. C. will find his plans less expensive and
more generous of good results in the future than they have been in the
past." See Simmons letter dated Canton, Aug. 26, 1885, *FMJ*, 17.5:4
(December 1885); and Crawford reply dated Richmond, Nov. 7, 1885,
FMJ, 17.6:4 (January 1886). See also criticism of Crawford by R. H.
Graves of Canton, *FMJ*, 17.9:1 (April 1886).

This type of criticism—that he actually spent large board sums to
little apparent effect, while denouncing subsidizers who spent less—was
particularly troublesome to Crawford. One element here was that
Crawford was always in some respects a subsidizer himself, as of his
scholarly research staff and crew of domestic servants, and by investing in

business ventures with his church members. One of his worst torments, he stated, was that circumstances had compelled him "to excite pecuniary expectations among the people," while his Baptist convictions simultaneously "compelled [him] to disappoint and rebuke them." See letter to C. W. Pruitt dated March 30, 1889, cited in Foster, pp. 220–223.

51. See Tupper, *A Decade of Foreign Missions, 1880–1890*, pp. 69–70.

52. *EMMV*, pp. 75–79.

53. *EMMV*, pp. 81–82.

54. Editorial in *FMJ*, 18.1:4 (August 1886). See also *EMMV*, p. 83. Later Baptist appraisals of Crawford's activities in the 1880s are more blunt. For a typical view—one that sees him "tearing up the foundations" of China missions—see Frank K. Means, *Southern Baptist Foreign Missions: Digest of Project Reports Made by Students in Southwestern Baptist Theological Seminary* (Seminary Hill, Texas, 1941). p. 20.

55. *EMMV*, p. 85; and *SBC Proceedings, 1888*, App. B, p. *xxxviii*.

56. See ibid., p. *xl*; Martha Crawford, "A Call to North China," dated Tengchow, Sept. 28, 1888, in Tupper, *A Decade of Foreign Missions, 1880–1890*, p. 668; letter dated Tengchow, March 4, 1889, *FMJ*, 20.10:3 (March 1889); and Foster, p. 225.

57. T. P. Crawford to C. W. Pruitt, March 30, 1889, in Foster, pp. 220–223; and *EMMV*, pp. 90–94.

58. See *EMMV*, pp. 86–89, 94–95.

59. See *EMMV*, pp. 98–104.

60. See G. P. Bostick letter dated Tengchow, Nov. 10, 1890, *FMJ*, 22.7:209 (February 1891).

61. On the importance of Martha Crawford to her husband's popularity see Anna S. Pruitt, *Up from Zero*, pp. 55, 59. On the 1890 mission meeting see *EMMV*, pp. 107–108.

62. See "Churches, To the Front!" reprinted in T. P. Crawford, ed., *The Crisis of the Churches. A Collection of Earnest Articles and Extracts from Earnest Men on Matters of Vital Concern to Baptists* (Chefoo, 1894), pp. 64–78.

63. See *FMJ*, 23.10:291–292 (May 1892); 23.12:358 (July 1892); 24.1:4 (August 1892); and article "Our Board and the 'Gospel Mission,'" 25.2:37–41 (September 1893). See also *EMMV*, p. 113.

64. See *EMMV*, pp. 107–130; and W. D. King letter, *FMJ*, 23.12:371 (July 1892).

65. See *EMMV*, pp. 138–141; Foster, p. 237; Anna B. Hartwell in Forsyth, p. 183; and J. B. Hartwell in *SBC Proceedings, 1894*, App. A, p. *xxviii*.

66. See *EMMV*, pp. 138–147; and Foster, pp. 234–257.

67. See ibid., pp. 300–309; and *EMMV*, pp. 146–147.

68. *EMMV*, pp. 149–150.

69. Foster, p. 276; facing p. 296 is a touching photograph taken at the 1907 Centenary Conference, showing Martha Crawford—looking more weatherbeaten than old—standing at the exact center of a group of

twenty-four attending senior Protestant missionaries in China, between W. A. P. Martin and Calvin Mateer.

The Gospel Mission hung on fitfully until well into the twentieth century. In 1920 the name changed to China Baptist Direct Mission, and later it changed again to Independent Baptist Direct Mission, Inc. The field remained around T'ai-an-fu. See *Encyclopedia of Southern Baptists,* I, 572.

70. See ibid., I, 462; J. B. Hartwell letter dated Tengchow, May 18, 1903, *FMJ*, 54.1:52 (July 1903); and C. W. Pruitt, "Twenty-Six Years in Our North China Mission," *New East*, 3.3:19–20 (April 1908).

71. See W. R. L. Smith, "Sick of Unions," and E. T. Hiscox, "The Organization Craze," both in T. P. Crawford, ed., *Crisis of the Churches,* pp. 15–22; and preface by J. A. Scarboro to *EMMV*, p. 6. Dissemination of Crawfordite ideas among Southern Baptists was accomplished both by literature and through lectures by G. P. Bostick and others. As was remarked by a journal sympathetic to the FMB, it was ironic that a group which professed not to need secretaries and organizers seemed to have at least one of its members constantly on tour on the home circuit. See "The Wreckers," *Religious Herald,* June 18, 1896, p. 2, cited in Barnes, pp. 115–116. On the Landmarkers see Chapter 1, notes 8 and 10 above.

72. See E. J. Grant, "The Church vs. Societies"; Francis Wayland, "Independence of the Churches"; and George Whitman, "The Authority of the Local Church," all in T. P. Crawford, ed., *Crisis of the Churches,* pp. 23–49.

73. Introduction by H. T. Cook to Foster, p. *xv*. See also Barnes, pp. 116–117; and *Encyclopedia of Southern Baptists,* I, 363. One also observes that T. P. Crawford so occupied himself attacking heathen "parasites, paupers, camp-followers, and moral weaklings" that the point of his message could easily be taken to be the uselessness of any missionary work at all. Devoting his energies so much to proving missions a waste, he not unnaturally received few contributions to his own self-denying efforts. By attacking the board system and its "artificially created enthusiasms"— all the "bewildering procession of societies, unions, circles, guilds, bands, etc., filing into the average church"—he was of course moreover making war on the process to which the whole mission movement largely owed its existence. See *Crisis of the Churches,* pp. 10, 38.

74. See W. J. Cash, *The Mind of the South* (originally published 1941; reprinted New York, 1954), pp. 54–58, 131.

75. Quotations from Larry L. King, "Bob Jones University: The Buckle on the Bible Belt," *Harper's Magazine,* 232.1393:51–58 (June 1966).

76. See *EMMV*, pp. 95, 153; and Foster, pp. 292, 295.

77. Ibid., pp. 331–335. The fairest extant view of Crawford seems to be that of C. W. Pruitt, who thought him genuinely entertaining and even attractive when taken in small doses. Crawford's problem, as Pruitt saw it, was his "very narrow and ungenerous" underlying attitude; his self-support fixation was "true enough if it had been held relatively to

other precious ideals, but when made to dominate all his life could not but fail." See "Some Recollections," p. 5.

78. Foster, p. 275.

4. Woman's Work in East Shantung

1. See Hunter Corbett, "Shepherd and Lambs," sermon dated Shanghai, Dec. 6, 1903 (offprint in Missionary Research Library, New York); and *Chin-hui tsai Hua pu-tao nien lüeh shih* (Shanghai, 1936), p. 145.

2. R. Pierce Beaver, *All Loves Excelling: American Protestant Women in World Mission* (Grand Rapids, 1968), p. 11.

3. Page Smith, *Daughters of the Promised Land: Women in American History* (Boston, 1970), p. 181.

4. Ibid., p. 201.

5. *Western Women in Eastern Lands: An Outline Study of Fifty Years of Woman's Work in Foreign Missions* (New York, 1910), pp. 3–4, 8. Mrs. Montgomery's book appeared as number 10 in a series inaugurated in 1900 by the interdenominational Central Committee on the United Study of Missions. This series, which was aimed at "the hosts of women who must have something especially attractive to enlist them," had by 1910 sold almost 600,000 books. One of the series's other volumes, entitled *Rex Christus*, was specifically about China. The author of *Rex Christus* was Shantung's Arthur H. Smith (ABCFM), concerning whom Mrs. Montgomery said, "There is no better authority on matters Chinese." On Helen Montgomery herself, see Beaver, pp. 137, 150–153, 163–164.

6. Montgomery, p. 10; and Henry Otis Dwight et al., eds., *The Encyclopedia of Missions*, second ed. (New York, 1910), pp. 790–791.

7. See Montgomery, pp. 45, 69, 73, 75.

8. Abundant data on east Shantung women missionaries is available not only in SBCP and APMP, but (for Baptists) in *FMJ* and in individual biographical notices in Tupper, *The Foreign Missions of the Southern Baptist Convention* and *A Decade of Foreign Missions, 1880–1890*, and (for Presbyterians) in OMF and WWW. For a good recent appraisal of American missionary calls see Valentin H. Rabe, "Evangelical Logistics: Mission Support and Resources to 1920," in Fairbank, ed., *The Missionary Enterprise in China and America*, esp. pp. 75–81.

9. Figures for China as a whole are taken from D. MacGillivray, ed., *A Century of Protestant Missions in China, 1807–1907* (Shanghai, 1907), App. I, p. 1. Shantung data is from *Record of American Presbyterian Mission Work in Shantung Province, China, 1861–1913*, first ed., (n.p., n.d.), pp. 73–75, and Ann S. Pruitt, *Up from Zero*, pp. 179–181.

10. For Martha Crawford's views see "Woman's Work for Woman," pp. 147–152. Julia Mateer's letter, dated Tengchow, Aug. 27, 1877, is in *WWC*, 1.1:7–11 (November 1877).

11. See Martha Crawford, "A Call to North China," p. 671; and

Julia Mateer letters in *WWW*, 8.10:277 (October 1878) and *WWFE*, 12.2:161 (May 1882).

12. Julia Mateer letter, *WWFE*, 12.2:161 (May 1892). Pay scale information is from her "Life in Shantung—I. A Chapter in Economics," *WWW*, 8.2:43–45 (February 1893).

13. Ida Tiffany Pruitt, "A Word of Encouragement," *WWC*, 7.1:31ᵗ-33 (November 1883); and Tupper, *A Decade of Foreign Missions, 1880–1890*, p. 842.

14. One of the most famous of these accounts was Martha Crawford's "The Chinese Daughter In Law," a tale well calculated to excite the young matrons of home mission bands. Here were their direct Chinese counterparts virtually enslaved either to tyrannical mothers-in-law or "miserable old men." Mrs. Crawford says, "Though the picture I have drawn may seem very dark, it must not be supposed that there is no domestic happiness . . . no affectionate families among the Chinese." From what she says in this particular article no other conclusion could be drawn. See *CR*, 5.4:207–214 (July-August 1874). The "Daughter In Law" was originally written in 1873 for presentation before the Tengchow Literary Association; see note in reprint of *OMF*, 4.3:1 (June 1875).

For other samplings of this kind of writing see especially Calista B. Downing, "Chinese Customs," *WWW*, 4.4:192–194 (September 1874) and 4.5:232–236 (November 1874); "Chinese Superstition" and "The Unwelcome Little Daughter," 5.5:169–171 (July 1875); and John L. Nevius, "Barbarous Chinese Custom," *OMF* (June 1876), pp. 58–60. A distinct anti-male element surfaces from time to time, as in the satisfaction with which Helen Nevius commented on her famine work: "As I write, I can see numbers of women and children coming up the hills and across the fields . . . We give only to women and girls, and for the first time, I suspect, in China, girls are *above par;* and many a poor hungry boy would be glad for the moment to change places with his despised little sister." *OMF* (August 1877), p. 64.

15. *OMF* (February 1884), p. 264; Jennie Anderson Laughlin to F. F. Ellinwood, Yenchiafang (near Wei-hsien), Jan. 15, 1888, APMP 23.2; and Julia Mateer, "The Ladies' Question," *WWC*, 6.2:91–99 (May 1883).

16. Martha Crawford, "Woman's Work for Woman," p. 147.

17. On the peepscopes see Maggie Brown Capp, "An Itinerating Tour," *OMF* (July 1878), pp. 52–55; and for an interesting first encounter with a village see Miss A. D. H. Kelsey, M.D., in *OMF* (November 1879), p. 83. For follow-up work see especially Fanny Corbett Hays, "Chefoo and Woman's Work at Chefoo," *WWW*, 10.2:35–37 (February 1886). For general information on village work, etc., see Mrs. Crawford's "Woman's Work for Woman." When itinerators arrived in a village, they could comprise anything from one woman (with native guide) up to a virtual safari. One 1879 expedition left Tengchow with 8 American women, 5 muleteers, 4 chairbearers, 2 cooks, 9 mules, and 3 donkeys, to

go to a village forty miles away. Such journeys might keep the women on the road up to two months and cover two to three hundred miles. See Julia Mateer letter, Tengchow, Aug. 27, 1877, *WWC*, 1.1:8 (November 1877).

18. From Mrs. J. B. Neal in *WWW-OMF*, 1.2:35–36 (February 1886).

19. See "Visits among the China Missions," *WWW*, 14.2:37–40 (February 1884); Jennie Anderson, "Inn Hospitality in Shantung," *WWW*, 13.9:303–304 (September 1883); letter in *WWW*, 15.4:126 (April 1885); and "Woman's Work in the Villages," *Foreign Misionary*, 40.11:476–478 (April 1882). See also Dr. Kelsey in *OMF* (November 1879), p. 82; and Mrs. Neal in *WWW-OMF*, 1.2:35–36 (February 1886).

20. See Maggie Capp, "An Itinerating Tour," p. 52; Ida R. Tiffany letter in *WWW*, 12.9:297 (September 1882); and comment by C. R. Mills in *Conference Records 1877*, p. 153.

21. From an anonymous BFM Secretary, introduction to Mrs. W. B. Hamilton, "The Chinese Bible Woman" (New York, n.d.), p. 3. Mrs. Hamilton's text (p. 5) has a more sensible description of the Bible woman and her duties.

22. Jennie Anderson, "Woman's Work in the Villages," p. 477. The *k'ang* is the brick bed commonly used in Shantung.

23. Helen S. C. Nevius, *Our Life in China* (New York, 1868), pp. 405–408.

24. See Martha Crawford, *FMJ*, 18.7:4 (February 1887); "A Call to North China," pp. 669–673; and "Woman's Work for Woman," p. 150.

25. R. M. Mateer to F. F. Ellinwood, Tengchow, Feb. 14, 1888, APMP, 23.3.

26. Julia Mateer, "Cleanliness Next to Godliness," *WWFE*, 12.2: 85–92 (May 1892). See also Martha Crawford, "A Call to North China," p. 671.

27. Martha Crawford, "Woman's Work for Woman," p. 150. See also Fanny Corbett Hays, "Chefoo and Woman's Work at Chefoo," p. 36.

28. Jennie Anderson, "Woman's Work in the Villages," p. 478.

29. Martha Crawford, "Paper from Tengchow," *WWC*, 3.2:93–95 (May 1880).

30. Helen Nevius, "Personal Report of Helen S. Coan Nevius for 1908," APMP, 129; "How Can We Reach the Heathen Women?" in *WWFE*, 21.1:1–4 (May 1900); and letter in *WWW*, 5.4:111 (June 1875).

31. W. A. P. Martin, "Tribute [to Mrs. Nevius]," in *CR*, 41.8:553–554 (August 1910).

32. Helen Nevius, letter in *WWW*, 5.4:112 (June 1875).

33. Martha Crawford, "Paper From Tengchow," pp. 93–94.

34. See Helen Nevius, "How Can We Reach the Heathen Women?" p. 3, and Martha Crawford, "Woman's Work for Woman," pp. 149–150.

35. Helen Nevius, *A Descriptive Catalogue of Books and Tracts by the Rev. John Livingston Nevius, D.D. and Helen S. Coan Nevius* (Shanghai, 1907), p. 28.

36. See Hunter Corbett, tribute to Mrs. Nevius in *The Presbyterian*, Nov. 16, 1910, p. 22; and APMP, 121.154, Helen S. C. Nevius to A. J. Brown, Chefoo, Dec. 11, 1906. The tract was issued both as *Yeh-su chiao wen-ta* and *Yeh-su chiao kuan-hua wen-ta*. The edition I have used is the first (Shanghai, 1863), and the latest I have seen is one printed in 1917. Editions of 1868 and 1874 are noted in *CR*, 8.5:395–397 (September-October 1877), and another is supposed to have been issued in 1898. Length varied according to whether the Ten Commandments section was confined to the main idea of each (Mrs. Nevius's method) or given a full treatment (the Presbyterian Press method).

37. *Yeh-su chiao kuan-hua wen-ta*, p. 9b.

38. Helen Nevius, *Descriptive Catalogue*, p. 29.

39. Reports of such usages came from as far away as Hangchow, and Shantung Christians were often badgered for copies by heathen friends. See ibid., pp. 40–42; and Helen Nevius, *Our Life in China*, pp. 410–413.

40. Helen Nevius, *Descriptive Catalogue*, pp. 30, 36.

41. Helen Nevius, *Mei Mo-shih hsing lüeh* (Shanghai, 1875), pp. 1, 15. See also *Descriptive Catalogue*, pp. 30–31 (English text). For a similar account of Mrs. Mills's life in English, probably by her husband, see "Memoir of the Late Mrs. Mills," *CR*, 5.5:274–279 (September-October 1874).

42. Helen Nevius, translator, *Hai-t'ung ku-shih* (Shanghai, 1883), pp. 1–2.

43. Helen Nevius, "How Can We Reach the Heathen Women?" p. 3.

44. Mary Nixon Corbett, "Paper From Chefoo," *WWC*, 4.1:31–34 (November 1880).

45. Mrs. J. B. Neal, letter dated Chefoo, July 28, 1885, *WWW*, 15.11:387 (November 1885). See also *OMF* (February 1884), p. 264; and Annetta T. Mills, "Guiding Influences of the Spirit on the Mission Field," *WWW*, 14.2:42–43 (February 1899). The pathos of some of these incidents defies paraphrase. On the eve of leaving "the old Kentucky home" for north China, Mrs. G. P. Bostick wrote in her diary, "May 8, 1889. Tomorrow, to-morrow, I shall say good-bye, perhaps forever, to the scenes of my happy childhood. My dear, dear home. How can I leave it? Papa, mamma, all the children and grandchildren are here. We have had such a delightful evening. When shall we meet again?" A year later to the day she died of smallpox in Tengchow. From Emma M. Connelly, "In China Land. In Memory of Mrs. Bertha Bryan Bostick," *FMJ*, 23. 6:171–174 (January 1892).

46. For censoring see C. R. Mills to F. F. Ellinwood, Tengchow, Feb. 21, 1882, APMP 16.96. Most of John Nevius's own Shantung letters are missing from the BFM files, from which they were withdrawn and almost

certainly destroyed with his diaries by Mrs. Nevius after her husband's death in 1893. The withdrawal (if not destruction) seems to have been authorized by BFM Corresponding Secretary Ellinwood, a close Nevius friend; see F. W. Jackson, Jr., to F. F. Ellinwood, New York, July 18, 1894, APMP 27.2.61; and APMP 9, typed notation in index concerning letter no. 5. Mrs. Nevius said she needed her husband's letters for his biography, which she did write (*The Life of John Livingston Nevius, For Forty Years a Missionary in China,* 1895). It seems a minor tragedy, however, that the record of one of the most unusual and fascinating American lives ever spent in China has been so critically weakened.

47. Hunter Corbett in *Record of American Presbyterian Mission Work,* first ed., p. 1. See also Anna S. Pruitt, *Up from Zero,* p. 17.

48. Helen Nevius, *Hai-t'ung ku-shih,* pp. 11a–b.

49. See Mary I. Bergen, "Mothers of a Chinese Revolution," *WWW,* 21.8:175–177 (August 1906).

50. See Robert McCheyne Mateer, *Character-Building in China: The Life Story of Julia Brown Mateer* (New York, 1912), pp. 67, 142.

51. See her letters dated Tengchow, Aug. 27, 1877, *WWC,* 1.1:7 (November 1877), and (undated) quoted in R. M. Mateer, *Character-Building in China,* p. 167.

52. See Calista B. Downing, "The Unwelcome Little Daughter," pp. 170–171; Mrs. J. M. Shaw, letter in *WWW,* 5.6:182 (August 1875); and J. K. Wight, "Chefoo," *WWW–OMF,* 2.2:35–36 (February 1887).

53. Calista B. Downing letter dated March 1872, cited in Margaret E. Burton, *The Education of Women in China* (New York, 1911), pp. 45–46; Martha Crawford, "The Chinese Daughter In Law," p. 214; and R. M. Mateer, "Primary Education for Girls," *Records of the First Shantung Missionary Conference, at Ch'ingchowfu, 1893* (Shanghai, 1894), pp. 70–76.

54. Ibid., p. 72.

55. Ibid., pp. 70–76.

56. Ibid., p. 75.

57. See ibid., pp. 73, 75–76; Mary E. Barr, "The Closing Exercises of Mrs. Capp's School," *OMF* (March 1882), pp. 307–308; and Miss A. D. H. Kelsey, M.D., "Tungchow Schools," *WWC,* 2.2:97 (May 1879). For a good description of the beginning of systematic female education in Shantung missions (Presbyterian), see "Report of the Annual Meeting of the Shantung Mission for 1886," APMP, 22.103. For a description of the problems which arose with this program, see Emma F. Boughton, "Village Schools for Girls," *Records of the Second Shantung Missionary Conference, at Weihsien, 1898* (Shanghai, 1899), pp. 56–59.

58. Title variously translated *Three School Girls, Three Little Daughters,* and *The Story of Three Little Girls.* The Chinese text was published at Shanghai in 1872.

59. Ibid., p. 27.

60. Dr. W. F. Seymour wrote in 1910 that the ratio of male to female patients in Tengchow dispensary was still almost six to one, and

that when the native women came they still preferred his non-M.D. wife to himself. The only period of large attendance by females had been when he briefly had a Western-trained Chinese female doctor as assistant; when she died the native women were greatly disturbed and ceased coming for some time. See "China Wants Women Doctors and Nurses," *WWW*, 25.2:38–39 (February 1910).

61. C. R. Mills to F. F. Ellinwood, Tengchow, June 26, 1877, APMP, 13.157.

62. Julia Mateer to F. F. Ellinwood, Tengchow, Aug. 6, 1877, APMP, 13.190.

63. The second Mrs. Hunter Corbett describes an incident of this type. She had been teaching "Jesus Loves Me" and basic doctrine to a certain woman, who fell ill and sent begging Mrs. Corbett's help. Mrs. Corbett went but was understandably reluctant: "What a place her home was, back of her husband's opium store. I was obliged to enter by the front door. All the men laughed as I passed. What with mud and dirt, flies and smoke from an herb burning to drive out the flies and mosquitoes, it was the dirtiest place I ever was in." After a number of visits Mrs. Corbett eventually nursed the woman back to health. See "Chefoo Incidents," *WWC*, 7.1:24–26 (November 1883).

64. C. R. Mills to F. F. Ellinwood, Tengchow, June 26, 1877, APMP, 13.157.

65. M. P. Barker, M.D., "Female Medical Missions: The Force in the Field—China," *WWW*, 14.3:83–85 (March 1884). Dr. Barker's article is an excellent summary of how female medical work developed in China, through various stages and by training Chinese women to be assistants and ultimately Western-style doctors themselves.

66. Lottie Moon in *WWFE*, 16.1:38 (May 1895). See also Mrs. Mills, "Guiding Influences of the Spirit on the Mission Field," p. 42; "Helping the Helpless," *WWW*, 25.8:177–179 (August 1910); and Anita E. Carter, *Sketch of the Life of Annetta Thompson Mills, Founder of the Chefoo School for the Deaf* (Chefoo, 1938), p. 12. Miss Carter was Mrs. Mills's niece, longtime assistant, and successor as chief of the school; her book gives the fullest discussion of Mrs. Mills and the work. Of further interest are Mrs. Mills's own *China Through a Car-Window: Observations on the Modern China, Made in the Course of a Four Months' Journey in Behalf of the Chinese Deaf; with Some Account of the School at Chefoo* (Washington, 1910), and her many essays and articles, particularly "Our School for Deaf Mutes in China." *WWW*, 8.2:37–39 (February 1893) and "Work among the Deaf and Dumb," *Conference Records 1907*, pp. 97–98, 508–509.

67. Paul D. Bergen, "Unoccupied Mission Fields of China," *WWW*, 26.1:8–9 (January 1911); and C. W. Mateer to F. F. Ellinwood, Tengchow, Oct. 14, 1878, APMP, 14.129. Figures are from Forsyth, pp. 234, 237–239.

68. C. W. Pruitt, "Some Recollections," pp. 6, 10.

69. Martha Crawford, *Discouragements and Encouragements of the Misionary Situation in China,* pp. 15–16.

70. C. W. Pruitt, "Some Recollections," p. 11. See also Foster, p. 240.

71. Helen Nevius, "How Can We Reach the Heathen Women?" p. 1; also letter to F. F. Ellinwood, Chefoo, Aug. 15, 1883, APMP, 17.113.

72. See "Chao shih san ku lieh-chuan," in Lien Chih-to (Martin Lien), *Kuo Hsien-te mu-shih hsing chuan ch'üan chi* (Shanghai, 1940), II, 478–479.

73. See Martin C. Yang, *A Chinese Village: Taitou, Shantung Province* (New York, 1945), pp. 188–189.

74. Ida Pruitt, pp. 192–194. On Mr. Lan see also Julia Mateer, "History of the Tungchow Mission," dated April 17, 1886, in APMP, 20.174, p. 8.

75. The T'ao Chu referred to here (also known as Fan Li) was a merchant-statesman who lived in the state of Yüeh in the fifth century B.C. The point of the comparison is that T'ao Chu became wealthy but gave much of his fortune to the poor ("This is what is meant by a rich man who delights in practicing virtue"). See *Records of the Grand Historian of China, Translated from the Shih chi of Ssu-ma Ch'ien,* tr. Burton Watson (New York, 1961), II, 479–481.

76. See "Liu Shou-shan chang-lao lieh-chuan," in Lien Chih-to, II, 497–502; also Hunter Corbett, "Shepherd and Lambs."

77. Ida Pruitt, pp. 189–191.

78. See Mary I. Bergen, "Mothers of a Chinese Revolution," pp. 175–177.

79. Mary Seymour, et al., "Missions and High Life at Tengchow," *WWW,* 20.2:27–29 (February 1905).

80. Ida Pruitt, pp. 63–65; see also p. 150.

5. *A Woman of Energy and Self-Respect*

1. From a letter to me from Mrs. Robert C. Fling, President, Woman's Missionary Union, SBC, Jan. 13, 1966.

2. See Lawrence, pp. 13–24; and C. W. Pruitt, "In Memoriam. Miss Lottie Moon," *CR,* 44.4:241–242 (April 1913).

3. See Lawrence, pp. 25–33.

4. Anna Mary Moon, comp., *Sketches of the Moon and Barclay Families* (n.p., 1939), pp. 40–41. See also Lawrence, pp. 29–30, 33.

5. Ibid., pp. 31–32, 52–53; and Anna Mary Moon, pp. 41–42. Inquiries to the National and Virginia State Archives have found no documentation of Orianna's Confederate officer status, although other evidence proves that she did treat wounded soldiers in Charlottesville. My own suspicion here is that Mrs. Lawrence is accepting family legend that has confused Orianna with Captain Sally Tompkins, a famous and authentic Confederate girl doctor from Richmond. Orianna's medical reputation is

also a matter of some disagreement; for an unflattering (in fact insulting) appraisal, by a former Confederate chief medical inspector, see Edward Warren, M.D., *A Doctor's Experiences in Three Continents* (Baltimore, 1885), pp. 279–280.

6. Lawrence, pp. 34–48; and Tupper, *The Foreign Missions of the Southern Baptist Convention,* pp. 217–218.

7. Anna Mary Moon, pp. 25–34; and Lawrence, pp. 48, 53.

8. Tupper, *The Foreign Missions of the Southern Baptist Convention,* p. 219; and Lawrence, pp. 53–58. Apropos to Lottie Moon's postwar teaching is an observation in one recent study that "increasing interest in education coincided with the need of large numbers of women to find paid employment. Schoolteaching had always been a respectable thing to do, and now it was the first thought of many upper-class women who needed to earn money." Anne Firor Scott, *The Southern Lady: From Pedestal to Politics, 1830–1930* (Chicago, 1970), pp. 110–111.

9. Lawrence, pp. 58–63.

10. Scott, pp. 86, 94, 106.

11. Quoted in Lawrence, p. 66. See also p. 49.

12. For an interesting sketch of Miss Safford's life and personality, see John W. Davis, "In Memoriam—Miss Anna Cunningham Safford," *CR,* 21.11:483–487 (November 1890).

13. During Miss Moon's early Tengchow years schools were very popular with the Baptist women. In 1875 Mrs. Crawford was teaching 20 boys, Mrs. Holmes 17 girls, and Edmonia Moon 14, the three schools being separate and in different parts of the city. See Lawrence, p. 81.

14. MFCD VI: Jan. 28, 1876.

15. J. B. Hartwell to H. A. Tupper, Jul. 2, 1872, SBCP (J. B. Hartwell Folder No. 1). See also MFCD VI: June 14, 1872.

16. For Mrs. Crawford's views see MFCD VI: Jan. 28, 1876. For accounts more sympathetic to Edmonia see Lawrence, pp. 79, 81–82, 191; and Anna Mary Moon, p. 45.

17. Quoted in Lawrence, p. 93.

18. The story of Miss Moon's lover has been a subject of some dispute among Baptists. One view is that there never really was one, as in Charles E. Maddry, *Christ's Expendables* (Nashville, 1949), pp. 31–32. Una Lawrence, in her standard biography of Miss Moon, accepts the story repeated by me but coyly avoids naming the man. The name is, however, in her original research notes. See "Notes taken at Atlanta" and draft outline "Chapter III," both in Una Roberts Lawrence Papers, vol. 5, Southern Baptist Theological Seminary Library, Louisville, Ky. Note also how events in Mrs. Lawrence's published account (*Lottie Moon,* pp. 91–96) correlate with Toy's biography in *Encyclopedia of Southern Baptists,* II, 1423. See also "The Romance of Lottie Moon," *Baptist Intermediate Union Quarterly,* 33.1:29–31 (January-March 1941). One of the quotations in my text's paragraph is from T. P. Crawford, *The Patriarchal Dynasties,* p. 6.

19. Lawrence, pp. 94, 96; *Encyclopedia of Southern Baptists,* II,

1423; and Lottie Moon letter dated Nov. 24, 1888, *FMJ*, 20.7:3 (February 1889).

20. See Lawrence, p. 94.

21. See ibid., pp. 94, 96.

22. Lottie Moon letter, *WWC*, 2.2:91–96 (May 1879).

23. Ibid., pp. 93–96.

24. Lottie Moon letter, Tengchow, June 4, 1880, *FMJ*, 12.6:3–4 (September 1880).

25. Lottie Moon, "Shantung Province," *WWC*, 5.2:79–94 (May 1882). See also her report in *WWC*, 2.2:91–96 (May 1879).

26. Ibid., pp. 92–93.

27. Ibid., pp. 91–92, 96.

28. Lottie Moon letter, Tengchow, June 4, 1880, *FMJ*, 12.6:3–4 (September 1880).

29. See Lottie Moon, "Shantung Province," pp. 79–85, 89.

30. Ibid., p. 93.

31. "Advantages and Disadvantages of Wearing the Native Dress in Missionary Work" appeared in *WWC*, 5.1:14–22 (November 1881). See also Ida Tiffany Pruitt, "A Word of Encouragement," pp. 31–33.

32. Lottie Moon, "Advantages and Disadvantages," pp. 15, 17–18, 20–21.

33. Ibid., pp. 21–22. For some scathing remarks on Gilbert Reid's affectations see C. W. Mateer to (Presbyterian) Board of Foreign Missions, Chefoo, June 18, 1887, APMP, 21.81.

34. Lottie Moon, "Advantages and Disadvantages," p. 20.

35. For a detailed description of Miss Moon's Tengchow life style at this time, see Lawrence, pp. 87–90.

36. See citations and comments in ibid., pp. 90–105; and Lottie Moon, "The Woman's Question Again," *WWC*, 7.1:47–55 (November 1883).

37. Lottie Moon, "Shantung Province," pp. 86–88.

38. See ibid., pp. 85, 88.

39. Lottie Moon, "The Woman's Question Again," pp. 50–53. For background see Julia Mateer, "The Ladies' Question," *WWC*, 6.2:91–99 (May 1883).

40. Lottie Moon, "The Woman's Question Again," pp. 48–54.

41. The lines are quoted from Dr. Porter's "The Ballad of Li Hua Ch'eng" (24 stanzas), in *CR*, 18.1:12–21 (January 1887).

42. Mrs. Smith's article ("Must the Single Lady Go?") appeared in *WWC*, 7.2:170–175 (May 1884). Miss Moon's reply (very restrained) is in *WWC*, 8.1:32–33 (November 1884).

43. Lottie Moon, "The Woman's Question Again," pp. 51, 55. See also R. M. Mateer to (Presbyterian) Board of Foreign Missions, Weihsien, Oct. 14, 1901, APMP, 41.6 (Appendix).

44. See Lottie Moon letter cited in Lawrence, p. 133.

45. Quotations are from ibid., p. 100.

46. John L. Nevius, "Religious Interest in Ping-tu," *CR*, 3.5:140

(October 1870). See also C. W. Mateer letter, Oct. 6, 1874, *CR*, 5.5:299 (September-October 1874).

47. Lottie Moon letter dated April 1885 cited in Lawrence, p. 133. See also pp. 109, 122–123. R. Pierce Beaver has perceptively called attention to the feminism of Miss Moon's position here, as distinct from her personal disagreements with T. P. Crawford. At one point in 1885 the FMB criticized Miss Moon for the spirit of independence displayed in her woman's question articles and specifically denied mission voting rights to women. Miss Moon countered by threatening to quit mission work, whereupon the board "backed down." See Beaver's sketch of Miss Moon in Edward T. James, ed., *Notable American Women 1607–1950: A Biographical Dictionary* (Cambridge, Mass., 1971), II, 570–571; and Lawrence, pp. 135–136. The resignation episode is also emphasized in E. Luther Copeland's recent tape cassette, "The Life of Miss Lottie Moon" (Kansas City, Mo., 1972).

48. Lottie Moon, "Work in Pingtu," *WWFE*, 11.1:1–11 (November 1890). See also Anna S. Pruitt, *Up from Zero*, p. 50; and Lawrence, pp. 126–127, 140.

49. Ibid., pp. 127–128; and Lottie Moon, "Work in Pingtu," p. 2.

50. Ibid., p. 3.

51. Lottie Moon letter, P'ingtu, Mar. 30, 1888, *FMJ*, 20.1:3 (August 1888).

52. Lottie Moon, "Work in Pingtu," p. 4; also Lawrence, pp. 129, 150.

53. On Miss Moon's reliance on these books see ibid., p. 115. See also Sally Holmes and Chou Wen-yüan, *Hsün erh chen yen* (Shanghai, 1865), and the English-language original by Favell L. (Mrs. Thomas) Mortimer. The edition of the latter that I have used is the third (Toronto, 1911).

54. Lottie Moon letter, P'ingtu, March 30, 1888, *FMJ*, 20.1:3 (August 1888). See also Martha Crawford, *Hsiao wen-ta* (Shanghai, 1874), pp. 22b–26b, 33, 35a–b; and Julia Mateer, "Fragments," *WWC*, 6.1:12–17 (November 1882).

55. See Lottie Moon letter, Tengchow, Jul. 10, 1886, *FMJ*, 18.3:3 (October 1886); P'ingtu, Dec. 13, 1886, *FMJ*, 18.8:2 (March 1887); and Tengchow, March 19, 1887, *FMJ*, 18.11:2 (June 1887).

56. Lottie Moon letter, P'ingtu, Oct. 3, 1887, *FMJ*, 19.6:2 (January 1888).

57. Lottie Moon, "Work in Pingtu," p. 4.

58. Ibid., pp. 3–4.

59. Lottie Moon letter, P'ingtu, Oct. 3, 1887, *FMJ*, 19.6:2 (January 1888). See also Lawrence, p. 150.

60. Lottie Moon letter, P'ingtu, Dec. 13, 1886, *FMJ*, 18.8:2 (March 1887). See also letters dated March 20, 1886, and May 4, 1887, in *FMJ*, 17.12:3 (July 1886) and 19.1:2 (August 1887).

61. See Lottie Moon letters dated Tengchow, July 29, 1890, *FMJ*, 22.4:107 (November 1890), and P'ingtu, March 30, 1888, *FMJ*, 20.1:3 (August 1888).

62. Lottie Moon, "Work in Pingtu," p. 4. See also Lawrence, pp. 263–264, and Lottie Moon letters dated Tengchow, July 10, 1886, *FMJ*, 18.3:3 (October 1886); P'ingtu, March 20, 1886, *FMJ*, 17.12:3 (July 1886); P'ingtu, Dec. 13, 1886, *FMJ*, 18.8:2 (March 1887); Tengchow, March 19, 1887, *FMJ*, 18.11:2 (June 1887); and Tengchow, June 19 and July 27, 1887, *FMJ*, 19.3:2 (October 1887).

6. *Lottie Moon at Sha-ling and in History*

1. Lottie Moon, "Work in Pingtu," p. 5; also Lawrence, p. 148.
2. Lottie Moon, "Work in Pingtu," pp. 5–6.
3. Ibid., pp. 6–10. See also Lawrence, pp. 129, 158, 161–164; and autobiographical sketch by Li Shou Ting (tr. T. O. Hearn) in *FMJ*, 61.8:243–244 (February 1911).
4. *Religious Herald* (May 22, 1884), quoted in Barnes, p. 145.
5. The friend was a former teaching associate in Danville, Ky. See Lawrence, p. 66; Barnes, p. 143; and Isa-Beall W. (Mrs. William J.) Neel, *His Story in Georgia W.M.U. History* (Atlanta, 1939), pp. 9–12, 82–83. On contributions to the Moon sisters see also Alma Hunt, *History of Woman's Missionary Union* (Nashville, 1964), p. 14.
6. Lottie Moon letter, P'ingtu, Jan. 12, 1886, *FMJ*, 17.10:3 (May 1886).
7. See Lawrence, pp. 149–152.
8. Lottie Moon letter, Tengchow, Sept. 15, 1887, *FMJ*, 19.5:2 (December 1887).
9. Lawrence, p. 154. For the WMU account see Ethlene B. Cox, *Following in His Train* (Nashville, 1938), pp. 105–108.
10. Lottie Moon, "Woman's Work in Shantung," dated Shanghai, June 22, 1888, *FMJ*, 20.3:3 (October 1888).
11. See Lawrence, pp. 157–158, 160. Information on the amount of money is in the letter to me from Mrs. Robert C. Fling, President, Woman's Missionary, SBC, Jan. 13, 1966. Una Lawrence's account is a little misleading here in that the WMU had in fact already undertaken one project earlier in 1888, before the Lottie Moon offering. This was a collection of money for the Home Mission Board to aid the First Baptist Church of Havana, Cuba. See Hunt, pp. 43–44.
12. See Lottie Moon to Annie Armstrong, P'ingtu, Jan. 9, 1889, SBCP (Lottie Moon Folder No. 2); and letter dated P'ingtu, Jan. 8, 1889, *FMJ*, 20.9:2 (April 1889).
13. Lawrence, p. 157.
14. Lottie Moon to H. A. Tupper, Aug. 23, 1888, SBCP (Lottie Moon Folder No. 2).
15. Lottie Moon to T. P. Bell, Feb. 11, 1889, SBCP (Lottie Moon Folder No. 2). Compare the letter of Aug. 23, 1888, to Dr. Tupper to the version in Lawrence, p. 155.
16. Lottie Moon letter, P'ingtu, Nov. 1, 1889, *FMJ*, 21.7:2 (February 1890).

17. Lottie Moon letter, undated, *FMJ*, 21.5:2 (December 1889). See also letters dated P'ingtu, Feb. 29, 1888, *FMJ*, 19.11:2 (June 1888); June 27, 1889, *FMJ*, 21.2:2 (September 1889); Nov. 1, 1889, *FMJ*, 21.7:2 (February 1890); and Tupper, *A Decade of Foreign Missions, 1880–1890*, p. 842.

18. Lottie Moon, "Work in Pingtu," pp. 8–10; letter dated Tengchow, June 27, 1889, *FMJ*, 21.2:2 (September 1889); and Lawrence, p. 165.

19. Lottie Moon, "Work in Pingtu," pp. 8–10. See also Li Shou Ting autobiography, *FMJ*, 61.8:243–244 (February 1911). Nevius's "Truth Manifested" (or "True Doctrine Explained") was one of his best and most frequently revised works. Written in classical Chinese, it deals with monotheism, salvation, and reconciling Christian duties with loyalty to family, the emperor, etc. See Helen Nevius, *A Descriptive Catalogue of Books and Tracts*, pp. 21–22.

20. See Lawrence, pp. 166–167; and Lottie Moon, "Work in Pingtu," pp. 8–10.

21. Lottie Moon, "Sa-ling Diary," Oct. 24, 1890, *FMJ*, 22.9:271 (April 1891). See also letters dated Aug. 25, 1890, *FMJ*, 22.6:176 (January 1891), and Oct. 13, 1890, *FMJ*, 22.8:237 (March 1891).

22. Lottie Moon, "Work in Pingtu," pp. 9–10. See also letter dated Jan. 8, 1894, cited in Lawrence, p. 193.

23. Cited in ibid., p. 171.

24. J. F. Love, *Southern Baptists and Their Far Eastern Missions* (Richmond, n.d. [*ca* 1922]), p. 170. See also *FMJ*, 22.9:271 (April 1891); and T. O. Hearn on Li Shou Ting, *FMJ*, 61.8:243 (Feb. 1911). The statement by Li himself is from his "Account of Miss Moon's Work in Pingtu," in Una Roberts Lawrence Papers, Vol. 5. Located in James P. Boyce Centennial Library, Southern Baptist Theological Seminary, Louisville, Ky. Used with permission.

25. Lottie Moon, "Shantung Province," pp. 79–84.

26. According to Anna Seward Pruitt, Miss Moon left the P'ingtu field out of "consideration for the young and new missionaries," from a feeling that "her presence there [would] hamper the younger women." While probably true enough, this alone hardly seems adequate to explain why she would give up so completely a work in which she had such a great emotional investment. See Anna S. Pruitt to Una R. Lawrence, Huang-hsien, April 22, 1923, in Una Roberts Lawrence Papers, vol. 4. Located in James P. Boyce Centennial Library, Southern Baptist Theological Seminary, Louisville, Ky. Used with permission.

27. See Lottie Moon letters, Tengchow, undated, *FMJ*, 25.12:365 (July 1894); Tengchow, Oct. 1, 1894, *FMJ*, 26.6:176 (January 1895); Tengchow, undated, *FMJ*, 46.2:15 (November 1895); and Tengchow, undated, *FMJ*, 46.3:15 (December 1895). See also Lottie Moon to Margaret Burruss Harrison, Tengchow, Oct. 22, 1894 (in Harrison correspondence, Virginia Baptist Historical Society, University of Richmond).

28. Lottie Moon letter, Tengchow, June 29, 1905, *FMJ*, 56.3:108

(September 1905). See also letters dated Tengchow, Oct. 5, 1898, *FMJ*, 49.7:253–254 (January 1899); undated, *FMJ*, 56.3:88 (December 1902); Sept. 8, 1905, *FMJ*, 58.2:54 (August 1907); undated, *FMJ*, 62.6:174 (December 1911); and Lawrence, esp. pp. 213–220.

29. Julia Mateer to Mrs. John P. Patterson, Feb. 5, 1896 (in Patterson correspondence, Presbyterian Historical Society, Philadelphia). See also Forsyth, p. 183.

30. Lottie Moon letter, Tengchow, Oct. 1, 1894, *FMJ*, 26.6:176 (January 1895). See also an undated letter in *FMJ*, 25.12:365 (July 1894), and one dated June 29, 1905, *FMJ*, 56.3:108 (September 1905).

31. Cited in Lawrence, p. 204. See also reminiscences by the Reverend W. W. and Mrs. Adams, Mrs. C. W. Pruitt, and Mrs. J. McF. Gaston, in "Miss Moon as We Knew Her" (Birmingham, n.d.), pp. 1–4.

32. See Mr. Adams in ibid.; and Lawrence, pp. 267, 284, 288.

33. Mrs. C. W. Pruitt in "Miss Moon as We Knew Her." See also Thomas W. Ayers, M.D., "Miss Lottie Moon—As I Knew Her" (Birmingham, n.d.), pp. 1–6.

34. Cited in Lawrence, pp. 256, 267, 273, 293. See also C. W. Pruitt, "In Memoriam. Miss Lottie Moon," pp. 241–242.

35. See "Miss Moon as We Knew Her"; and Lawrence, pp. 263–266.

36. Lottie Moon, "Our China Mission," *FMJ*, 18.4:2 (November 1886). See also undated letter, *FMJ*, 18.12:2 (July 1887).

37. Lottie Moon, "Our China Mission," p. 2; and Lottie Moon to Margaret Burruss Harrison, Oct. 22, 1894 (in Harrison correspondence).

38. Lottie Moon to Bettie Fowlkes, Tengchow, Sept. 20, 1905 (at Virginia Baptist Historical Society, Richmond). See also Miss Moon's articles, "Our China Mission," p. 2, and "The Colored People," *FMJ*, 24.3:89 (October 1892).

39. Lottie Moon to Margaret Burruss Harrison, Feb. 24, 1898 (in Harrison correspondence). See also Julia Mateer to Mrs. John P. Patterson, Feb. 5, 1896 (in Patterson correspondence); C. W. Pruitt, "In Memoriam. Miss Lottie Moon," p. 241; and Lawrence, pp. 248–252.

40. Cited in ibid., pp. 257–258. See also C. W. Pruitt, "In Memoriam. Miss Lottie Moon," p. 241.

41. Cited in Lawrence, p. 272. See also pp. 299–305. On the cost of living see Arthur Judson Brown, *Report on a Second Visit to China, Japan, and Korea, 1909, With a Discussion of Some Problems of Mission Work* (New York, 1909), p. 168.

42. See Lawrence, pp. 185, 290–291, 301–305.

43. See ibid., pp. 306–310; and C. W. Pruitt, "In Memoriam. Miss Lottie Moon," p. 242.

44. Lawrence, p. 317.

45. Lucy Hamilton Howard, "Her Lengthened Shadow: Scenes from the Life of Lottie Moon, 1840–1912" (Birmingham, 1964), p. 16.

46. Cited in Barnes, p. 154.

47. See *FMJ*, 24.4:01 (November 1892), which notes that the Christmas offering for 1892 is going to Japan.

48. See Lawrence, pp. 181–191.
49. See Neel, pp. 16–22; and *FMJ*, 23.11:344 (June 1892).
50. See *Encyclopedia of Southern Baptists*, I, 323–324; and II, 1515, 1518, 1524. See also "Lottie Moon Christmas Offerings" (a two-page mimeographed handout prepared by the Treasurer's Office, SBC Foreign Mission Board, listing amounts of annual Christmas collections; originally prepared 1960, updated annually). For a description of FMB financial difficulties developing in the later 1920s see Hill, "Administering Southern Baptist Foreign Missions," pp. 35ff. The disaster threatened by such embarrassments was very real. Hill's article graphically documents how the overall foreign mission effort had in some ways grown greatly, as from a total FMB income of $679,699 in 1915, supporting 298 missionaries in nine fields (382 churches and 819 outstations), to $1,413,920 in 1928, supporting 489 missionaries in fifteen fields (1275 churches and 2861 outstations). But at the same time the board had fallen more than a million dollars in debt, and the force in the field had already begun to decline seriously.
51. *Encyclopedia of Southern Baptists*, II, 1515, 1523.
52. See ibid., p. 1516; and Lawrence, p. 7.
53. Ibid., pp. 7, 9, 317; and (on *Lottie Moon* sales) a letter to me from William J. Fallis, editor, Broadman Press, Nashville, Dec. 31, 1965.
54. Howard, p. 2.
55. Dorothy Lehman Sumerau, "Make His Name Glorious: A Dramatic Service of Worship on the Life and Work of Lottie Moon" (Nashville, 1958), pp. 15, 19–20. See also Miriam Robinson, "Faithful Unto Death: Narration of the Life of Lottie Moon" (Birmingham, 1964), pp. 2–3.
56. Howard, pp. 2–3, 7–9, 11–12.
57. See *Lottie Moon in Pictures* (Richmond, 1961).
58. See Claude Rhea, comp., *Lottie Moon Cook Book: Recipes Used by Lottie Moon 1875–1912* (Waco, 1969). Citation is from dust jacket.
59. For additional information on the children's books see bibliographic entries for Helen A. Monsell and Jester Summers. The tape cassette, which has been prepared and narrated by a distinguished Baptist historian (see Chapter 5, note 47), is much more restrained and thoughtful than other versions of the Lottie Moon story. The tape was made, so I was told at the Atlanta Baptist Book Store, because the Lottie Moon movie is not available in sufficient quantity to accommodate all the groups wanting audiovisual aid.
60. Hunt, p. 169. It should be noted that foreign missions were not the only aspect of Southern Baptist activity to become big business. In twenty years the "total amount given to all [Southern] Baptist causes . . . increased from $178,337,207 in 1949 to $809,608,812 in 1969." By 1972 the total had passed the billion-dollar mark. See Hill, "Administering Southern Baptist Foreign Missions," p. 53; and Owen Cooper, president, SBC, quoted in *The Atlantic Constitution*, June 14, 1973.
61. Figures are from "Lottie Moon Christmas Offerings" and from

a letter to me from Nancy Nell Stanley, director, FMB Library and Archives, Richmond, July 18, 1974. The centennial, booklet, entitled "In the Spirit of Christmas" (n. p., 1973), has some fascinating photographs of Lottie Moon, of Tengchow scenery, and of Baptist mission work in north China up to (apparently) around 1920. The notecards feature twelve of the same pictures.

62. Information from Baker J. Cauthen, "The Lottie Moon Christmas Offering: Praise and Thanksgiving!" (Richmond, 1973); "The Lottie Moon Christmas Offering: Where Does the Money Go?" (Richmond, 1970); and from a letter to this writer from Virginia Anderson, assistant to Eugene Hill, secretary, FMB Department of Missionary Education and Promotion, Richmond, June 29, 1971. Other support of FMB activities—income not derived from the Christmas offering—comes chiefly from the SBC's Cooperative Program, a year-round sharing plan. Since the Cooperative Program's income has to be divided with "every agency and institution of the Southern Baptist Convention," the Lottie Moon offering—given exclusively for foreign missions—remains the key element without which the FMB would "inescapably be forced to reduce the foreign mission effort drastically." See Cauthen, ed., *Advance: A History of Southern Baptist Foreign Missions*, pp. 305–307. For the SBC's newest and most ambitious plan (doubling number of foreign missionaries to 5000, increasing domestic staff, greater use of mass media) see statements attributed to the Reverend Bill Self, FMB member, *The Atlanta Constitution*, December 19, 1975. Mr. Self says the proposed program will more than double the SBC's mission budget.

63. Rhea, from the dust jacket.

64. Mrs. J. McF. Gaston in "Miss Moon As We Knew Her," p. 3.

65. Cash, p. 97.

66. See Lawrence, pp. 231–232, 267; and Love, p. 170.

67. Scott, pp. 147, 149.

68. Church statistics are from Jessyca Russell Gaver, *"You Shall Know the Truth": The Baptist Story* (New York, 1973), pp. 242, 263.

69. Lawrence (citing a notation by Lottie Moon), p. 23.

70. Fiedler's celebrated essay "Come Back to the Raft Ag'in, Huck Honey!" appeared originally in *Partisan Review* (June, 1948). It is reprinted in *An End to Innocence: Essays on Culture and Politics* (Boston, 1955), pp. 142–151. See also comment on Fiedler by Michael Halberstam, "Are *You* Guilty of Murdering Martin Luther King?" *The New York Times Magazine*, June 9, 1968, pp. 27–29, 54–66.

71. See Lillian Smith, *Killers of the Dream* (New York, 1963), esp. pp. 120–135, 190–191; also Fiedler, p. 149.

72. See letter to "My own precious Fan," dated Jan. 8, 1894, reproduced with commentary in Lawrence, pp. 192–194.

73. See Fiedler, "Adolescence and Maturity in the American Novel," in *An End to Innocence*, pp. 191–210, esp. p. 202.

74. Scott, p. 218n9.

75. See Carol Tomlinson and Doris Standridge, "It Cannot End at

Kobe: How Lottie Moon Lives in Missions in the 1970's" (Birmingham, n.d.).

76. *The New York Times*, June 5, 1970, and Aug. 19, 1973. For a typical longer treatment of the "new" SBC see "We're Really World Baptists," *Newsweek*, 76.3:52–53 (July 20, 1970).

77. See Catherine Allen, *Baptist Women Member Handbook* (Birmingham, 1972), pp. 5–13.

78. Tomlinson and Standridge, esp. pp. 9–10.

79. Gaver, p. 246. One still cannot help comparing the cornucopia-like dimensions of the present SBC missionary effort with that of Crawford's time. Between 1846 and 1893—roughly his years of association with the FMB—total SBC contributions for foreign missionary work amounted to $1,958,928, and at the end of that half-century only 92 missionaries (including wives and unmarried women) were in all fields. See Hill, "Administering Southern Baptist Foreign Missions," pp. 28–30, 33.

80. Lottie Moon's feelings of aloneness at the end of her life, as expressed by the notation in her bank book, compares interestingly to what Leslie Fiedler sees as the subject of Carson McCullers's *The Heart Is a Lonely Hunter*. Miss McCullers's theme, he states, is "the impossibility of reciprocal love, the sadness of a world in which growing up means only learning that isolation is the fate of every one of us" (see "Adolescence and Maturity in the American Novel," p. 203).

81. See Lawrence, pp. 311–316, for all citations in this paragraph.

82. Fiedler, "Come Back to the Raft Ag'in, Huck Honey!" p. 151; and Lawrence, p. 316.

7. A Call and the Struggle to Interpret It

1. On the influence of Mateer and his work, one mission official wrote at his death that "he was one of the makers of the new China, and his life forms a part of the history of Christian missions which no student of that subject can afford to overlook." See Arthur Judson Brown, cited in Daniel Webster Fisher, *Calvin Wilson Mateer, Forty-Five Years a Missionary in Shantung, China: A Biography* (Philadelphia, 1911), p. 9. For less extravagant modern appraisals see especially K. C. Liu, "Early Christian Colleges in China," *The Journal of Asian Studies*, 20.1:71–78 (November 1960); and Wang Shu-huai, *Wai-jen yü wu-hsü pien-fa* (Taipei, 1965), pp. 20–24.

2. See Samuel Couling, *The Encyclopaedia Sinica* (Shanghai, 1917; reprinted Taipei, 1964), p. 20; and C. E. Scott letter to A. J. Brown, Tsingtao, Sept. 29, 1908, in "Calvin Wilson Mateer Publicity Folder" (United Presbyterian Church, Commission on Ecumenical Mission and Relations, Central Files, New York).

3. See W. A. P. Martin, "A Tribute to Dr. Mateer," *CR*, 39.12: 694–695 (December 1908); and F. W. Baller, "The Rev. C. W. Mateer, D.D.—An Appreciation," *CR*, 39.11:630–633 (November 1908).

4. See Martin, "A Tribute to Dr. Mateer," p. 695.

5. Wang Yüan-te, "Ti K'ao-wen hsien-sheng chuan," in *WHKC*, pp. 1–10.

6. After Calvin had gone away to college the Mateers moved to western Pennsylvania and later to Illinois. See Fisher, pp. 21–22.

7. Ibid., p. 23.

8. Ibid., pp. 20, 23–24.

9. Cited in ibid., p. 90.

10. Cited in Ernest M. Hayes, "Draft Outline for a Biography of Watson M. Hayes" (in John D. Hayes papers), p. 5. See also Wang Yüan-te, "Ti K'ao-wen hsien-sheng chuan," p. 1.

11. Fisher, p. 93. See also pp. 19, 22, 24–25.

12. Of the seven children, the four who went as missionaries to China were Calvin, Robert, John, and Lillian. Jennie was also appointed to go, but poor health canceled her plans. She was married first to a Presbyterian minister, and after his death to Professor J. M. Kirkwood of Wooster College. Horace Mateer, the sixth child, became a Wooster professor also, as well as a practicing physician. William Mateer wound up in business, although according to the family he too had wanted to be a missionary at one time. See ibid., pp. 17–19, 41–42.

13. See Wang Yüan-te, "Ti K'ao-wen hsien-sheng chuan," p. 1; and Fisher, pp. 20, 30–31.

14. Cited in ibid., p. 32.

15. See ibid., p. 38; and Ernest M. Hayes, "Draft Outline for a Biography of Watson M. Hayes," pp. 1, 3–4.

16. Cited in Fisher, p. 43.

17. See ibid., pp. 40, 44–45, 50–51.

18. Ibid., pp. 48, 51, 56, 94–100. I have been unable to locate Calvin Mateer's journals, and all passages from them are cited either from Fisher or from John J. Heeren, *On the Shantung Front: A History of the Shantung Mission of the Presbyterian Church in the U.S.A., 1861–1940, in its Historical, Economic, and Political Setting* (New York, 1940). The journals (according to Heeren) covered a twenty-year period from October 1856 to November 1876; after the latter date Mateer kept copy books instead, which were much less revealing. At the time Fisher used the journals (*ca* 1910) they were in the United States and consisted of "many thousands of pages"; when Heeren saw them (1937), they were in the Augustine Library, Cheeloo University, Tsinan. Heeren believed that by the time he got to them a large portion of the original manuscript had been deliberately destroyed; still, he felt, the journals constituted sources of great value on Shantung missions in general. J. J. Heeren is now deceased, and letters I have written to various living members of the Mateer family have produced no information on the whereabouts of the journals since 1937. See Heeren, pp. 49n11, 77n56, 245; and Fisher, p. 90.

19. Cited in ibid., pp. 54–55.

20. See ibid., pp. 57–69; R. M. Mateer, *Character-Building in China,*

pp. 23–31; and Harold F. Smith, *Hunter Corbett and His Family* (Claremont, Calif., 1965), pp. 16–17.

21. Heeren, p. 92. The Tsungli Yamen considered missionary housing in Tengchow to be an important matter at this time, i.e., a possible precedent, and the difficulties of Mateer and other Americans are well documented in Chinese as well as English. For the American diplomatic side of Mateer's problems, with source references, see Heeren, pp. 87–91. For representative Chinese views see Chang K'ai-yün, comp., *T'ung-shang yüeh-chang lei ts'uan* (Tientsin, 1886), chüan 22:15b–16b, and Hsü Chia-kan, comp., *Chiao-wu chi-yao* (Hupei, 1898), chüan 2:13. For three additional references see Wu Sheng-te and Ch'en Tseng-hui, comps., *Chiao-an shih-liao pien-mu* (Peiping, 1941), p. 27. Students of such incidents should also see Heeren's entire section on "Early Difficulties and Methods of Dealing with Them," pp. 86–103; though based entirely on missionary writings and U.S. diplomatic sources, this is a highly informative short study of typical cases in one Chinese province.

22. Fisher, p. 77; Heeren, p. 92; and R. M. Mateer, *Character-Building in China*, pp. 33–34.

23. Fisher, pp. 107–110.

24. See ibid., pp. 78–81; and Heeren, p. 92.

25. Fisher, p. 105; and Ernest M. Hayes, "Draft Outline for a Biography of Watson M. Hayes," p. 4.

26. Information on quotations are from Fisher, pp. 105–127.

27. Ibid., pp. 175–176, 181–182; C. R. Mills, letter in *Home and Foreign Record*, 15.9:203 (September 1864); and Julia Mateer, "History of the Tungchow Mission," dated April 17, 1886, in APMP, 20.174, pp. 3–6.

28. See Fisher, pp. 279–280; and Julia Mateer, "History of the Tungchow Mission," p. 5.

29. See "Chefoo-Tientsin Consular Records, 1863–1869," esp. Mills, Corbett, and Mateer to Anson Burlingame, Tengchow, June 2, 1864, pp. 19–30; E. T. Sandford to S. W. Williams, Chefoo, April 30, 1866, pp. 115–118; Mateer, Crawford, Hartwell, and Mills to Burlingame, Tengchow, Oct. 23, 1866, pp. 227–232; Crawford to S. A. Holmes, Tengchow, Dec. 18, 1868, pp. 359–366.

30. "Chefoo-Tientsin Consular Records, 1863–1869," Prince Kung to S. W. Williams (English translation), Peking, Sept. 21, 1866, pp. 205–210. See also Sandford to Williams, Chefoo, Aug. 2, 1866, pp. 185–187; and two letters from Sandford to Williams dated Chefoo, Aug. 28 and Sept. 11, 1866, pp. 215–221.

31. For immediate background on the grave desecrations (which were directed also at Crawford and J. B. Hartwell) see "Chefoo-Tientsin Consular Records, 1863–1869," esp. statement by Hartwell dated Tengchow, Feb. 5, 1866, pp. 99–105; and C. R. Mills to Sandford, Tengchow, May 14, 1866, pp. 123–127. See also Heeren, pp. 92–93.

32. See "Chefoo-Tientsin Consular Records, 1863–1869," esp. Sandford to S. W. Williams, Chefoo, Aug. 11, 1866, pp. 161–167; Sandford

to Tengchow *chih-fu* (English translation), Tengchow, July 14, 1866, pp. 169–172; Prince Kung to Williams (English translation), Peking, Aug. 10, 1866, pp. 197–200; Prince Kung to Williams (English translation), Peking, Sept. 21, 1866, pp. 205–210.

33. "Chefoo-Tientsin Consular Records, 1863–1869," letter from Mateer, Crawford, Hartwell, and Mills to Burlingame, Tengchow, Oct. 23, 1866, pp. 227–232. See also Prince Kung to Williams (English translation), Peking, Aug. 10, 1866, pp. 197–200; Prince Kung to Williams (English translation), Peking, Sept. 21, 1866, pp. 205–210; Prince Kung to Williams (English translation), Peking, Aug. 30, 1866, pp. 211–214; Williams to Sandford, Peking, Aug. 3, 1866, pp. 189–192; Williams to Sandford, Peking, Aug. 22, 1866, pp. 193–196.

34. On Holmes see "Chefoo-Tientsin Consular Records, 1863–1869," Prince Kung to Williams (English translation), Peking, Dec. 3, 1867, pp. 307–309; Sandford to Williams, Chefoo, Dec. 12, 1867, pp. 311–312; Prince Kung to Williams (English translation), Peking, Jan. 5, 1868, pp. 319–321. For Crawford's activities refer to Chapter 1, note 51 above.

35. See *Death Blow to Corrupt Doctrines: A Plain Statement of Facts*, tr. "Tungchow Missionaries" (Shanghai, 1870), pp. *iv–vii*; Paul A. Cohen, *China and Christianity: The Missionary Movement and the Growth of Chinese Antiforeignism, 1860–1870* (Cambridge, Mass., 1963), pp. 293n83; and Heeren, pp. 62–63, 97–98.

36. Fisher, pp. 280–282; and Heeren, pp. 63–64.

37. Information on this episode, with quotations from Mateer's journal and from U.S. diplomatic documents, are in ibid., pp. 62–65, 97, and in Fisher, pp. 281–283. For additional official criticism of the missionaries see "Tientsin-Chefoo Consular Records, 1868–1874," esp. Nevius to S. A. Holmes, Tengchow, Aug. 29, 1870, pp. 775–779; statement by Adm. Henry Kellett, RN, dated Chefoo, Aug. 31, 1870, pp. 783–785; S. A. Holmes to W. F. Mayers, Chefoo, Sept. 2, 1870, pp. 791–793; Chefoo Taotai Liu to S. A. Holmes (English translation), Chefoo, Sept. 2, 1870, pp. 795–801.

38. Heeren, pp. 99, 103n171.

39. Fisher, pp. 184–185.

40. Ibid., pp. 186–187; also "Tientsin-Chefoo Consular Records, 1868–1874," Mateer and Nevius to S. A. Holmes, Aug. 17, 1869, pp. 661–670; Chefoo Taotai Liu to Holmes (English translation), Aug. 22, 1869, pp. 681–686.

41. Cited from *The Presbyterian Banner*, in Fisher, p. 188. See also p. 187; and "Tientsin-Chefoo Consular Records, 1868–1874," Mateer and Nevius to Holmes, Aug. 17, 1869, pp. 661–670; Chefoo Taotai Liu to Holmes (English translation), Sept. 19, 1869, pp. 709–721.

42. See ibid.; and Mateer and Nevius to Holmes, Aug. 17, 1869, pp. 661–670; Holmes to Chefoo Taotai Liu (English translation), Chefoo, Aug. 20, 1869, pp. 671–679; Chefoo Taotai Liu to Holmes (English translation), Aug. 22, 1869, pp. 681–686.

43. Williams to Holmes, Peking, Feb. 28, 1870, in "Tientsin-Chefoo Consular Records, 1868–1874," pp. 752–756. See also Chefoo Taotai Liu to Holmes (English translation), Sept. 19, 1869, pp. 709–721.

44. Heeren, p. 100: also Fisher, pp. 189–191.

45. Julia Mateer, "History of the Tungchow Mission," p. 5.

46. Heeren, pp. 99–100.

47. Ibid., p. 103n171; *Death Blow to Corrupt Doctrines*, p. *viii*; and Fisher, p. 121.

48. Ibid., p. 191.

49. In 1886, writing about the *Death Blow* and books like it, Mateer said they actually showed simply the "mental and moral apathy of the Chinese." In his judgment all these works were variations on a single xenophobic theme; they were not rational attacks, and for that reason they were more an immediate than a long-term danger. They indicated (to Mateer) that the Chinese "have hatred enough to persecute the Christians in every quarter, and passion enough to raise mobs and burn chapels, but not intelligent energy enough to assail Christianity by means of [rational] books and tracts. The day will come, however, when they will do so." See C. W. Mateer, "The Agency of Chinese Authors in Preparing a Christian Literature for China," *CR*, 17.3:93–101 (March 1886).

50. Julia Mateer, "History of the Tungchow Mission," p. 7.

8. The Tengchow School

1. Cited in Fisher, p. 129.

2. Ernest M. Hayes, "Draft Outline for a Biography of Watson M. Hayes," p. 4. See also Fisher, p. 129; R. M. Mateer, *Character-Building in China*, p. 43; and Forsyth, p. 192.

3. An interesting angle here is that Mateer, Mills, Nevius, Corbett, and other American missionaries had themselves been molded at small denominational schools in isolated American environments. Mills suggests the analogy and reflects on Tengchow as a college town in a letter dated Feb. 9, 1885, *CR*, 16.2:118–119 (March 1885).

4. C. W. Mateer to Board of Foreign Missions, April 18, 1865, APMP, 7.129. See also Charles Hodge Corbett, *Shantung Christian University (Cheeloo)* (New York, 1955), pp. 11–12; and Lien Chih-to, II, 155n.

5. Charles H. Corbett, pp. 13–14.

6. For the school's first year see Charles H. Corbett, pp. 12, 14; Julia Mateer, "The Tungchow Boys' Boarding School," *ca* 1885, in APMP, 52; and C. W. Mateer to Board of Foreign Missions, April 18, 1865, APMP, 7.129; Walter Lowrie, May 27, 1865, APMP, 7.146; J. C. Lowrie, Nov. 4, 1865, APMP, 7.207. Apart from Wang Ch'un-ling, the first-year students were Li Shih-kuang (baptized 1870, attended school six years, returned to Ch'i-hsia and eventually apostatized); Ch'iu Tao-ho (dismissed for dull-

ness); Hou Ch'eng-hsin and Kuan Chu (withdrawn by fathers); and Hsing Tao-ming (see text). Teacher Chang Kan-ch'en's two sons also attended for part of the year. See *WHKC*, p. 20.

7. Chou Wen-yüan reportedly told the boys that the school was "all of no use" and would only "hinder their getting positions as teachers among their own people, and effectually prevent their getting a literary degree." Among the school's books that presumably would "only spoil their *wun-le*" was the *Peep of Day* translation that Chou himself had done for Sally Holmes.

8. Julia Mateer, "Report of Tungchow Boys' Boarding School for the Year 1869," APMP, 9.3:398. See also *WHKC*, pp. 22, 52.

9. See Julia Mateer, "Report of Tungchow Boys' Boarding School for the Year 1869"; "Report of the Tungchow Boys' School for the Year Ending Jan. 17th, 1873," APMP, 11.329; letter to F. F. Ellinwood, March 12, 1877, APMP, 13.82; and R. M. Mateer, *Character-Building in China*, p. 48. See also *WHKC*, pp. 21–22.

10. Ibid., p. 26.

11. "The Teng Chow Fu College," in *A Record of American Presbyterian Mission Work*, second ed., pp. 81–88. Chai-li was the actual home of most of the early members of the Tengchow church. It was a promising field up to around 1871, when work terminated due to bad conduct by the lay preacher. This Christian leader was reportedly an individual "of more zeal than prudence or self control. His unhappy temper incurred the ill will of his neighbors and, after a while, made it impossible for him to do any good in that place." See Julia Mateer, "History of the Tungchow Mission," p. 5.

12. *WHKC*, p. 35. The contract reproduced here is one of the later types (1880s), whereby the school does not furnish as much to the pupils as in earlier years. The Mateers sometimes translated *yü-wan* as vicious, in the sense meaning habituated to vice. See R. M. Mateer, *Character-Building in China*, pp. 41–42.

13. Samuel Couling, "Some Experiments in Conducting a Boarding School for Boys," *Records of the Second Shantung Missionary Conference, at Weihsien, 1898* (Shanghai, 1899), pp. 116–121.

14. *WHKC*, pp. 22–24. For a good discussion of the unenforceability of school indentures see Charles A. Litzinger, "Patterns of Missionary Cases Following the Tientsin Massacre, 1870–1875," *Papers on China*, 23:87–108 (1970). In his section on "The Chi-mo Case" (pp. 98–99), which occurred in Shantung in 1873, the author shows that "while it was true that indenturing was sanctioned by Chinese custom, it was also true that children committed under such an arrangement were usually destined for 'disreputable occupations,' " and that American diplomatic representatives in China "would not support the missionaries in cases of breach."

Also interesting, incidentally, is the main point of Mr. Litzinger's article, which is that "In the history of anti-missionary disturbances in China . . . perhaps the entire period from 1870 to 1890 appears as a trough between two surging waves. The common assumption of a sustained, organized, constantly developing anti-missionary movement during the last 40 years of the nineteenth century needs to be further examined. Rather, the constant factor in such disturbances seems to have been the offensive nature of the missionary activity itself." An investigation of American Presbyterian and Baptist experience in east Shantung sustains this thesis. In the light of incidents that did occur further west in the 1880s—most notably at Tsinan and Wei-hsien—I would offer one corollary: missionary "offensiveness" (or inoffensiveness) seems throughout the 1860–1900 period to have been connected very often both to the age and/or China experience of the missionaries involved, and to the amount of prior exposure to missionaries in the pertinent Chinese communities. One of the clearest points about relations in Tengchow is that the foreigners and the Chinese, after great mutual hostility in the 1860s, learned subsequently to tolerate, to cooperate with, and in many cases even to like each other. At the newer Shantung stations, on the other hand, one sees a succession of aggressive younger missionaries and suspicious Chinese having to learn the same lessons over and over again.

15. Julia Mateer, "History of the Tungchow Mission," pp. 3–4; also Heeren, p. 98.

16. "The Teng Chow Fu College," p. 84. See also R. M. Mateer, *Character-Building in China*, pp. 76–79.

17. See ibid., pp. 75–83; and Fisher, pp. 141-142.

18. The *i-yeh* course consisted of woodwork, bricklaying, lithography, etc., taught on the job by Calvin Mateer to well-behaved academic failures. The term seems in the early years to have been largely a euphemism for Mateer's project of the moment, though some of the boys did make careers out of such training. Of the sixty-two students lost by the school, my total differs from that (fifty-seven) given in *WHKC*; this is because *WHKC* omits entirely two names mentioned elsewhere and fails to add to the dropout total three who are listed among the first five boys of 1864. See *WHKC*, pp. 21–26.

19. Julia Mateer to F. F. Ellinwood, March 12, 1877, APMP, 13.82.

20. Fisher, pp. 152–154. For interesting background on the press see Suzanne W. Barnett, "Silent Evangelism: Presbyterians and the Mission Press in China, 1807–1860," *Journal of Presbyterian History*, 49.4:287–302 (Winter 1971).

21. Fisher, p. 155.

22. Ibid., pp. 156–158; and *WHKC*, p. 20.

23. C. W. Mateer to F. F. Ellinwood, Oct. 29, APMP, 10.318. See also Fisher, p. 138; Julia Mateer, "Report of the Tungchow Boys' School for the Year Ending Jan. 17th, 1873," APMP, 11.329; and "The Teng Chow Fu College," p. 84.

24. See ibid., p. 84; R. M. Mateer, *Character-Building in China*, pp. 42–44; Julia Mateer, "The Tungchow Boys' Boarding School," APMP, 52; and *WHKC*, p. 35.

25. See Julia Mateer to F. F. Ellinwood, March 12, 1877, APMP,

13.82; "The Teng Chow Fu College," pp. 83–84; and Julia Mateer, "The Tungchow Boys' Boarding School."

26. Ibid.; and Julia Mateer to F. F. Ellinwood, March 12, 1877, APMP, 13.82.

27. Julia Mateer to F. F. Ellinwood, March 1, 1875, APMP, 12.47. See also her letter dated March 12, 1877, APMP, 13.82; and *WHKC*, p. 53.

28. See Charles H. Corbett, pp. 13–14, 17.

29. The Christian primers used in the 1870s remained more or less standard, at least in the preparatory department, for the duration of the school's history. These began with Helen Nevius's *Mandarin Catechism* and moved up through *Peep of Day, Old Testament History*, etc. See ibid., p. 15; and Fisher, p. 139.

30. Charles H. Corbett, p. 15; Fisher, p. 144; and W. A. P. Martin review of Mateer's *Arithemetic* in *CR*, 10.3:397–398 (September–October 1879).

31. Julia Mateer to F. F. Ellinwood, March 12, 1877, APMP, 13.82. See also "The Teng Chow Fu College," p. 85; Julia Mateer, "The Tung-chow Boys' Boarding School"; and Julia Mateer to F. F. Ellinwood, March 1, 1875, APMP 12.47.

32. C. W. Mateer to F. F. Ellinwood, Oct. 29, 1872, APMP, 10.318. Mateer's journal entry for April 9, 1869, tells an interesting story of one of these cases. A youth named "Leon Chin Chi" (not identifiable in *WHKC*) had here taken poison because of a personal problem of which the Mateers were ignorant; they were ignorant because it involved be-trothal, which was against the school's rules. Calvin Mateer pumped out Leon's stomach and tried unsuccessfully to make him talk. Failing in this, he decided "it was my duty" to whip the boy "formally and severely" in front of the assembled student body. The boy turned out to be a dis-appointment, and Mateer brooded over his case a good deal. See Fisher, pp. 141–142; and R. M. Mateer, *Character-Building in China*, pp. 74–75.

33. Wang Yüan-te, "Ti K'ao-wen hsien-sheng chuan," p. 4.

34. Ibid., p. 6.

35. There were six classes of *t'iao-kuei* at Tengchow from 1876 on, of which *chin-ling* were specifically the fifth. Other regulations covered worship (*li-pai*); dormitory life (*chai-she*); class routine (*chiang-t'ang*); vacations (*fang-chia*); and rewards and punishments (*shang-fa*). Re-wards (books, toys, coins, etc.) for good work had actually been discon-tinued by 1876, because "deceits arose." For descriptions of all see *WHKC*, pp. 31–34.

36. Chu Pao-chen, "Ti fu-jen Pang Chiu-lieh shih-lüeh," in ibid., pp. 11–14.

37. Ibid., p. 12.

38. Ibid., p. 12. See also Forsyth, p. 192.

39. Chu Pao-chen, "Ti fu-jen," pp. 12–13; and R. M. Mateer, *Character-Building in China*, pp. 49, 58.

40. Ibid., pp. 9, 59; and Chu Pao-chen, "Ti fu-jen," p. 11–14.

41. See R. M. Mateer, *Character-Building in China*, pp. 21–22.

42. Ibid., pp. 53, 58; Wang Yüan-te, "Ti K'ao-wen hsien-sheng chuan," p. 4; and Julia Mateer, "The Tungchow Boys' Boarding School."

43. R. M. Mateer, *Character-Building in China*, p. 58.

44. Charles H. Corbett, p. 18.

45. Julia Mateer to F. F. Ellinwood, March 12, 1877, APMP, 13.82.

46. See Julia Mateer, "The Tungchow Boys' Boarding School"; and *WHKC*, pp. 29–32.

47. Julia Mateer letter dated February 1877, in *Foreign Missionary*, 36.1:23 (June 1877); and *WHKC*, pp. 32, 48–49.

48. Julia Mateer letter dated February 1877, in *Foreign Missionary*, 36.1:24 (June 1877).

49. See ibid., p. 24; C. R. Mills to F. F. Ellinwood, Feb. 7, 1877, APMP, 13.58; Fisher, p. 144; and MFCD VII: Feb. 9, 1877. There is some confusion as to when the school's first class graduated (some accounts say class of 1876 and others say 1877). The exercises were held February 2, 1877, but the class is properly that of 1876, as it is listed in *WHKC*. Charles H. Corbett explains here that "the school term which began in the autumn of 1876 did not follow the Western calendar, and so did not end in December but ran on into January 1877, when the approach of Chinese New Year's indicated a fitting time to close. The work was practically finished in 1876, but the actual ceremonies of graduation took place one evening in January, 1877." Corbett's final date seems to be wrong (assuming Mrs. Mateer's to be right), but otherwise his account appears correct. See C. H. Corbett, p. 18.

50. See *WHKC*, p. 73; Fisher, p. 144; Julia Mateer letter dated February 1877, in *Foreign Missionary*, 36.1:24 (June 1877); and "Weihsien, Shantung, China," in APMP, 121.17.

51. Hsing's story is told at length in R. M. Mateer, *Character-Building in China*, pp. 84–87. See also *WHKC*, p. 74; and Julia Mateer letter in *Foreign Missionary*, 36.1:23 (June 1877).

52. R. M. Mateer, *Character-Building in China*, p. 180; *WHKC*, pp. 20, 26; Julia Mateer, "The Tungchow Boys' Boarding School"; and C. R. Mills to F. F. Ellinwood, Feb. 7, 1877, APMP, 13.58, and Feb. 4, 1878, APMP, 13.282.

53. See *A Record of American Presbyterian Mission Work*, second ed., pp. 75–76; also *Conference Records* 1877, pp. 1–18, 471–478, and Introduction (by Mateer), pp. *i–ii*.

54. The citation is from Alice H. Gregg, *China and Educational Autonomy: The Changing Role of the Protestant Educational Missionary in China*, 1807–1937 (Syracuse, 1946, p. 18.)

55. See C. W. Mateer to F. F. Ellinwood, June 15, 1874, APMP, 11.147; and an undated Julia Mateer letter in *The Church at Home and Abroad*, 5.29:423 (May 1889).

56. Gregg, p. 18.

57. Ibid., p. 18.

58. Ibid., p. 232, note 21 (citing Sheffield in *Conference Records*

1877, p. 203). See also p. 17. For a contrasting example of steady (though not unopposed) growth in educational work in another mission field see James A. Field, Jr., *America and the Mediterranean World, 1776–1882* (Princeton, 1969), esp. pp. 345–459. Cyrus Hamlin here seems a sort of Calvin Mateer among the Turks.

59. C. W. Mateer to F. F. Ellinwood, Jan. 30, 1877, APMP, 13.52; C. R. Mills to F. F. Ellinwood, Feb. 7, 1877, APMP, 13.58; C. W. Mateer to F. F. Ellinwood, June 15, 1874, APMP, 11.147; and C. W. Mateer to "Dear Brethren" (Board of Foreign Missions), Aug. 21, 1876, APMP, 12.304.

60. See C. W. Mateer to F. F. Ellinwood, April 2, 1874, APMP, 11.126; to Board of Foreign Missions, Aug. 21, 1876, APMP, 12.304; and Fisher, p. 134.

61. Julia Mateer letter dated February 1877, in *Foreign Missionary*, 36.1:24 (June 1877).

62. See C. W. Mateer to F. F. Ellinwood, April 2, 1874, APMP, 11.126; Julia Mateer to F. F. Ellinwood, Sept. 30, 1873, APMP, 11.77; and C. W. Mateer to Board of Foreign Missions, Aug. 21, 1876, APMP, 12.304.

63. Ibid.; C. W. Mateer to F. F. Ellinwood, June 15, 1874, APMP, 11.147; C. W. Mateer to F. F. Ellinwood, Jan. 30, 1877, APMP, 13.52; and C. W. Mateer to F. F Ellinwood, Aug. 22, 1876, APMP, 12.305.

64. *Conference Records 1877*, pp. 171, 174.

65. All citations of the conference speech are from the printed text of "The Relation of Protestant Missions to Education." See ibid., pp. 171–180.

66. See comments by J. Butler; L. H. Gulick, M.D.; G. W. Painter; H. Mackenzie; D. Z. Sheffield; and J. V. N. Talmage, all in ibid., pp. 197–203. For further objections to the teaching of science see D. N. Lyon, Griffith John, and J. Hudson Taylor, pp. 236, 239. The Reverend R. Lechler, it should be said, gave another speech in support of education (pp. 160–171).

67. C. W. Mateer, "School Books for China," *CR*, 8.5:427–432 (September-October 1877). For information on the committee see *Conference Records 1877*, p. 18; and *Conference Records 1890*, pp. 713, 718.

68. See ibid., p. 718; and *Conference Records 1877*, p. 240.

69. Gregg, p. 18. See also *Conference Records 1890*, pp. 715–718; and *The China Mission Hand-Book* (Shanghai, 1896), II, 311.

70. See ibid., p. 311; D. MacGillivray, ed., *A Century of Protestant Missions in China (1807–1907), Being the Centenary Conference Historical Volume* (Shanghai, 1907), p. 442; and *Conference Records 1890*, pp. xlviii, 550–551, 578.

71. See C. W. Mateer, "School Books for China," p. 427; Fisher, p. 159; and Gregg, p. 19. Gregg points out that the committee's published books were actually treatises, for the most part, rather than textbooks. Mateer's contributions (his mathematics books) seem not guilty of such abstruseness.

72. See Fisher, p. 145; Charles H. Corbett, p. 24; R. M. Mateer, *Character-Building in China*, p. 52; Hunter Corbett to F. F. Ellinwood, June 1, 1880, APMP, 15.81; and C. R. Mills to F. F. Ellinwood, Feb. 7, 1877, APMP, 13.58 (includes reference to Martin) and Feb. 4, 1878, APMP, 13.82. Calvin Mateer's degree, a D.D., was awarded by Hanover College in 1880 (Fisher, p. 293).

73. Quotations are from the petition, written by Mateer and signed by himself and five others, dated Feb. 14, 1881, APMP, 15.205. On the financial implications see C. R. Mills to F. F. Ellinwood, Feb. 4, 1878, APMP, 13.82; and Charles H. Corbett, p. 24.

74. *WHKC*, p. 51. The college's claim to historical priority is disputed, particularly by supporters of Hangchow and St. John's Universities. As schools both were in fact much older (1845 and 1847 respectively), and St. John's began styling itself a college as early as 1879. Neither St. John's nor Hangchow, however—nor any other Protestant school in China—offered as Tengchow did "work of collegiate grade (as understood in America at that time)" until the 1890s. A number of "Anglo-Chinese colleges" also existed prior to 1882, but they were similarly "not of full college grade" by American standards. Tengchow's claim seems legitimate. See Charles H. Corbett, pp. 26–27.

75. C. W. Mateer, "Missionary Work In and From Tungchow," in *Presbyterian Monthly Record*, 33.10:348–349 (October 1882); also C. W. Mateer to Board of Foreign Missions, Dec. 31, 1881, APMP, 16.50; Julia Mateer, "The Tungchow Boy's Boarding School"; and *WHKC*, p. 53.

76. C. W. Mateer, "Missionary Work In and From Tungchow," p. 349; also C. W. Mateer to F. F. Ellinwood, Feb. 15, 1881, APMP, 15.206; C. W. Mateer to Board of Foreign Missions, Dec. 31, 1881, APMP, 16–50; and Fisher, p. 146.

77. The preparatory department also had two parts, a primary (*meng-hsüeh*) and a higher primary (*kao-teng hsiao hsüeh-t'ang*). Entrance tests were waived for boys recommended by certain mission schools, and those exceptionally qualified in classical studies could finish the upper course in less than six years. See *WHKC*, pp. 26, 35; and C. W. Mateer to F. F. Ellinwood, Feb. 15, 1881, APMP, 15.206.

78. Fisher, pp. 146–147; C. W. Mateer to Board of Foreign Missions, Dec. 31, 1881; APMP, 16.50; C. W. Mateer, "Mission Work In and From Tungchow," p. 349; Julia Mateer, "The Tungchow Boys' Boarding School"; and *WHKC*, pp. 74–75.

79. Ibid., pp. 35, 54.

80. C. W. Mateer, "How May Educational Work Be Made Most to Advance the Cause of Christianity in China?" *Conference Records 1890*, pp. 456–467. See also R. E. Speer in R. M. Mateer, *Character-Building in China*, pp. 10–11.

81. C. W. Mateer, "What is the Best Course of Study for a Mission School in China?" *Records of the Second Triennial Meeting of the Edu-*

cational Association of China, Held at Shanghai May 6–9, 1896 (Shanghai, 1896), pp. 48–55. See also *Conference Records 1890*, pp. 457–459; and C. W. Mateer to F. F. Ellinwood, April 24, 1894, APMP, 27.2.36.

82. Course information is from W. M. Hayes, "Course of Study— Tungchow College," dated Jan. 17, 1891, APMP, 26.A.8; Charles H. Corbett, pp. 30–32; and *WHKC*, pp. 28–31. For a list of library holdings see ibid., pp. 38–41.

83. Broad knowledge was particularly important, Mateer believed, in the Chinese situation: "In any community the educated men are the influential men. They control the sentiments and opinions of society . . . The bulwark of Confucianism is its educated men. If we are going to displace it in the minds of the people and wrest from its educated men the position they now hold, we must provide men educated in Christianity and in Western science, who will be able to outshine them." See C. W. Mateer, "Missionary Colleges," in *The Church at Home and Abroad*, 2.129:200–202 (September 1897); and *Conference Records 1890*, pp. pp. 459–460.

84. C. W. Mateer, "Chinese Education," *CR*, 14.6:463–469 (November-December 1883); "The Agency of Chinese Authors in Preparing a Christian Literature for China," *CR*, 17.3:93–101 (March 1886); and *Conference Records 1890*, p. 461.

85. Tengchow missionaries to Board of Foreign Missions, Feb. 14, 1881, APMP, 15.205; also *Records of the Second Triennial Meeting of the Educational Association of China*, pp. 52, 112.

86. Charles H. Corbett, pp. 28–29. See also *WHKC*, pp. 28–31; and W. M. Hayes, "Course of Study—Tungchow College."

87. C. W. Mateer, "Chinese Education," pp. 466, 468.

88. Julia Mateer, "The Tungchow Boys' Boarding School."

89. *Conference Records 1890*, p. 462. See also C. W. Mateer, "What Is the Best Course of Study for a Mission School in China?" pp. 49–51.

90. Ibid., pp. 49–50.

91. Ibid., p. 51. See also C. W. Mateer, "The Agency of Chinese Authors in Preparing a Christian Literature for China," p. 96; and W. M. Hayes, "The Aim of a Christian School in China," *Records of the Third Triennial Meeting of the Educational Association of China, Held at Shanghai, May 17–20, 1899* (Shanghai, 1900), pp. 60–66.

92. See *Conference Records 1877*, p. 171.

93. *Conference Records 1890*, p. 466; C. W. Mateer, "What Is the Best Course of Study for a Mission School in China?" p. 54; and letter to F. F. Ellinwood, June 28, 1884, APMP, 18.292.

94. See *WHKC*, pp. 28–32; W. M. Hayes, "The Aim of a Christian School in China," p. 65; and W. M. Hayes, "Course of Study—Tungchow College."

95. Other school organizations were the Total Abstinence Society (Chieh yen chiu hui) and the Chinese Independent Schools Society (Chung-kuo tzu-li hsüeh-shu hui). The Abstinence Society, says the

Alumni History, totally reformed all students with vicious inclinations. The Independent Schools Society was an organization for prospective teachers and patrons of self-supporting Christian schools; founded in 1898, it also seems to have been the last purely local organization at Tengchow. For information on all the groups see *WHKC*, pp. 32, 47–50; and R. M. Mateer, *Character-Building in China*, pp. 59–60.

96. See *WHKC*, pp. 32–36; W. M. Hayes, "The Aim of a Christian School in China," p. 64; Julia Mateer letter in *Foreign Missionary*, 36.1:23 (July 1877); *Conference Records 1890*, p. 463; and Fisher, pp. 140, 147.

97. See C. W. Mateer in *CR*, 13.2:150–152 (March-April 1882); W. M. Hayes, "The Aim of a Christian School in China," pp. 62–63; and Julia Mateer letter in *Foreign Missionary*, 36.1:23 (July 1877).

98. The monitor system is covered in *WHKC*, pp. 31–34. For information on the debating societies see *WHKC*, pp. 20, 48, 62–65; R. M. Mateer, *Character-Building in China*, pp. 18, 44–45 (last page gives an interesting list of typical debate topics); and C. W. Mateer to J. C. Lowrie, Feb. 17, 1868, APMP, 8.118 (on origins of Tengchow debating).

99. *WHKC*, p. 61; and C. R. Mills letter dated Feb. 9, 1885, in *CR*, 16.2:119 (March 1885).

100. *WHKC*, pp. 20, 47.

101. See *WHKC*, p. 49.

102. See Julia Mateer, "What School Songs and Songs for Recreation and Amusement Should We Teach and Encourage in Our Schools? Have Such Songs Been Tried, and If So with What Result?" in *Records of the Second Triennial Meeting of the Educational Association of China*, pp. 105–109; *WHKC*, pp. 8, 31, 61–65; and "Wen hui-kuan ch'ang-ko hsüan ch'ao shih-p'ien," an unpaginated insert following *WHKC*, p. 66. The songs seem to prove quite conclusively that Mrs. Mateer did encourage a "spirit of life and growth."

103. Feng's song, entitled "Hui-fu chih" (Recovery), is included in ibid.; for information on his life see C. W. Mateer in *The Westminster*, Feb. 15, 1908, p. 11, and *WHKC*, p. 86. A sketch of Wang I-ch'eng's career is also in *WHKC*, p. 88.

104. See Ada Haven Mateer, cited in Fisher, p. 334; and C. W. Mateer, "Chinese Education," p. 467.

9. The Missionary as Enterpreneur

1. See *Conference Records 1890*, p. 466.

2. *The Presbyterian Banner*, Nov. 26, 1908, p. 32; also *Conference Records 1877*, p. 174.

3. Fisher, pp. 211–213; also Ernest M. Hayes, "Draft Outline for a Biography of Watson M. Hayes," p. 5.

4. *WHKC*, pp. 41–45.

5. See Fisher, pp. 213–214; and C. W. Mateer to R. E. Speer, June 5, 1903, APMP, 115.18.

6. See Fisher, pp. 236–251; and *WHKC*, p. 5.

7. F. W. Baller, "The Rev. C. W. Mateer, D.D.—An Appreciation," pp. 630–633; and Chauncey Goodrich, cited in Fisher, p. 321.

8. Hunter Corbett, "In Memoriam: Calvin Wilson Mateer," cited in ibid., pp. 239–240 (or see *The Presbyterian Banner,* Nov. 26, 1908, p. 32).

9. See Fisher, pp. 236–251.

10. C. W. Mateer in *Records of the Second Triennial Meeting of the Educational Association of China,* p. 112.

11. Ada Haven Mateer, cited in Fisher, p. 334.

12. Ibid., pp. 246–248; and C. W. Mateer in *Records of the Second Triennial Meeting of the Educational Association of China,* p. 112.

13. See Fisher, pp. 86–87, 236–251; H. R. Williamson, *British Baptists in China, 1845–1952* (London, 1957), p. 34; and *WHKC,* p. 6.

14. For information on Mateer's evangelistic writings see *CR,* 8.5: 395–397 (September-October 1877); and Fisher, pp. 160–161. The Nevius-Mateer *Hymnal,* a Presbyterian standby for over fifty years, was an updating of Nevius's *Sung-yang chen-shen ko* (1862), which was itself a Mandarin reworking of several Ningpo hymnals dating back to *ca* 1857. See Wylie, pp. 195, 225; and Helen Nevius, *Descriptive Catalogue,* pp. 7–8.

15. *CR,* 10.5:397–398 (September-October 1879).

16. *CR,* 8.5:427–432 (September-October 1877).

17. See Fisher, pp. 163–164; W. A. P. Martin in *CR,* 17.8:314–316 (August 1886); and C. W. Mateer, "Mathematics in Chinese," *CR,* 9.5: 372–378 (September-October 1878).

18. Reviewed by Martin in *CR,* 17.8:314–316 (August 1886), and by an anonymous critic in *CR,* 25.3:135–137 (March 1894).

19. Fisher, p. 164; Julia Mateer, "The Tungchow Boys' Boarding School."

20. Fisher, pp. 163–164; and *CR,* 25.3:135–137 (March 1894).

21. *Conference Records 1890,* pp. 549–550.

22. Martin in *CR,* 10.5:397–398 (September-October 1879).

23. *Descriptive Catalogue and Price List of the Books, Wall Charts, Maps, etc., Published by the Educational Association of China* (Shanghai, 1909), p. 11. See *Records* of the first five EAC triennial meetings (1893, 1896, 1899, 1902, 1905) for membership and composition of the Committees on Publication and on Technical and Scientific Terms.

24. Fisher, pp. 167–168.

25. Ibid., pp. 169–170; and C. W. Mateer, *A Course of Mandarin Lessons, Based on Idiom,* 1906 rev. ed. (Shanghai, 1909), pp. *vii–viii.*

26. Wang Yüan-te, "Ti K'ao-wen hsien-sheng chuan," p. 3. See also Fisher, pp. 168–169; *Mandarin Lessons,* pp. *i–ii;* and C. W. Mateer, "Lessons Learned in Translating the Bible into Mandarin," *CR,* 39.11: 603–609 (November 1908).

27. Wang Yüan-te, "Ti K'ao-wen hsien-sheng chuan," p. 3; *Mandarin Lessons,* pp. *vi–viii, xxxvii–lv;* and Fisher, pp. 169–170.

28. See *Mandarin Lessons,* pp. *xiii–xxix,* 282–285, 525–527, 609.

29. Ibid., pp. *iv,* 1.

30. See *Conference Records 1890*, p. 732; and Harlan P. Beach, "The History of Christian Missions in China," in G. H. Blakeslee, ed., *China and the Far East* (New York, 1910), pp. 245–276. See esp. p. 274.

31. *Mandarin Lessons*, p. *iv*.

32. See *Conference Records 1907*, pp. 275–283, 673; also Fisher, pp. 252–274.

33. Wang Yüan-te, "Ti K'ao-wen hsien-sheng chuan," p. 8; and C. W. Mateer, "Lessons Learned in Translating the Bible into Mandarin," pp. 608–609.

34. Ibid., pp. 605–609. On use of *wen-li* nomenclature, see C. W. Mateer, "School Books for China," p. 429, and "Mathematics in Chinese," p. 373.

35. See Wang Yüan-te, "Ti K'ao-wen hsien-sheng chuan," p. 10; Mateer obituary by George Owen, *The Bible in the World*, 4.12:374 (December 1908); and K. S. Latourette, *A History of Christian Missions in China* (originally published 1929; reprinted Taipei, 1966), p. 647.

36. Wang Yüan-te, "Ti K'ao-wen hsien-sheng chuan," p. 5.

37. Ibid., p. 5; and Fisher, pp. 165–166.

38. C. W. Mateer, "Lessons Learned in Translating the Bible into Mandarin," pp. 607–609. See also his "School Books for China," p. 429; comments in *Conference Records 1877*, p. 223; his "The Revised List of Chemical Elements," *CR*, 29.2:87–94 (February 1898); review by "A.P.P." [A. P. Parker?] of C. W. Mateer et al., *A Glossary of Chemical Terms*, *CR*, 34.6:306–307 (June 1903); and Loren Eiseley, *Darwin's Century: Evolution and the Men Who Discovered It* (New York, 1961), pp. 25–26.

39. Paul A. Cohen, "Wang T'ao and Incipient Chinese Nationalism," *The Journal of Asian Studies*, 26.4:559–574 (August 1967).

40. C. W. Mateer, "Lessons Learned in Translating the Bible into Mandarin," p. 606.

41. See esp. C. W. Mateer, "Mathematics in Chinese," pp. 372–378.

42. Mateer comment, *Conference Records 1877*, p. 222. See also, for example, Mateer vs. Edkins on "relative precision of the Mandarin and the Wen-li" (ibid., p. 223); Mateer vs. Chalmers and Reid on translating style in C. W. Mateer, *The Meaning of the Word* [*shen*] (Shanghai, 1913), p. 15, and in "The Use of [*ni*] in Prayer.—II," *CR*, 23.5:224–229 (May 1892); and Mateer vs. Martin on apologetic adaptations, *CR*, 30.12:607–609 (December 1899).

43. Fisher, pp. 165, 213–214, 258; C. W. Mateer to F. F. Ellinwood, June 15, 1874, APMP, 11.147; *Conference Records 1877*, p. 222; *Mandarin Lessons*, pp. *vii–viii*; and *Conference Records 1890*, pp. 275–283.

44. George Owen in *The Bible in the World*, 4.12:374 (December 1908), and C. W. Mateer, "Lessons Learned in Translating the Bible into Mandarin," p. 605.

45. See Fisher, pp. 259; and Lottie Moon to Margaret Burruss Harrison, Feb. 24, 1898 (in Harrison correspondence).

46. *WHKC*, pp. 52–53.

47. *WHKC*, pp. 53, 73–90.

48. *WHKC*, pp. 52–53.

49. C. W. Mateer, "Plans for the Future," in *Records of the Third Triennial Meeting of the Educational Association of China*, pp. 121–123.

50. Ibid., p. 122; Fisher, pp. 305–318; and George W. Chalfant, "A Friend's Recollection of Dr. Mateer," *The Westminster*, 33.51:16 (Dec. 19, 1908). See also Gregg, pp. 22–28, 42–50.

51. See, for instance, how Mateer used reports from graduates teaching at Shanghai and Hangchow, in C. W. Mateer to F. F. Ellinwood, June 28, 1884, APMP 18.292.

52. See *Records* of EAC triennials, 1893–1909.

53. Cited in Fisher, pp. 255–256.

54. Cited in ibid., pp. 256–257.

55. On the New Testament see especially ibid., pp. 252–274; *Conference Records 1890*, pp. 513–514; and C. W. Mateer to F. F. Ellinwood, Feb. 9, 1893, APMP, 27.1.18. On Mateer vs. John Fryer see *Conference Records 1890*, p. 550; citation from C. W. Mateer and W. M. Hayes, "Letter to the Committee of Educational Association on Terms" and "The Committee on Terminology's Report," both in Adrian A. Bennett, *John Fryer: The Introduction of Western Science and Technology into Nineteenth-Century China* (Cambridge, Mass., 1967), pp. 32–33; C. W. Mateer, "The Revised List of Chemical Elements," *CR*, 29.2:87–94 (February 1898). This would appear to qualify a citation from John Ferguson in Bennett (p. 33) suggesting that Fryer was a major participant in this project. See also "A.P.P.", review of C. W. Mateer et al., *A Glossary of Chemical Terms*, pp. 306–307.

56. See Fisher, pp. 171–172; Wang Yüan-te, "Ti K'ao-wen hsien-sheng chuan," p. 6; and C. E. Scott letter to A. J. Brown, Sept. 29, 1908, in "Calvin Wilson Mateer Publicity Folder" (United Presbyterian Mission Library, New York).

57. Julia Mateer, "Life in Shantung—I. A Chapter in Economics," *WWW*, 8.2:43–45 (February 1893).

58. F. W. Baller, "The Rev. C. W. Mateer, D.D.—An Appreciation," pp. 630–633.

59. W. M. Hayes, "School Management and Methods," summarized in *Records of the [First] Triennial Meeting of the Educational Association of China, Held at Shanghai, May 2–4, 1893* (Shanghai, 1893), p. 54.

60. See C. W. Mateer, "The Agency of Chinese Authors in Preparing a Christian Literature for China," pp. 93–101.

61. See Wang Yuan-te, "Ti K'ao-wen hsien-sheng chuan," p. 9; Goodrich, cited in Fisher, p. 320; and C. E. Scott to A. J. Brown, Sept. 29, 1908, in "Calvin Wilson Mateer Publicity Folder."

62. Goodrich, cited in Fisher, p. 320.

63. Baller, "The Rev. C. W. Mateer, D.D.—An Appreciation," p. 632.

64. *WHKC*, p. 34.

65. Wang Yüan-te, "Ti K'ao-wen hsien-sheng chuan," pp. 1, 9;

Fisher, pp. 90–91; and C. W. Mateer, "Tungchow High School," *Foreign Missionary*, 44.3:127–128 (August 1885).

66. Wang Yüan-te, "Ti K'ao-wen hsien-sheng chuan," p. 10; and Fisher, pp. 259–260.

67. Wang Yüan-te, "Ti K'ao-wen hsien-sheng chuan," pp. 4, 6–7.

68. Ibid., pp. 1, 5–6, 8, 10; and Chu Pao-chen, "Ti fu-jen," p. 11.

69. Wang Yüan-te, "Ti K'ao-wen hsien-sheng chuan," pp. 1–2, 4, 7–9; and Fisher (citing Goodrich), p. 333.

70. *CR*, 39.11:593–594 (November 1908).

71. Wang Yüan-te, "Ti K'ao-wen hsien-sheng chuan," p. 9.

72. This quotation apparently involves two of Wang's many plays on words. *Chüeh-chiang* (written *chüeh-ch'iang*) is a term of insult applied in ancient times to *ti* (originally barbarians but now also Mateer's Chinese surname) by a commentary to the "Wei Capital *Fu*," a *Wen hsüan* poem. *Chih-yao*, a reversal of a more normal compound, is a quality attributed in the Sung *Hsü T'ung-chien* to the unorthodox minister Wang An-shih. See ibid., pp. 5, 7–10; and *Tz'u-hai* (Taipei, 1965), I, 249, 693.

73. C. W. Mateer, "Chinese Education," pp. 643–649.

74. Comments by Mateer in *Records of the First Shantung Missionary Conference*, pp. 41–42. See also "Chinese Education," p. 468.

75. Ibid., p. 465.

76. See, for example, comment by Ada Haven Mateer cited in Fisher, pp. 333–334.

77. "The Teng Chow Fu College," pp. 81–88.

78. Ida Pruitt, p. 25. In Ning Lao T'ai-t'ai's version of this incident it will be noted that no date is given, except that part of it occurred on a Sunday and that Lao T'ai-t'ai was at the time about eleven years old. In Chinese terms this would be a year off Martha Crawford's placement in November-December 1876. It seems unquestionable, however, that the incidents are the same; the stories are too similar and the times are too close together for the case to be otherwise.

79. Ibid., pp. 25–26.

80. Ibid., pp. 26–27; and MFCD VII: Nov. 25, 1876. Ida Pruitt confirms Ning Lao T'ai-t'ai's Dr. Deemster as Calvin Mateer in a letter to me dated Feb. 8, 1968. Mateer's Chinese peacemaking counterpart, however, could not possibly have been Yüan Shih-k'ai, since Yüan did not arrive in Tengchow until 1880. Lao T'ai-t'ai was seventy years old when Miss Pruitt knew her in Peking, and her recall of nineteenth-century Tengchow chronology (as distinct from her recall of people) sometimes seems hazy. See also Foster, pp. 173–174; and Heeren, p. 73.

81. MFCD VII: Nov. 25, 1876.

82. MFCD VII: Dec. 7, 1876; and Wang Yüan-te, "Ti K'ao-wen hsien-sheng chuan," pp. 6–7.

83. Ibid.; and MFCD VII: Dec. 7, 1876.

84. Ibid.; and Wang Yüan-te, "Ti K'ao-wen hsien-sheng chuan," pp. 6–7.

85. Ibid.; and MFCD VII: Dec. 7, 1876. It will be noted that Wang,

like Ning Lao T'ai-t'ai, does not give a date in his account of this story, except as an incident long past but still remembered in Tengchow in 1912. That it is again the same case as that described by Lao T'ai-t'ai and the Crawfords is practically certain. No evidence of any other student-soldier fight, or of such a yamen experience by Mateer, exists in Mateer's correspondence in APMP.

86. See C. W. Mateer, "The Missionary and Public Questions" (address and resolutions), *Conference Records 1907*, pp. 335–352, 743–744; and comments in *Records of the First Shantung Missionary Conference*, p. 51.

87. C. W. Mateer, "Tungchow High School," p. 128.

88. C. W. Mateer to F. F. Ellinwood and A. J. Brown, Feb. 8, 1896, APMP, 35.14.

89. C. W. Mateer, "Chen-hsing hsüeh-hsiao lun," in *Wan-kuo kung-pao*, 14:23–48 (1881–1882), extensively quoted and discussed in Wang Shu-huai, pp. 20–24.

90. See Wang Shu-huai, p. 23; *Records of the Second Triennial Meeting of the Educational Association of China*, p. 46; and *Records of the Third Triennial Meeting of the Educational Association of China*, p. 17.

91. *Conference Records 1907*, p. 352.

92. Fisher, p. 313.

93. Ibid., p. 313 (citing an otherwise unidentified article by C. W. Mateer, "Education in China," dated *ca* 1907).

94. C. W. Mateer to A. J. Brown, Jan. 14, 1899, APMP, 41.3.1.

95. Wang Yüan-te, "Ti K'ao-wen hsien-sheng chuan," p. 8.

96. On Hayes at Tsinan, see Heeren, p. 136; Hayes, "Foreign Instructors and Intolerance," *CR*, 34.5:230–235 (May 1903); *A Record of American Presbyterian Mission Work*, second ed., p. 91; and J. B. Neal and others in *WWW*, 18.1:1 (January 1903). See also Gregg, p. 27.

97. Editorial in *CR*, 39.11:593–594 (November 1908).

98. George Owen in *The Bible in the World*, p. 374. See also Fisher, p. 293.

99. Goodrich, cited in ibid., p. 333.

100. See ibid., pp. 83–85; R. M. Mateer, *Character-Building in China*, p. 181; and Hunter Corbett, "In Memoriam: Calvin Wilson Mateer," p. 32.

101. Ida Pruitt, p. 24. See also Fisher, p. 83.

102. Ida Pruitt, in a letter to me, March 27, 1968, and in a conversation earlier in the same month. Mateer's talent for shouting came out mostly at mission meetings, where John Nevius was reportedly a favorite target. They disagreed on many things, and Nevius's "little high-pitched voice" perhaps made him easy to out-shout (from a conversation with Mrs. John D. Hayes, November 1965).

103. J. H. Laughlin to F. F. Ellinwood, Nov. 16, 1885, APMP, 19.32.

104. R. M. Mateer, *Character-Building in China*, p. 21.

105. J. P. Irwin to A. J. Brown, Feb. 15, 1899, APMP, 41.4.

106. See statistics in *A Record of American Presbyterian Mission Work*, second ed., pp. 73–74.

107. W. M. Hayes to F. F. Ellinwood, May 15, 1893, APMP, 27.1.39. See also Ernest M. Hayes, "Draft Outline for a Biography of Watson M. Hayes," p. 3.

108. C. W. Mateer, W. M. Hayes, and C. R. Mills to F. F. Ellinwood, May 30, 1891, APMP, 26.A.42. See also J. H. Laughlin to F. F. Ellinwood, Nov. 16, 1885, APMP, 19.32.

109. C. W. Mateer to F. F. Ellinwood, Aug. 22, 1883, APMP, 17.145.

110. The statement is actually made on the physician's behalf, in J. P. Irwin to A. J. Brown, Feb. 15, 1899, APMP, 41.4.

111. C. W. Mateer to F. F. Ellinwood, Aug. 22, 1883, APMP, 17.145.

112. Cited in R. M. Mateer, *Character-Building in China,* p. 170.

113. R. M. Mateer to F. F. Ellinwood, March 20, 1884, APMP, 18.119. See also C. W. Mateer to F. F. Ellinwood, Aug. 22, 1883, APMP, 17.145, and Feb. 23, 1884, APMP, 18.94; and W. B. Hamilton to A. J. Brown, Jan. 6, 1904, APMP, 119.1.2.

114. A. D. H. Kelsey to F. F. Ellinwood, Jan. 14, 1882, APMP, 16.76. Information and quotations regarding Dr. Kelsey come also from C. W. Mateer to F. F. Ellinwood, Jan. 9, 1880, APMP, 15.13 and April 12, 1881, APMP, 15.234; Kelsey to F. F. Ellinwood, July 5, 1880, APMP, 15.101; and from letters from Dr. Kelsey in *OMF* for March, 1879 (p. 37); November, 1879 (pp. 82–84); May 1880 (p. 50); September 1880 (pp. 93–95); and June 1882 (pp. 29–30).

115. See David Riesman, "Peace Corps and After," in *The Harvard Crimson,* Dec. 6, 1967.

116. Ibid.

117. Information on J. B. Neal comes from C. W. Mateer to F. F. Ellinwood, Feb. 23, 1884, APMP, 18.94; from Neal's *Annual Report[s] of the Tungchow Dispensary, in Charge of the American Presbyterian Mission, Tungchow, China* (Shanghai, 1886–1887–1888); and from a conversation with Mrs. Norwood F. (Mary Louise Hamilton) Allman, October, 1965.

118. Information on Mary Snodgrass comes from C. W. Mateer to A. J. Brown, April 6, 1904, APMP, 119.1.44; Heeren, p. 84; *The Presbyterian Banner,* June 22, 1916, p. 24; and *Minutes of the Annual* [1916] *Meeting, Shantung* [*Presbyterian*] *Mission* (Shanghai, 1916), p. 8.

119. See Fisher, p. 328.

120. Hunter Corbett, "In Memoriam: Calvin Wilson Mateer," p. 23. See also R. M. Mateer to F. F. Ellinwood, Jan. 23, 1889, APMP, 24.1.10; and C. W. Mateer to A. J. Brown, Nov. 27, 1905, APMP, 120.149.

121. Fisher, pp. 103–104.

122. Cited in ibid., p. 331. See also p. 104.

123. Cited in ibid., p. 332.

124. Cited in Harold F. Smith, *May Corbett Smith* (Claremont, Calif., 1965), p. 123.

Conclusion

1. See especially Wang Yüan-te, "Ti K'ao-wen hsien-sheng chuan," pp. 1–10; and George Cornwell to A. J. Brown, May 25, 1900, APMP, 41.5.36.

2. For convenience see the series in its book (reprint) form: C. W. Mateer, *The Meaning of the Word* [*shen*]. For usage trends and typical criticism of Mateer's views see *CR*, 25.11:552 (November 1894); *CR*, 33.4:204–205 (April 1902); *CR*, 35.1:5–18 (January 1904); and *CR*, 35.8:429 (August 1904).

3. Charles H. Corbett, p. 61. For background on the railroad see John E. Schrecker, *Imperialism and Chinese Nationalism: Germany in Shantung* (Cambridge, Mass., 1971), pp. 104–124, 171–179.

4. Ernest M. Hayes, "Draft Outline for a Biography of Watson M. Hayes," pp. 1–3. To cite Hayes more fully, he says that the theory advocated by Mateer and by his own father (Watson Hayes) was "that a combination of scientific knowledge and religious indoctrination at the mass level, with a maximum of personal application and a minimum of social application, would do the most to propagate Christian belief to the greatest number of souls, coupled with the theory that any man could teach himself anything by assiduous work especially at studies that inherently developed thinking capacity. The opposing theory (e. g., Luce) that grew into S.C.U. aimed to attract the intellectual, social, and cultural elite by qualitative education imbued with Christian ideals whose prestige would carry Christian belief to the greatest number . . . Both theories aimed at quantity in numbers and quality in Christian living, but one was from the bottom out, the other from the top down; the one stressed the individual gospel, the other the social gospel." See also Charles H. Corbett, pp. 60–64; Bettis A. Garside, *One Increasing Purpose: The Life of Henry Winters Luce* (New York, 1948), pp. 100–127; and Jessie Gregory Lutz, *China and the Christian Colleges, 1850–1950* (Ithaca, N.Y., 1971), pp. 69–71, 103, 108–109.

5. For a heartfelt defense of the logic and necessity of the changes that were made to the old Tengchow College program, read Charles H. Corbett, beginning at p. 51. For a Marxist (but remarkably Mateer-like) criticism of the effects of such "imperialistic" liberalization in mission school curricula—that it operated to denationalize Chinese students and turn them into an incipient bourgeois elite—see A. A. Volokhova, *Inostrannye Missionepy v Kitae (1901–20)*, tr. and ed. Ellen Widmer (unpublished data paper, Cambridge, Mass., 1971), pp. 13–15. For a caustic view, by a Cheeloo faculty member of the 1930s, of the "extravagant" and "arrogant" elitism eventually characteristic of many of the students, see Martin M. C. Yang, *Chinese Social Structure: A His-*

torical Study (Taipei, 1969), p. 275. For an excellent and unbiased general discussion of problems and policies in early twentieth-century Christian education in China, read Lutz, *China and the Christian Colleges,* pp. 80–129.

6. For pithy statements of Mateer's views on English teaching see C. W. Mateer to A. J. Brown, Feb. 26, 1907, APMP, 122.30; and his comments in *Conference Records 1890,* pp. 506–507. For a sampling of his resentment and contempt for the young missionary "tinkerers" who came to his school, see C. W. Mateer to F. F. Ellinwood, March 8, 1893, APMP, 27.1.28; C. W. Mateer to Mrs. John P. Patterson, Jan. 18, 1901 (in Patterson correspondence); and C. W. Mateer to A. J. Brown, Feb. 7, 1905, APMP, 120.25. See also Robert Mateer's revealing remarks in R. M. Mateer to F. F. Ellinwood, Jan. 23, 1889, APMP, 24.1.10.

7. H. W. Luce to A J. Brown, Dec. 28, 1904, APMP, 119.2.49.

8. See Charles H. Corbett, pp. 74–78; P. D. Bergen and E. W. Burt, "A Sketch of the Trouble at the College," dated Wei-hsien, Nov. 7, 1906, APMP, 121.142; and Wang Yüan-te, "Ti K'ao-wen hsien-sheng chuan," pp. 7–8.

9. W. O. Elterich to A. J. Brown, Oct. 5, 1908, APMP, 123.116.

10. All information and figures are from *WHKC,* pp. 73–95.

11. From a letter dated Sept. 1, 1907, cited in Fisher, pp. 316–318.

12. See ibid., p. 318; and *WHKC,* p. 66.

13. Today's American view of the historical importance of such Christian Chinese as Mateer's graduates seems to be that "outside the religious field" they "could have little influence and could contribute relatively little to the modernization of China," with the qualification that the Christian colleges, upon the 1905 abolition of the traditional examinations, were "only briefly a primary source of teachers and administrators in the new educational system" (Lutz, *China and the Christian Colleges,* pp. 495–496). For a contrary Chinese appraisal, based on observation in Shantung ("The alumni of the mission schools played a significant role in popularizing the knowledge of modern sciences and the ideas of Western democracy"), see Martin M. C. Yang, *Chinese Social Structure,* pp. 274–275.

14. For examples of Luce's skill in easing Mateer out of the college, see Luce's letters to A. J. Brown dated June 15, 1907, APMP, 122.86; and Aug. 7, 1907, APMP, 122.103.

15. See Ray Allen Billington, "Frontiers," in C. Vann Woodward, ed., *The Comparative Approach to American History* (New York, 1968), pp. 75–90.

16. Fisher, p. 242.

17. C. W. Mateer, "Missionary Colleges," *The Church at Home and Abroad,* 22.129:200–202 (September 1897).

18. See C. W. Mateer, *The Meaning of the Word* [*shen*], esp. pp. 1–6, 51, 114–115; "The Use of [*ni*] in Prayer," *CR,* 22.7:308–310 (July 1891); and *CR,* 23.5:224–229 (May 1892). See also W. T. A. Barber in *CR,* 22.8:387 (August 1891); Gilbert Reid in *CR,* 22.10:458

(October 1891); and I. J. Atwood in *CR*, 33.4:204–205 (April 1902). For excellent background on foreign interpretations of *shen* and *shang-ti*, and on the original term controversy of the 1840s, see Douglas G. Spelman, "Christianity in Chinese: The Protestant Term Question," *Papers on China*, 22A:25–52 (1969). For a provocative exposition of the idea that the American (including missionary) self-image with regard to China turned imperialistic at the turn of the century—and that to some this meant assuming a specifically Britannic posture—see Marilyn Blatt Young, *The Rhetoric of Empire: American China Policy, 1895–1901* (Cambridge, Mass., 1968), esp. pp. 76–87, 219–231.

19. Oscar Handlin, *The Americans: A New History of the People of the United States* (Boston, 1963), p. 230. I have seen no evidence at all that Mateer was specifically influenced by Bushnell; I am just impressed by the congeniality of their views.

20. See Horace Bushnell, *Christian Nurture* (New York, 1861), pp. 90–122, 366–384.

21. Stanley Loomis, "The Man, the Office, the Age," review of *Louis XIV*, by John B. Wolf, in *The New York Times Book Review*, March 24, 1968.

22. See Christopher Jencks and David Riesman, "Where Graduate Schools Fail," *The Atlantic Monthly*, 221.2:49–55 (February 1968). Both the thoughts suggested by me are really from Jencks and Riesman.

23. Handlin, pp. 228–230.

24. Horace Bushnell, *Views of Christian Nurture, And of Subjects Adjacent Thereto* (Hartford, 1847), pp. 64–65.

25. See Barnes, pp. 100–113.

26. Charles W. Mensendiek, "The Protestant Missionary Understanding of the Chinese Situation and the Christian Task from 1890–1911" (Ph.D. dissertation, Columbia University, 1958).

27. "Observer," *Missionary Characteristics* (reprinted from *The Shanghai Mercury*; Shanghai, 1902), pp. 62–63.

28. *WHKC*, p. 55.

29. John K. Fairbank, "Virtues That Bring Disaster," review of *Stilwell and the American Experience in China, 1911–1945*, by Barbara W. Tuchman, in *The New Republic*, 164.13:25–26 (March 27, 1971).

30. Richard Rhodes, "Mattie Ross' True Account," review of *True Grit*, by Charles Portis, in *The New York Times Book Review*, July 7, 1968.

31. Paul Mus, "Commitment," review of *Last Reflections on a War*, by Bernard Fall, in *The New York Times Book Review*, Dec. 10, 1967.

32. Ibid.

Bibliography

Allen, Catherine. *Baptist Women Member Handbook*. Birmingham, Woman's Missionary Union, 1972.

Alumni History of Tengchow College. See *WHKC*.

American Presbyterian Mission Papers. See APMP.

Anderson, Jennie. "Woman's Work in the Villages," *Foreign Missionary*, 40.11: 476–478 (April 1882).

———— "Inn Hospitality in Shantung," *Woman's Work for Woman*, 13.9: 303–304 (September 1883).

APMP: American Presbyterian Mission Papers. Manuscript correspondence from and relating to members of the (East) Shantung Mission; in microfilmed papers of the Board of Foreign Missions, Presbyterian Church in the U.S.A., Houghton Library, Harvard University. Document numbering refers to volume and number of document within that volume.

"A. P. P." (probably A. P. Parker). Review of *A Glossary of Chemical Terms* (Hua-hsüeh ming-mu 化學名目), by C. W. Mateer et al., in *The Chinese Recorder*, 34.6: 306–307 (June 1903).

Armstrong, Alexander. *Shantung (China): A General Outline of the Geography and History of the Province; a Sketch of its Missions; and Notes of a Journey to the Tomb of Confucius*. Shanghai, 1891.

Ayers, Thomas W., M.D. "Miss Lottie Moon—As I Knew Her." Birmingham, Woman's Missionary Union, n.d.

Baller, Frederick William. "The Rev. C. W. Mateer, D.D.—An Appreciation," *The Chinese Recorder*, 39.11: 630–633 (November 1908).

Barker, M. P., M.D. "Female Medical Missions: The Force in the Field—China," *Woman's Work for Woman*, 14.3: 83–85 (March 1884).

Barnes, William W. *The Southern Baptist Convention, 1845–1953*. Nashville, Broadman Press, 1954.

Barnett, Suzanne W. "Silent Evangelism: Presbyterians and the Mission Press in China, 1807–1860," *Journal of Presbyterian History*, 49.4: 287–302 (Winter 1971).

Barr, Mary E. "The Closing Exercises of Mrs. Capp's School," *Our Mission Field* (March 1882).

Beach, Harlan P. "The History of Christian Missions in China," in George H. Blakeslee, ed., *China and the Far East. Clark University Lectures*. New York, Thomas Y. Crowell, 1910.

Beaver, R. Pierce. *All Loves Excelling: American Women in World Mission*. Grand Rapids, William B. Eerdmans Publishing Co., 1968.

Bennett, Adrian A. *John Fryer: The Introduction of Western Science and Technology into Nineteenth-Century China*. Cambridge, Mass., East Asian Research Center, 1967.

Bergen, Mary I. (Mrs. Paul D.). "Mothers of a Chinese Revolution," *Woman's Work for Woman*, 21.8: 175–177 (August 1906).

Bergen, Paul D. "Unoccupied Mission Fields of China," *Woman's Work for Woman*, 26.1: 8–9 (January 1911).

———— and E. W. Burt. "A Sketch of the Trouble at the College," American Presbyterian Mission Papers 121.142. Document dated Wei-hsien, Nov. 7, 1906.

Billington, Ray Allen. "Frontiers," in C. Vann Woodward, ed., *The Comparative Approach to American History*. New York, Basic Books, Inc., 1968.

Bostick, George Pleasant. "In Memoriam. The Late T. P. Crawford, D.D.," *The Chinese Recorder*, 33.9: 456–458 (September 1902).

Boughton, Emma F. "Village Schools for Girls," in *Records of the Second Shantung Missionary Conference*.

Brown, Arthur Judson. *Report of a Visitation of the Missions in China of the Board of Foreign Missions of the Presbyterian Church U.S.A.* New York, Board of Foreign Missions, 1901.

———— *Report on a Second Visit to China, Japan, and Korea, 1909, With a Discussion of Some Problems of Mission Work*. New York, Board of Foreign Missions of the Presbyterian Church U.S.A., 1909.

Burton, Margaret E. *The Education of Women in China*. New York, Fleming H. Revell and Co., 1911.

Bushnell, Horace. *Views of Christian Nurture, And of Subjects Adjacent Thereto*. Hartford, Conn., 1847.

———— *Christian Nurture*. New York, 1861.

Calvin Wilson Mateer Publicity Folder. News clippings, obituary notices, letters, photographs, etc., relating to Mateer. Compiled and held by the United Presbyterian Church, Commission on Ecumenical Mission and Relations, Central Files, New York.

Capp, Maggie Brown (Mrs. Edward P.). "An Itinerating Tour," *Our Mission Field* (July 1878).

Carter, Anita E. *Sketch of the Life of Annetta Thompson Mills, Founder of the Chefoo School for the Deaf.* Chefoo, 1938.

Cash, Wilbur J. *The Mind of the South.* Originally published 1941; reprinted New York, Doubleday Anchor Books, 1954.

Cauthen, Baker J., ed., *Advance: A History of Southern Baptist Foreign Missions.* Nashville, Broadman Press, 1970.

———— "The Lottie Moon Christmas Offering: Praise and Thanksgiving!" Richmond, Foreign Mission Board of the Southern Baptist Convention, 1973.

A Century for Christ in China. Richmond, Foreign Mission Board of the Southern Baptist Convention, 1936.

Chalfant, George W. "A Friend's Recollection of Dr. Mateer," *The Westminster,* 33.51: 16 (December 19, 1908).

Chang K'ai-yün 張開運, comp. *T'ung-shang yueh-chang lei ts'uan* 通商約章類纂 (Collected stipulations of commercial treaties). 35 chüan. Tientsin, 1886.

"Chao shih san ku lieh-chuan" 趙氏三姑列傳 (Biographies of the three Chao sisters), in Lien Chih-to, *Kuo Hsien-te mu-shih hsing chuan ch'üan chi,* II.

"Chefoo Consular Archives, 1868–1874." Bound ms. correspondence. National Archives, Washington, D.C.

"Chefoo-Tientsin Consular Records, 1863–1869." Bound ms. correspondence. National Archives, Washington, D.C.

Chin-hui tsai Hua pu-tao pai nien lüeh shih 浸會在華佈道百年略史 (Brief Historical Sketches of Baptist Missions in China, 1836–1936). Shanghai, 1936.

The China Mission Hand-Book. 2 vols. bound in one. Shanghai, 1896.

The Chinese Recorder. See *CR.*

Chu Pao-chen 朱葆琛. "Ti fu-jen Pang Chiu-lieh shih-lüeh" 狄夫人邦就列事略 (Sketch of the life of Mrs. Julia Brown Mateer', in *Wen hui-kuan chih.*

Cohen, Paul A. *China and Christianity: The Missionary Movement and the Growth of Chinese Antiforeignism, 1860–1870.* Cambridge, Mass., Harvard University Press, 1963.

———— "Wang T'ao and Incipient Chinese Nationalism," *The Journal of Asian Studies,* 26.4: 559–574 (August 1967).

Conference Records 1877: Records of the General Conference of the Protestant Missionaries of China, Held at Shanghai, May 10–24, 1877. Shanghai, 1878.

Conference Records 1890: Records of the General Conference of the Protestant Missionaries of China, Held at Shanghai, May 7–20, 1890. Shanghai, 1890.

Conference Records 1907: Records, China Centenary Missionary Conference, Held at Shanghai, April 25 to May 8, 1907. New York, American Tract Society, n.d.

Connelly, Emma M. "In China Land. In Memory of Mrs. Bertha Bryan Bostick," *Foreign Mission Journal,* 23.6: 171–174 (January 1892).

Copeland, E. Luther. "The Life of Miss Lottie Moon." 45-minute tape cassette. Kansas City, Mo., Christian Cassettes (Onesimus Incorporated), 1972.

Corbett, Charles Hodge. *Shantung Christian University (Cheeloo)*. New York, United Board for Christian Colleges in China, 1955.

Corbett, Hunter. *Sheng-ching yao-tao* 聖經要道 (Important scripture truths). Chefoo, n.d.

———— "Shepherd and Lambs." 23-page printed text of a sermon preached by Dr. Corbett at the Shanghai Union Church, Dec. 6, 1903, N.p., n.d.

———— "In Memoriam: Calvin Wilson Mateer," *The Presbyterian Banner*, Nov. 26, 1908.

Corbett, Mary Nixon (Mrs. Hunter). "Paper From Chefoo," *Woman's Work in China*, 4.1: 31–34 (November 1880).

———— "Chefoo Incidents," *Woman's Work in China*, 7.1: 24–26 (November 1883).

Coughlin, Margaret M. "Strangers in the House: The First Baptist Missionaries from America to China, J. Lewis Shuck and Issachar Roberts." University of Virginia, Ph.D. dissertation, 1972.

Couling, Samuel. *The Encyclopaedia Sinica*. Originally published 1917; reprinted Taipei, 1964.

———— "Some Experiments in Conducting a Boarding School for Boys," in *Records of the Second Shantung Missionary Conference*.

Cox, Ethlene Boone. *Following in His Train*. Nashville, Broadman Press, 1938.

CR: The Chinese Recorder and Missionary Journal. Foochow, 1868–1872; Shanghai, 1874 et seq.

Crawford, Martha Foster (Mrs. T. P.). *Tsao yang-fan shu* 造洋飯書 (Foreign cookery in Chinese). Shanghai, 1866.

———— *San-ko kuei nü* 三個閨女 (The three maidens). Shanghai, 1872.

———— *Hsiao wen-ta* 小問答 (Scripture catechism). Shanghai, 1874.

———— "The Chinese Daughter-in-Law," *The Chinese Recorder*, 5.4: 207–214 (July-August 1874).

———— "Woman's Work for Woman," in *Conference Records 1877*.

———— "My School," *Woman's Work in China*, 3.1: 7–10 (November 1879).

———— "Paper From Tengchow," *Woman's Work in China*, 3.2: 93–95 (May 1880).

———— "History of Missions in Tungchow for the First Thirteen Years," condensed in Tupper, *The Foreign Missions of the Southern Baptist Convention*.

———— *Discouragements and Encouragements of the Missionary Situation in North China*. N.p., 1883.

———— "A Call to North China," in Tupper, *A Decade of Foreign Missions, 1880–1890*.

Crawford, Tarleton Perry. *Lüeh-lun tsa-chi* 略論袱集 (Christian ritual [or Catechism of general information]). N.p., 1870.

———— "Ch'in-mu chih chun-sheng" 親睦之準繩 (Rule for keeping on good terms), in his *Lüeh-lun tsa-chi*.

———— "Hui-t'ang li ti kuei-chü" 會堂裏的規矩 (Church regulations), in his *Lüeh-lun tsa-chi.*

———— *Ku kuo chien lüeh* 古國鑑略 (Brief history of the ancient world [or Epitome of ancient history]). Tengchow, 1873.

———— "What Caused the Sudden Death of Christ?" *The Chinese Recorder,* 5.4: 199–204 (July-August 1874).

———— "Advantages and Disadvantages of the Employment of Native Assistants," in *Conference Records 1877.*

———— "Report of Tungchow Baptist Mission for 1877," in Foster, *Fifty Years in China.*

———— *The Patriarchal Dynasties from Adam to Abraham, Shown to Cover 10,500 Years, And the Highest Human Life Only 187.* Richmond, 1877.

———— "The Ancient Dynasties of Berosus and China Compared with Those of Genesis," *The Chinese Recorder,* 11.6: 411–429 (November-December 1880).

———— "A Compendium of History 鳳洲綱鑑 in Thirty Volumes. By Wong Shi-ching 王世貞, an Eminent Scholar of the Ming Dynasty, A.D. 1526–1590," *The Chinese Recorder,* 12.2: 77–86 (March-April 1881). Further installments under the same title are *The Chinese Recorder,* 12.3: 193–201 (May-June 1881) and 12.4: 294–297 (July-August 1881).

———— "A System of Phonetic Symbols for Writing the Dialects of China," *The Chinese Recorder,* 19.3: 101–110 (March 1888).

————, ed. *The Crisis of the Churches. A Collection of Earnest Articles and Extracts from Earnest Men on Matters of Vital Concern to Baptists.* Chefoo, 1894.

———— "Churches, To the Front!" Rev. ed., in his *The Crisis of the Churches.*

———— "A Poem for the Churches," in Foster, *Fifty Years in China.*

———— *Evolution in My Mission Views.* See *EMMV.*

Crawley, J. Winston. "East Asia," in Cauthen, ed., *Advance: A History of Southern Baptist Foreign Missions.*

Davault, Enos Elijah. "First Impressions," *Foreign Mission Journal,* 16.9: 2 (April 1885).

Davis, John W. "In Memoriam—Miss Anna Cunningham Safford," *The Chinese Recorder,* 21.11: 483–487 (November 1890).

Death Blow to Corrupt Doctrines: A Plain Statement of Facts, tr. "Tungchow Missionaries." Shanghai, 1870. A translation of the *Pi-hsieh shih-lu* 辟邪實錄 (A true record to ward off heterodoxy). N.p., n.d.

Descriptive Catalogue and Price List of the Books, Wall Charts, Maps, Etc., Published by the Educational Association of China. Shanghai, 1909.

"Despatches from United States Consuls in Chefoo, 1863–1906." Washington, D.C., National Archives Microfilm Publications, 1965.

Downing, Calista B. "Chinese Customs," *Woman's Work for Woman,* 4.4: 192–194 (September 1874) and 4.5: 232–236 (November 1874).

———— "Chinese Superstitions," *Woman's Work for Woman,* 5.5: 169–170 (July 1875).

——— "The Unwelcome Little Daughter," *Woman's Work for Woman,* 5.5: 170–171 (July 1875).

Dwight, Henry Otis, H. Allen Tupper, Jr., and Edwin Munsell Bliss, eds. *The Encyclopedia of Missions.* Second edition. New York, Funk and Wagnalls Co., 1910.

Eiseley, Loren. *Darwin's Century: Evolution and the Men Who Discovered It.* New York, Doubleday Anchor Books, 1961.

EMMV: T. P. Crawford. *Evolution in My Mission Views, or Growth of Gospel Mission Principles in My Own Mind.* Fulton, Ky., J. A. Scarboro, 1903.

Encyclopedia of Southern Baptists. 2 vols. Nashville, Broadman Press, 1958.

Fairbank, John King. "Virtues That Bring Disaster." Review of *Stilwell and the American Experience in China, 1911–1945,* by Barbara W. Tuchman, in *The New Republic,* 164.13: 25–26 (March 27, 1971).

———, ed. *The Missionary Enterprise in China and America.* Cambridge, Mass., Harvard University Press, 1974.

Feng Chih-ch'ien 馮志謙. "Hui-fu chih" 恢復誌 (Recovery), in "Wen hui-kuan ch'ang-ko hsüan ch'ao shih-p'ien."

Fiedler, Leslie A. *An End to Innocence: Essays on Culture and Politics.* Boston, Beacon Press, 1955.

——— "Adolescence and Maturity in the American Novel," in his *An End to Innocence.*

——— "Come Back to the Raft Ag'in, Huck Honey!" in his *An End to Innocence.*

Field, James A., Jr. *America and the Mediterranean World, 1776–1882.* Princeton, Princeton University Press, 1969.

——— "Near East Notes and Far East Queries," in Fairbank, ed., *The Missionary Enterprise in China and America.*

Fisher, Daniel Webster. *Calvin Wilson Mateer, Forty-Five Years a Missionary in Shantung Province, China: A Biography.* Philadelphia, The Westminster Press, 1911.

FMJ: Foreign Mission Journal. Organ of the Foreign Mission Board of the Southern Baptist Convention; Richmond, Va., 1851–1916.

Foreign Mission Journal. See *FMJ.*

The Forty-Ninth Annual Report of the Board of Foreign Missions of the Presbyterian Church in the United States of America, Presented to the General Assembly, May, 1886. New York, 1886.

Forsyth, Robert Coventry, ed. *Shantung: The Sacred Province of China in Some of Its Aspects.* Shanghai, 1912.

Foster, Lovelace Savidge. *Fifty Years in China: An Eventful Memoir of the Life of Tarleton Perry Crawford, D.D.* Nashville, Bayless-Pullen Co., 1909.

Frady, Marshall. "Growing Up a Baptist," *Mademoiselle,* 70.5: 156, 225–229 (March 1970).

Garrett, Shirley Stone. "Why They Stayed: American Church Politics and Chinese Nationalism in the Twenties," in Fairbank, ed., *The Mis-*

sionary Enterprise in China and America.

Garside, Bettis A. *One Increasing Purpose: The Life of Henry Winters Luce.* New York, Fleming H. Revell and Co., 1948.

Gaver, Jessyca Russell. *"You Shall Know the Truth:" The Baptist Story.* New York, Lancer Books, 1973.

Grant, E. J. "The Church vs. Societies," in T. P. Crawford, ed., *The Crisis of the Churches.*

Gregg, Alice H. *China and Educational Autonomy: The Changing Role of the Protestant Educational Missionary in China, 1807–1937.* Syracuse, N.Y., Syracuse University Press, 1946.

Halberstam, Michael. "Are *You* Guilty of Murdering Martin Luther King?" *The New York Times Magazine,* June 9, 1968.

Hamilton, Mrs. William B. "The Chinese Bible-Woman." New York, Woman's Board of Foreign Missions of the Presbyterian Church U.S.A., n.d.

Handlin, Oscar. *The Americans: A New History of the People of the United States.* Boston, Little, Brown, and Co., 1963.

Harrison Correspondence. A collection of letters from Lottie Moon to Margaret Burruss (Mrs. William Henry) Harrison, a personal friend. Deposited at the Virginia Baptist Historical Society, Richmond University Library, Richmond, Va.

Hayes, Ernest M. "Draft Outline for a Biography of Watson M. Hayes," in John D. Hayes Papers.

Hayes, John D. Papers. A Collection of letters, notes, photographs, outlines of proposed books, etc., relating to American Presbyterian mission work. Owned by Mrs. John D. Hayes, New York.

Hayes, Watson MacMillan. "Course of Study—Tungchow College," American Presbyterian Mission Papers 26.A.8. Document dated Jan. 17, 1891.

———— "School Management and Methods," summarized in *Records of the [First] Triennial Meeting of the Educational Association of China.*

———— "The Aim of a Christian School of China," in *Records of the Third Triennial Meeting of the Educational Association of China.*

———— "Foreign Instructors and Intolerance," *The Chinese Recorder,* 34.5: 230–235 (May 1903).

Hays, Fanny Corbett (Mrs. George). "Chefoo and Woman's Work at Chefoo," *Woman's Work for Woman,* 10.2: 35–37 (February 1886).

Heck, Fannie E. S. *In Royal Service: The Mission Work of Southern Baptist Women.* Richmond, Foreign Mission Board of the Southern Baptist Convention, 1913.

Heeren, John J. *On the Shantung Front: A History of the Shantung Mission of the Presbyterian Church in the U.S.A., 1861–1940, in its Historical, Economic, and Political Setting.* New York, Board of Foreign Missions of the Presbyterian Church U.S.A., 1940.

"Henry R. Luce, 1898–1967," *LIFE,* March 10, 1967.

Hill, Eugene L. "Administering Southern Baptist Foreign Missions," in

Cauthen, ed., *Advance: A History of Southern Baptist Foreign Missions.*

Hiscox, E. T. "The Organization Craze," in T. P. Crawford, ed., *The Crisis of the Churches.*

Holmes, Sally Little (Mrs. James Landrum), and Chou Wen-yüan 周文源. *Hsün erh chen yen* 訓兒眞言 (Peep of Day). Shanghai, 1865.

Howard, Lucy Hamilton. "Her Lengthened Shadow: Scenes from the Life of Lottie Moon, 1840–1912." Birmingham, Woman's Missionary Union, 1964.

Hsü Chia-kan 徐家幹, comp. *Chiao-wu chi-yao* 教務輯要 (Selected documents on church affairs). 4 chüan. Hupei, 1898.

Hunt, Alma. *History of Woman's Missionary Union.* Nashville, Convention Press, 1964.

Hyatt, Irwin T., Jr. "The Missionary as Entrepreneur: Calvin Mateer in Shantung," *Journal of Presbyterian History,* 49.4: 303–327 (Winter 1971).

"In the Spirit of Christmas." N.p., Woman's Missionary Union, 1973.

James, Edward T., ed. *Notable American Women 1607–1950: A Biographical Dictionary.* 3 vols. Cambridge, Mass., Harvard University Press, 1971.

Jencks, Christopher, and David Riesman. "Where Graduate Schools Fail," *The Atlantic Monthly,* 221.2: 49–55 (February 1968).

Kates, George N. *The Years That Were Fat: The Last of Old China.* Originally published 1952; reprinted Cambridge, Mass., M.I.T. Press, 1967.

Kelsey, Adeline de Haven, M.D. "Tungchow Schools," *Woman's Work in China,* 2.2: 97 (May 1897).

Latourette, Kenneth Scott. *A History of Christian Missions in China.* Originally published New York, Macmillan Co., 1929; reprinted Taipei, 1966.

Lawrence, Una Roberts (Mrs. Irvin). *Lottie Moon.* Nashville, Sunday School Board of the Southern Baptist Convention, 1927.

———— Papers. 5 vols. Notes, correspondence, outlines, section drafts, and other manuscript materials generated by Una Lawrence in writing and publishing her *Lottie Moon.* Deposited at the Southern Baptist Theological Seminary Library, Louisville, Ky.

Li Shou Ting. Autobiographical Sketch, tr. T. O. Hearn, in *Foreign Mission Journal,* 61.8: 243–244 (February 1911).

Lien Chih-to 連之鐸 (Martin T. Lien). *Kuo Hsien-te mu-shih hsing chuan ch'üan chi* 郭顯德牧師行傳全集 (Hunter Corbett and the Presbyterian Church in Shantung). 2 vols. bound in one. Shanghai, 1940.

Litzinger, Charles A. "Patterns of Missionary Cases Following the Tientsin Massacre, 1870–1875," *Papers on China,* 23: 87–108 (1970). Cambridge, Mass., East Asian Research Center.

Liu, Kwang-Ching. "Early Christian Colleges in China," *The Journal of Asian Studies,* 20.1: 71–78 (November 1960).

"Liu Shou-shan chang-lao lieh-chuan" 劉壽山長老列傳 (Biography of

Elder Liu Shou-shan), in Lien Chih-to, *Kuo Hsien-te mu-shih hsing chuan ch'üan chi*, II.

Liu T'ieh-yün, *The Travels of Lao Ts'an*, tr. and annotated Harold Shadick. Ithaca, N.Y., Cornell University Press, 1952.

Loomis, Stanley. "The Man, the Office, the Age." Review of *Louis XIV*, by John B. Wolf, in *The New York Times Book Review*, March 24, 1968.

"The Lottie Moon Christmas Offering: Where Does the Money Go?" Richmond, Foreign Mission Board of the Southern Baptist Convention, 1970.

"Lottie Moon Christmas Offerings." Two-page mimeographed handout prepared by the Treasurer's Office, Foreign Mission Board of the SBC, listing totals of annual Christmas offerings. Originally issued 1960, updated annually.

Lottie Moon in Pictures. Richmond, Foreign Mission Board of the Southern Baptist Convention, 1961.

Love, J. F. *Southern Baptists and Their Far Eastern Missions*. Richmond, Foreign Mission Board of the Southern Baptist Convention, n.d.

Lutz, Jessie Gregory. *China and the Christian Colleges, 1850–1950*. Ithaca, N.Y., Cornell University Press, 1971.

Maddry, Charles E. *Christ's Expendables*. Nashville, Broadman Press, 1949.

Malraux, André, *Man's Fate*, tr. Haakon M. Chevalier. New York, Modern Library, 1934.

Martin, William A. P. "A Tribute to Dr. Mateer," *The Chinese Recorder*, 39.12: 694–695 (December 1908).

——— "Tribute" (obituary testimonial to Helen S. C. Nevius), *The Chinese Recorder*, 41.8: 553–554 (August 1910).

Mateer, Calvin Wilson. "School Books for China," *The Chinese Recorder*, 8.5: 427–432 (September-October 1877).

——— "The Relation of Protestant Missions to Education," in *Conference Records 1877*.

——— "Mathematics in Chinese," *The Chinese Recorder*, 9.5: 372–378 (September-October 1878).

——— "Missionary Work In and From Tungchow," *Presbyterian Monthly Record*, 33.10: 348–349 (October 1882).

——— "Chinese Education," *The Chinese Recorder*, 14.6: 463–469 (November-December 1883).

——— "Tungchow High School," *Foreign Missionary*, 44.3: 127–128 (August 1885).

——— "The Agency of Chinese Authors in Preparing a Christian Literature for China," *The Chinese Recorder*, 17.3: 93–101 (March 1886).

——— "How May Educational Work Be Made Most to Advance the Cause of Christianity in China?" in *Conference Records 1890*.

——— "The Use of 你 [*ni*] in Prayer," *The Chinese Recorder*, 22.7: 308–310 (July 1891).

———— "The Use of 你 [*ni*] in Prayer—II," *The Chinese Recorder,* 23.5: 224–229 (May 1892).

———— "What Is the Best Course of Study for a Mission School in China?" in *Records of the Second Triennial Meeting of the Educational Association of China.*

———— "Missionary Colleges," *The Church at Home and Abroad,* 22.129: 200–202 (September 1897).

———— "The Revised List of Chemical Elements," *The Chinese Recorder,* 29.2: 87–94 (February 1898).

———— "Plans for the Future," in *Records of the Third Triennial Meeting of the Educational Association of China.*

———— *A Course of Mandarin Lessons, Based on Idiom.* 1906 rev. ed. Shanghai, 1906.

———— "The Missionary and Public Questions," in *Conference Records 1907.*

———— "Lessons Learned in Translating the Bible into Mandarin," *The Chinese Recorder,* 39.11: 603–609 (November 1908).

———— *The Meaning of the Word* 神 [*shen*]. Shanghai, 1913.

Mateer, Julia Brown (Mrs. Calvin Wilson). "Report of Tungchow Boys' Boarding School for the Year 1869," American Presbyterian Mission Papers 9.398.

———— "Report of the Tungchow Boys' Boarding School for the Year Ending Jan. 17th, 1873," American Presbyterian Mission Papers 11.329.

———— "Fragments," *Woman's Work in China,* 6.1: 12–17 (November 1882).

———— "The Ladies' Question," *Woman's Work in China,* 6.2: 91–98 (May 1883).

———— "The Tungchow Boys' Boarding School," American Presbyterian Mission Papers 52. Document dated *ca.* 1885.

———— "History of the Tungchow Mission," American Presbyterian Mission Papers 20.174. Document dated April 17, 1886.

———— "Cleanliness Next to Godliness," *Woman's Work in the Far East,* 12.2: 85–92 (May 1892).

———— "Life in Shantung—I. A Chapter in Economics," *Woman's Work for Woman,* 8.2: 43–45 (February 1893).

———— "What School Songs and Songs for Recreation and Amusement Should We Teach and Encourage in Our Schools? Have Such Songs Been Tried, and If so with What Result?" in *Records of the Second Triennial Meeting of the Educational Association of China.*

Mateer, Robert McCheyne. "Primary Education for Girls," in *Records of the First Shantung Missionary Conference.*

———— *Character-Building in China: The Life Story of Julia Brown Mateer.* New York, Fleming H. Revell and Co., 1912.

Matthews, T. S. ". . . tall, balding, dead Henry R. Luce . . . ," *Esquire,* 68.3: 131–132, 183 (September 1967).

McGillivray, D., ed. *A Century of Protestant Missions in China, 1807–1907,*

Being the Centenary Conference Historical Volume. Shanghai, 1907.

Means, Frank K. *Southern Baptist Foreign Missions: Digest of Project Reports Made by Students in Southwestern Baptist Theological Seminary*. Seminary Hill, Tex., Seminary Book Store, 1941.

"Memoir of the Late Mrs. Mills," *The Chinese Recorder*, 5.5: 274–279 (September-October 1874). Obituary testimonial to Rose MacMaster Mills; appears to have been written by her husband, Charles Rogers Mills.

Mensendiek, Charles William. "The Protestant Missionary Understanding of the Chinese Situation and the Christian Task From 1890–1911." Columbia University, Ph.D. dissertation, 1958.

MFCD: Martha Foster Crawford Diaries. 7 vols. Manuscript journals covering period 1847–81. Held by the Perkins Library of Duke University (Manuscript Department).

Mills, Annetta Thompson (Mrs. Charles Rogers). "Our School for Deaf Mutes in China," *Woman's Work for Woman*, 8.2: 37–39 (February 1893).

—— "Guiding Influences of the Spirit on the Mission Field," *Woman's Work for Woman*, 14.2: 42–43 (February 1899).

—— "Work Among the Deaf and Dumb," in *Conference Records 1907*.

—— *China Through a Car-Window: Observations on the Modern China, Made in the Course of a Four Months' Journey in Behalf of the Chinese Deaf; with Some Account of the School at Chefoo*. Washington, D.C., Volta Bureau, 1910.

—— "Helping the Helpless," *Woman's Work for Woman*, 25.8: 177–179 (August 1910).

Minutes of the [1916] Annual Meeting, Shantung [Presbyterian] Mission. Shanghai, 1916.

"Miss Moon as We Knew Her." Birmingham, Woman's Missionary Union, n.d.

Monsell, Helen Albee. *Her Own Way: The Story of Lottie Moon*. Nashville, Broadman Press, 1958.

Montgomery, Helen Barrett. *Western Women in Eastern Lands: An Outline Study of Fifty Years of Woman's Work in Foreign Missions*. Central Committee on the United Study of Missions Series. New York, The Macmillan Co., 1910.

Moon, Anna Mary, comp. *Sketches of the Moon and Barclay Families*. N.p., 1939.

Moon, Charlotte (Lottie) Diggs. "Advantages and Disadvantages of Wearing the Native Dress in Missionary Work," *Woman's Work in China*, 5.1: 14–22 (November 1881).

—— "Shantung Province," *Woman's Work in China*, 5.2: 79–94 (May 1882).

—— "Sketch of Tungchow," *Woman's Work in China*, 6.2: 141–148 (May 1883).

—— "The Woman's Question Again," *Woman's Work in China*, 7.1:

47–55 (November 1883).

—— "Our China Mission," *Foreign Mission Journal,* 18.4: 2 (November 1886).

—— "Woman's Work in Shantung," *Foreign Mission Journal,* 20.3: 3 (October 1888).

—— "Work in Pingtu," *Woman's Work in the Far East,* 11.1: 1–11 (November 1890).

—— "Sa-ling Diary," *Foreign Mission Journal,* 22.9: 271 (April 1891).

—— "The Colored People," *Foreign Mission Journal,* 24.3: 89 (October 1892).

Mortimer, Favell L. *The Peep of Day.* Third ed. Toronto, Ward, Lock and Co., Ltd., 1911.

Murphey, Rhoads. *Shanghai: Key to Modern China.* Cambridge, Mass., Harvard University Press, 1953.

Mus, Paul. "Commitment." Review of *Last Reflections on a War,* by Bernard Fall, in *The New York Times Book Review,* Dec. 10, 1967.

Neal, James Boyd, M.D. *First Annual Report of the Tungchow Dispensary, in Charge of the American Presbyterian Mission, Tungchow, for the Year 1885.* Shanghai, 1886.

—— *Second Annual Report of the Tungchow Dispensary, in Charge of the American Presbyterian Mission, Tungchow, for the Year 1886.* Shanghai, 1887.

—— *Third Annual Report of the Tungchow Dispensary, in Charge of the American Presbyterian Mission, Tungchow, for the Year 1887.* Shanghai, 1888.

Neel, Isa-Beall Williams. *His Story in Georgia W.M.U. History.* Atlanta, Woman's Missionary Union of the Georgia Baptist Convention, 1939.

Nevius, Helen S. Coan (Mrs. John Livingston). *Yeh-su chiao kuan-hua wen-ta* 耶穌教官話問答 (Mandarin catechism [or Catechism of Christian doctrine]). Shanghai, 1863.

—— *Our Life in China.* New York, 1868.

—— *Mei Mo-shih hsing lüeh* 梅莫氏行略 (The life of Rose Mills). Shanghai, 1875.

—— *Hai-t'ung ku-shih* 孩童故事 (The Swiss boy, or the story of Sah-pe). Shanghai, 1883.

—— "How Can We Reach the Heathen Women?" *Woman's Work in the Far East,* 21.1: 1–4 (May 1900).

—— *A Descriptive Catalogue of Books and Tracts by the Rev. John Livingston Nevius, D.D., and Helen S. Coan Nevius.* Shanghai, 1907. A Chinese translation (very rough), entitled *Shu mu ts'e* 書目冊, is bound into the book as an appendix.

—— "Personal Report of Helen S. Coan Nevius for 1908," American Presbyterian Mission Papers 129.

Nevius, John Livingston. "Religious Interest in Ping-tu," *The Chinese Recorder,* 3.5: 140 (October 1870).

———— "Barbarous Chinese Custom," *Our Mission Field* (July 1875).
"Observer." *Missionary Characteristics*. Shanghai, 1902. Document consists of semi-satirical articles reprinted from *The Shanghai Mercury,* written in reply to Arthur H. Smith, *Chinese Characteristics* (New York, 1894).
OMF: Our Mission Field. Organ of Women's Foreign Mission Societies, Presbyterian Church in the U.S.A.; New York, 1871–1885. Many issues not visibly numbered by either issue or volume.
"Our Board and the 'Gospel Mission,'" *Foreign Mission Journal,* 25.2: 37–41 (September 1893).
Our Mission Field. See *OMF*.
Owen, George. "Personalia" (obituary testimonial to Calvin W. Mateer), *The Bible in the World,* 4.12: 374 (December 1908).
Patterson Correspondence. A collection of letters from Calvin and Julia Mateer, Hunter Corbett, and other Shantung missionaries to Mrs. John P. Patterson, a onetime (1871) member of the Tengchow Presbyterian station. Deposited at the Presbyterian Historical Society, Philadelphia.
Porter, Henry D., M.D. "The Ballad of Li Hua Ch'eng," in "A Modern Shantung Prophet," *The Chinese Recorder,* 18.1: 12–21 (January 1887).
Proceedings of the Southern Baptist Convention. See *SBC Proceedings*.
Pruitt, Anna Seward (Mrs. C. W.). *The Day of Small Things*. Richmond, Foreign Mission Board of the Southern Baptist Convention, 1929.
———— *Up From Zero*. Nashville, Broadman Press, 1939.
Pruitt, Cicero Washington. "Twenty-Six Years in Our North China Mission," *The New East,* 3.3: 19–20 (April 1908).
———— "In Memoriam. Miss Lottie Moon," *The Chinese Recorder,* 44.4: 241–242 (April 1913).
———— "Some Recollections of Dr. T. P. Crawford and Wife," Southern Baptist Convention Papers (Martha F. Crawford Folder). Document is unsigned, but handwriting and other features identify it as C. W. Pruitt's. Consists of 11 ms. pp., dated Philadelphia, Dec. 22, 1917.
Pruitt, Ida. *A Daughter of Han: The Autobiography of a Chinese Working Woman*. Originally published 1945; reprinted Stanford, Stanford University Press, 1967.
Pruitt, Ida Tiffany (Mrs. C. W.). "A Word of Encouragement," *Woman's Work in China,* 7.1: 31–33 (November 1883).
Rabe, Valentin H. "Evangelical Logistics: Mission Support and Logistics to 1920," in Fairbank, ed., *The Missionary Enterprise in China and America*.
A Record of American Presbyterian Mission Work in Shantung Province, China, 1861–1913. Two editions exist, both n.p., n.d.
Records of the General Conference of the Protestant Missionaries of China, Held at Shanghai, May 10–24, 1877. See *Conference Records 1877*.
Records of the General Conference of the Protestant Missionaries of China, Held at Shanghai, May 7–20, 1890. See *Conference Records 1890*.

Records, China Centenary Missionary Conference, Held at Shanghai, April 25 to May 8, 1907. See *Conference Records 1907.*

Records of the First Shantung Missionary Conference, at Ch'ingchowfu, 1893. Shanghai, 1894.

Records of the Second Shantung Missionary Conference, at Weihsien, 1898. Shanghai, 1899.

Records of the [*First*] *Triennial Meeting of the Educational Association of China, Held at Shanghai, May 2–4, 1893.* Shanghai, 1893.

Records of the Second Triennial Meeting of the Educational Association of China, Held at Shanghai, May 6–9, 1896. Shanghai, 1896.

Records of the Third Triennial Meeting of the Educational Association of China, Held at Shanghai, May 17–20, 1899. Shanghai, 1900.

Records of the Fourth Triennial Meeting of the Educational Association of China, Held at Shanghai, May 21–24, 1902. Shanghai, 1902.

Records of the Fifth Triennial Meeting of the Educational Association of China, Held at Shanghai, May 17–20, 1905. Shanghai, 1906.

Records of the Sixth Triennial Meeting of the Educational Association of China, Held at Shanghai, May 19–22, 1909. 2 vols. bound in one. Shanghai, 1909.

"Report of the Annual Meeting of the Shantung [Presbyterian] Mission for 1886," American Presbyterian Mission Papers 22.103.

Rhea, Claude, comp. *Lottie Moon Cook Book: Recipes Used by Lottie Moon 1875–1912.* Waco, Tex., Word Books, 1969.

Rhodes, Richard. "Mattie Ross' True Account." Review of *True Grit,* by Charles Portis, in *The New York Times Book Review,* July 7, 1968.

Riesman, David. "Peace Corps and After," *The Harvard Crimson,* Dec. 6, 1967.

Robinson, Miriam. "Faithful Unto Death: Narration of the Life of Lottie Moon." Birmingham, Woman's Missionary Union, 1964.

"The Romance of Lottie Moon," *Baptist Intermediate Union Quarterly,* 33.1: 29–31 (January-March 1941).

SBCP: Southern Baptist Convention Papers. Manuscript correspondence from and relating to members of the Southern Baptist North China Mission, 1864–1912. Arranged chronologically in numbered folders by individual missionary, at the Foreign Mission Board, Richmond.

SBC Proceedings: Proceedings of the Southern Baptist Convention. Minutes, addresses, board reports, etc., of the annual Southern Baptist Convention. Published yearly since 1845.

Schrecker, John E. *Imperialism and Chinese Nationalism: Germany in Shantung.* Cambridge, Mass., Harvard University Press, 1971.

Scott, Anne Firor. *The Southern Lady: From Pedestal to Politics, 1830–1930.* Chicago, University of Chicago Press, 1970.

Seymour, Mary (Mrs. Walter F.), et al. "Missions and High Life at Tengchow," *Woman's Work for Woman,* 20.2: 27–29 (February 1905).

Seymour, Walter F., M.D. "China Wants Women Doctors and Nurses," *Woman's Work for Woman,* 25.2: 38–39 (February 1910).

Smith, Mrs. Arthur Henderson. "Must the Single Lady Go?" *Woman's Work in China*, 7.2: 170–175 (May 1884).

Smith, Harold Fred. *Hunter Corbett and His Family*. Claremont, Calif., College Press, 1965.

———— *May Corbett Smith*. Claremont, Calif., College Press, 1965.

Smith, Lillian. *Killers of the Dream*. New York, Doubleday Anchor Books, 1963.

Smith, Page. *Daughters of the Promised Land: Women in American History*. Boston, Little, Brown and Co., 1970.

Smith, W. R. L. "Sick of Unions," in T. P. Crawford, ed., *The Crisis of the Churches*.

Southern Baptist Convention Papers. See SBCP.

Spelman, Douglas G. "Christianity in Chinese: The Protestant Term Question," *Papers on China*, 22A: 25–52 (1969). Cambridge, Mass., East Asian Research Center.

Ssu-ma Ch'ien, *Records of the Grand Historian of China, Translated from the Shih chi,* tr. Burton Watson. New York, Columbia University Press, 1961.

Su Tung-p'o: Selections from a Sung Dynasty Poet, tr. Burton Watson. New York, Columbia University Press, 1965.

Sumerau, Dorothy Lehman. "Make His Name Glorious: A Dramatic Service of Worship on the Life and Work of Lottie Moon." Nashville, Broadman Press, 1958.

Summers, Jester. *Lottie Moon of China*. Nashville, Broadman Press, 1971.

Teng, Yuan Chung. "Reverend Issachar Jacox Roberts and the Taiping Rebellion," *The Journal of Asian Studies,* 23.1: 55–67 (November 1963).

Tengchowfu—A Model Station in China. New York, Board of Foreign Missions of the Presbyterian Church U.S.A., 1913.

"The Teng Chow Fu College," in *A Record of American Presbyterian Mission Work in Shantung Province, China, 1861–1913,* second ed.

Thompson, Virginia M. "Extracts from the Diary of Martha E. Foster Crawford, 1852–1854. Edited, With Notes, An Introduction, and Some Historical Comments on the Role of Mrs. Crawford as a Christian Emissary from the United States to China." Duke University, M.A. thesis, 1952.

Tomlinson, Carol, and Doris Standridge. "It Cannot End at Kobe: How Lottie Moon Lives in Missions in the 1970's." Birmingham, Woman's Missionary Union, n.d.

Tupper, Henry Allen. *The Foreign Missions of the Southern Baptist Convention*. Philadelphia, 1880.

———— *A Decade of Foreign Missions, 1880–1890*. Richmond, 1891.

"Visits Among the China Missions," *Woman's Work for Woman,* 14.2: 37–40 (February 1884).

Volokhova, A. A. *Inostrannye Missionepy v Kitae, 1901–20* (Foreign Missionaries in China 1901–1920), tr. and ed. Ellen Widmer. Unpublished data paper. Cambridge, Mass., East Asian Research Center, 1971.

Wang Shu-huai 王樹槐. *Wai-jen yü wu-hsü pien-fa* 外人與戊戌變法 (Foreigners and the 1898 reform movement). Institute of Modern History Monographs. Taipei, 1965.

Wang Yüan-te. "Ti K'ao-wen hsien-sheng chuan" 狄考文先生傳 (Biography of Mr. Calvin Mateer), in *Wen hui-kuan chih*.

Warren, Edward, M.D. *A Doctor's Experiences in Three Continents*. Baltimore, 1885.

Watson, C. N. "Overdoing Organization," in T. P. Crawford, ed., *The Crisis of the Churches*.

Wayland, Francis. "Independence of the Churches," in T. P. Crawford, ed., *The Crisis of the Churches*.

"Weihsien, Shantung, China," American Presbyterian Mission Papers 121.17.

"Wen hui-kuan ch'ang-ko hsüan ch'ao shih-p'ien" 文會館唱歌選抄十篇 (Ten selected songs of Tengchow College), in *Wen hui-kuan chih*. Document is an unpaginated 24-pp. insert following p. 66.

Wen hui-kuan chih. See *WHKC*.

"We're Really World Baptists," *Newsweek*, 76.3: 52–53 (July 20, 1970).

Whitman, George. "The Authority of the Local Church," in T. P. Crawford, ed., *The Crisis of the Churches*.

WHKC: Wang Yuan-te 王元德 and Liu Yü-feng 劉玉峰, eds., *Wen hui-kuan chih* 文會館志 (Alumni history of Tengchow College). Weihsien, 1913.

"Why Didn't You Come Last Year?" Richmond, Foreign Mission Board of the Southern Baptist Convention, 1968.

Wight, J. K. "Chefoo," *Woman's Work for Woman and Our Mission Field*, 2.2: 35–36 (February 1887).

Williamson, H. R. *British Baptists in China, 1845–1952*. London, Carey Kingsgate Press, 1957.

Woman's Missionary Union Year Book 1974–75. Birmingham, Woman's Missionary Union, 1974.

Woman's Work for Woman. See *WWW*.

Woman's Work for Woman and Our Mission Field. See *WWW-OMF*.

Woman's Work in China. See *WWC*.

Woman's Work in the Far East. See *WWFE*.

Wu Sheng-te 吳盛德 and Ch'en Tseng-hui 陳增輝, comps. *Chiao-an shih-liao pien mu* 教案史料編目 (A bibliography of Chinese source materials dealing with local or international cases involving Christian missions). Yenching School of Religion Series. Peiping, 1941.

WWC: *Woman's Work in China*. Interdenominational organ of Protestant woman's workers; Shanghai, 1877–1889.

WWFE: *Woman's Work in the Far East*. Successor (1890–1921) to *Woman's Work in China*.

WWW: *Woman's Work for Woman*. Organ of Women's Foreign Mission Societies, Presbyterian Church in the U.S.A.; New York, 1886–1924.

WWW-OMF: *Woman's Work for Woman and Our Mission Field*. A transition title used in 1885–86, as *Our Mission Field* was succeeded by *Woman's Work for Woman.*

Wylie, Alexander. *Memorials of Protestant Missionaries to the Chinese: Giving a List of Their Publications, and Obituary Notices of the Deceased. With Copious Indexes.* Shanghai, 1867.

Yang, Martin C. *A Chinese Village: Taitou, Shantung Province.* New York, Columbia University Press, 1945.

———— *Chinese Social Structure: A Historical Study.* Taipei, 1969.

Young, Marilyn Blatt. *The Rhetoric of Empire: American China Policy, 1895–1901.* Cambridge, Mass., Harvard University Press, 1968.

Glossary

Names, Places, and Terms

Chai-li 寨裏
chai-she 齋舍
Chang Kan-ch'en 張幹臣
Chang P'ei-ling 張佩令
Ch'ang-lo 昌樂
Chao-yüan 招遠
Cheeloo (Ch'i-lu) 齊魯
Chefoo (Chih-fu) 芝罘
"Chen-hsing hsüeh-hsiao lun" 振興
　學校論
Chen tao chieh 眞道解
cheng-chai 正齋
chi-ho 幾何
"Chi-lieh hsien" 基列縣
Chi-mei (Chi-mo) 卽墨
Ch'i chia p'aï-fang chiao-hui 戚家牌
　坊教會
Ch'i-hsia 棲霞
chiang-t'ang 講堂
chiao-an 教案
chiao-min 教民
Chieh yen chiu hui 戒煙酒會
chien-ch'en 奸臣
chien-tu 監督
Ch'ien-pai tao-kao wen 淺白禱告文

chih-fu 知府
chih hsi-i 治西醫
chih-jih-sheng 值日生
chih-tsao chia 製造家
chih-tsao so 製造所
chih-yao 執拗
chin-ling 禁令
Ch'ing-chou-fu 青州府
Ch'ing Mei Hong 清美行
Ch'ing-nien hui 靑年會
Ch'iu Tao-ho 丘道和
Chou Li-wen 鄒立文
Chu Feng-tan 朱鳳丹
chu-tso teng-shen 著作等身
Ch'uan-tao hui 傳道會
Ch'uang-shih chi wen-ta 創世紀問答
Chung-kuo tzu-li hsüeh-shu hui
　中國自立學塾會
Chung Wei-i 仲偉儀
chü-jen 舉人
chüeh-chiang 倔彊
chüeh-ch'iang 倔彊
fang-chia 放假
Fen tzu lüeh chieh 分字略解
feng-ch'ao 風潮

314

fu-jen 夫人
fu-kuo ts'e 富國冊
Fu-nü fu-chu hui 婦女輔助會
fu-sheng 附生
Hai-tzu shou-hsi li lun 孩子受洗禮論
Han-wen 漢文
Hou Ch'eng-hsin 侯誠信
Hsi-hsüeh 西學
hsiang-yü kuan-mo 相與觀摩
Hsiao shih-tzu ko 小十字閣
hsien-k'ao 縣考
hsien-sheng 先生
Hsin-wen hui 新聞會
hsing 行
hsing-hsüeh 形學
Hsing Tao-ming 开道明
Hsiu Chi 修己
hsiu-shen 修身
hsiu-ts'ai 秀才
Hsü t'ung-chien 續通鑑
hsün-hsü 循序
hua-pien 花邊
hui-t'ou 會頭
i hui 以惠
i-yeh 肄業
Kang-yü 崗嵛
k'ang 炕
kao-teng hsiao hsüeh-t'ang 高等小
　學堂
Kiaochow (Chiao-chou) 膠州
kou-ku hsüeh 勾股學
Kuan Chu 關住
kuan-fu 官府
kuan-hua chih t'ung hsing 官話之
　通行
Kuan-yin T'ang 觀音堂
kung-chü 公局
kung-hsüeh 公學
Lai-chou 萊州
Lai-wang-kou 來王溝
Lan-ti 蘭底
lao-hui 老會
Lao-t'ien hui 老天會
li 理
Li chi 禮記
Li Chin-yü 李進玉
Li Hung-chang 李鴻章
Li Hung-chung 李洪中

Li-jen 里仁
Li Kuang-nai 李光鼐
li-pai 禮拜
Li Ping-i 李秉義
Li Shan-ch'ing 李山青
Li Yüan-k'ai 李元愷
Li Yüan-t'ung 李元通
Li Yün-lu 李雲路
lin-sheng 廩生
Liu Mei-ch'ing 劉梅卿
Liu Wang-shih 劉王氏
Lo-an 樂安
Lu-chia-ch'iu 魯家邱
Lu Ming-chao 盧鳴韶
meng-hsüeh 蒙學
Miao Hua-yü 苗化育
Mien-li hui 勉勵會
ming 名
Nan-t'ung 南通
"Ni hsing shen-ma?" 你姓甚麼
P'ang-chia-chuang 龐家庄
pei-chai 備齋
pei-chih 備旨
P'eng-lai 蓬萊
pi mei hao chih chan-cheng 彼美好
　之戰爭
Pi-suan shu-hsüeh 筆算數學
Pien-lun hui 辯論會
P'ingtu (P'ing-tu) 平度
pu k'o pu li 不可不立
Sha-ling 沙嶺
San-tzu ching 三字經
shan-tzu 苫子
Shang-chuang 上庄
shang-fa 賞罰
Shang-ti 上帝
sheng-yüan 生員
shih-fei hsüeh 是非學
Shou-kuang 壽光
shuo-ho-ti 說和的
su-hwa (su-hua) 俗話
Sung-yang chen-shen ko 頌揚眞神歌
ta-kuan 大宮
T'ai-an-fu 泰安府
T'ai-shan 泰山
tao 道
te 德
t'e-hsüeh 特學

Tengchow (Teng-chou) 登州
ti-tzu 弟子
t'iao-kuei 條規
Ting Li-huang 丁立黃
Ting Li-mei 丁立美
ting-yüeh 定約
Tsan-shen sheng-shih 讚神聖詩
Tsan-yang fu-yin hui 讚揚福音會
tsao-chiu jen-ts'ai 造就人材
ts'e-pu 冊簿
Tsinan (Chi-nan) 濟南
Tsingtao (Ch'ing-tao) 青島
tsung-chen 總鎮
tu-shu jen 讀書人
T'ung-chou 通州
t'ung-hsüeh 同學
t'ung-jen 同人
tzu-yüan 自願.
Wan-kuo kung-pao 萬國公報
wan-sui 萬歲
Wang An-shih 王安石
Wang Ch'un-ling 王春齡
Wang Hsi-en 王錫恩

Wang I-ch'eng 王以成
Wei-hsien 濰縣
"Wei tu fu" 魏都賦
Wen hsüan 文選
wen-li 文理
wen-yen 文言
Wong Ping-san (Huang P'in-san) 黃品三
wu-chih kun-t'u 無知棍徒
Yeh-su wei shei 耶穌爲誰
Yen-t'ai 煙臺
yin-ch'in, erh tzu 殷勤二字
yung-yüan shih-chin 永遠示禁
Yü Hsi-chin 于錫晉
yü-wan 愚頑
yü ying shou mu 育英壽母
yüan-fen 緣分
Yüan Hsün 元勳
Yüan Shih-k'ai 袁世凱
Yüan T'ing-chen 阮廷珍
yüan-ya 淵雅
Yüan Yüeh-chün 袁月俊
yüeh-hui 約會

Chinese Names of Major American Figures

Bostick, George Pleasant — Pao Chih-p'i 包治丕
Corbett, Hunter — Kuo Hsien-te 郭顯德
Crawford, Tarleton Perry — Kao Ti-p'i 高第丕
Kao Lo-fu 高樂福
Kao T'ai-p'ei 高泰培
Goodrich, Chauncey — Fu Shan 富善
Hartwell, Jesse Boardman — Hai Ya-hsi 海雅西
Hayes, Watson MacMillan — Ho Shih 赫士
Holmes, James Landrum — "Hua Erh" 花二
Holmes, Matthew G. — Hua Ma-t'ai 花馬太
Holmes, Sally Little — Hua Sa-lai 花撒剩
Kelsey, Adeline de Haven — K'o Li-ssu 克利斯
Mateer, Calvin Wilson — Ti K'ao-wen 狄考文
Ti Tung-ming 狄東明
Mateer, Julia Brown — Ti Pang Chiu-lieh 狄邦就烈
Mateer, Robert McCheyne — Ti Lo-po 狄樂播
Mills, Charles Rogers — Mei Li-shih 梅理士
Moon, Charlotte (Lottie) Diggs — Mu La-ti 幕拉第
Nevius, Helen S. Coan — Ni Ko-shih 倪戈氏
Nevius, John Livingston — Ni Wei-ssu 倪維思
Pruitt, Cicero Washington — P'u Ch'i-wei 浦其維
Yates, Matthew Tyson — Yen Ma-t'ai 晏馬太

Index

Abbott, E. L., 51
Albemarle Female Institute, 95
Allegheny Seminary. *See* Western Theological Seminary
Allen, Y. J., 217
Alumni, Tengchow College, careers of, 174–175, 204–205, 229–230
Anderson, Jennie, 72
Anti-Christianity: and Shantung missionaries, 150, 279n14; at Sha-ling, 115–116; and Mateer, 146–147, 150–158, 213–218, 278n49. *See also* Property disputes, missionary
Arithmetic (Mateer), 168, 194–195, 207
Armstrong, Annie, 114–115, 125
Ayers, Dr. T. W., 125, 127

Baller, Frederick William, 201–202, 209, 211
Beaver, Pa., 144
Beaver, R. Pierce, 268n47
Bergen, Paul, 227–228
Bergen, Mrs. Paul, 91
Bible women, 72, 91
Big Hatchie Association, 6, 54, 233, 244n10
Board of Foreign Missions (BFM), Presbyterian, and Mateer, 145, 161, 177–179, 181
Bostick, Bertha Bryan (Mrs. George P.), 262n45
Bostick, George P., 56–57, 246n31
Bryant, William Cullen, 129
Bushnell, Horace, 232–233

Cabaniss, A. B., 42, 245n24
Capp, Edward, 178
Capp, Maggie Brown (Mrs. Edward), 79, 165, 196, 214, 222
Carter, Anita, 264n66
Cartersville, Ga., 96, 104

Cash, W. J., 60
Chai-li, 160, 162–163, 279n11
Chalmers, John, 201
Chang Kan-ch'en, 160–161
Chang, Mrs. (Presbyterian worker), 89
Chang P'ei-ling, 167
Chang Yun Who, 15, 33
Chao Shang Ching, 29
Chao sisters (Presbyterian activists), 88
Chao Teh Shin, 107
Chao Ting Ching, 13–15, 19
Chao-yüan, 33, 39–40, 153–157, 213
Cheeloo (Shantung Christian University), 89, 225–228, 293nn4 and 5
Chefoo: as site for missionary work, 26, 175–176; school for the deaf at, 85–86; taotai of, 154–155, 217
Chefoo Convention, 214
Chi-mo, 88
Ch'i-hsia, 153–158
Chicago World's Fair (1893), 192
Chih-tsao-so. See Manufactory, Mateer's
Chinese Recorder, The, 177, 193, 218–219
Ch'ing Mei Hong, 26–27
Chinkiang, 115, 135
Chou Li-wen: as Mateer student, 166–167, 174, 178; as assistant to Mateer, 196–197, 203–204, 207
Chou, Mrs. (Helen Nevius' pupil), 77
Chou Wen-yüan, 108, 161–162, 164, 166–167
Christian Endeavor (Mien-li hui), 188
Christmas Offering, Lottie Moon, 112–115, 124–136
Chu Feng-tan, 204
Chung Wei-i, 203
"Churches, To the Front!" (Crawford), 57
Classics, Chinese, at Tengchow College, 186–187. *See also* Han-wen; Wen-li
Clopton, Samuel C., 3, 244n2

Li-jen village, 88
Li Kuang-nai, 161–162
Li Ping-i, 174, 178
Li Shan-ch'ing, 174, 178
Li Shih-kuang, 175
Li Shou Ting (Pastor Li), 112, 116–117, 127
Li-tzu-yuan village, 112
Li Yüan-k'ai, 164
Li Yüan-t'ung, 164
Li Yün-lu, 162, 167
Liang Wei Shing, 28–29
Linnaeus, 200
Litzinger, Charles A., 279n14
Liu Mei-ch'ing (Mrs. Liu Shou-shan), 89–91
Liu, Mrs. (Crawford employee), 14, 31, 246n35
Liu Shou-shan, 89–90
Liu Wang-shih, 89–90
Lord, Edward C., 252n27
Lottie Moon (Lawrence), 127, 133
Lottie Moon Cook Book (Rhea), 129, 131
Lottie Moon in Pictures, 129
"Lottie Moon Story, The," 124–136
Low, F. F., 153
Lu Ming-chao, 15, 17–18, 32, 61
Luce, Henry Winters, 228–230, 293n4

Macao, Southern Baptist missionary work at, 4
Ma-chia village, 15
McCullers, Carson, 133, 274n80
"Make His Name Glorious" (Sumerau), 128
Mandarin Catechism (Yeh-su chiao [kuan-hua] wen-ta; Helen Nevius), 76–77, 160
Mandarin Lessons (Mateer), 139, 193, 196–198, 202, 207, 235
Malraux, André, 135–136
Manufactory (*chih-tsao-so*), Mateer's, 192
Margary, A. R., 214
Martin, W. A. P., 75, 217; and Mateer, 139–140, 182, 193–195, 201
Mateer, Ada Haven (Mrs. Calvin Wilson), 220
Mateer, Calvin Wilson: background and missionary decision of, 140–145; early evangelistic and pastoral work of, in China, 106, 145–158; and Tengchow Boys' School and College, 139–140, 159–190, 209–212; defends missionary education at 1877 General Conference, 175–182; as mechanic and scientist, 147–148, 191–193; linguistic competence and lit-

erary work of, 147–148, 160, 181, 186–187, 193–202, 231–233; as organizer and director, 165–166, 202–209, 235–236; and Julia Mateer, 145, 149, 159, 170–172, 219–220, 235; and Crawford, 48, 51, 174, 214–215, 233–237; and Miao Hua-yü, 153–158, 213, 234; relations of, with non-Christian Chinese, 146–147, 150–158, 212–218, 278n49, 290n85; relations of, with students and Christian Chinese, 169, 171–172, 192–193, 209–212, 281n32; relations of, with fellow missionaries, 218–226; reputation of, 139–140, 218–219, last years and death of, 227–230; career appraised, 231–237
Mateer, Jennie (sister), 141, 275n12
Mateer, John (father), 140–143
Mateer, John (brother), 166
Mateer, Julia Ann Brown (Mrs. Calvin Wilson): background and marriage of, 145; as woman's worker, 68–71, 79, 81–83; and Tengchow school, 159–190, 203; as husband's literary coworker, 196–197; affection for husband of, 145, 219; has health problems, 81, 146–147, 165, 203; final illness and death of, 92, 122–123
Mateer, Lillian (sister), 221–222
Mateer, Mary Diven (mother), 141–144
Mateer, Robert (brother), 105, 171, 222; on education for Chinese women, 82–83, 91
Mathematics, as aspect of Mateer's work, 185, 194–195
Medhurst, W. H., 176, 201–202
Medical missionaries: Southern Baptist, 125; Presbyterian, 221, 224. *See also* Woman's work
Mell, Patrick H., 54
Melville, Herman, 133
Meng-chia-chuang village, 15, 33
Meng Kyü Wha, 15, 22, 31, 33
Miao Hua-yü, 153–158, 162, 213, 234–235
Miller, Cynthia, 123
Mills, Annetta Thompson (Mrs. Charles R.), 68, 85–86, 264n66
Mills, Charles R.: and Crawford, 19–21; and Mateer, 146–147, 150–151, 158, 175–178, 182, 221; on medical work by female missionaries, 84
Mills, Rose MacMaster (Mrs. Charles R.), 77–78, 84
Milne, W. C., 76
Mission study, Southern Baptist, 126–127
Missions. *See* Protestant missions in China

Harvard Studies in American-East Asian Relations